Slurp! A Social and Culinary
History of Ramen – Japan's
Favorite Noodle Soup

Slurp! A Social and Culinary History of Ramen – Japan's Favorite Noodle Soup

By

Barak Kushner

GLOBAL
ORIENTAL

LEIDEN · BOSTON
2014

Cover illustration: (from top left and down): Author's photo of an exhibition poster for the 2009 Noodle Industry event held in Tokyo; Tokugawa era soba salesman selling noodles from his urban stall, reprinted with permission from the University of Cambridge owned volume Adachi Ginkō, *Ōedo shibai nenchū gyōji*, Tokyo, Hasegawa Hisami publishers (1897), no pagination; author's photo of the storefront of a popular ramen shop called Fukuya, in Mita-ku, Tokyo, Japan (2011); author's photo of a bowl of ramen noodle soup (2011).

This paperback was originally published in hardback under ISBN 978-90-04-21845-1.

Library of Congress Cataloging-in-Publication Data

Kushner, Barak, 1968-
 Slurp! : a social and culinary history of ramen, Japan's favorite noodle soup / by Barak Kushner.
   p. cm.
 Includes bibliographical references and index.
 ISBN 978-90-04-21845-1 (hardback : alk. paper) 1. Noodles--Japan. 2. Noodles--Japan--History. 3. Pasta products--Japan--History. I. Title. II. Title: Social and culinary history of ramen, Japan's favorite noodle soup.
 TP435.M3K87 2012
 664'.7550952--dc23

                                    2012027430

This publication has been typeset in the multilingual "Brill" typeface. With over 5,100 characters covering Latin, IPA, Greek, and Cyrillic, this typeface is especially suitable for use in the humanities. For more information, please see www.brill.nl/brill-typeface.

ISBN 978 90 04 21845 1 (hardback)
ISBN 978 90 04 22098 0 (e-book)

Copyright 2012 by Koninklijke Brill NV, Leiden, The Netherlands.
Koninklijke Brill NV incorporates the imprints Brill, Global Oriental, Hotei Publishing, IDC Publishers and Martinus Nijhoff Publishers.

All rights reserved. No part of this publication may be reproduced, translated, stored in a retrieval system, or transmitted in any form or by any means, electronic, mechanical, photocopying, recording or otherwise, without prior written permission from the publisher.

Authorization to photocopy items for internal or personal use is granted by Koninklijke Brill NV provided that the appropriate fees are paid directly to The Copyright Clearance Center, 222 Rosewood Drive, Suite 910, Danvers, MA 01923, USA.
Fees are subject to change.

This book is printed on acid-free paper.

This book is dedicated to Mami "Tiny Minister" Mizutori, who sacrificed much so that we could spend the second half of our lives together. I endeavor daily to repay that debt.

CONTENTS

Preface xi
Note on Transliteration xv
List of Figures.. xvii

Introduction – The Temple of Noodledom... 1
    The Ramen Question 8
    Ramen – An International Force 9
    Noodles and Nationalism 12

1 Three Sages Walk into a Restaurant and ... Noodles 15
    The Arrival of Noodles in China – Noodle Loaf? 18
    Food Legends and the Roots of Noodle Worship........................... 21
    Premodern Noodles 27

2 Court Food versus Common Food... 33
    Shinto and Food 35
    Chinese Food Technology.. 37
    The Rise of Samurai and Medieval Japanese Food 44

3 International Japan, Foreign Foods and Isolation........................... 47
    The Rise of New Leaders and New Japanese Foodways 49
    Edo is Not the Only City – Tokugawa Peace and a
       Piece of the Pie 51
    Nagasaki and Chinese Food 53
    Food and the Chinese 58
    Passion for Noodles – *Soba* and *Udon*.. 62
    Banning Noodle Consumption 64

4 Early Modern Noodles and the Myth of Ramen.............................. 71
    Japan's First Chinese Chef – Shu Shunsui?..................................... 73
    Edo – Feast and Famine 79
    Kansai versus Kantō Taste 80
    Edo and Meat Eating... 84

5 The Meiji Restoration: Menu Renovation on the
    Road to Ramen 89

   Treaty Ports 91
   Barbarians and Banquets 95
   Japanese and Meat Eating 104
   The Militarization of Food 107
   Sources of *Bunmei Kaika* – Civilization and Enlightenment 113
   Nagasaki and *Champon* Noodles 115

6 Diplomacy and the Desire to Impress 119

   Imperial Dining 123
   Health, Hygiene and Food 128
   Chinese in Meiji Japan 134
   Imperialism and Food 139

7 Empire and Japanese Cuisine 143

   Time is the Meter of Civilization – the Birth of Delicious 144
   Food and Excrement 149
   Raising the Standard 151
   Ramen Debuts on the Japanese Stage 155
   Other Theories 157
   Nighttime Dining, Students and Erotic, Grotesque Nonsense 160
   The Rise of "Nutrition" 163
   Edo Started the Process, Meiji Promoted and Taisho Finalized 165

8 World War II Cuisine: A World Adrift 169

   Starving Japan and Bountiful America 171
   The Path to War 172
   Wartime Cuisine and the Nation 173
   Japanese Soldiers and Food 175
   Food and Victory 177
   Japanese Identity and Rice 180
   Battle Zones and Prisoners of War 183
   Food and the Home Front 187
   Surrender and the Dissolution of Imperial Food 188

9 History at the Dining Table: Postwar Instant Ramen 191

   The Sudden Postwar 195
   A Land without Food 197

Repatriates and Food..199
　　A Dream Come True – Instant Ramen 204
　　Why Invent Instant Ramen?...208
　　Japan and Instant Ramen 213
　　The Ramen Boom..215
　　Ramen and Food Tourism 217
　　Branding the Local 220
　　Ramen Finds Its Way Abroad – First to America.....................220
　　You Are *Not* What You Eat...222
　　"Fighting for a Share of the Stomach".....................................223
　　Is Ramen Part of Japanese Cuisine?..224
　　Ramen Is Japan 227

10　Ramen Popular Culture 229
　　How to Eat Ramen – Slurp!..229
　　Comedy and Ramen 231
　　Ramen Fanatics...235
　　Musée de Ramen 237
　　Ramen Stadiums...238
　　Manga and Ramen Music...241
　　For the Love of Sushi 248
　　Ramen – With a New York State of Mind.................................251
　　The Global Impact of Japanese Food..252
　　The Rise of Ramen and Japanese Popular Culture..................254
　　Competition for Original Ramen 255

Conclusion...257
　　The Dark Side of Food Greatness..260
　　The Future of Food in Japan..262
　　Changes in the Contemporary Japanese Diet..........................263
　　Did Japanese Food Create Japanese Identity?.........................265
　　Ramen and History 268
　　Now Go Eat History!..269

Bibliography 271
Index..285

PREFACE

This book would long ago have been lost had it not been for the support and cajoling of my friend Gwen Robinson, who saw something there when others just offered rejection. My colleagues in the Department of East Asian Studies at the University of Cambridge who tolerate my research into fringe topics always enjoy a good discussion over a pint, or several; for me the move to the UK was one of happenstance that proved to be the best life choice. John Swenson-Wright's love for coffee is only overwhelmed by his enthusiasm for gathering people together and pushing the boundaries of scholarship. Professor Roel Sterckx offered suggestions and immense improvements, while Professor Richard Bowring, Master of Selwyn College, made immeasurably useful comments on religion and food (though I fully understand that he may want to distance himself from this project and any criticism it invites). Professor Peter Kornicki and emeritus professor Dr. Stephen Large offered extensive comments on much of the work. Brigitte Steger was supportive. Thanks for all the snacks and for reading various iterations, a big shout out to Anna Boermel who has been a true friend over the years. Thanks to Dr. Lora Saalman for dealing with my obsessions in China and Japan – the travel was fun. Yoshii Mika, who regretfully passed away, discussed Tokugawa food with me and explained what exactly was funny about comedian Matsumoto Hitoshi's "*suberanai hanashi*." The kind words of Hu Xiao-ping and the everlasting friendship and camaraderie of Hsiao Hui-fen in Taipei remain key. Tony Tavares and Marc and Kara Abramson have shared many long discussions about food. A lovely afternoon with cultural historian Mark Swislocki was also eye-opening. Nicole Rousmaniere's excitement about the research led to interviews with a major manga publisher and I hope to future interviews with ramen chefs as well. Paul Dunscomb and Michael Baskett have read and critiqued more versions of the manuscript for this book than should have been permitted, as have my parents and extended family. My Chinese tutor Dr. Yin Zhiguang, who knows every postmodern Chinese term in existence, was helpful in many ways. Professor Ishige Naomichi met with me for an afternoon in his office stacked high with books and set me on the right path; I thank Professor Katarzyna Cwiertka for that introduction. Fuchsia Dunlop offered much appreciated advice, as did Dr. Lizzie Collingham in several conversations, while working on her bestseller on wartime food. Dr. Robert Fish from the Japan Society has been consistently helpful, Roger Brown was intrigued by the project, while Steve Covell and his lovely family in Michigan hosted me for one of the talks. My former student Sven Palys lent his needed expertise to fiddle with maps and assorted graphics. National Taiwan University professor Dr. Yi Jolan led me through some articles on Ming dining, while Dr. Thomas Jansen pored over early versions but never grew irritable with my relentless questions. Librarian John Moffet at the Needham Research Institute in Cambridge pointed me to Chinese student diary collections.

The Cambridge University Library is lucky to have the phenomenal Japanese librarian Koyama Noboru whose knowledge of where to locate any Japanese book on food, no matter how obscure, is as infinite as his patience with annoyingly persistent researchers like me. Our tireless faculty librarian Francoise Simmons has been a true source of support, always supplying hungry researchers with a selection of tasty cookies in the Faculty Library. The staff in the faculty administrative offices filled in numerous financial forms to get fellowships processed in time.

Corpus Christi College generously provided travel and research funds, and the Japan Foundation Endowment Committee enabled me to spend a summer in Japan in 2007 carrying out extensive research in Tokyo and Nagasaki. I also thank the Cambridge University Travel Fund, Dr. Shelley Rigger and the Freeman Foundation, and the Faculty of Asian and Middle Eastern Studies, for money that supported various trips to China and Japan.

Talks presented at venues in the US, UK, Japan and Taiwan helped me develop my thoughts on ramen through the Q&A sessions. These talks included a presentation at the Modern Japan Workshop at Waseda University, a translation conference at Normal University in Taipei, Taiwan, and a presentation in the Department of History at National Taiwan University in Taipei. A 2007 Oxford-Princeton conference where I was the only one to speak on food was a great enterprise. The Royal Asiatic Society in London, the SOAS Food Studies Centre, the Soga Japan Center Speaker Series at Western Michigan University, the World History Seminar at St. Catharine's College, University of Cambridge, the Japan Research Centre at the School of Oriental and African Studies in London, the History of Design Seminar at the Royal College of Art, London, and the Sainsbury Institute for the Study of Japanese Arts and Cultures in Norwich all kindly invited me to speak on various occasions and heard portions of this material. I am grateful for the suggestions given to me at all of these places.

Business scholar and ramen historian Okuyama Tadamasa started me on the road to ramen in 2004, when I interviewed him and he generously spent several hours with me discoursing on the meaning of noodles. Okuyama-san's deep interest in the economic and social implications of ramen was infectious; I cannot thank him enough. My understanding was also developed by many other enlightening interviews with museum staff and people from the food industry around Japan, especially Osaka and Nagasaki, as well as an afternoon set of interviews at the Maesawa Cattle Museum.

I would like to thank Professor Bill Tsutsui and Dr. Chris Gerteis for their comments on my manuscript and also to extend my appreciative thanks to publisher Paul Norbury from Global Oriental who decided to take a risk on this book and kept smiling while doing so. Lucy North and Zoe Swenson-Wright were equally helpful with editing.

I should acknowledge with grateful thanks, permission to use parts of Chapter 7 which first appeared in my essay, "Imperial Cuisines in Taishō Foodways," in Eric Rath and Stephanie Assmann, editors, *Past and Present in Japanese Foodways*, Chicago: University of Illinois Press, 2010, pp. 145–165.

To answer everyone's question – Why write a book on ramen? – I have this to say: It seemed like a good idea at the time! But actually, a bowl of ramen noodle soup is not merely a wad of noodles served in a flavorsome broth with a variety of toppings and seasonings: it is also a microcosm of East Asian history, and as such a most delicious amalgamation of lowbrow and highbrow. Writing about ramen opens up a unique perspective on the history of Japan, and researching ramen has allowed me to combine the pleasures of the table (or ramen shop) with the joy of examining the past. What could be more fun than that? I hope that readers enjoy the experience as much as I appreciated the process of delving into the mysteries of ramen noodle history.

Slurp!

Barak Kushner

NOTE ON TRANSLITERATION

Japanese, Chinese and Korean names appear in the East Asian order, with family name first. Japanese words are normally printed in italics, except when the word, such as saké, anime, daimyo, samurai, manga and miso have entered the English language. Long vowels in Japanese are indicated by a macron, as in *shōyu*, although this rule has not been applied to commonplace names, as in Tokyo, Osaka and Kyoto.

LIST OF FIGURES

1. Standard bowl of *ramen*, or noodle soup 2
2. Cook straining noodles with a flourish for the visual entertainment of his customers 5
3. Inside view of an average ramen shop 5
4. Foodstall vendor in contemporary China selling modern breakfast *bing* 19
5. Noodle-makers on the street in western China 28
6. Small stone obelisk in the front garden of Jōten Temple Hakata, recording the temple's history as the birthplace of *udon* and *soba* noodle technology in Japan 38
7. Picture of the Miso Shrine, "Miso Tenjin," also known as the Motomura Shrine 39
8. A 1792 Japanese hand-colored scroll depicting Nagasaki harbor 52
9. Front view of Kōfuku Temple in Nagasaki 55
10. Inner entrance to Sōfuku Temple, Nagasaki 56
11. Japanese drawing of Chinese diners using a *shippoku* table 57
12. Japanese rendition of a Chinese trading ship, *Tōsen* – literally a "Tang Ship," pulling into port 58
13. Tokugawa-era map of the large Chinese enclosure, Nagasaki 59
14. Chinese banquet in Nagasaki, hosted in the Chinese enclosure 60
15. Print featuring a Chinese man in his own quarters with a courtesan 61
16. Edo food-seller carrying his wares in baskets 64
17. Edo food-seller with portable foodstall 65
18. Example of Edo noodle stalls 65
19. Stone marker featuring four Chinese characters, stating "Soba is not permitted" 67
20. "Half moon bridge" in Kōrakuen, northern Tokyo 74
21. Memorial stele to Shu Shunsui, University of Tokyo 78
22. Official Meiji declaration announcing foreigners' rights to travel for a limited time to attend a cultural exhibition in Kyoto 93
23. Drawings from Fukuzawa's book, *Western Food, Clothing and Living Habits,* featuring Western cutlery 97

LIST OF FIGURES

24. Compilation of the different ways in which the word for "coffee" has been translated into Japanese over the centuries 98
25. Article 7, stating: "It is forbidden to knowingly sell fake or spoiled foods and drinks" 100
26. Article 45, stating: "It is illegal to butcher and skin a dead cow or horse in the street" 101
27. Article 61, stating: "It is forbidden to defecate or urinate on a city street where there is no bathroom" 102
28. Drawing of beef-stew restaurants and noodle shops (*soba-ya*) in Tokyo 107
29. Image of Yōwaken restaurant where "*Nanking soba*" was supposedly first served in 1884 117
30. and 31. Images from the instruction manual for imperial evening events 120, 121
32. Drawing of life at Enryōkan and a glimpse of former US President Ulysses S. Grant's tour of Japan in 1879 122
33. Picture of a "leftovers stand" in Tokyo 130
34. Front page of a Japanese government publication entitled "How Koreans Dress, Eat and Live" 135
35. 1894 caricatures of Chinese depicted as pigs 137
36. Picture of a housewife and maid discussing kitchen tasks from the book "Renovating Kitchens" 153
37. US World War II "Eat the Right Food" poster 176
38. Postwar playbill for the song, "The Apple Song" 192
39. Package of the first type of instant ramen for sale (chicken-flavored) 207
40. Cartoon from a 1950 American occupation report entitled, "Survey of Bread and Flour Utilization by the Japanese People" 209
41. Traveling "Kitchen Bus" 212
42. Banners stating "Village of store houses" hanging on the platforms in Kitakata rail station 219
43. Author with *rakugo* star Hayashiya Kikuzō in Tokyo 233
44. Advertisement for a ramen competition hall 240
45. Front cover of a popular manga about ramen with Mantarō enjoying a bowl of noodle soup 242
46. Mantarō literally falling in love with the naked female character of the story 243
47. Contestants are asked to pick out the plate of noodles that are made in Tokyo 245

48. The female contestant who is about to win but a cheater loosens her top and so she fails at the last moment...........................246
49. Typical Japanese-style ramen shop in downtown Seoul, Korea 255
50. Large sign outside the Fukuya Ramen Shop, Tokyo 256
51. Poster for a newly launched series called "Soba-master," in which the protagonist undertakes "noodle adventures" 258
52. Noodle dishes are commonplace in the average corner convenience store 265
53. Poster touting a 2009 show promoting new ramen tastes and stores 267
54. Typical weekly and monthly magazines which review restaurants, recipes, food travel tours and guidebooks 268

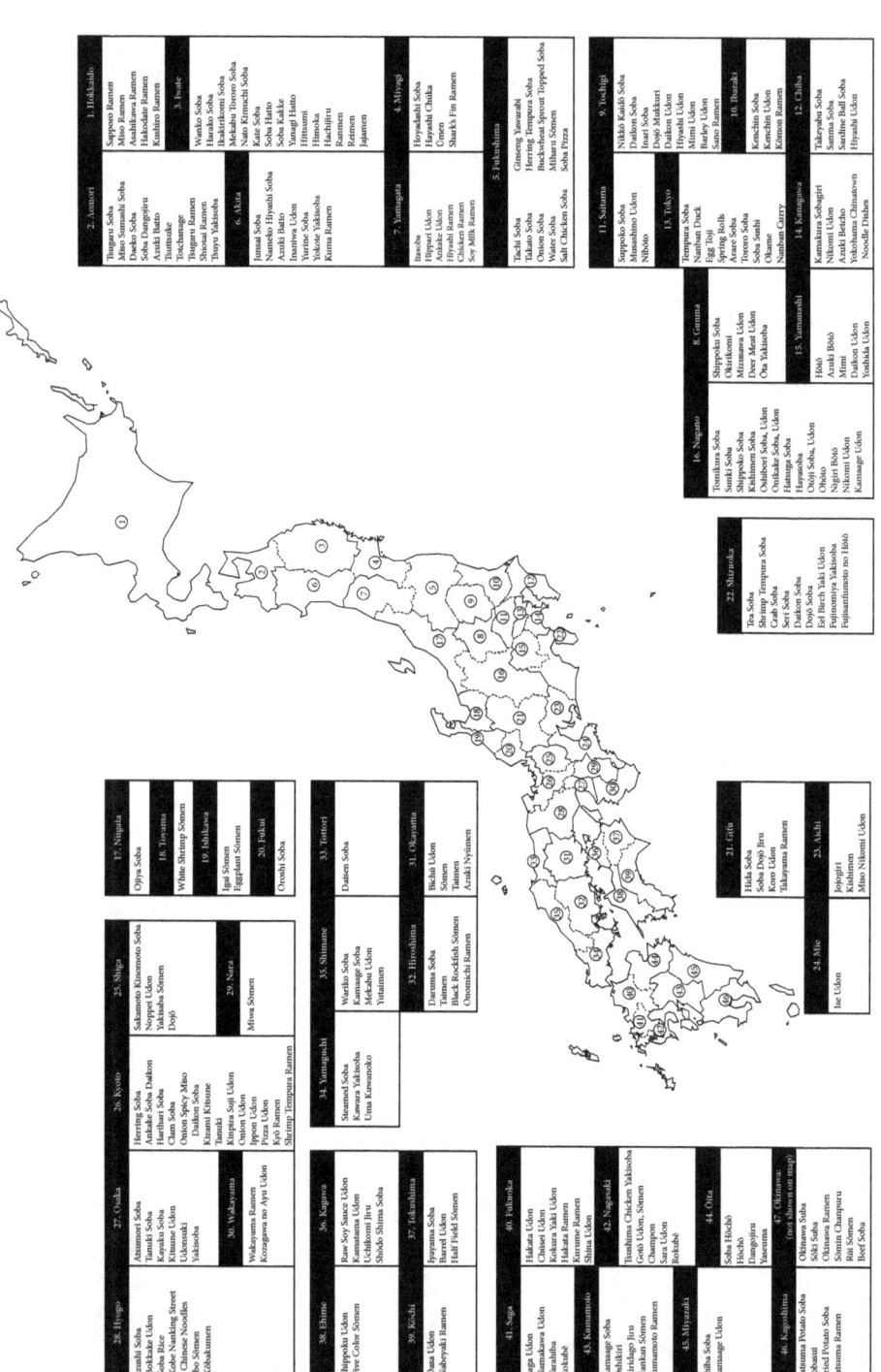

(Map adapted from Okamura Ayao, *Nihon menshoku bunka no sensanbyakunen*, pp. 522–523.)

INTRODUCTION

THE TEMPLE OF NOODLEDOM

In Japan, ramen is not merely food but a path to serious gastronomic enlightenment. I learned this one summer several years ago in Hakata, a humid and sunny city in western Japan on the island of Kyushu, when I decided to try the Ichiran ("The Orchid") ramen restaurant, housed in a nondescript one-story building. At first, it was hard to believe that I was really in a noodle shop. Normally, in Japan, when you enter a shop or restaurant, you are greeted with a hearty "*Irasshaimase*!" meaning "Welcome" in Japanese. Ichiran, in contrast, was eerily quiet. I purchased a ticket for a bowl of standard pork-broth ramen from one of the vending machines at the entrance. Just inside the door was a large sign with a lengthy explanation in Japanese for customers about the restaurant's unique eating "system." Under these instructions were two rows of red lights that indicated which seats along the counters in the restaurant were empty – necessary in this establishment because all exits and entrances in the eating area are sectioned off with curtains, preventing diners from any view through the restaurant, a "hidden" effect that Ichiran's corporate owners (it is part of a franchise system) have patented. Dining here is carried out in solitary isolation and the interior is designed to encourage customers to focus on the ramen experience.

 I chose a stool somewhere along the middle of the counter, feeling as if I were in a monastery rather than at an eating establishment. Each stool was separated from the next by a wooden partition, which might have cramped the style of a larger eater, forming in effect a kind of cubicle. A red curtain hung two feet in front of my face, cutting off the view into the kitchen, and preventing me from watching the noodles and soup being prepared. On the wall was a detailed explanation in Japanese of the Ichiran customer code of behavior: it looked as if it would take at least ten minutes to read. I gave up halfway through and assumed I would understand what to do. It turned out I was wrong.

 Leaning back from my partition, I tried to engage my fellow diners in a conversation. I soon realized, however, that while this was not exactly forbidden, it was definitely not appreciated. Angry looks from passionate diners studying their bowls of hot noodle soup prompted me to shut up and simply wait silently for the moment of truth – chopsticks to noodles, to lips, to hopefully ... bliss. I had understood from my brief perusal of the code of behavior that I should also refrain from speaking to the staff. I therefore placed my order slip on the counter and a waiter appeared from behind the red curtain to pick it up. He gave me another slip on which I was now supposed to indicate exactly how I wanted my ramen noodles prepared: soft, medium or firm; I also had to specify a soup base. At Ichiran (as in other ramen shops), one can choose from a long list of possibilities, including salty, miso, and soy sauce flavors. There was no talking; all ordering was processed by paper and by pushing buttons. At the end of the meal I had some soup left but no noodles, however, I was not worried. Another patented feature of the Ichiran system allowed me to press a red button on the counter, which illuminated a blinking light to indicate an order for an additional small portion of noodles (called *tamagae*) to soak up the remaining soup. In the competitive world of ramen, where every chef believes his ramen is superb, leftover noodles border on the blasphemous: they suggest to the manager that the meal did

Figure 1. A standard bowl of *ramen*, or noodle soup. The meal is served in a deep bowl called a *donburi* and eaten with chopsticks to capture the noodles, and usually a large spoon to enjoy the tasty soup.[1]

---

[1] Unless otherwise noted, all photographs are the author's.

not suit the taste of the customer. In the end, my experience at Ichiran was both delicious and a bit overwhelming. A simple bowl of noodles and soup had been elevated to a near religious experience.

Contemporary Japan almost floats on a sea of noodle soup. You can buy computer software that allows you to search the whole country for details on your favorite ramen shop. You can register your cell phone for directions and the train schedule toward a destination that will provide the exact type of ramen for which your heart yearns. In a similar fashion, guidebooks assist Japanese in finding the right ramen shop when they travel abroad to Korea, Taiwan and parts of China. Today, there are almost no taboos in the gastronomic world of ramen and any number of stores offer something for virtually any type of customer taste – from salty to bland and from soy sauce to tomato sauce.

Noodle-soup restaurants in Japan, popularly known as *ramen-ya*, or ramen shops, dominate the urban and rural landscape. Statistics vary but according to industry estimates, ramen accounts for twenty-six percent of all meals eaten outside the home.[2] There are more ramen restaurants in Japan than any other kind of eating establishment, some 30,000 at last government count.[3] Ramen shops dot cities from the western tip of Japan in Kurume and Fukuoka to the northern cities of Kitakata and Sapporo. Every small village or hamlet boasts at least one or two ramen shops. Without exaggeration, ramen is surely the emperor of food in Japan. In Hakata, on the western island of Kyushu, a Ramen Stadium feeds thousands daily. There is a Ramen Sumo Hall in Sendai, a large northern city, and a Ramen Theater in Chiba Prefecture, near Tokyo, where diners consume prodigious quantities in a huge arena devoted to the ramen experience. In contrast to the Ichiran environment, these versions include both the joy of eating a tasty meal and the pleasure of watching it being prepared.

In addition to ramen shops, there are museums of ramen. Yokohama, a modern coastal city near Tokyo, boasts an elaborate museum devoted to the evolution of the famous noodle soup. A small town outside Osaka in central Japan erected a memorial hall celebrating the life of Andō Momofuku, the inventor of instant ramen – lifeblood of students, late-night workers and busy people.

---

[2] "Rāmen daikenkyū," *Shūkan Tōyō keizai*, November 30, 2002, p. 108.
[3] Julia Moskin, "Here Comes Ramen, the Slurp Heard Round the World," *The New York Times*, November 10, 2004.

I first encountered ramen when I lived in a small fishing village, Yamada machi, on the eastern coast of northern Japan. The village overlooked a picturesque bay studded with scallop, sea urchin and seaweed beds. I was working as an English teacher, and every day for several months I used to walk past a squat, unremarkable building. I could not yet read Japanese signs and had no idea what the building was. The door was always closed and I never saw anyone go in or out. All became clear one night when a colleague took me out for ramen at 2 am after late-night drinks. The enigmatic building turned out to be a pub-like ramen establishment called *Rokumon*, or "Sixpence." Ramen is the *de rigueur* late-night Japanese meal for revelers; all the clients in the Rokumon looked as inebriated as we were. It would never have occurred to me that a small fishing village could have eateries that opened after midnight.

Drinking with friends or colleagues after work is something of a national pastime in Japan. Imbibing is an activity that has a long history, and is indulged in by most members of society. Sometimes drinking sessions go late into the night, forcing carousers to choose between cutting short their evenings to catch the last bus or train or staying out until the morning to catch the first train home. Either way, many Japanese will tuck into a final bowl of ramen. One Japanese physiologist explains that long sessions of drinking alcohol deaden the tongue to flavors, making the drinker crave food with a strong taste. Drinking also makes you crave hearty carbohydrates. Nothing provides a better, stronger taste, filled with starch and protein, than a meaty broth of ramen noodle soup.[4] Stalwarts believe the noodles help absorb alcohol and prevent hangovers. There is something almost decadent about eating a bowl of hot, steaming noodles after a night of beer and saké. I discovered that ramen is not consumed only for lunch, dinner, or as the last stop on the way home after midnight – the Japanese love eating ramen at almost any time of the day or night.

The first kind of ramen that many non-Japanese come into contact with in their own countries is "instant ramen," known as "pot noodles" in Europe and *"fangbian mian"* (noodles of convenience) in China. These

---

[4] "Rāmen daisuki," *SPA!* May 2, 1992, p. 48. Ramen has become an icon of modern Japan to the point that scholars are writing PhD dissertations about various aspects of its history and its anthropology. For a modern understanding concerning the phenemenon of ramen in mostly postwar Japanese society see George Solt, "Taking ramen seriously: food, labor, and everyday life in modern Japan," PhD dissertation in the History Department, University of California, San Diego, 2009; an anthropological analysis of contemporary trends can be studied in Satomi Fukutomi, "Connoisseurship of B-grade culture: Consuming Japanese national food Ramen," PhD dissertation in the Department of Anthropology at the University of Hawai'i Manoa, 2010.

Figure 2. A cook straining the noodles with a flourish for the visual entertainment of his customers. The spectacle of watching your ramen being made is half the fun of dining at Shiodome, in central Tokyo.

Figure 3. Inside view of an average ramen shop.

noodles bear some relation to the ramen served in special-purpose restaurants but essentially ramen and instant ramen are two completely different foods with similar origins. As of 2010, the world devours over 95 billion packages of instant ramen a year, according to the World Instant Noodles Association. The Chinese slurp up more than 42 billion portions, while Indonesians eat about 14 billion cups. Japan ranks a mere third, with slightly more than 5 billion bowls a year.[5] Moreover, in the world today there are literally hundreds of different styles and flavors of instant ramen. The French boast that their country produces over four hundred varieties of cheese, but many of these can only be purchased locally. Ramen is available globally, in its classic regular store-made form and instant versions.

Real ramen, the elder brother to instant ramen, is a savory noodle soup. Ramen is not limited to one flavor; many variations have grown up around Japan and each reflects different regional influences. Fundamentally, ramen is a dish where the noodles are usually made from wheat and swim in a flavorful soup. While it is now considered a Japanese dish, ramen did not actually evolve from Japan's domestic cuisine. In fact, the oily and rich taste of the meaty soup is almost heretical within the world of traditional Japanese cuisine. Traditional Japanese cuisine rested on a fishy palate, with a taste arising from the use of bonito flakes, *katsuobushi*, and *niboshi*, small crunchy fish, with a thick seaweed essence known as *konbu*. Ramen noodle soup, on the other hand, is a dish based on meat flavors and oil, creating in the process more of what most would consider a classic Chinese taste.

The broth is cooked from a stock comprising various ingredients – often including pork, chicken, garlic, seaweed, soy sauce, and other natural flavors. The taste varies by region, and cooking times depend on the complexity of the soup, with some broths taking more than half a day to prepare. There are certain regional markers that have historically placed ramen in one of several camps. Soy sauce-flavored soup, or *shōyu ramen*, from Tokyo, probably developed due to the region's preference for the heavy soy sauce that was native to cuisine around the shogun's former capital. *Shio ramen*, a transparent salt-based soup, originally particular to Yokohama, competed with *miso ramen* from Sapporo on the northern island of Hokkaido, which offers a heavier flavor. *Tonkotsu ramen* from Kyushu is the furthest from a traditional Japanese taste because the broth

---

[5] This organization used to be called the International Ramen Manufacturers Association but changed its name in 2007. For the latest data see, http://instantnoodles.org/noodles/expanding-market.html.

is made mostly from pork meat and bones that reveal a white, milky-looking soup after stewing for several hours.

Good ramen is difficult and time-consuming to make. The springy wheat noodles that bathe in the soup are freshly boiled when the orders are placed. Upon receiving an order, the chef throws a wad of noodles into a boiling cauldron to cook, and then places them, along with several ladles of the broth and other flavorings, into a large, deep bowl called a *donburi*. The soup is garnished with a variety of toppings according to the customer's wishes: bean sprouts, pork slices, onions, spinach, egg, *naruto* (thin slices of a gelatinous fish paste that sounds better in Japanese and is tastier than one might assume) and combinations of these and many other delicacies. *This* is the real ramen.

Instant ramen, on the other hand, is essentially a packet of dried noodles over which you sprinkle some mixed spices that come sealed in a small, foil envelope and then add boiling water. The attraction of instant ramen, in an age when time is of the essence, is firstly that it is cheap, and secondly that it can provide a quick, hot meal, simply by adding water. There are historic similarities between fresh and instant ramen, and some crossover appeal as well. Both have exerted a mass international impact and altered the Japanese diet in the process. However, to truly appreciate instant ramen one must first grapple with the history of traditional ramen.

Why is Japanese culture so apparently obsessed with ramen? Even in corporate establishments such as Ichiran, eating ramen noodle soup symbolizes more than just having a simple meal. As a character in the 1985 film *Tampopo*, an international hit directed by the late Itami Jūzō, explains: "Good ramen represents all that is good in life." A collection of vaguely connected stories exploring the place of food in modern Japanese life, the plot of this film centers on the story of a truck driver Gorō who befriends the heroine Tampopo, and teaches her how to make the best ramen in all Japan. The film is filled with *Rocky*-style scenes in which Gorō trains Tampopo up, mentally and physically, so that she can attain top culinary form. Wiping the sweat from her brow, with a determined expression Tampopo dunks a portion of noodles into a large tub of boiling water. She quickly ladles out two large bowls of soup from a larger pot that keeps the broth simmering continuously over a gas burner, lifts the noodles from the water and places them in the soup, and then deftly reaches over the counter to add spices and garnishes. Gorō, relaxed in a chair, makes her go through the process repeatedly, until she is almost exhausted. Then suddenly, after her repeated labors, she understands – she has reached ramen enlightenment! Movie viewers are delighted when, physically and emotionally almost at the end of her tether, she finally smiles.

Ramen looks easy to make but in fact it requires care, assiduousness, patience, an understanding of the ingredients and the timing of their interaction, and physical prowess. To purists, Gorō's mantra that tasty ramen represents "goodness" also holds true conversely. Tasteless ramen, like the noodles Tampopo made before encountering Gorō, represents all that is bad in life. No soup noodle devotee wants to eat bad ramen.

The Ramen Question

Ramen speaks volumes about the complex relationship between Japan and China. It also teaches us about the enduring history of East Asia and helps to explain modern Japan. Although most foreigners and many Japanese believe that ramen has long historical roots in China, it has somehow mysteriously transformed into a Japanese product. What began as an offshoot of Chinese cooking has ended up, almost a thousand years later, as an emblem of modern Japanese cuisine. The history of ramen also illustrates Japan's transformation into a food-obsessed nation capable of producing hit TV shows such as *The Iron Chef*, a cook-off competition that has acquired a comprehensive following both nationally and internationally. So how did a Chinese noodle dish become one of the most popular foods in Japan and why is ramen such a big international business now? To answer this we need to explore the political and cultural interactions between Japan and the rest of East Asia.

◊

Historically, the Japanese ate little meat. However, during centuries of exchange with the rest of East Asia they steadily adopted an entirely different set of eating habits that were expressed in banquets, taste and various dishes. These changes reoriented Japanese culinary practices, or foodways as historians like to term them. In the generations leading up to the nineteenth-century, China was Japan's classical model; its cultural products, language, law and history had an immense impact on the smaller nation's development. After the Meiji Restoration in 1868, however, the Japanese developed a pronounced disdain for China. As Japan modernized during the nineteenth century, profound new debates about national diet centered on cuisine as a symbol of national identity. These discussions, along with improved trading routes, a shifting economic landscape and changes in lifestyles, were the keys to the diffusion of ingredients and creation of hybrid dishes which ultimately led to the production of ramen.

The ingredients necessary to create ramen – noodles, meat and various flavorings – took centuries to reach Japan, either as discrete items associated with the transmission of Buddhism or as the result of trade, colonialism and imperialism. During the nineteenth century, the components of ramen reflected the Japanese belief that a new cuisine could boost the physical health of the nation. Elites and government authorities championed a national program for health as the key to avoiding colonization by the West. In the mid-nineteenth century, Westerners seemed physically bigger and stronger. Many Japanese suspected that their historically own poor eating habits had resulted in a smaller stature that would make them unable to fend off encroaching European and American colonial interests.

Ramen – An International Force

All societies, not just Japan and China, define themselves through food. We may not always want to admit it, but cultural identity is tied inextricably to traditions of cooking, eating and producing food. The noted British food historian, Ben Rogers, once observed that, "it is no exaggeration to say that, after language, food is the most important bearer of national identity."[6] Anyone who prizes "Mom's home cooking" or can relate to the term "comfort food" will understand the issues at stake. Paradoxically, however, although we may believe that our own national cuisines are rooted in history, they are actually in constant flux. It is a myth that the French have always enjoyed rich stews and velvety sauces; it is equally wrong to believe that the Japanese have always loved raw fish and the beautiful presentation of aesthetically pleasing yet bland dishes. Britain's "nice cup of tea" is fixed in popular consciousness as the national drink, although it was not originally British. The concept of the "full *English* breakfast" is also relatively recent, as is the popular meal of fish and chips. The "traditional English meal," emblazoned in store windows across well-known tourist towns in the UK today, could just as easily be a chicken masala or kebab. What people call their national "cuisine" reflects certain ideas about the food their countrymen consume on a daily basis. Although ramen is different from traditional Japanese dishes, it does not belong to any Western

---

[6] Ben Rogers. *Beef and Liberty. Roast Beef, John Bull and the English Nation*, p. 3.

culinary category or even to classical Chinese cuisine, defying attempts to categorize it.

For a clearer view on this question, I consulted Ōsaki Hiroshi, a man who has turned the eating of ramen for virtually every meal into a full-time consulting business, the Ramen Data Bank. One hot afternoon, I visited Ōsaki's headquarters in a small office building just off a busy main street in the Meguro district of Tokyo. A cheery man of about fifty, Ōsaki looks healthy for someone who, by his own admission, has already eaten close to 17,000 bowls of ramen. I had pursued Ōsaki not only to try to discover what drives a man to dedicate his career and life to a single dish, but also to ask whether he considers ramen to be Japanese, Chinese or Western. A seemingly innocuous question; yet, when I put it to Japanese food industry executives and experts around the country, it had always elicited a blank surprised response that puzzled me. Did they consider ramen Japanese food or not, I wondered? Most Japanese have a preconceived notion about their national diet. To many, rice, vegetables and a side bowl of miso soup constitute the traditional Japanese meal, never mind that meat, potatoes, eggs, hamburgers and curry rice are also very popular choices. Rice is considered the central element of the Japanese diet, but some food industry representatives allowed that they also daily consumed items that are completely alien to traditional Japanese cooking, including bread, steak and cake. The response to my question led me to think that Japanese seemed to believe that any food they ingested automatically became part of Japanese cuisine. What were the real origins of ramen, though? I was hoping that Ōsaki-san could clear up the issue for me. He offered the following explanation:

> Ramen represents Japanese culture in that the main pillars of its origin are Chinese but later, Japan nurtured these elements for itself and created something completely different from Chinese culture. As Japan did with American semiconductors, we took a product and improved on the original, making it in the process a reflection of our own culture. I think ramen shows Japan's talented side, our *kiyōsei*, the ability to recraft anything. Ramen is the result of this skill.

So is ramen Japanese, Chinese, or what? I asked. Ōsaki barely paused before replying: "Ramen is not part of either *washoku* or *Nihon ryōri*. Those terms do not really help in classifying noodle soup."[7] We should similarly

---

[7] Interview, July 3, 2009. See also his website, www.ramendatabank.co.jp.

hesitate when talking about "Japanese food" – *washoku*. The cuisine of Japan's main islands has seen enormous changes over the millennia, as the Japanese borrowed food from the Chinese, Indians, English, Spanish and Portuguese. Tempura, castella cake, beer, noodles, curry rice, fried pork cutlet and ramen are all popular dishes in Japan and staples of the diet today, although they are not "home grown."

"*Washoku*" is a word normally used to describe traditional Japanese food that many believe is homegrown: a cuisine that evolved within Japan from the medieval era, and was not influenced by other countries. "*Nihon ryōri*" is a somewhat more expansive term for Japanese cuisine that includes many dishes that were imported and then adapted from abroad but that are now consumed in Japan. Confusingly, both terms in English signify "Japanese cuisine," while in the Japanese language they distinguish between traditional and more international types of food. To Ōsaki, ramen is constantly changing and evolving to the point where it has become its own category, belonging neither to traditional "washoku" nor to China, which spawned its noodle great-grandparents. The fact that Westerners are taking to it with such ease, he adds, shows that ramen has created an entirely new classification of cuisine. Pizza, spaghetti and curry have ancient roots in their native lands, but they have all morphed into something virtually unrecognizable since being replanted to the US and Great Britain. In a way, says Ōsaki, Japanese ramen is similar.

As ramen pushes the boundaries of the notion of "national cuisine" the world over, we must also consider that some Chinese dishes, often regarded as traditional mainstays, may not have been created in China. Fuchsia Dunlop, a British expert on Chinese cuisine, has explored the origins of the American Chinese restaurant staple, "General Tso's Chicken," discovering that the creator of this spicy Hunanese dish, Peng Chang-kuei, fled the mainland after the revolution in 1949 and lived for a while in Taiwan, before moving to the United States where he established several restaurants. At one of these eateries (near the United Nations Headquarters), US Secretary of State Henry Kissinger took a shine to Peng's cooking, so that it suddenly attracted a lot of attention. Peng's efforts to lure in American customers prompted him to create one dish that caught on in a big way: General Tso's Chicken. According to Dunlop, other restaurants copied Peng's creation and the dish began to appear on Chinese restaurant menus throughout the West. General Tso's Chicken is not native to China and is still virtually unheard of in its supposedly "native" Hunan province.

One of the most well-known "Chinese food" dishes in the United States, therefore, is arguably not Chinese at all.[8]

This is not to say that differences between the cuisines of different cultures do not exist. The emotions and cultural weight attached to eating vary greatly across East Asia. Jia Huixuan, a well-known Chinese historian of food culture, is on target when he argues that Chinese historical texts discuss food and drink with much more reverence and frequency than Japanese documents. In Japan, however, a different myth exists and is promoted by government agencies. Japan's Ministry of Agriculture, Forestry and Fisheries (MAFF) continues to promulgate the dubious claim that Japanese traditional cuisine has always been healthy and tasty, and the envy of the world from the outset. To be sure, modern Japanese cuisine is excellent and Tokyo, arguably, has more internationally acclaimed restaurants than any other comparable city. However, the multi-layered and exciting Japanese cuisine of today is far different from what the Japanese historically ate. This type of amnesia about cuisine history needs to be untangled to understand where ramen fits in. Official documents published by the "Delicious Japan!" campaign (a program that MAFF underwrites) promote the idea that Japanese cuisine centers on a bowl of rice accompanied by soup and a side dish. The claim is that this style of cuisine embodies the supposed Japanese "spirit of frugality" adopted throughout the nation centuries ago. The ministry pushes the idea that the essence of Japanese cuisine involves preparing seasonal foods in a simple manner, making the most of their natural flavors and allowing nothing to go to waste.[9]

It sounds appealing – but it is not quite accurate, especially given that the way the Japanese eat today is not the way they did before the sweeping reforms of the post-1868 Meiji era. There are forms of Japanese cuisine that have evolved over the centuries but there is no one unchanging set of dishes that remain constant since time immemorial. Japanese food has been constantly in flux and the richness of its flavors and dazzling presentation are much more a recent phenomenon than an enduring tradition.

Noodles and Nationalism

In 1949, the historian Redcliffe Salaman published an innocuous-sounding book, entitled *The History and Social Influence of the Potato*. It was not a

---

[8] Fuchsia Dunlop, "Hunan Resources," *The New York Times*, February 4, 2007, also detailed in her book *Revolutionary Chinese Cookbook: Recipes from Hunan Province*.

[9] http://www.maff.go.jp/e/oishii/index.html.

best-seller but it highlighted some crucial issues. Until recently, the potato as a force of history has been otherwise ignored, perhaps unfairly. The Irish know its political impact all too well because of the horrific potato famine of the mid-nineteenth century. However, history books have tended to limit the discussion of potatoes and other food issues to just a few lines, preferring to recount the succession of kings and political parties.[10] Yet, the potato's history is precisely about power politics because it helped make possible the industrial revolution. It also may have helped Japan's western feudal domains acquire wealth and lead the Meiji Restoration in the mid-nineteenth century, by providing ample nutrition when competing regions were left with poor harvests and an inadequate food supply. Simply put, if the population of a country is famine-stricken, the government falls and the masses rebel, as Jared Diamond argues in his work on the interaction between the environment and culture, *Collapse: How Societies Choose to Fail or Succeed.* In this context, the evolution of what comes to be called "national cuisine" has significant social and political implications. Ramen illustrates this evolving concept of "national cuisine." East Asian dietary habits now affect the larger world, as can be seen in the late-twentieth century explosion of interest in Asian gastronomic traditions. From Tokyo to New York, Paris and Manchester, supermarkets and restaurants now offer the latest East Asian foods. Ramen is a central part of this trend.

The evolution of ramen is the result of an astoundingly complex process of cultural transmission, agricultural development, national shifts of eating patterns and serendipity, mixed together in almost equal amounts. The history of ramen does not start, as is sometimes claimed, with Chinese "pulled noodles" (*la-mian*) in Lanzhou, China. Nor did the arrival of the well-known European traveler to China, Marco Polo, have much impact on the situation. Another popular story with mythical elements is the immigrant narrative whereby nineteenth-century Chinese emigrants traveled to Japan in search of work and carried the recipes with them. Had the Chinese actually imported such a dish before the twentieth century, few in Japan would have dared to eat it; foreign food did not meet Japanese food preferences. For ramen to be created and accepted, the Japanese had to undergo a revolution in their eating and cooking habits, and that took centuries, if not almost a millennium. The elements to make and market ramen were invented or developed during various eras and across various

---

[10] One recent exception to the avoidance of the potato in history is John Reader, *The Untold History of the Potato.*

regions but did not really all come together in Japan until the early twentieth century.

The truth of the matter is that the story behind the birth of ramen starts in ancient times. A staggering assortment of flavors and components needed to appear precisely at the right time and these resources needed to be manipulated in a certain manner to satisfy a complex new set of consumer demands. It is quite difficult to produce an item that no one knows they will enjoy. Once both the demand and the supply conditions were met, the ingredients had to find delivery systems, not only in terms of geographical transport (to be cooked in a region where people appreciated the taste), but also in terms of bowl and spoon (essential for eating). For the ingredients and appliances to come together in one bowl in a specific mixed form is close to a culinary miracle. None of the items crucial to the birth of ramen – the noodles, meat broths, soy sauce, seaweed, bowls, spoons and toppings – occurred without human intervention between China and Japan.

To fathom the complex process of how all these items arrived in Japan to be used in the development of one of the most popular dishes on earth, we will start at the beginning. Before we discover how ramen was made, we need to investigate why Japanese even wanted to eat it and that story begins in ancient East Asia.

◊

To recount how flour became noodles and noodles became ramen only speaks to the story's skeleton. The real narrative describes the cultural development, travels, people and events that shaped how the Chinese and Japanese ate. We must begin, therefore, with the origins of noodle eating and East Asian food culture – and that means tackling the myths of eating in premodern times.

CHAPTER ONE

THREE SAGES WALK INTO A RESTAURANT AND ... NOODLES

Whatever type of noodle you wished to make in ancient China, you first needed to mill flour. No milling tools, no noodles. The technology to grind grains into flour, mix dough and shape it into noodles long predates the central Chinese state, originally unified under the first emperor, Qin Shihuang (who reigned 221-210 BCE). As the Chinese scholar H.T. Huang notes in an exhaustive history of Chinese science, recipes and practices from Central Asian peoples influenced the rise of the noodle/bread items that grew popular in China.[1] The technology to make and use flour is ancient. Flour for bread has been uncovered in archeological digs in Turkey dating from 5500 BCE, and the technology probably traveled east and north through Mongolia to China. Traces of flour have been carbon-dated to 3000 BCE in various Chinese provinces, including eastern Anhui, western Qinghai and southern Yunan. In 2005, the Chinese media reported that 4,000-year-old noodles, the oldest ever found, had been unearthed in the Lajia archaeological dig in northwestern China. It appears that the Chinese might have been eating fairly well when most others were not. The expertise needed to take grains and crush them into flour might have been guarded technology, because it only arrived in Japan through Korea centuries later – around the fourth or fifth century CE.

Japan was slow to acquire Chinese food technology and in ancient times seemed very distant from its cultured and sophisticated neighbor. Third-century Chinese dynastic records, when they refer at all to the small island country to their east, noted that the Japanese still ate with their hands, a practice considered by ancient Chinese to be grossly uncouth.[2] In ancient China, cuisine and the manner of eating were not considered superficial or unimportant; they demonstrated and symbolized a culture's level of civilization. The Chinese liked to claim that they had already stopped eating with their hands and started using chopsticks by the Spring

---

[1] H.T. Huang, *Science and Civilisation in China Series*, Vol. 6, Biology and Biological Technology, part 5, Fermentations and Food Science; Silvano Serventi and Francoise Sabban. *Pasta: The Story of a Universal Food*.
[2] Harada Nobuo, *Washoku to Nihon bunka*, p. 61.

and Autumn period (900–600BCE). In ancient China, food was served at dining tables for the elite, who also often employed culinary vocabulary as political metaphors in discussions. Regardless of your background or uncouth upbringing, you could become more civilized by following Chinese dietary rituals and the rules of Confucianism that grew in importance after the fifth century BCE. The ideology of Confucianism lay at the root of ancient Chinese society and it set out a strict set of five relationships in which the vassal obeyed his ruler, the father followed his ancestors and the son complied with the father's wishes – and so on down the social ladder. Women, not so fortunate in this male-oriented environment, obeyed male commands. The patriarch was the law of house and home. These five relations, if followed correctly, were thought to encourage the establishment of a harmonious society over which the leader had authority, guiding his subjects with his superior behavior. Part of correct Confucian conduct included knowing the precise arrangements and etiquette for rituals and festivals, and for eating and drinking. The *Analects*, Confucius' manual and exposition on the harmonious society, detailed the need to eat and drink in moderation, claiming that proper mealtime ritual helped to create and maintain a just and equal society. For the early Chinese, as the old adage explained, "to eat correctly was as much an instrument of virtue as an expression of it."[3] Even today, eating is a part of how Chinese people relate to one another – it is a form of social lubricant. There is an old Chinese saying that translates as, "the origin of politesse is found in food and drink."[4] The fundamentals of etiquette and the proper development of society derive from how one eats and drinks at the table.

Japanese cuisine developed differently and few metaphors for politics connected with cooking can be found in Japanese historical texts, though eating obviously retained many aspects of pleasurable socializing. It was not that the Japanese did not eat – of course they did. The process of preparing and consuming a meal in Japan, the art of cuisine, simply did not occupy the same vital social and moral role in ancient society. It did not become the means to express wider political issues as it did in China. In the premodern era, Japanese foodways often remained relegated to fantasy. According to historian of Japanese cuisine Eric Rath, chefs would

---

[3] Reay Tannahill, *Food in History*, p. 127.
[4] Jia Huixuan, "Zhongri yinshiguan bianyi," in Li Shijing, edited, *Zhonghua shiyuan*, Vol. 6, p. 349. For views on ancient and modern Chinese views on food see Judith Farquhar's *Appetites, food and sex in post-socialist China* and Roel Sterckx's *Food, Sacrifice, and Sagehood in Early China*.

create elaborately beautiful works of art from a variety of ingredients that could never be consumed and these would be placed on the dining table as a decoration.[5] This divergence between the political and social roles played by cuisine in ancient China and premodern Japan might explain why the Chinese experimented with a much wider variety of tastes and ingredients than the Japanese, who essentially were satisfied with bland and mainly vegetarian food until well into the fifteenth century.

Eating in Japan does contain religious significance and the early vocabulary used for talking about the dining ritual is related in part to Shinto, the Japanese indigenous religion. Harada Nobuo, a well-known Japanese food historian, explains that in Japan popular rituals emphasized food as part of a process of sharing offerings with the gods.[6] Ancient Shinto tracts mentioned noodles that had to be prepared and placed in various formations and containers to meet ceremonial guidelines. These religious texts emphasized the appearance of food rather than its taste, because beauty was important in the ceremony for the gods, *kami matsuri*.[7] To over-generalize, the Chinese focused on taste while the Japanese specialized in the aesthetics of presentation. Despite this, once the Japanese (who loved *tsuru tsuru* or "slurpy" foods) actually came into contact with Chinese noodles, it was only a matter of time before a fascination with them developed.

In ancient times, Japanese peasants learned to digest a range of foods. Many were prized for their medicinal value and some also offered excellent nutrition.[8] Chinese meals usually consisted of some grains, a few vegetables and some fruits, with occasionally a small amount of meat, brought together in a stew-like concoction. Japanese meals were similar, although usually without the meat. In China, there were manuals of instruction explaining how to cook properly. Jia Sixie, one of the leading agronomists in Chinese history, penned a massive agricultural encyclopedia, better known as the famous sixth-century manual for cooking, entitled "Essential Skills for the Common People" (*Qinmin Yaoshu*). It is the earliest and most complete treatise on preparing food ever found in the lands that made up ancient China. Jia's tome was one of the first to print the recipe for a type of noodle called *bing*.

---

[5] Eric Rath, *Food and Fantasy in Early Modern Japanese Foodways*.
[6] Harada Nobuo, *Washoku to Nihon bunka,* pp. 43–44. A whole scholarly debate surges around the origins of Shintoism and whether it is a religion.
[7] Harada Nobuo, *Washoku to Nihon bunka,* p. 72.
[8] E.N. Anderson, *The Food of China,* p. 106.

The Arrival of Noodles in China – Noodle Loaf?

Ramen connoisseurs in Japan today knowingly nudge their neighbors when a novice noodle-eater enters the room and makes the greatest of all mistakes: quiet noodle-eating. Nothing earns complete social disdain more quickly. Discerning customers understand that noodle soup needs to be eaten very hot and thus you need to slurp. A whoosh of the chopsticks, cradled by a large spoon, rising triumphantly toward the eager mouth as the steam rolls off noodles dripping with liquid, completes the action. In order to avoid scalding your tongue you must simultaneously suck in cool air. Sucking in air and slurping in noodles at the same time results in a delightful sound of *schlu, schlu*, a noise guaranteed to offend the ears of most Western mothers trying to raise polite offspring. In Japan, if noodles are not slurped it signals that they are not hot enough, or that they are not tasty ... in short, this means that the ramen chef has failed in his mission to deliver something worth tucking into. Noodles that are daintily eaten, noodles that are pecked at, noodles that are stared at, are not ramen. They are something else, something unmentionable to ramen purists. Slurping ramen has become such a common and popular midday meal for office workers that many Japanese men now slurp quite a few of their meals. Women slurp as well, although usually with not as much gusto in public. I once heard a Japanese colleague slurp a bologna sandwich and as I type these words on my laptop in a coffee shop in Shinjuku, downtown Tokyo, I can testify that the guy at the table next to me is slurping his chocolate muffin for breakfast.

Noodles were not always slurped in this way. In fact, they could not have been, because early noodles were probably not noodles at all but a food closer to bread. The forerunner of noodles was a flat, bread-like foodstuff known in the Chinese language as *bing*; the original word meaning to blend flour and water to make dough.[9] Early Chinese cooks produced *bing* by flattening a doughy mixture of flour and water and frying it on an oiled flat pan, or dropping it into a broth and boiling it. The Chinese considered *bing* a form of pasta, a food group that "covered a wide range of food made from grains. The dough from wheat flour could be unleavened or raised. It could be fried, baked, steamed or boiled."[10] As Francoise Sabban's

---

[9] David R. Knechtges, "Gradually Entering the Realm of Delight: Food and Drink in Early Medieval China," *Journal of the American Oriental Society*, Vol. 117, No. 2, April-June 1997, p. 234.

[10] H.T. Huang, *Science and Civilisation in China Series*, Vol. 6, Biology and Biological Technology, part 5, Fermentations and Food Science, p. 474.

academic history of pasta recounts, *bing* was so popular and widespread that, in the third century, a poet penned an "Ode to Bing."[11]

Today in China, *bing* are round flat dough cakes usually stuffed with something savory or sweet. Early *bing* were mostly made from wheat flour, the technology of milling having been slowly appropriated from Central Asia. According to most early Chinese accounts, over time *bing* was most likely flattened and lengthened, and came to resemble the longer and thinner shape we associate with noodles. One theory is that *bing* started as something rolled and then someone thought of the idea of unrolling the thin loaf and cutting it into strands – thus creating the ancestor of noodles. Exactly how and why this process took place is the subject of myriad

Figure 4. A foodstall vendor in contemporary China selling modern breakfast *bing*. Today, this warm treat is offered with a fried egg inside and a choice of spicy or salty toppings. It does not look anything like a noodle. Over the centuries *bing* changed shape drastically – it was stretched out and rolled, altering how it looked but not essentially what it was made of.

---

[11] Silvano Serventi and Francoise Sabban, *Pasta: The Story of a Universal Food*, pp. 281–296, details how early imperial Chinese high society loved *bing* products and how that aided their proliferation within Chinese society.

debates. Theories proliferate; some professional historians and archeologists have devoted their entire careers to the analysis of *bing* evolution and the search for evidence to support one theory over another. *Bing* products spread widely but, in China, their transformation into noodles did not really take place until the sixth century.[12] The modern Chinese term for noodles (pronounced *mian* in Mandarin) merely meant wheat flour in ancient times. (In Japanese, the equivalent term *men* is written with the same Chinese character 麵.) In ancient times, vocabulary relating to food was not always precise. Dishes did not always have particular names attached to them because there was little need to distinguish any one item. You were not going to buy it on the street – restaurants as such did not really come into existence until the late Song dynasty in China (960–1279) and these were among the earliest in the world. Not until the explosion of printed media did certain preconceptions of what a particular dish should look like and be called start to become more standardized.

Initially the word *bing* could have meant wheat flour or noodles, or a foodstuff of similar provenance. Free association of terminology is not uncommon even today in our heavily media-saturated world. In America, for example, when people in different states refer to pizza they may actually be thinking about remarkably different dishes and tastes – think deep-dish Chicago-style versus thin crust in New York. Such a problem grows exponentially over a very large country or where several countries are involved. Ask for pizza in Japan and it will quite often be topped with mayonnaise, heretical to most pizza-lovers in the West (particularly so in my home town of New Jersey where pizza fans are legion).

Not only did noodle vocabulary fluctuate on any given day but the shape of *bing* also varied greatly. In previous centuries, it could have been spherical, oblong or flat and it would still have been considered a noodle. Recipes were orally transmitted, with the first written recipe for something similar to our modern noodle recorded in the sixth-century Chinese cooking manual, "Essential Skills for the Common People." These noodles were yanked off a large *bing* in a process called *shuiyin*, or "wet drawn pulling," where cooks dipped an uncooked blob of dough into a bowl of water and, at the same time, peeled off string-like ends to make longer and

---

[12] We can use the definition of noodle from famed Japanese historian of food Ishige Naomichi, "a linear processed food made from the flour of cereals, beans and potatoes, which must be boiled for serving," as quoted in H.T. Huang, *Science and Civilisation in China Series*, Vol. 6, Biology and Biological Technology, part 5, Fermentations and Food Science, p. 490.

thinner strands. The result was probably a sort of flat, thin noodle akin to fettuccini. Who initiated this experimentation remains unknown.

Much of what we assume to be Chinese cuisine is really an amalgamation of tastes and recipes that have flowed in from the outside, from regions including India, Persia, Russia and Mongolia and from southern tribes and Central Asian empires such as the Sogdian and Khotan which no longer exist. For this reason, some food historians argue that the Silk Road should be known also as the "Noodle Road." While this term may not find favor everywhere, it does reflect a corrective view of how we should be looking at the growth of noodle-eating and technology in East Asia. Food, tastes and cooking methods followed business and the transmission of other knowledge, both religious and scientific, across national boundaries and along major trade routes. No single culture monopolized the invention of any one food – innovation emanated from interaction with surrounding neighbors and regions. Historically speaking, there is no one Chinese cuisine; it is a pastiche of many regional cuisines. If we consider it unique, that is mainly because food and taste help us identify with our own ethnicity and origins – we prefer to consider national cuisines as non-changing entities that make it easier for us to distinguish one culture from another.[13] While the noodle that was the forerunner of ramen acquired distinct traits in China, its roots belong just as much to Central Asia.

Food Legends and the Roots of Noodle Worship

Given the ambiguity surrounding who ate what in ancient East Asia, it should come as no surprise that prehistoric Japan (6000 BCE to 400 CE) remains clouded in mystery, even as new excavations continue to unearth evidence and use innovative methods to untangle the past. There are few records from this era and early accounts can be found only in Chinese and Korean documents. Recent archeological finds are beginning to shed light on Japan's origins, but contentious debates continue. One of the first official Chinese references to Japan comes from a famous third-century CE treatise, the "History of the Three Kingdoms."[14] Within this historical

---

[13] David Y.H. Wu and Sidney C.H. Cheung, eds., *The Globalization of Chinese Food*, p. 7.
[14] The three kingdoms denotes a time when the area we call China was actually composed of three separate realms – *Wei*, the largest with a capital at what is now the city of Luoyang in the central west, *Wu* with its seat in the city known in modern times as Nanjing on the eastern seaboard and *Shu* with a center at Chengdu, the modern capital of Sichuan province in the southwest.

record, a section entitled 'The Eastern Barbarian Dwarf Land,' describes a country that was the forerunner of Japan and probably located on the island of Kyushu, the westernmost of Japan's four main islands. It is important to remember that much of Japanese history begins in what is called western Japan, actually the southern region. It is called western Japan because rather than standing north–south on the earth, the Japanese archipelago sits along an east–west axis. Thus, southern Japan was historically and still is referred to as western Japan. This particular Chinese chronicle described a kingdom, Yamatai, that was probably located in western Japan and ruled by a Queen Himiko.[15] The exact historical location of Yamatai continues to bedevil scholars on all sides of the Pacific but as J. Kidder suggests in his book on the topic, it was a place where one thousand female attendants supposedly served Himiko and thus, while it may have been diminutive in comparison to China, it could not have been completely insignificant.[16] Yamatai, regardless of its exact placement and construct, was in a sense the first central stronghold and birthplace of ancient Japanese culture.

Based on archeological excavations, Chinese sources and semi-historical, semi-fictional military tales, we assume that before the seventh century the Japanese ate meat. They might never have been big consumers of beef or horse, but crane, deer and wild boar were popular at all levels of society. Buddhism slowly crept into Japan from China over the early centuries and took root during the seventh century, when the Yamato court (which may or may not have grown out of the Yamatai kingdom – no scholarly consensus having yet been reached) adopted it from China and established it as the state religion. Yamato was the early seat of imperial Japan in the *Kinki* or central plains of Japan, known today also as the Kansai region. Prince Shōtoku (who may or may not have existed) is reputed to have urged the adoption of the Chinese calendar and various government facilities in the early 600s. Regardless of the quality of the historical evidence and the academic debates that surround it, most scholars agree that a Japanese early kingdom of some type became established in

---

[15] For a fuller explanation see Gari Ledyard, "Galloping along with the Horseriders: Looking for the Founders of Japan," *Journal of Japanese Studies*, Vol. 1, No. 2., Spring 1975, pp. 230–232. Ledyard says we should understand the region as a Thallocracy, a region of interconnected islands with a semi-common administration and loyalty to the center, like the Minoan civilization.

[16] William Wayne Farris, *Sacred Texts and Buried Treasures*, p. 34. See also, J. Edward Kidder, *Himiko and Japan's Elusive Chiefdom of Yamatai: Archaeology, History and Mythology*.

this region and that it did adopt Chinese styles of administration. In 674, Emperor Tenmu announced a *sesshō kindanrei*, or "prohibition on killing live things" and Japan took steps toward discouraging the consumption of meat, thus creating the conditions for the state's promotion of vegetarianism in accordance with the tenets of Buddhism. Subsequent emperors would continue to make such exhortations for several centuries.[17] That, at least, is how the story is popularly told, although the actual original decree reads a bit differently from the ancient collection of myths and historical tracts. In the *Nihon shoki,* the ancient collection of myth and historical tracts, the emperor proclaimed that:

> Henceforth the fisherman and hunters are to be restrained from making pitfalls or using spear-traps and like contrivances. Moreover, from the 1st day of the 4th month until the 13th day of the 9th month, let no one set fish-traps, closing the space. Further, let no one eat the flesh of kine [cattle], horses, dogs, monkeys, or barn-door fowls. *This prohibition does not extend to other kinds of meat*. Offenders against this regulation will be punished.[18]

Tenmu may have been quite religious – he would not be the first or last regent with the desire to lead his people toward the path of moral righteousness – but he did not ban the consumption of all meat outright. Bans were placed on hunting some sources of meat during some seasons but others were obviously within the legal limits to butcher. One plausible scenario is that the ruling Japanese families wanted to organize the nascent Japanese state around agriculture, specifically wet-field rice paddies, and to push the farmers to focus on the production of food, namely rice and vegetables to be used to pay for taxes. In Han dynasty China the administration had paid its employees in various grains and the Japanese imperial family wanted to copy that idea. However, Japan's geography and demographics were not right for the production of all types of grain. Peasants needed to be urged into growing rice so the coffers of the government would be full enough to pay for the growing number of officials. Another equally important task was to distract the competing powerful families in the area. Buddhism was vital for accomplishing both requirements. Buddhism was power politics in the ancient world of early Japan and rice was the economic lubricant.

---

[17] In Japanese this is termed, *sesshō kindanrei,* (殺生禁断令); Itō kinen zaidan ed., *Nihon shokuniku bunkashi*, pp. 75–80; Kikkoman edited series, *Food Culture*, Vol. 1, Watanabe Zenjirō, "Sekai o kakeru Nihongata shoku seikatsu no henbō," p. 28.

[18] W.G. Aston (translation), *Nihongi: Chronicles of Japan from the Earliest Times to AD 697*, pp. 328–329.

This small Japanese kingdom did not have access to agricultural or mineral riches like its Chinese and Korean neighbors; nevertheless, food and the harvest played a significant role in government rituals. As historian Herman Ooms tells us in his book about rituals and symbols in ancient Japan: "Offering food was a gesture of seeking to ingratiate oneself with someone more elevated: district officials with provincial governors, they with the monarch and he or she with the *kami* [gods]."[19] The kingdom expanded both in power and territory, but the main shift came in 710, when the Japanese capital moved to a location now known as Nara, much more in the center of the main island of Japan than Yamatai may have been, not far from modern-day Kyoto. This new Japanese capital was a direct replica of the Chinese capital Chang'an; its bureaucratic structure was also a virtual copy. In 794, Emperor Kammu moved the capital again, this time a bit further north to the village of Heian, later known as Kyoto, where it remained the Japanese imperial seat for the next thousand years.

In contrast to the clearly-defined frontiers that separate countries in today's world, prior to the seventh century relations between kingdoms in northern China, Korea and western Japan were locally defined and less identifiable. There were no nations, in our modern sense of the word. Before the latter part of the sixth century CE, no defined boundary existed between the island of Kyushu and the Korean peninsula.[20] There was a rich exchange of cultures: ships and people of different nations frequented the seas. Food technology, cooks, recipes and eating styles all traveled easily within this region bounded by the East China Sea, the Yellow Sea and the Sea of Japan. One of the more popular gateways for the mixing of cultures was the city of Hakata on the northwest coast of Kyushu.[21] According to historian Bruce Batten, Hakata Bay is one of the finest natural harbors in Kyushu and so frequent was travel from one coast to the other that local officials erected watchtowers on hills overlooking the sea to announce the arrival of foreign ships and serve as sentry posts.[22] I was struck, while traveling for this research, by the great wealth western Japan historically produced and the strong links it maintained with the rest of East Asia. Although in our own time we tend to focus on Tokyo as the center of Japan and the source of electronic gadgets and opulent fashion, Tokyo had little influence on national culture until quite recently. The far west was where

---

[19] Herman Ooms, *Imperial Politics and Symbolics in Ancient Japan: The Tenmu Dynasty, 650–800*, p. 108.
[20] Bruce Batten, *Gateway to Japan: Hakata in War and Peace, 500–1300*, p. 24.
[21] Ibid., p. 24.
[22] Ibid., p. 33.

Japanese history began; Tokyo only became the central player from the 1600s onward.

Japan was not formally part of China's political and cultural orbit until the seventh century and it did not fully invest in appropriating Chinese culture until this time. Chinese texts describe a Japan that was relatively untouched by Chinese influence. The Japanese were said to enjoy a kind of dumpling soup, called *huntunjiao* in Chinese, although scholars are unclear about its contents. Once exchange grew more frequent, Chinese observed Japanese consuming grains as the main course of their meal, garnished with vegetable side dishes. This way of eating a central bowl of some starchy product with a small bowl of soup and several small plates of salted or pickled vegetables as side garnishes to help the rice go down appears to have a long history in Japanese culture.[23]

Native treatises about Japanese culture emerge around the eighth century. From what we gather from the remnants of these documents, Japanese food does not feature as it does in Chinese-style legends linking excessive eating and drinking with political decline, or as it does in Judeo/Christian biblical references such as the story of Adam and Eve's expulsion from the Garden of Eden with sexual downfall. By contrast, Japanese food myths create a positive link between food, sex and the rise of the nation. The historical record is notoriously incomplete when it comes to Japanese food and we have to make educated guesses based on some written but mostly archeological evidence. One primary source is the *Kojiki*, often translated as the *Record of Ancient Things* and thought to have been completed in 712 CE. This chronicle was essentially a compilation of events long since passed that had been transmitted orally through the centuries; even though written essentially in classical Chinese, the stories deal with the origins of things Japanese. There was also an "official history" called the *Nihon shoki*, or *Chronicles of Japan*, which was completed around 720, soon after the *Kojiki*. The two records are similar, except that the *Kojiki* focuses on origin myths while the *Nihon shoki* is more interested in historical accounts and the genealogical charts of rulers. Of course, neither is truly accurate in any historical sense since they both mythologize the development of Japan.

The birth of Japan in the legend-filled *Kojiki* is related to sexual intercourse between two gods, Izanagi and Izanami. The historic text, in one of

---

[23] Zako Jun, "Nihon ni okeru Chūgoku shokubunka," in Sai Ki edited, *Nihon ni okeru Chūgoku dentō bunka*, pp. 245–257. (The direct Chinese citation is: 新校本三國志/魏書/卷三十 魏書三十/東夷/ 倭人传, 854.)

the first English translations, rendered their dialogue in somewhat stilted terms. Izanagi says: "My body is formed but has one place that is formed to excess." To which Izanami coquettishly replies, "My body is formed but has a place that is formed insufficiently." In true omnipotent fashion Izanagi realizes his excess might just fit well into Inazami's insufficiency. They have sex several times, resulting in the birth of their children, the Japanese islands.[24] The original Japanese text was too scandalous for a nineteenth century Western audience. For example, when the two gods spoke to one another about their body parts, Izanagi actually exclaimed to his female partner that he would "thrust and fill you up," and she retorted in the affirmative, "that would be quite good."[25] When the first English translations were produced, prudish Victorian scholars rendered what they considered the more salacious parts into Latin so that only the scholastically gifted could grasp the meaning.

The *Record of Ancient Things* was very helpful in also explaining to the Japanese people the origins of the five grains on which their existence depended. As with many religions, the practice of belief was supported by ritualistic consumption of food. In ancient Japan, this was taken a step further. According to the legend, one of the principal gods, Susanoo, grew hungry and ordered Ugetsu, also known as Ukemochi, a name that means "to protect food," to make him a meal.[26] Presumably because she had god-like powers, instead of rustling up a meal Ugetsu turned away from Susanoo and started emitting foods from several of her orifices. Disgusted and insulted at the manner in which he had been served, Susanoo beat Ugetsu, and she died from his blows. Prone on the ground, she merged with the earth, and from her corpse grew the five grains that people relied on in their daily lives. After her demise, Ugetsu became an all-producing god: silkworms grew from her head, rice seedlings from her eye sockets, millet from her ears, and red beans from her nostrils. Wheat sprouted out of her vagina and soybeans from her anus. If Susanoo thought the meal Ugetsu originally produced came from unclean sources, the legend does not divulge what he made of this sequel to the meal.[27] While these gods

---

[24] *Kojiki*, translated and notes by Donald Philippi, p. 50.

[25] Kurano Kenji, Takeda Yūkichi, *Kojiki*, Nihon koten bungaku taikei, Vol. 1, p. 53.

[26] The transliterated spellings of Japanese god names vary widely so I standardize them here for the sake of readability.

[27] Jia Huixuan "Qianxi Zhongri yinshi wenhua zhi tedian," in Li Shijing, editor, *Zhonghua shiyuan*, Vol. 8, p. 313. Chinese and Japanese interpretations, as well as English, differ somewhat. Also see *Kojiki*, translated and notes by Donald Philippi, p. 87; and Kurano Kenji, Takeda Yūkichi, *Kojiki*, p. 85.

and myths no longer have any significant bearing in postwar, modern Japan, they were believed in for millennia and treated as sacrosanct.

Premodern Noodles

Anyone who has spent time in East Asia knows that the region is awash with noodley dishes. In China there are noodles of every shape. Dozens of verbs are used to describe noodle-making; they can be twisted, pulled, spooned-over twice and recooked, knife-sliced, steamed and kneaded. There are even "embarrassed noodles," though why they are embarrassed was not clear to me when I ate them. As with many noodles in western China these were shaved from large blocks of dough and flung into a tub of hot water. In 2004, when I visited Ningxia, a remote western province of China, on the same street two noodle vendors offered from their stalls thirty different variations of noodle soup, made mostly with similar ingredients. In China, especially in the western regions, noodles are ubiquitous.

The Japanese on the other hand consumed vast quantities of what eventually came to be known as *soba* and *udon*. *Soba* is a thinner easily breakable noodle, made from buckwheat flour, that is usually served cold on a plate and dipped into a sauce before slurping. *Udon* is a thick wheat noodle often served in a thin broth. Both of these noodles had their heyday during the Tokugawa era, but they were not produced in alkaline water and that made them less springy than the ramen noodles that evolved later. Nonetheless, both *soba* and *udon* remain popular today; they share in the history of noodle evolution that led to ramen. The first noodles that came to Japan were usually either served plain or with a cold vegetable side dish. They might not have been warm or even that tasty, but they were extremely popular and obviously fed an enthusiasm for culinary delights from the Chinese mainland that followed once Japan opened more in the later 1800s. The forerunner of what later turned into *udon* and *soba* probably made the journey from southeast China to Japan during the Nara period (710 to 794) and this noodle dish was called *hōtō* (a form of it can still be enjoyed in some of today's Yamanashi prefectural restaurants, located west of Tokyo in the Kantō region). *Hōtō* was a flat noodle cut like an *udon* noodle and served with a hot broth. The Chinese version of this dish was called *botuo* and the first reference as to how to cook it can be found in the *Essential Skills for the Common People* cookbook.

As with much technology and information exchange in premodern days, trade and commerce in food products and technology was mainly a

Figure 5. Noodle-makers on the street in western China. The small white blur leaving the cook's hands is the "flung noodle" that will land in the large barrel of boiling water.

by-product of the travels of itinerant Buddhist monks, who undertook hazardous journeys from various parts of Japan deep into the heart of China to study the intricacies of the human spirit and the source of enlightenment.[28] Buddhist monks traveling back and forth between Japan and China played a crucial role in the transmission of national tastes, as did officials and religious pilgrims from Korea.[29] The blandness of native Japanese cuisine must have made the foreign religion of Buddhism with its link to Chinese food seem all the more appealing. Even though Buddhism was originally an Indian religion, it took hold in China and spread eastward. The main tenets of its philosophy are that life is full of suffering; and that to ease that suffering we must rid ourselves of desire. We must also behave correctly and follow the five rules, which include not taking a life, wounding or causing anything to suffer.

In the seventh century, a Japanese Buddhist priest returned from China with the Nirvana Sutra. The Nirvana Sutra assists devotees in comprehending the five stages of understanding the world, a process that eventually leads to enlightenment. These stages are difficult for most laymen to fathom; one metaphor meant presumably to aid comprehension compared the five stages of enlightenment with various products derived from milk: as you rose on the scale toward enlightenment, the taste of the milk products got creamier and richer – you could taste your way into nirvana! Readers were taught to conceive of enlightenment as being similar to a process of making milk into cream, or taking a base ingredient and enhancing its texture and taste. In a world where a rich diet was beyond the means of most inhabitants, this analogy for illiterate followers must have been easy to grasp, with the taste of cream serving as an unattainable and yet extremely desirable aim. Believers began their practice as milk then advanced to the stage of curd or koumiss, then butter, then refined butter, and finally cream, the ultimate taste, referred to as *daigo* in Japanese.[30] In contemporary Japan, most people have forgotten its Buddhist origins, but the word *daigo* still means something like quintessence, or the *crème de la crème*.

---

[28] For excellent insight into the manner in which much of this culture started in India and made its way east through Buddhist travels, see John Kieschnick, *The Impact of Buddhism on Chinese Material Culture*.

[29] For reasons of clarity and space I have mostly left Korea out of this discussion concerning the transmission of ideas and technology from China to Japan but the early kingdoms on the Korean peninsula and the subsequent Yi dynasty after the fourteenth century played crucial roles in the evolution of exchange and thus the development of Japanese cuisine and identity.

[30] Ōchō Enichi, *Nehankyō to jōdokyō: hotoke no ganriki to jōbutsu no shin*, p. 102.

From eighth-century records found in temples in Nara, historians have discovered that members of the court of the Nara period frequently consumed large quantities of milk and buttery products, very different from what we are usually led to believe about a rice- and soy-dominated Japanese diet. No one is exactly sure what form the milk took but it was not likely to have resembled the processed milk drunk today because it was often refined, rendering it more like a custard or thick cream in texture.[31] Okamura Ayao, a professor of Japanese literature who has written extensively about ancient Japanese dietary practices, and hosted a popular television show that recreates these meals, has written that the Nara elite routinely drank gallons of refined buttermilk and other milk products. A popular ancient Japanese medical text, the "Ishinpō," copied Chinese medicinal practices and strongly recommended consuming dairy products in order to maintain strong bones and healthy muscles.[32]

In 805 CE, the Japanese Buddhist monk Eichū (743–816), who had studied in Tang dynasty China for about thirty years, returned home and was shocked at the poor fare his countrymen considered dinner. He had not realized how meager Japanese meals were compared with what was available in Chang'an (now the city of Xian), the then capital of the Tang dynasty. Eichū founded the Bonshaku Temple in what is now Shiga Prefecture, in western central Japan. He was also one of the first traveling Buddhist monks to bring green tea back to Japan. The failure of imported tea to captivate Japanese drinkers at the time can help us understand how the arrival of a new food or technology does not automatically mean that the product will be accepted in its new homeland. Green tea is now almost synonymous with Japan, so it is ironic that the brew found few takers when it was first introduced in the ninth century. No one liked it – it was too bitter and left an unpleasant aftertaste. The product itself was probably inferior, but more importantly the Japanese taste preferences were not yet prepared to accept tea, regardless of its supposed medicinal benefits and immense popularity in China. It was not until the rise of Zen Buddhism and Japan's reconnection with China in the thirteenth century that tea-drinking became a key element in Japanese dining. Attitudes changed and, more importantly, certain elements of the upper classes were prepared to pay for it.

---

[31] Sekine Shinryū, *Naracho shokuseikatsu no kenkyū*, p. 274.
[32] Okamura Ayao, "Kodaishoku no fukugen," *Chōri kagaku*, Vol. 24, no. 1, 1991, p. 70. See also the Japanese Buddhist explanation from the mid-Meiji era, Katō Eshō, *Nenbutsu daigo hyōzō*, pp. 2–4.

Buddhist travelers continued to be the main force behind much of the exchanges of culture in East Asia. On the noodle issue, Ennin, another well-known early Japanese Buddhist monk who participated in one of the last official Japanese missions to China in 838, mentions the *botuo* noodle in his diary of the journey and may have been responsible for bringing the recipe to Japan.[33] Ennin ate the noodle dish all over China – in what are now Jiangsu, Shandong and Hebei provinces. Depending on the region and its culinary style, *botuo* was like its noodle colleague *bing* in that it did not always have a predetermined shape. *Botuo* noodles were either similar to a dumpling, called *gyōza* in Japanese, or a thick noodle. Another noodle also appeared in Japan from China during the Nara period, something called *sakubei* (索餅), which was essentially anything rope-like and made from wheat flour. What is striking about this name is that the second of its two Chinese characters is the kanji used in Japanese to mean *mochi*, or sticky rice. It is also the character used in Chinese for *bing* (the noodle of indeterminate shape). The characters that described noodles were thus used for a variety of foods that included dumplings, thick and thin noodles and food items that were not noodley at all, like *mochi*. Some scholars suggest that this linguistic conflation of sticky rice and wheat noodles shows that noodles from the Nara period and before might not have been slippery and noodley at all but more what the Japanese call *neba neba*, or sticky, like chewy taffy, and probably not long and thin as we are used to today.

One other major peculiarity of Chinese noodles during the transition from the Tang to the Song dynasties was that the strands grew more springy, which made them very different from traditional domestic noodles in Japan. The Chinese had learned a new technique in noodle production, possibly gleaned from the foreigners arriving in great numbers from the surrounding regions. The Song era was a period of major disruption in China and saw the country split into northern and southern kingdoms; certain parts were even ruled by "barbarian tribes." It is during this innovative time that a new method to produce the noodles was introduced. This "Chinese" method used alkaline additives to the dough mixture to produce springy noodles, not ones that broke off easily when bitten into. Japanese *soba* and *udon* do not have this peculiar consistency, or *hagotae* ("teeth feel") as they say in Japanese. At the time, people boiled stewed

---

[33] Sakamoto Kazutoshi, *Dare mo shiranai Chūgoku rāmen no michi – Nihon rāmen no genryū o saguru*, p. 140.

vegetation with a bit of ash to create alkaline water. This water was added to flour to make dough for noodles. This new food technology produced a type of *al-dente* noodle that would slowly take over the market: it seemed heartier, could retain its shape and consistency in water and offered a more substantial "mouth-feel" when chewed.

Whatever the exact form was, generally speaking noodles were incorporated into a Japanese cuisine that was light and rather plain. This is in direct contrast to the numerous cooking styles involving spicy and syrupy sauces that China delighted in offering the world. Kumakura Isao, an expert on the historical evolution of Japanese food and the Japanese tea ceremony, once offered a decidedly simple explanation for this difference. Historically, Kumakura said, the essence of Japanese food was to do nothing: allow nature to provide its own taste and form; add nothing and let the natural flavors speak for themselves. Where the ancient Chinese viewed food as something to be manipulated, the Japanese focused more on the original state of the ingredients.[34] This difference may partly arise from the fact that historically the Chinese ate better, while the Japanese existed on what little they could and later refined a cooking style around the absence of abundant foodstuffs. During its early period of development, Japanese food, it would seem, was dull – neither plentiful, nor very satisfying. Acorns, a coarse mix of grains, and scant protein were standard features until well into the early modern era. It is no mystery why the Chinese never considered Japanese cuisine something to emulate: there was not much of it to digest. Ancient Japan was not known for its gourmet food. By the tenth century, however, the roots of noodle-making and noodle appreciation had already infiltrated all levels of society in Japan and heightened interest in the possibility of developing more nutritious and flavorsome foods.

---

[34] Kumakura Isao has organized a fundamental collection of essays detailing the history of Japanese cuisines, though not necessarily defining it, in Kōza shoku no bunka, Vol. 2, *Nihon no shokuji bunka*.

CHAPTER TWO

COURT FOOD VERSUS COMMON FOOD

The Heian period, which spanned the eighth to the twelfth centuries, was early Japan's artistic age. The era produced the world's first novel, *The Tale of Genji*, which epitomized unrequited love and melancholy: nobles seemed to have little to occupy their long days and nights but flirt with each other through poetry and occasionally indulge in courtly intrigue. Both men and women used cosmetics to beautify themselves: women shaved their eyebrows, painting a stylized form of them instead several inches higher up on their foreheads. At least for the upper classes, life must have been quite sterile. Heian court culture proscribed close and intimate contact: people rarely saw each other face-to-face and even members of the same sex, if not on close terms, met separated by a curtain. Such barriers to personal intimacy led to the use of incense as a way to charm one's lover. In the words of an historian regarding the aromatic interpersonal relations of the time, "[O]ne of the few means of forming an opinion on one's companion was the scent emanating from his or her quarters."[1] If you could not see your partner, it was probably best to smell them first. While other nobles were sniffing one another in the dark, the Fujiwara clan came to dominate the political landscape and they and the clergy amassed large estates outside the capital. Over the ensuing centuries, these estates were taken over by other power brokers who came to dominate the effete court nobles, establishing a militant and macho cult of the samurai with their seat at Kamakura, further east in an area not far from the modern city of Yokohama.

Even though the Heian court nobility produced fine literature and poetry, the quality of their life was less than brilliant. They gorged on rice with a few pickled side dishes and rarely exercised. It is doubtful whether the upper classes even made it outdoors, since most activities took place in the inner chambers of palace buildings. The men drank large quantities of a sweet alcoholic drink and developed a range of diabetic-related illnesses. People died from the slightest infections because their immune

---

[1] Aileen Gatten, "A Wisp of Smoke. Scent and Character in The Tale of Genji," *Monumenta Nipponica*, Vol. 32, No. 1, Spring, 1977, p. 36.

systems were so compromised. It is telling that Japanese fiction does not delight in descriptions of food, in the way that medieval Chinese fiction does – with, for example, plot lines linked to eating in the famous Qing dynasty novel, *Dream of the Red Chamber*. In *The Tale of Genji* and similar Japanese novels of the Heian period and later, there are no luscious descriptions of dining, banqueting, cooking or the beauty or taste of food. Such pleasures are completely absent. For Higuchi Kiyoyuki, an historian of Japanese literature, the Heian era is a "literature with no appetite."[2] This was essentially the situation until the seventeenth-century Tokugawa period. The Heian and subsequent medieval periods spawned a philosophy of life known as *mono no aware*, or an understanding of the pathos of things. It appears to originate from philosophical insight and the Buddhist reflection that life is fleeting and not always joyous. It is tempting to wonder whether this world view might not have been influenced by endless unpalatable meals eaten in dark corners under three-inch thick, multiple layers of silken robes weighing the courtly inhabitants down in body and soul. Needless to say, Heian courtiers were not eating ramen or many other noodles. They produced the world's first novel but no cookbooks.

During the Heian period, early Japanese administrations copied Chinese models of bureaucracy, and also created several *daizenshoku* positions for the court. Such positions mainly involved preparing meals for imperial residents.[3] As the government flourished and expanded its rule between the eighth and ninth centuries, important court positions were created to honor food-related functionaries in the Chinese fashion, regardless of what actually was required in the court in Japan. Holders of high office, therefore, included the "Steward of Sauce," responsible for a fish sauce that was a precursor of Japanese soy sauce and the "Brew Master," responsible for alcoholic drinks, from early on a crucial item at Japanese banquets.[4]

By the tenth century, through a combination of Chinese influences trickling in through trade and religion, combined with native Japanese ingredients and customs, the basic tastes of Japanese cuisine had put down roots. One core taste was based on the forerunner of soy sauce, written with the same Chinese characters but pronounced as *hishio* by the Japanese. It was a thick sauce-like substance with a fishy taste derived from seaweed and fish flakes. It is hard to tell if there was any difference

---

[2] Higuchi Kiyoyuki, *Taberu Nihonshi*, p. 90.
[3] Harada Nobuo, *Washoku to Nihon bunka*, p. 50.
[4] Ibid., p. 53.

between the historical forerunners of soy sauce and miso: both originated as a Chinese *jiang* (醬), which is a thick sauce. Confucius mentions something like soy sauce in the *Analects*, also calling it *jiang*. A recipe for *jiang* was included in the early Chinese cookbook "Essential Skills for the Common People." But we must assume that, like *bing* and noodles, *jiang* evolved through many forms.

Shinto and Food

While the transmission of Buddhism to Japan brought new technology and food traditions, early Japan also preserved the rituals of Shinto, its pre-Buddhist native belief system. Given the Japanese propensity to adopt and adapt, Shinto and Buddhism were not mutually exclusive. The nature of belief in Japan meant that many Shinto rituals survived or were combined with Buddhist elements to create alternative forms of ritual. Shinto was not merely a passing animist phase – it required diligence and attention to detail, as with any form of religion. The number of Shinto rituals, according to one major scholar, "staggers the imagination" although the ceremonies required by ancient texts may not have achieved in practice the stupendous scale called for in theory. The Japanese book of rituals, called the *Engishiki*, was a vast compendium of procedures and regulations for various ceremonies, published during the period 901–922 CE. The lists are obsessively precise and detailed, stipulating everything that royal participants could wear, say and eat during more than two hundred yearly rituals. "In brief," the Shinto historian Allan Grappard claims, "if one totalled up the amount of various materials needed for all the festivals and rituals at Shinto shrines throughout the year in the early centuries of Japan's development it necessitated: 1,810 or so yards of pongee (soft thin cloth of raw Chinese silk), 737 shields, 198 deer antlers, 316 gallons of saké, 81 pounds of bonito fish, 98 pounds of hard seaweed, 79 gallons of salt, etc."[5] Priests and lay people performed most of these ceremonies, praying to avert the frequent natural disasters that laid waste to fields and set epidemics raging amongst the population. Imperial families had virtually no time left for other engagements. These rituals are understood to form the basis of Shinto belief; as is the case in a religion like Judaism, these events also celebrate food and life. Shinto was preoccupied with purity and cleanliness, but food also played a central role in most major Shinto

---

[5] Allan Grappard, "The economics of ritual power," pp. 82–83.

ceremonies. Records from the *Engishiki* show that portions of noodles arranged as ropes of lighting were components of some ceremonies. The Japanese did not possess advanced milling technology at this stage, so anything made with flour was an expensive treat. Such foodstuffs were brought out for special festivals and events with particular religious meaning. On such days people feasted on noodles.

Shinto may have promoted religious values about certain foodstuffs in early Japan but this did not make the food taste any better. In fact, one hallmark of early Japanese society, from the dawn of Kamakura society in the twelfth century to the sixteenth, was a high mortality rate linked with a generally low production of food, and food that was of poor quality – or at least food that was not sufficiently remarkable for anyone to write positively about. However, noodles and noodle technology did proliferate; in fact, I would argue that noodles and the dishes that featured them began to dominate Japanese cuisine precisely because of this lack of appetizing competition. William Farris, a noted demographic historian, estimates that until 1100 CE, even with heavy immigration and technology imports from China and Korea, Japan experienced a massive crop failure on average every three years and hunger was common. Japanese land was notoriously poor for agriculture; Japan is a very mountainous country and not ideal for cultivating crops. Infant mortality before the seventeenth century may have reached 50–60% at certain times.[6] If diseases such as dysentery, smallpox and syphilis did not kill people, the lack of food did. The Japanese frequently suffered malnutrition and famine. Not only was arable Japanese land in short supply, but chronic civil war continually upset agricultural production. Famine and political struggle often go hand in hand. During the first ten months of 1180, a famine set off by a severe drought wracked the countryside. A Japanese aristocrat wrote in his diary in 1181 that "the roads are filled with dead bodies," and a townsperson recalled in his memoirs a few years later in 1212 that "officials counted within the boundaries of the capital [Kyoto] over 42,300 corpses lying in the streets."[7] At the dawn of Japanese society and its new samurai culture, not all of Japanese society was idly sitting around in a courtly manner. On the contrary, most of the population lived in varying degrees of squalor. Less than half a century later, in the early 1230s, during a famine around Kyoto, gangs of thieves and hoodlums ransacked parts of the town; it was said that sedan-chair porters for the rich were so weak from hunger that they died while transporting

---

[6] William Farris, *Japan's Medieval Population*, pp. 9–10.
[7] Ibid., p. 30.

their patrons.⁸ Supposedly honorable samurai behaved no better. Until 1310, it was not considered a crime for a samurai to seize a peasant's baggage on the road or enter fields or grain houses to "requisition" food.

Chinese Food Technology

While the majority of the population who tilled the fields experienced penury and hardship, Buddhist temples and the powerful ruling families consolidated their wealth, enjoying official banquets and privileges. This growth is reflected in their changing attitudes toward food and dining. During the early Kamakura era (1192–1333) the Japanese Buddhist priest Gen'e is credited with writing a book about etiquette and social interaction, entitled the "Book of Moral Instruction" (*Teikin ōrai*). In addition to describing imperial banquets in exquisite detail, he explained to the literati and other interested elite the new *udon* and noodle dishes. This era witnessed the first of many traveling Buddhist priests to bring back food technology from China after a long hiatus; for several centuries, missions to China had all but stopped, mainly it seems because Japanese leaders in various areas wanted to prove that they were civilized enough to stand on their own without borrowing from or paying constant homage to Chinese culture. In 1241 the monk Enni (1202–1280) brought to Japan from China the technology to grind buckwheat and to make flour for *soba* noodles.⁹ Enni returned to western Japan and established noodle-making classes at the Jōten Temple.

The technology to make noodles in zesty sauces entered Japan from China on the back of Buddhist study and, it seemed, at the right time. This was not the first wave of Japanese Buddhist scholars to bring recipes back, but Japan was now wealthier, if not more unified as a kingdom, and primed to incorporate these new eating habits and recipes. The population craved new dishes that were relatively simple to produce. Buddhism promoted the new learning, mixing it with missionary zeal and a bit of reading sutras on the side. During the Kamakura era, Japan began to develop the technology required to ferment soy sauce, another necessary ingredient in the development of an identifiable Japanese taste. The Zen monk Kakushin traveled to Song dynasty China and returned in 1254, having studied at a

---

⁸ Ibid., p. 36.
⁹ Yonezawa mengyō kumiai kyūjūnenshi kankō īnkai edited, *Yonezawa mengyōshi*, pp. 23–24. His posthumous Buddhist name was Shōichi Kokushi.

Figure 6. A small stone obelisk in the front garden of today's Jōten Temple, almost invisible from the pathway, highlights the temple's history as the birthplace of *udon* and *soba* noodle technology in Japan. According to the temple's scholars, the founder of Rinzai Zen in Japan, Enni, returned to Hakata, a port on the northern coast of Kyushu, armed with both Buddhist learning and the ability to make noodles. Buddhist priests were indispensable servants of enlightenment but the temples also had to be economically self-sufficient. It did not hurt to make a profit by selling goods.

temple in Jiangsu province called the Floating Dragon on the River Golden Mountain Temple, where he also learned how to make miso, a fermented flavoring paste. Kakushin established the Kōkoku Temple in Toyama Prefecture, which specialized in Zen and the art of making miso. You make miso by mixing soybeans, wheat and/or some rice with a fermenting agent. Add a bit of salt, mix and mash the compost and let it sit. The fermented mixture is pressed through a cloth that filters and collects the mush.

Miso was popular and people soon realized that the leftover juice at the bottom of an emptied barrel of miso was also a good condiment. Vegetables and other sundries stewed in the dregs of the miso were quite delicious. This miso juice contributed to the development of soy sauce, or *shōyu* in

Japanese.[10] Although the two condiments are produced differently, the Chinese ancestor sauce, *jiang*, was combined with miso juice to create soy sauce, a slightly salty sauce that could be poured over vegetables to improve their palatability. Soy sauce added a savory flavor to an otherwise bland cuisine; it became associated with Japanese food in the minds of diners and was produced on a large scale from the late sixteenth century.

What is important to remember about Japan's culinary exchanges with China is that Chinese dishes of the time were often not what we would now think of as "Chinese." During several Chinese dynasties the rulers

Figure 7. A picture of the Miso Shrine, "Miso Tenjin," also known as the Motomura Shrine. This shrine was established in 715 CE originally as a place to pray for protection against the epidemic raging at the time. Years later it became associated with miso because during a fire a relic from a main temple nearby was at risk of being burned and a quick thinker swiftly took the relic and stashed it nearby in a miso storehouse. Even afterwards the shrine became known as the miso shrine. It is currently the only such shrine in Japan. (Photograph taken in the city of Kumamoto.)

---

[10] Tatsuno shōyu kyōdō kumiai edited, *Tatsuno shōyu kyōdō kumiai yōran*, pp. 4–5.

were not ethnically Chinese, but Mongol, Turkic or something else. Even the great Yuan dynasty (1271–1368) perhaps should not be classified as a Chinese dynasty since the rulers were actually Mongolian. The great Khans of China, as they expanded westward creating the huge Mongol Empire, left an enormous footprint on Chinese cuisine. As the Japanese learned from China, they were also importing *de facto* Central Asian and Mongolian culinary influences. There is a record of the *haute cuisine* of the Mongol court in 1330, translated best as "Proper Essentials for the Emperor's Food and Drink," a dietary manual presented to the Mongolian Yuan emperor. The book included an enormous number of boiled dishes but, importantly, emphasized noodle soups and dumpling technology.[11] Japan could not have avoided becoming a noodle-loving nation given the eating habits of its neighbors and the influence that emanated from the great kingdoms next door.

Another element of "Japanese taste" that began to dominate the food scene in the medieval era was the use of thick seaweed or *konbu*. *Konbu* is kelp, mainly harvested north of the Sanriku coast, on the northeastern corridor of Japan. The seas surrounding the domains in the north of Honshu and south of Hokkaido Island were thick with *konbu*. It is full of glutamine acid that gives food a savory taste, *umami* in Japanese. *Konbu* harvesting and sales proliferated around the city of Osaka, later known as "the kitchen of Japan" for its massive production and consumption of foodstuffs.

A famous fourteenth-century *kyōgen* play, *Kobu uri*, or "Selling Konbu," depicts how food products and tastes traveled around Japan, mostly through itinerant peddlers. *Kyōgen* are comedic interludes between the acts in Noh theater. Although Noh is a very serious, highbrow form of Japanese theatre, where actors wear hardened masks painted in the Heian tradition and speak in a nearly impossibly lyrical, drawn-out eleventh-century dialect, *Kyōgen* are light-hearted and entertaining. The central character of the *konbu* skit is a peasant seaweed salesman traveling to peddle his wares. On the road he runs into a samurai and the two have a comic altercation, demonstrating the friction between classes.[12] The samurai is making a religious pilgrimage to a famous shrine in the Kansai region for a particular festival. His attendants are all busy running errands so he has to carry his own sword. Fourteenth-century samurai had high social status and did not generally carry their own belongings; someone of

---

[11] Paul D. Buell and Eugene N. Anderson, *A Soup for the Qan: Chinese Dietary Medicine of the Mongol Era as Seen in Hu Szu-Hui's Yin-Shan Cheng-Yao*, introduction.

[12] Harada Nobuo, *Washoku to Nihon bunka*, pp. 83–84.

a lower status followed behind with swords, a satchel for money, and other sundry items such as an umbrella. When the samurai encounters the *konbu* salesman he forces the peasant to carry his sword. Because the samurai belongs to a higher social rank and could harm him, the salesman resigns himself to carrying the samurai's sword, even though he is occupied with his own business and will lose money by wasting time on the doltish warrior. As the hours drag on during the trek, the degradation of being forced into menial servitude and being subjected to the samurai droning on haughtily about the proper way to carry a sword becomes more than he can tolerate, and the salesman finally loses his patience. He suddenly draws the samurai's sword out of the scabbard and challenges him to try a hand at *his* job, singing out sales pitches for seaweed. The comedy pivots on how the samurai is forced to try and sing songs of praise to customers about delicious seaweed. The medieval audience would have relished watching a reversal of the deeply entrenched social hierarchy in what the Japanese call *gekokujō*, or "bottom overcoming the top." Satisfied with his revenge, the salesman flees with the sword and the story ends.[13] This play provides us with a window on evolving samurai culture and shows how ingredients moved around medieval Japan.

If theater demonstrated how new food practices and tastes traveled from region to region, Buddhism was also influencing the production of food and the way it was discussed. It is highly likely that *sōmen* appeared during this era. *Sōmen* are long thin noodles made of wheat flour, but the word reflects the profound Buddhist influence that penetrated Japan in the early medieval period. Some scholars assert that "simple noodles," *somian* in Chinese, could have evolved into *sōmen*. The word *sōmen* may also have come from Zen Buddhism and a Japanese mispronunciation of the Chinese word *sucai*, which referred to a simple vegetable meal common to Buddhist temples. Temples were centers for the transmission of food technology, not to mention sales of noodles and other goodies. Lay people often ate simple meals on the temple grounds, during feasts, fairs and other events.

---

[13] Because it is such an old performance authorship is attributed to a whole range of famous and also less well-known writers. A full dialogue is reprinted in an early twentieth-century collection of kyōgen in Yamawaki Izumi, *Izumiryū kyōgen daisei*, Vol. 4, pp. 210–216. Koyama Hiroshi, et al., eds., Iwanami kōza nō kyōgen, Vol. 7, *Kyōgen kanshō annai*, pp. 90–92 details the play *Kobu uri*. For more on the theatre of kyōgen see Iwanami kōza Nō kyōgen, Vol. 5, *Kyōgen no sekai*, pp. 113–150. For the history and trade routes of konbu all over Japan, see Yunoki Manabu, eds., *Nihon suijō kōtsūshi ronshū*, Vol. 2, pp. 49–123, which details the range of konbu sales and historic trade routes.

Regardless of the preferred noodle – *udon, soba,* or *sōmen* – it was not really tasty if you just ate it plain. Noodles needed to be dipped into some kind of broth. There is no doubt that the advent of soy sauce increased the spread of the noodle across Japan. Not all soy sauce, however, is created equal; even today there is a lot of regional variation. To investigate regional soy sauce production and unlock the mysteries behind regional taste differences, I journeyed to Tatsuno City to interview staff at the Kamigata Soy Sauce Museum. Soy sauce technology arrived in Tatsuno City, close to the famous Himeji Castle and just south of Kyoto on the Ibo River, around the late fifteenth to early sixteenth century. The curator Sawa-san and I discussed soy sauce and its special place in Japanese cuisine. What did Sawa-san think of Kikkoman? I asked provocatively. After all, Tatsuno-style soy sauce, called *usukuchi* or "thin taste" in Japanese, dominated national cuisine until the early 1600s and memories last long in Japan. Kikkoman, which produces a thicker eastern flavor, is now the largest manufacturer of soy sauce in the world and the most commonly known brand outside Japan, so a bit of jealous rivalry exists between manufacturers. Sawa responded: "Perhaps Kikkoman [the eastern brand] is more popular abroad because as a taste it envelops foods and fits the heavier food and tastes of foreign countries." "Light soy sauce, the original taste of Japan's western region," he explained to me, piling scientific papers on the table, "doesn't envelop food because it has a higher salt density and therefore enhances the taste already inherent in the food."[14] Sawa's commentary reminded me that during the late Kamakura period of the thirteenth to fourteenth centuries, there was no national consensus on "Japanese taste." The far west of Japan felt the influence of Chinese food technology, while the central regions near the imperial capital of Kyoto retained lighter, blander food that suited court culture. The eastern hinterland that was Edo, modern-day Tokyo, was a culinary backwater until the seventeenth century. The Japanese palate, and therefore cuisine in general, was extremely varied and people held to their regional identities strongly, with little concept of a national identity expressed through diet.

As we have seen, Buddhist monks journeying from China brought noodles, food and sauces to Japan. Like Western missionaries to the Far East during the eighteenth and nineteenth centuries, Japanese monks making the arduous journeys to China and Chinese monks visiting Japan and Korea during the medieval era were not just importing and exporting

---

[14] Interview with director of Tatsuno Shōyu Museum, Higashimaru Company, August 17, 2006; Watanabe Zenjirō, "Sekai o kakeru Nihongata shoku seikatsu no henbō," p. 15.

religion, but technology, news, new ideas and learning. Expanding trade routes within the Japanese-ruled islands allowed for the development of a "Japanese" palate by combining and synthesizing tastes from various domains. However, these tastes, as can be seen in the two styles of soy sauce, were still far from being unified. Meals that incorporated these dishes were initially served in a traditional form of dining called *honzen* cooking, a practice of the upper classes during the 1400s. In the *honzen* dining manner, samurai and nobles would sit in front of small trays on which food would be served individually to each person. This form later expanded into a form of banqueting called *kaiseki* (会席), where domain lords, rich merchants, and aristocrats would be served many courses on several trays which accompanied "many days of hospitality for many guests – drinking saké, amusements of all kinds, and gambling." These activities continued into the Meiji era and *kaiseki* restaurants are also popular today, albeit "on a slightly less lavish but more decorative scale."[15] At the same time, there is another sort of *kaiseki* cuisine that developed along with the expansion and growth of Zen temples, adding a new strand to the mix of different foodways. This *kaiseki* cuisine is written with the Chinese characters for "stone for the belly" (懐石) and evolved into a form of aesthetic Zen meditation where you would consume one small soup and three side dishes as a meal. The "stones in the belly" was a reference to Buddhist monks who would put warm stones in their cloaks to stave off hunger while they meditated. This *kaiseki* mostly remained the preserve of the leisurely class and first appeared in the later seventeenth century as an offshoot of the tea ceremony. In early forms, the meal was "designed to instill among guests a feeling of austerity of 'barely enough,' but also to lead them, through an insufficient but beautifully prepared and arranged meal, to a realization of the profound beauty of simplicity." The famous originator of the Japanese tea ceremony, Rikyū, kept the meal to a particularly austere standard. When asked how much food one should serve he supposedly replied: "Barely enough to prevent you from starving."[16] *Kaiseki* written with the "stone belly" characters exists today as a form of tea cuisine and Zen temple dining.

---

[15] Gary Sōka Cadwallader and Joseph R. Justice, "Stones for the Belly: *Kaiseki* Cuisine for Tea during the Early Edo Period," in Eric Rath and Stephanie Assmann, eds., *Past and Present in Japanese Foodways*, pp. 68–69; Eric Rath, *Food and Fantasy in Early Modern Japanese Foodways*, pp. 28–29.

[16] Herbert Plutschow, *Rediscovering Rikyu and the Beginnings of the Japanese Tea Ceremony*, pp. 134–135.

The Rise of Samurai and Medieval Japanese Food

Japan's medieval era saw the rise of an aristocratic warrior class, the samurai, protecting large domains that resembled small countries within the larger geographic space known as Japan. The upper classes and clerics, who represented a very small percentage of the total population, consumed noodles and kept track of new recipes – but for most people, their "food life" remained dull and tasteless. An ambassador from Korea in 1429 noted: "In Japan, where there are many people and little to eat, they sell lots of slaves. In some cases in secret they sell children."[17] Not only were most people poor and constantly on the verge of starvation, but the city of Kyoto in the final years of the fifteenth and early sixteenth centuries "was still one of the filthiest and smelliest places in Japan, reminiscent of the shantytowns in the industrializing Third World today."[18] Up until the late 1500s, bloodshed and power struggles created unstable social and political conditions throughout the archipelago. During times of strife, peasants were afraid to be in the fields, where they might be dragooned into the various militias or used for corvée labor. They dreaded the samurai who passed through their villages, raping, pillaging and taking whatever agricultural products they desired.

By the dawn of Japan's early modern period and the expansion of samurai culture in the fifteenth and sixteenth centuries, Japanese cuisine had completely changed. In the view of Chinese food historian Jia Huixuan, the goal of Chinese food was to harmonize taste, while Japanese food was oriented around the idea of retaining freshness and naturalness.[19] But what was "Japanese taste?" What was the flavoring? An aesthetically beautiful and predominantly vegetarian, if not Zen, cuisine developed during the Muromachi period (1333–1573). Before the Edo era, the Japanese ate mostly cold meals arranged in a Chinese style, on small, low individual tables placed in front of each diner.[20] No one is in complete agreement on any aspect of Japanese food history, although many scholars have ignored the formative force of noodles. For example, Susan Hanley, the esteemed expert on the history of Japanese daily life, estimates that "by the late Muromachi years, all of the major elements of what can be considered traditional Japanese cuisine were present, from the staple foods to

---

[17] William Farris, *Japan's Medieval Population*, p. 159.
[18] Ibid., p. 161.
[19] Jia Huixuan, *Zhongri yinshi wenhua bijao yanjiu*, p. 80.
[20] Hayashi Reiko and Amamo Masatoshi, *Nihon no aji shōyu no reskihi*.

seasonings and combinations of how foods were served. Changes that occurred in the Tokugawa period were primarily refinements in production and changes in fashion."[21] The problem with this view is that it skims over many delicious elements of Japan's exciting contemporary cuisine that began to emerge during the Tokugawa period, including noodles and sushi, which really comes into its own during the early modern era. More importantly, Edo-dwellers developed an obsession with *soba* that we need to consider when discussing the emergence of Japanese cuisine. Edo period *soba* noodle markets had a profound impact on the later development of ramen.

The Muromachi era saw the noodle market expand with a new product called *kirimen*. Like most noodles, *kirimen* has its own origin myth and presents a linguistic nightmare. As was the case with *bing*, the word was initially written in Chinese characters that now possess two meanings: either *wonton* or *udon* (饂飩). At the outset, during the Nara era, this word was read as *konton* in the Japanese language and by the Chinese as something closer to *wonton*, the dumpling found on today's Chinese menus. *Kirimen* was a slightly thicker noodle that was rolled with a pin, boiled and then cooled and served in hot broth. It is possible that this noodle was the precursor to *udon*, or was once a dumpling, like a modern *wonton*.

During the massive upheaval and changes in Japanese foodways during the medieval period, *bing* as the forerunner of noodles, together with soy sauce and miso had already made the journey over the sea from China to Japan. With the addition of *umami,* a savory taste made from seaweed and fish flakes, to Japan's nascent noodle culture, ramen's future success was essentially set by the 1500s. One crucial element, however, was still missing – meat, or at least the desire to consume it. As we shall see in the next chapter, Chinese travelers fleeing the fall of the Ming dynasty (1368–1644) brought a taste for noodles and an appetite for meat to the western islands of Japan where they disembarked.[22] The Chinese may not have created Japanese ramen but their presence was certainly instrumental, once Chinese ingredients had been adapted and incorporated into basic Japanese cuisine.

As samurai and peasants slowly made the transition from the medieval era, the stage was set for the creation of the precursor to ramen. Japan had evolved over eighteen hundred years from a land that knew no noodles, to

---

[21] Susan Hanley, *Everyday Things in Premodern Japan*, p. 85.
[22] Qiu Zhonglin (Chi-u Chung lin), Huangdi de canzhuo: mingdai de guanshan zhidu ji qi xiangguan wenti," *Taida lishi xuebao*, di 34 qi, December 2004, pp. 1–42.

one where Buddhist priests had introduced the technology for milling flour and for making noodles. The Japanese were producing miso and had developed an offshoot, soy sauce, which expanded their repertoire of tastes and increased the desire to eat better. Japanese society was finally prospering, even if not at peace (it actually stood on the verge of a long, drawn-out series of civil wars). At the same time, the curtain was ready to lift on an emerging national cuisine and one of its most popular noodle dishes.

CHAPTER THREE

INTERNATIONAL JAPAN, FOREIGN FOODS AND ISOLATION

Following the collapse of the Kamakura shogunate in the fourteenth century, Japan slowly sank into a period of internecine warfare that eventually fed a long and vicious civil war among fiefs. During the ensuing Muromachi period, however, rice production improved and small-scale commerce began in the growing number of castle towns across the archipelago. The Buddhist influence on cuisine propelled *shōjin ryōri*, a type of vegetarian Zen cuisine, into the public eye, and fish was considered the top "meat" of choice, though very little animal meat was actually consumed. Religious temples provided sanctuary and solace from calamities – both natural and man-made – but the Muromachi period witnessed more than just catastrophic events. The era also saw the emergence of the Japanese tea ceremony and a masterpiece of Japanese architecture and landscape – the Golden Pavilion, a landmark building in Kyoto. The development of a refined sense of aesthetics, in part promoted by the expansion of Zen Buddhism and supported by expanding wealth, furthered the austere *kaiseki* cuisine as a feature of Japanese elite dining. This growth encouraged the traditions now prized as hallmarks of Japanese culture. Near the middle of the fifteenth century, the estate system threatened to crumble under the weight of mutual antagonism among competing fiefs, lords vying for supremacy and constant political disagreement. Indeed, this era spanning the mid fifteenth century until 1600 is known in Japanese history as the *sengoku* era, or warring states period. For a century and a half, no leader remained dominant. The chiefs of regional domains strove to amass as many men as possible under their vassalage, to strengthen their castle defenses and secure their surrounding holdings.

Fortunes began to shift as the wind blew in trading ships from the West, thirsty for Japanese silk, silver and other finely made goods. In 1543, the first Portuguese traders arrived and in 1549, famed missionary Francis Xavier came ashore, declaring that while he thought the Japanese a very proper and advanced civilization, their language was "the devil's tongue." Portuguese missionaries and traders brought an exciting new brand of religion with them to Nagasaki, a soon-to-be major urban enclave of Kyushu. Several key Japanese lords became enamored of the idea of a single savior and permanent salvation in the afterlife. In 1580, the ruler of Nagasaki, Ōmura Sumitada, was baptized and became the first "Christian daimyo," or Christian lord of a fief. Following his conversion, Nagasaki became an essentially Christian city, handing city management over to church leaders and a quorum of Portuguese traders. While the Dutch and British struggled with their small trading outposts in Hirado, on the northwestern edge of Kyushu, Nagasaki became the golden port. More importantly, it "was a city of only 50,000 odd inhabitants, and far from the centers of power. It took about as long to get there from Edo as it did from Batavia [the city of Jakarta in present-day Indonesia]."[1] When Dutch traders who lived in Nagasaki made their pilgrimages to Edo to demonstrate fealty to the shogun they would leave in February and not arrive in the shogun's capital to the north until mid-May, such was the difficulty of traveling overland. Japan was not yet unified under one ruler, and the daimyo of the west, rulers of large landholdings, were reaping huge profits in trade, commerce and technology transfer from their expanding contacts with the outside world, especially China and the seafaring nations of Western Europe.

One Western missionary who resided in Japan for a long time during the transition from war to peace in the mid-to–late-sixteenth century was Luis Frois, a Portuguese Jesuit from Lisbon. He arrived in Japan in 1563 and was a keen observer of Japanese customs, befriending the masses as well as the top leaders. He died in Nagasaki in 1597, just as the expulsion of Christians was beginning. Frois became a fluent speaker of Japanese and was thus well placed to comment on their customs. At one point in his writings he could not resist saluting the vast gulf of differences that separated Japanese dining habits from European ones. While he took note of the fact that dishes often consisted of very little actual substance, he also lamented that:

> We like milk products, cheese and butter, and bone marrow; the Japanese abhor all of that, and for them it has a bad smell. We think rotten fish entrails are revolting; the Japanese use them as *sakana* [snacks] and eat them with real relish. We make food tasty with various seasonings; the Japanese with *miso*, that is, rotten [fermented] grains, mixed with salt. For us it is regarded as filthy manners, to chew the food loudly, and to noisily slurp the wine to the last drop; the Japanese consider both to be polite. For us belching at the

---

[1] Timon Screech, annotated and introduced, *Secret Memoirs of the Shoguns: Isaac Titsingh and Japan, 1779–1822*, p. 7

table in front of guests is considered bad breeding; in Japan it is a very common occurrence, and they pay not attention to it.[2]

THE RISE OF NEW LEADERS AND NEW JAPANESE FOODWAYS

By the mid-1500s, one leader advanced through sheer cunning, ruthless battle tactics and political savvy, not to mention intimidation, to gain the respect of a majority of the semi-powerful rulers in the central plains of Japan. His name was Oda Nobunaga and, although his life ended abruptly, his armies fought to bring national unity, enabling his successor, Toyotomi Hideyoshi, to promote the idea of a national realm under a single ruler. Hideyoshi was ultimately unsuccessful in seating himself at the top of the political administration of his grand scheme, but the spread of his power and final defeat at the hands of the Tokugawa clan in 1600 on the battlefield of Sekigahara (modern Gifu Prefecture) led to the founding of the Tokugawa era. The two-hundred-and-fifty years of ensuing peace and prosperity during the Tokugawa period helped shape Japan until the mid-nineteenth century.

The Tokugawa house ruled Japan as a family of shoguns under what is known as the *bakuhan* system. It was a complex arrangement because while the shogun served as the essential ruling authority in Edo "the daimyo enhanced their own powers of private control over their local domains," and "borrow[ed] support from the very central authority that sought to constrain them." What this meant in practice was that daimyo domains gave up a portion of their autonomy to survive and profit by remaining a part of the larger whole.[3] The first shogun, Ieyasu, supported international exchange and expanded the trading agreements established several decades earlier. Once the Tokugawa clan established dominance over disparate fiefs in the early 1600s, international trade flourished for three decades. Tallies of ships and port records show that by the late sixteenth and early seventeenth centuries, the Japanese were traveling all over East Asia, as well as welcoming travelers.[4] At the outset of the Tokugawa era Japan was anything but a closed country and this internationalism was clearly reflected in the national diet.

---

[2] As quoted in William McOmie, ed., *Foreign Images and Experiences of Japan*, Vol. 1, First Century AD to 1841, pp. 222–223.
[3] John Whitney Hall, "The Bakuhan system," *Cambridge History of Japan*, Vol. 4, Early Modern Japan, p. 129.
[4] Hirosi Nakamura, "The Japanese Portolanos of Portuguese Origin of the XVIth and XVIIth Centuries," *Imago Mundi*, Vol. 18, 1964, p. 25.

The rise of the city of Edo also changed the face of Japanese foodways and taste. Eager to divorce themselves from court power and intrigue, the Tokugawa shoguns moved the seat of administrative power from imperial Kyoto to the swampy backwater known as Edo (modern-day Tokyo). Within a century, the Tokugawa planners had transformed this insignificant village into one of the world's largest cities. Urban expansion brought about a dramatic change in Japanese cuisine. Although the Tatsuno soy sauce trade had spread across many regions and catered for courtly appetites in Kyoto, there was a significant difference between the soy sauce of the Kyoto region and the heavier sauce developed in Kantō, the region around Tokyo. Noda city in Chiba Prefecture, about an hour north of Tokyo by train today, is the birthplace of Edo-style soy sauce. Well-placed in its proximity to Edo, the castle city of Noda became a holding of the Tokugawa rulers. By 1558, the locally made soy sauce had won accolades. Word spread that a premium sauce was available in the hinterlands of Edo, although with most wealth and power still concentrated in Kyoto and Osaka (home to many merchant markets), the Noda soy sauce did not acquire a national reputation. That quickly changed with the advance of the Tokugawa peace. By the early 1600s, shipping facilities had improved so that boats could be loaded in the morning in Noda on the Edo River, and by evening the barrels would be on the banks of the shogun's new capital.[5] The heavier soy sauce even won over Buddhist priests, who claimed that the taste enhanced vegetarian meals. Soldiers appreciated its durability in transport.[6] The lighter soy sauce of the Kansai region, despite its popularity at the court in Kyoto, was just too geographically remote to compete economically with the heavier tasting Noda soy sauce made so close to Edo.

By the time the Tokugawa family had installed itself more firmly in the shogun's seat, ruling over a peaceful Japan, the social class structure was codified and people were assigned to the social milieu that would adhere for virtually the next two and a half centuries. An ever-increasing number of laws defined which classes could wear particular colors and footwear and whether they should walk or ride a horse. People were also told what they could and could not eat as members of a specific level of hierarchy in Japanese society. In 1649, for example, the Tokugawa administration passed an ordinance decreeing that peasants could cook *daikon* (Japanese radish), chestnut, wheat, millet and similar grains and vegetables but

---

[5] Kikkoman shōyu kabushikigaisha edited, *Kikkoman shōyushi*, p. 434.
[6] W. Mark Fruin, *Kikkoman*, p. 15; Hayashi Reiko and Amamo Masatoshi, *Nihon no aji shōyu no reskihi*.

"were not to eat rice." The government wanted to limit the consumption of rice because the peasants used it to pay taxes, providing the upper classes with their stipends and livelihoods.[7] Also, despite Tokugawa Japan being officially "closed" to the rest of the world, the Edo era was the period when foreign foods were fully integrated into the Japanese diet. Items such as castella cake, tempura, sweet bean paste and the sweet potato all entered Japan during this time and continue to be mainstays of Japanese cuisine to this day. In the early 1600s, people finally stopped feeding potatoes to their animals and ate them themselves, sharply reducing famine. Edo, the shogun's enclave, may have been shut off to most foreigners but its peripheral borders remained porous and eager to accept outside culinary recipes.

The Kyoto court did not disappear when the national administration shifted north, but its role as the engine of innovation and wealth slowly dimmed. It appears, however, that even this court became captive to the noodle phenomenon that was slowly making its way across Japan over the centuries. The diaries of various Japanese emperors, written by female attendants, record various imperial activities from 1477 to 1687, and from these carefully kept documents we know that on July 7, 1676, the emperor ate *sakubei*, the noodle (as described in Chapter 1) extruded from a roll of dough that rose to popularity during the Nara period.[8] From the 1600s onward regional disparities intensified. Historically, as we have seen, Japanese food had been fairly bland in the west; in the east efforts were made to enhance it using soybeans to create miso, soy sauce and *nattō* (a fermented dish made from beans) and radishes to make pickles, known as *takuan*.[9] The culinary competitiveness between Kyoto and Tokyo continues today; many Japanese claim that the favored noodle of western Japan is *udon*, while in eastern Japan it is *soba*, both claiming theirs to be the national noodle.

Edo is Not the Only City – Tokugawa Peace and a Piece of the Pie

At the very western tip of the southwestern tentacle of the island of Kyushu lies the city of Nagasaki. From earliest times, many of the ports of Japan's western coasts have served as gateways for the import and export of

---

[7] Morisue Yoshiaki, edited, *Taikei Nihonshi sōsho*, Vol. 16, Seikatsushi II, p. 202.
[8] Itō Hiroshi, *Tsuru tsuru monogatari*.
[9] Koyanagi Kiichi, *Nihonjin no shokuseikatsu: kiga to hōyō no hentenshi*, p. 15. Takuan was a famous Buddhist monk (1573–1645) who had urged his followers to eat simple food in reasonable quantities.

Figure 8. A 1792 Japanese hand-colored scroll depicting the harbor of Nagasaki. The bottom right corner is the Dutch trading enclosure known as *Deshima*. In the middle of the picture, colorful Chinese junks are drawn anchored at port. Closer to the top right a Dutch ship is poised to sail out to sea. The larger Chinese enclosure, the *Tōjin yashiki*, can be seen on the left side in the middle.[10]

culture. In the early Nara and Heian eras, ships set sail from ports nearby like Hakata to China in search of knowledge, law and religion. When the late Ming dynasty (1368–1644) closed China off from the outside world, Japan waited. In 1684, its patience paid off and the newly-formed Qing dynasty, run by Manchus from the north, reawakened Chinese interest in shipping exchanges with Japan. Unofficially, trade had never stopped because Japan's trading partners in the southern Chinese regions rarely followed official policy anyway. In the 1630s, the shogun grew anxious about spreading heterodoxy through Christianity and expelled all Europeans except the Dutch, who were granted a tiny mission on a man-made island in Nagasaki harbor called *Deshima* (island-that-juts-out). By contrast, China faced few obstacles in enjoying free trade with Japan and

---

[10] Nagasaki Museum of History and Culture, (長崎港湾図 3/680).

Chinese junks continued to exchange silk threads, medicines and sugar for seafood products and copper.

Nagasaki and Chinese Food

During the seventeenth century, as in previous centuries, the westernmost island of Kyushu was brimming with Chinese travelers, businessmen and tourists. Visitors were so numerous that businessmen from Satsuma (a large fief on the island of Kyushu) accepted coins from the Chinese continent as currency. By 1688, the population of Nagasaki reached slightly over 50,000 and included about 10,000 Chinese. Of the 194 ships that entered the harbor that year, 117 had sailed from China.[11] Initially, the Chinese were free to live where they wanted and to conduct trade as they wished but the Tokugawa administration feared the encroachment of foreign ideas. To curb instability and block the spread of Christianity, the shogun initially outlawed Westerners. He later ruled that Chinese visitors had to stay in the Tang Visitors Center, or *Tōjin yashiki*. Japan had borrowed so much from the Tang dynasty that the Chinese character for "Tang" read as *tō* in Japanese, referred to anything Chinese or foreign. A lively trade in prostitution served the Chinese mission in Japan, where men often stayed for several months without their wives or concubines.[12]

After 1689, the permanent Chinese center in Nagasaki housed all traveling Chinese and they were no longer permitted to walk around town without prior approval. Local Chinese were asked to stay in their residences, but the Japanese in town all noted their presence. The diaries of several Chinese businessmen reveal that they held the Japanese in high regard for their excellent hygienic standards and the fact that couples dined separately, in accordance with correct Confucian etiquette. Perhaps this positive view of Japan also stemmed from the fact that these men spent many evenings consorting with professional ladies, who were in fact the only Japanese legally authorized to stay overnight in the Chinese quarters.[13] Courtesans who mingled with Ming and later Qing visitors could spend the night, but only Chinese male guests were allowed in the quarters after dark. Prostitutes who consorted with the Chinese were called *tōjin-yuki*, "those going to visit a Chinese person," or in this case the Chinese

---

[11] Nagasaki kyōikuīnkai, *Chūgoku bunka to Nagasakiken*, pp. 167–168.
[12] Tō Ken, "Yūkō toshi Nagasaki e," *Nihon kenkyū*, 23, Kokusai Nihon bunka sentā kiyō, March 2001, p. 77.
[13] Bu Anryū, Yū Tatsuun, editors, *Chūgokujin no Nihon kenkyūshi*, pp. 95–97.

enclosure.¹⁴ Those who frequented the Dutch enclosure were called *Oranda-yuki*, or "those going to Holland." Hishiya Heishichi, a Japanese traveler who visited Kyushu in the early 1800s, noted that Nagasaki was a special city even in the late Tokugawa period and that one needed a special passport for entry. You could get a sightseeing visa for up to 180 days; women in the entertaining business were eligible for a five-year pass.¹⁵ The location was so strange and different from the rest of Japan that Hishiya chose a consort and wrote that he stayed with her during the evening "because I wanted to hear from her the details of how the Chinese make love. This was one of the rare experiences one can enjoy in such a distant and exotic place."¹⁶

Chinese traders and tourists were numerous and their visits frequent enough to warrant erecting their own places of worship. The first Chinese temple in Nagasaki was the Kōfuku Temple erected in the 1620s. Soon after, Chinese from other regions established the Fukusai Temple and later the Sōfuku Temple. At the outset of the Tokugawa era, culture did not bloom in Edo but rather in Nagasaki, a hub of activity due to the vast influx of products and knowledge pouring in from China and elsewhere.¹⁷ Nagasaki was smaller in terms of trade and consumption than the merchant city of Osaka and the old imperial capital of Kyoto – cities with Japan's largest economies during the late medieval and early modern era – but it had greater access to information and exchange. Those Japanese who visited Nagasaki to dine with the Dutch or Chinese, or to study translation, would have observed foreign food customs, partaking of Dutch roasted boar and pork dishes as well as Chinese banquets that might feature swallow's nest soup and other exotic delicacies.¹⁸ Dutch and Western food at this juncture was known to the Japanese as "southern barbarian cuisine," *nanban ryōri*, and lumped together with the mass of Portuguese and some Spanish dishes that had become popular before the Tokugawa

---

¹⁴ Tō Ken, "Yūkō toshi Nagasaki e," p. 99. After the Meiji restoration in 1868 when destitute Japanese could travel freely abroad, Japan's exported prostitutes were called *karayuki-san*, those going to China from Japan. In the complex Japanese reading system for Chinese characters, *kara* is another way of reading the same kanji for *tō*, the character Japanese used to identify Tang-era China. Many of Japan's nineteenth-twentieth-century *karayuki-san* were from Kyushu – oddly where Chinese influence had been the greatest.

¹⁵ This is taken from an interesting collection of semi-translated travelogues included in Herbert Plutschow, *A Reader in Edo Period Travel*, p. 252.

¹⁶ Herbert Plutschow, *A Reader in Edo Period Travel*, p. 254.

¹⁷ Ōba Osamu, "Kinsei shinjidai no Nitchū bunka kōryū," p. 270.

¹⁸ Reinier H. Hesselink, "A Dutch New Year at the Shirando Academy," *Monumenta Nipponica*, Vol. 50, No.2, Summer 1995, pp. 189–234.

Figure 9. The front view of Kōfuku Temple in Nagasaki. The Chinese priest Zhengyuan founded the temple in 1620 on land owned and managed by the Chinese community in Nagasaki. As with other Chinese temples in Nagasaki, this one maintained a separate hall off to the left for guarding the spirit of Mazu, or Maso in Japanese. Mazu was the ocean deity worshipped by the Chinese; most ships carried some form of statue of her across the tempestuous straits to Japan. After arriving safely at port, the Chinese would transport the statue from the ship and walk it all the way up to the temple in a ceremonious procession. It would then be hauled back for the journey home to China.

rulers expelled Christians in the 1630s. The intrepid traveler Hishiya scrawled in his travel diary that Nagasaki residents enjoyed their unique cuisine. "The food is adapted," he wrote, "to the Chinese style and they have a special liking for fish, pork, chicken and goat (a kind of sheep). Therefore, many suffer from skin rashes. The language is similar, but there are many things that are difficult to understand, in particular the daily speech of wives and the poor."[19]

Chinese cuisine spread throughout western Japan due to the significant Chinese presence and the trade relationship. A main feature of

---

[19] Herbert Plutschow, *A Reader in Edo Period Travel*, p. 256.

Figure 10. The inner entrance to Sōfuku Temple in Nagasaki. The temple was specifically founded for religious practices of the Chinese community living in Nagasaki.

contemporary ramen in Japan is that the Kyushu style is modeled on a pork-based soup with a rich meaty taste, quite different from traditional Japanese cuisine and unlike the ramen that developed elsewhere on the other three main islands. This probably originated in Nagasaki, where inhabitants were exposed to strong Chinese influence. Two kinds of hybrid Chinese food that evolved in Nagasaki later influenced Japanese cuisine and the growth of ramen. While Chinese Buddhist priests and returning Japanese priests brought back simple vegetarian Zen-style cooking, the Chinese businessmen who traveled on ships introduced *shippoku* dining, where one ate at a low table with colleagues, friends or the evening's female entertainment.[20] *Shippoku* is the Japanese pronunciation of the Cantonese word for dining table. Historical records describe it as a large table where diners served themselves from common dishes with shared spoons and chopsticks, placing portions onto smaller plates to eat with

---

[20] This form of table was quite common until the 1920s in Japan.

Figure 11. Japanese drawing of Chinese diners using a *shippoku* table.

personal utensils.[21] In traditional Japanese dining, each diner would be provided with his own small table or tray and food already apportioned onto smaller plates. The term stuck; near the end of the Tokugawa era in 1860, when the Chinese were released from the enclosure to move freely once again in Nagasaki, *shippoku ryōri,* or Chinese table cuisine, became more widely known as *Shina ryōri* or "Chinese cuisine."[22] *Shippoku* cuisine is still appreciated in Nagasaki and available at local restaurants as a hybrid Chinese and western Japanese-style of food preparation and dining.[23]

---

[21] Wada Tsuneko, *Nagasaki ryōri*, p. 52.
[22] Ibid., p. 214.
[23] Nishiyama Matsunosuke, *Edo Culture: daily life and diversions in urban Japan, 1600–1868* (translated by Gerald Groemer), p. 146. The author claims that during his childhood in Kansai, around the city of Akō in Harima, his family used to call a dining table a "shippoku-dai."

Figure 12. A Japanese rendition of a Chinese trading ship, *Tōsen* – literally a "Tang Ship," pulling into port.[24]

Food and the Chinese

The way in which the Chinese were regarded in Japan during most of the Tokugawa era and before is radically different from the Chinese experience in the United States during the mid-nineteenth century when thousands arrived as little more than indentured servants. For centuries, Chinese entrepreneurs traveling to Nagasaki received a first-class

---

[24] Nagasaki Museum of History and Culture (長崎港湾図3/87-1).

reception. Kyushu was international and this vibrancy propelled changes in foodways that urged a transformation in Japanese cuisine.

During the Ming and Qing Dynasties, the Chinese ate quite differently from the Japanese. The Chinese dined at the same table and food was set on the table in large bowls or on big plates; diners took a portion and placed it on their own plate. This may not seem astounding today, but for the Japanese it was; travelers constantly commented on these strange dining habits. Even today in Japan, at formal banquets or at a traditional inn (*ryokan*), the diner often sits in front of his own little table, eating carefully arranged food from an array of small personal dishes. Japanese visiting the Chinese enclosure were also shocked to discover that the Chinese conversed during meals and turned any gathering into a banquet, formalized but festive. Japanese samurai and nobles of all ranks ingested food primarily to maintain health and did not regard it as cause for a party. Talking or chatting was frowned upon and considered only suitable for women. Certainly, Chinese cuisine was different, but it surely did not seem as

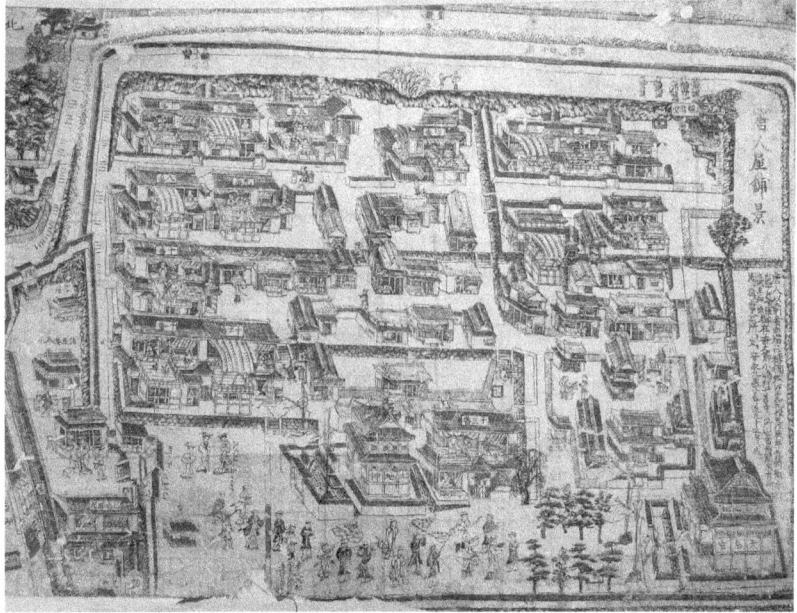

Figure 13. A detailed Tokugawa era map of the large Chinese enclosure in Nagasaki.[25]

---

[25] Nagasaki Museum of History and Culture, (唐人屋鋪景 3/163-2).

foreign as the Dutch meals with their creamy ingredients and large steaks of cooked animal flesh. The "dog shogun" Tokugawa Tsunayoshi, so-called because he was a devout Buddhist opposed to taking life in any form and very fond of dogs, proclaimed a special edict forbidding the killing of living things. Nevertheless, he granted the Dutch and Chinese special dispensation to continue eating their pork and chicken.[26]

The Chinese influence in Nagasaki during the Tokugawa era not only made a deep impression on the food culture of western Japan, but also altered political and religious attitudes. Chinese temples, owned and operated by the Chinese themselves, remain standing in Nagasaki and elsewhere in Kyushu as living testaments to the multicultural nature of society and the importance of international trade in western Japan. The overseas Chinese community in Nagasaki imported products not previously known

Figure 14. A Chinese banquet in Nagasaki, hosted in the Chinese enclosure. Note the very different style compared to a Japanese celebratory meal. Here, groups of gentlemen sit around tables and are hosted by courtesans. Large bowls of food form the centerpieces, with smaller personal dishes in front of each diner.[27]

---

[26] Yamamoto Noritsuna, *Nagasaki Tōjin yashiki*, p. 309. See also Beatrice M. Bodart-Bailey, *The dog shogun: the personality and policies of Tokugawa Tsunayoshi*.

[27] *Nagasaki meishō zue*, no pagination.

Figure 15. The Chinese were avid fans of the red light district but due to conflicts with the locals and administrative fears they outgrew their welcome in the public area and were confined to their quarters to wait for courtesans to visit.[28]

to the Japanese and encouraged an enthusiasm for experimentation that became a motivating political force in Japan's reconstruction during the early Meiji Restoration in the mid-nineteenth century. A taste for pork and the influence of Chinese food emporia, channeling these latent culinary forces, helped to create new noodle dishes in Nagasaki that opened the future market for ramen.

[28] Ibid.

We should not forget that the Chinese were not the only major group of foreigners influencing Japanese life in the western regions. The Dutch excelled at making friends with foreign leaders through their commercial *savoir-faire* and their preference for profit over proselytizing. Generally, Dutch food appealed to few Japanese people but their pastries and sugary confections made a lasting impact. The eighth shogun, Tokugawa Yoshimune, who became leader in 1716 at the age of thirty-one, was intrigued by Dutch goods. In 1724, he asked the Dutch traders, during their yearly tribute visit to Edo, to bring biscuits and butter because he wanted to see what they were. In 1725, they brought napkins, meat knives and other oddities. In 1726, they prepared a complete Dutch meal for him, or at least for part of the shogun's staff, with the Dutch at a table and the Japanese sitting on a tatami mat.[29] It was, in a sense, a precursor to Japan's successful "food diplomacy" at the dawn of the modern era in the mid-nineteenth century.

Passion for Noodles – *Soba* and *Udon*

While Nagasaki flourished, the main national urban enclave of Edo was attracting ever larger crowds to enjoy a greater variety of foods than most Japanese had ever known. Japan's first domestic cookbook, entitled "Tales of Cookery" (*Ryōri monogatari*), was published in 1643 and included a recipe for *udon*. By 1657, Edo was already providing numerous guidebooks to restaurants and brothels.[30] If Nagasaki residents marveled at Chinese cuisine and pork delights, Edoites were enamored with noodles, primarily *soba*. Saitō Gesshin, a well-known author and inveterate traveler, wrote an extensive series of eighteenth-century guidebooks, including "Handbook for the Great Sights of Edo." In this early modern tourist guide, Saitō constantly referred to the enormous number of *soba* noodle-sellers who peddled their wares all over the city at all hours of the day and night. The new city-dwellers' preferred style of eating also encouraged noodle worship

---

[29] Ego Michiko, *Nanban kara kita shokubunka*, p. 20. A similar fascinating episode of how such an exchange worked can be seen in Reinier Hesselink, "A Dutch New Year at the Shirando Academy: 1 January 1795," *Monumenta Nipponica*, Vol. 50, no. 2, Summer 1995, pp. 189–234.

[30] Watanabe Zenjirō, "Sekai o kakeru Nihongata shoku seikatsu no henbō," p. 1. For more see Harada Nobuo, "Culinary Culture and its transmission in the late Edo period," in Susanne Formanek and Sepp Linhart, eds., *Written Texts – Visual Texts: Woodblock printed Media in Early Modern Japan*, pp. 141–158.

during this era. Edoites considered the shogun's castle a refined urban setting, in contrast to Osaka. They consequently ate smaller meals more frequently, to distinguish themselves from what they considered to be gaudy merchants of the western areas of Japan. Edo urbanites snacked all day and night because small meals were quickly digested leaving the snack-seeker hungry for the next culinary delight. When you were hungry, which was often, it was said that "your stomach had arrived," *hara ga kita*.

The rise of restaurants is an historical anomaly during the Edo period because, in theory, the Tokugawa government was enforcing strict sumptuary laws that controlled who could wear and eat what according to their class. Nonetheless, Edo's urban style of living encouraged the availability of hot foods for sale on the streets. Guides to the city described the sights and sounds, directing travelers, gourmands and itinerant pilgrims to the stalls and shops that sold the latest in fashion and the best noodles. Edo quickly became a city that never slept and entrepreneurs responded by increasing night sales and keeping stalls open until the small hours of the morning. The sheer number of peddlers exceeded what the shogun's advisors considered an acceptable level, and in 1670 the *bakufu*, the shogun's administrative arm, banned night sales. The authorities also worried about the stoves used by urban noodle-sellers, fearing a repeat of the great Meireki fire of 1657 that burned down almost two-thirds of the new capital. After the *bakufu* banned night sales, noodle-sellers walked around at night selling their wares, to avoid being categorized as "restaurants" and being forced to follow proper licensing procedures. The *bakufu*'s efforts to control how food was sold, and thereby putting the lid on any potential threat to the fixed social hierarchy it sought to preserve, brought about the quite unexpected birth of a new entrepreneur: the wandering noodle salesman. The original ban had been against "selling stewed goods": noodle soup was not exactly stewed, in the legal sense.[31] Streetwalkers, or nighthawks (*yotaka*) as they were known at the time, were also big customers for the late-night noodle-peddlers, and some historians assume that the authorities' move to cut off noodle sales was actually designed to curtail the trade in unlicensed evening pleasure. So prevalent at one time were nighthawks and the peddlers who served them that the stalls were called "nighthawk soba stands."[32]

---

[31] Yonezawa mengyō kumiai kyūjūnenshi kankō īnkai edited, *Yonezawa mengyōshi*, p. 26.
[32] Niijima Shigeru and Satsuma Uichi, *Soba no sekai*, p. 74.

By the 1680s, there were already thousands of stalls in Edo selling *soba* – the buckwheat noodle that broke easily and was one of the city's four delicacies, the other three being eel, tempura and sushi. No one flavor was associated with a "national taste" and food preferences varied greatly between Osaka, Kyoto and Edo, the three great cultural cities of central Japan. As Edo's power grew, its food preferences began to dominate the market.

Banning Noodle Consumption

Soba was becoming so popular as a temple snack that many clerical and administrative officials questioned whether this was a good thing. A main Jōdo Buddhist temple in Edo, known as Shōōin, took the extreme measure of banning the sale of noodles outright, arguing that this commerce detracted from the serious work of Buddhist monks, and that clerics should not be selling *soba*.[33] One area of the compound had become so

Figure 16. A food-seller carrying his wares in baskets in Edo.

---

[33] Nihon menruigyō dantai rengōkai, *Soba udon hyakumi hyakudai*, p. 17.

INTERNATIONAL JAPAN, FOREIGN FOODS AND ISOLATION   65

Figure 17. A small and portable foodstall in Edo.

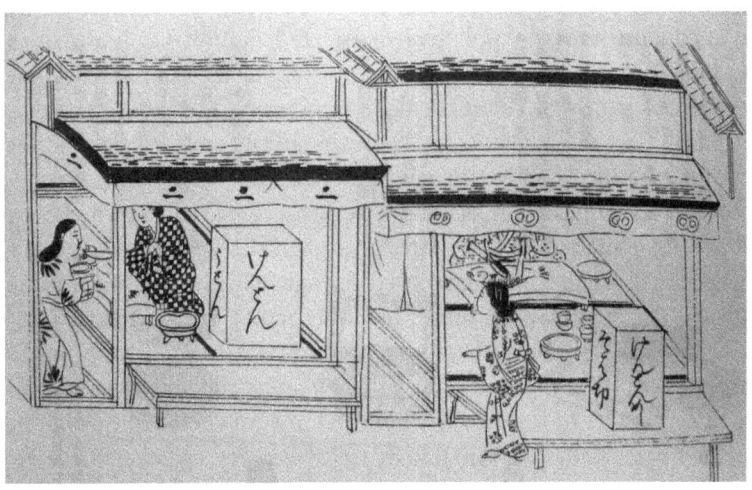

Figure 18. An example of noodle stalls in Edo.

busy that it was known as the "Soba Temple." Initially, the temple compound was located in Asakusa, an area filled with shops and restaurants serving the entertainment business. Several centuries later, the compound moved to a more peaceful enclave outside the city. Inside the temple walls was a hermit's cell called the *Dōkōan* (the suffix *an* means small dwelling). The Chinese character for *an* (庵) is associated with *soba* noodles and many contemporary shops carry on the tradition linked to this temple by putting the character *an* in their stores' names. Ramen shops, to distinguish themselves, would usually not use the same characters. The Buddhist monk who resided in this small residence hailed from a town in what is now Nagano Prefecture, a region renowned for its delicious *soba*. The monk was a *soba*-maker extraordinaire and his noodles were famous. His less noodle-oriented bosses felt that making *soba* all day interrupted his Buddhist study sessions so they erected a stone obelisk engraved with the words "Soba-making is forbidden here!" in front of his cell. The stone marker fell over during an earthquake and was lost, but was recently found and re-erected on the temple grounds to remind us of just how much Edo residents loved their noodles and the efforts authorities took to limit their consumption.

Throughout the Tokugawa era, the Japanese demand for noodles continued to grow and urban markets were able to meet the demands of an exploding population. However, we should not assume that the Japanese liked noodles that much or that the *soba* itself was so unusually delicious. The fact of the matter is that noodles were a welcome addition to a monotonous diet. Today, Japanese steamed rice is a treat. However, stoves capable of cooking rice were only really perfected about a hundred years ago. Previously, cooking good rice required a great deal of time management, since it took nearly two hours to make a single pot. A growing debate rages within the historical East Asian food community concerning the precise manner of eating rice. One thing is clear: rice was not consumed or cooked in the same manner today as it was several hundred years ago. Today, most people in Japan assume that perfectly cooked rice will have a slightly glutinous consistency. This rice is used to make sushi or served on dinner tables; it is tasty and a bit soft. A few hundred years ago this variety was quite rare and the more common product was *kowaī*, or "strong rice." "Strong Rice" was prevalent during the Heian period and consumed until the mid-nineteenth century. It is believed to have been a somewhat hard, steamed rice, not as delicious or easy to eat as today's glutinous rice. Some historians believe that in earlier times men ate steamed rice, while women

Figure 19. At the top of the stone marker are four Chinese characters, which mean "Soba is not permitted."

dined on a form of rice gruel.[34] One of the biggest changes between early medieval Kamakura times and the Tokugawa era was the shift in emphasis – from eating as a way of merely filling your stomach to dining for pleasure on food that tasted good. Noodles, at this point mainly *soba* and *udon*, offered a tastier alternative to poorly cooked rice for a person of any class who could afford such treats.

Once Edo culture was established, noodles flourished and laid the foundation for modern Japanese cuisine. Edo was a male enclave, enriched by domainal lords required to visit the shogun's capital every two years in alternative attendance, a duty called *sankin kōtai*. The lords of all the domains across Japan traveled to make their appearance at the shogun's offices and reside in Edo for several months. Their travel route generally involved one of several major trunk roads, and they would journey with massive retinues, including baggage carriers, cooks, hairdressers and personal physicians. The towns along the way, where these entourages stopped for the evening or for several days to rest and take on provisions, grew in size to meet consumer demand, often selling souvenirs and regional food products. Constantine Vaporis, an historian who has spent a career analyzing the impact of this system on the formation of Japanese culture, suggests that these roads, markets and travel "created an instant class of consumers."[35] In traveling to Edo and returning home, lords, samurai and attendants functioned as "carriers of culture" who brought back customs and dining habits from Edo and transplanted them to their home fiefs.[36] In this way, noodle eating and noodle cuisine spread through the archipelago.

The Eastern Sea road, *Tōkaidō*, was one of Japan's five great trunk roads. At four-hundred-and-eighty-eight kilometers long, it connected Edo to Kyoto and was thus of great political importance. Along the way, fifty-three post-stations dotted the route, making the road one of the most traveled and popular. There were stores in the post-station areas, tea shops, restaurants and, of course, noodle shops. Towards the end of the Tokugawa era, a *soba*-loving traveler, Yamazaki Eizan, published a book of his travels on this road down to Osaka and wrote in great detail about all the *soba* noodle shops. The book, entitled "A Soba Road Diary" (*Soba dōchūki*), is a detailed account of Yamazaki's travels and love affair with *soba*, as well as

---

[34] Kawakami Kōzō, *Nihon ryōri jibutsu kigen* (2 Vol. combined version), pp. 358–360.
[35] Constantine Vaporis, *Tour of duty: samurai, military service in Edo and the culture of early modern Japan*, p. 192.
[36] Ibid., p. 206.

an important piece of historical evidence demonstrating the spread of noodle cuisine around Japan at this time. Engelbert Kaempfer, a German physician who lived in the Dutch enclosure in Nagasaki and was allowed a privileged visit to Edo and other places in Japan, noted during his travels the innumerable food stalls that lined the trunk roads, even in forests and mountains. Kaempfer, a keen observer, recorded that the stalls served all kinds of food, including *manjū* (bread rolls), small pieces of fried eel and Chinese *karoutsu*, a kind of wheat dough thinly rolled up, folded, cut into narrow strips and then boiled. This was akin to wheat noodles, or *sobakiri* in Japanese.[37]

From the start of the Japanese love affair with noodles to the temple ban, the Edo period saw a great rise in the production of simple foods sold to samurai, townspeople and the growing number of travelers between regions. As Tokugawa Japan flourished and the consumption of noodles spread, wealthier sections of the population began to want tastier food, and to look at cuisine in new and interesting ways. Edo culture prepared the way for a national cuisine in Japan through the sheer dominance of the city and the regular visits that the nation's elite were required to make to the shogun's domain. Noodles were on the rise and the population could almost taste the next innovation, so hungry were they for new and exotic fare.

---

[37] Beatrice Bodart-Bailey, edited and translated, *Kaempfer's Japan: Tokugawa Culture Observed*, pp. 268–269. For more general observations on what the Japanese ate in the late eighteenth century, see Timon Screech, annotated and introduced, *Japan Extolled and Decried: Carl Peter Thunburg and the Shogun's Realm, 1775–1796*, pp. 210–211.

CHAPTER FOUR

EARLY MODERN NOODLES AND THE MYTH OF RAMEN

As Japan's affinity with *soba* and *udon* grew, it was only a matter of time before other noodle dishes caught the public's fancy. Chinese culture was, as ever, a strong influence. As art historian Timon Screech explains, Edo in the Tokugawa period was not just the seat of government where the shoguns managed the whole country, but a site that based its power on the age-old Japanese custom of appropriating Chinese symbols of authority and urban landscape.[1] This inclination toward Chinese representations of power, combined with the emergence throughout Japan of larger capital markets for food and eating, pushed the food revolution forward toward the production of ramen.

Just slightly to the north of the imperial palace in modern-day Tokyo lies an expansive tract of greenery, one of the few surviving Edo-period parks in the city, complete with flower gardens, several ponds and waterways, meandering paths, and many lush beautiful trees, bounded now by busy traffic lanes and convenience stores. As you enter the Koishikawa Kōrakuen, or "Garden of Deferred Leisure," you are instantly transported back to a time when social class was fixed, and every citizen of Japan had a permanent status as an aristocrat, peasant, merchant, or artisan.[2]

The Tokugawa shogun, or "Barbarian Subduing Generalissimo" (the full Japanese meaning of the term), built his new capital in Edo and ruled in the name of the emperor, an effete monarch with no power and little (at times no) money who remained ensconced with his court in Kyoto. Various lords around the country – between 200 and 250, depending on wealth or the whim of the shogun – pledged varying degrees of allegiance to the shogun, effectively uniting Japan under a common set of federal and state-like laws. Political and economic fortunes waxed and waned, and families withered, according to the shogun's pleasure: he could summarily confiscate their landholdings and allocate them to more supportive clans. People did not think of themselves as Japanese or as members of a nation.

---

[1] Taimon Sukurīchi, *Edo no ōbushin: Tokugawa toshi keikaku no shigaku*, pp. 68–67.
[2] In fact, peasants were supposedly ranked high in the social hierarchy of Tokugawa Japan because they worked the fields but in actuality their lives were fraught with poverty and they were looked down upon by merchants and samurai.

However, peace made economic and social progress possible within fiefs. Identity was more regional, less national, and often depended on where you lived – west, east or close to the cities of Osaka, Edo or Nagasaki. Lords from all areas had to travel to Edo and stay for several months while they conducted administrative affairs with the central *bakufu*, or shogun's government. This alternative attendance system put a tremendous food burden on Edo, requiring the constant delivery of large amounts of provisions and supplies. To meet demand, the shogun's administrators were constantly regulating the peasants, encouraging them to till the land rather than take waged labor, forcing them to pay taxes in the form of rice. This wealth was measured in bushels (called *koku*), hence the historical references to how many *koku* a lord owned, or "was worth." The amount of rice available to a leader determined how many retainers and foot soldiers he could afford to keep and feed. During their sojourns in Edo, lords and their retinues of up to several hundred people, depending on the fief's agricultural output and wealth, resided in their own residences, which were like embassies in the shogun's city. The "Garden of Deferred Leisure" was part of the estate of the Mito fief.

Each lord had a large residence. The Mito fief, or *han* in Japanese, was not far from Edo and the lord of Mito was a relative of the Tokugawa family. Familial proximity to the Tokugawa administration did not always translate into greater wealth, but it did not diminish business options either. Mito was a fairly prosperous fief, but more importantly by the mid-1600s clan leaders had launched a project to write a national history of Japan. Following the Chinese tradition of writing history to support national leadership, the leader of the Mito fief, Mito Kōmon and his group embarked on an ambitious program of collecting, organizing and inscribing a sixty-volume series – the first attempt of its kind.[3] The Mito scholars looked for help and who better to assist than a Chinese scholar who was based in Nagasaki after fleeing the fall of the Ming dynasty in 1644? Nagasaki was already home to thousands of Chinese conducting business and trade, and Japan was keen to exploit their experience and prestige.

After decades of internal corruption in China, and growing Manchu power in the north, the Ming emperor committed suicide and the Ming dynasty collapsed. Non-Chinese invaders from the barbarian north occupied Beijing and established the Qing dynasty. This shift of power was deemed unacceptable to the imperial loyalists around Nanjing – some

---

[3] Mito was how he was popularly known but his real name was Tokugawa Mitsukuni.

Chinese fled and others rebelled, while millions grumbled but acquiesced. To consolidate their power, the Manchus or Qing rulers moved their imperial court from the city of Shenyang in deep Manchuria to Beijing. The Qing dynasty was China's last imperial leadership and it was a foreign one. Hundreds of thousands of Ming officials, still loyal to the administration where they had earned their salaries and written their imperial memoranda, fled south. For close to a century, they searched for sources of military and financial largesse within Asia to assist their struggle against the Qing overlords. In the ensuing years, dozens of groups claiming to be Ming embassies also traveled to Japan to ask for military support to restore the Ming court.[4]

One of the many loyalist Ming scholars who sought refuge in Nagasaki, Shu Shunsui (Zhu Shunshui), taught Confucian ethics to interested Mito scholars and, because he was multi-talented, also helped with various other projects such as planning the gardens of leisure. Shu designed part of Kōrakuen, the Mito garden in Tokyo, including the graceful "half moon bridge," which arches over a section of the interior lake, as well as other aspects of the Mito residence in the capital. Mito Kōmon incorporated many other traditional Chinese garden features and replicated famous Chinese settings. The interior lake was designed to resemble the Western Lake in the city of Hangzhou – a renowned beauty spot the Mito leader would have read about in classical texts. Even the name Kōrakuen comes from the Chinese classics. In his poetic account, Fan Zhongyan described how those in power worry first about maintaining authority and only later about enjoying it. The three-character name pronounced *kō-raku-en* in Japanese derives from this idea and incorporates the idea of a garden for "enjoying life after power."

Japan's First Chinese Chef – Shu Shunsui?

To understand the impact of a Confucian scholar like Shu Shunsui it is necessary to untangle the complex web of history that formed Sino-Japanese political relations, which in turn influenced the evolution of Japanese noodle cuisine. To achieve this, we must delve below the modern stereotypes that have been thrust onto the historical figure of Mito Kōmon. Turn on the TV any late afternoon in Japan and you will see reruns of a remarkably long-running television show called *Mito Kōmon*. In this

---

[4] Ronald Toby, *State and Diplomacy in Early Modern Japan*, pp. 119–130.

Figure 20. The "half moon bridge" in Kōrakuen, in the north part of Tokyo.

program, Mito, traveling in disguise around the Japanese countryside, rights wrongs and assists peasants in distress, while foiling the efforts of dastardly elite officials and village heads abusing their positions. It is in some ways a modern version of the fourteenth-century *kyōgen* comedy play about the peasant seaweed salesman who turns the tables on a hapless samurai when ordered to carry his sword. The final scene of every episode is a predictable climax: one of Mito's loyal assistants reaches into his pocket and pulls out the official Mito seal. Thrusting the round emblem into the faces of the evil-doers, he shouts: "Cast your eyes upon this seal, do you not recognize the authority that lies behind it?" Mortified and struck dumb, the villains belatedly realize that the band of misfits that has trounced them is none other than the lord of Mito and his minions. Generations of Japanese have grown up with this fairly cheesy show, so the name Mito Kōmon is quite familiar to them.

Notwithstanding the popularity of Mito Kōmon as an after-school TV hero, his appearance in popular lore as an inventor of Japanese ramen should give us pause. Open many popular Japanese books on ramen or visit a ramen-related museum, such as the one in Yokohama, and you will be presented with a persistent myth about the origin of ramen in Japan.[5]

---

[5] Japanese are not the only ones to promote this myth. A lengthy feature on ramen in the *New York Times* from January 26, 2010 repeated the false charge.

It is a good story, in the sense that it contains some historical truth, but it is also flawed. Mito Kōmon was a well-known figure and did invite Shu to teach Confucian doctrine in the Mito domain. According to the myth, Shu later taught Mito to make ramen, making Mito Kōmon the first Japanese to eat ramen. Mito did mention in his diaries that he enjoyed soba but that is a far cry from *ramen*. As a member of the literati class, Shu would have been a very unlikely teacher of cooking. Pictures drawn of him at the time reveal a slightly aging yet elegant figure with a traditional wispy beard and long fingernails. It is true that Chinese officials loved to eat, but Shu probably had little experience of actual cooking methods – that would have been quite below his station. His mind was preoccupied with more pressing matters of etiquette, moral behavior and a proper understanding of neo-Confucian thought, which could only be obtained through long, careful years of intense study.

The possibility that Shu Shunsui would have been willing to spend his time teaching Mito how to make ramen is made more unlikely when we consider the sheer effort that was required to advance in imperial Chinese society. Boys in China who wished to attain success for themselves and their families worked hard for the civil service exams, hoping to gain a position as an official. As historian David Nivison explains, the "examinations played a very large part in a literary man's life, molding his education from early youth."[6] Exams were held every three years at three levels: the county, provincial and metropolitan. At the highest level they were administered in the capital, where the emperor presided over the grading. To pass such higher level exams, a daunting amount of intense study was required. Scholars estimated that they had to memorize 626,000 words (the equivalent of six thick and weighty books) of complicated Chinese; this effort required about fifteen steady years of study.[7] After digesting that material, students worked on perfecting their calligraphy, the sign of a learned man. Scholars who passed any exam but failed to gain a position in government became teachers. This was not out of choice: as the Chinese proverb says, "no one with enough grain to get through the winter becomes a schoolteacher."[8] Life in the poor official-scholar class was tough: wages were low, certainly too low to maintain a standard of living adequate to their status. Shu was such a scholar and after the fall of the Ming dynasty he needed a new patron. The Mito leaders in Japan offered a perfect opportunity.

---

[6] David S. Nivison, *The Life and Thought of Chang Hsueh-ch'eng (1738–1801)*, p. 8.
[7] Henrietta Harrison, *The Man Awakened from Dreams*, p. 26.
[8] Ibid., p. 41.

A mid-seventeenth century portrait of Shu depicts him as a stereotypical upright Confucian gentleman who has evidently risen in Ming Chinese society through careful study and the application of Confucian doctrine. In one image he is wearing a long gown, his stern eyes staring straight ahead and his pointy face layered with a sparse, jutting beard. You can almost imagine him stroking his chin with his long, thin fingers. He might have known something about cooking and would certainly have instructed cooks, but Shu hailed from a region not known for its soup or noodles. Shu came from Zhejiang, an eastern province in China that was home to the Neo-Confucian hero Wang Yangming. He was a father by the age of eighteen and pursued Confucian studies rather than training for the civil service exams because he believed the grading system to be rife with corruption. He never officially joined the Ming bureaucracy until it became an exiled government in the south. Shu traveled widely in the 1640s and 1650s, visiting Vietnam and Japan. In 1651, he formally asked the shogun for permission to reside permanently in Japan where "poetry and history are honored" and "propriety and righteousness are valued," as he wrote.[9] However, the Japanese authorities declined to grant Shu residence, which may have reflected the *bakufu's* ambivalence over whether to support fallen Ming officials or build relations with the new Qing court from Manchuria. Shu traveled back and forth several times between Japan and Vietnam and at one point corresponded with Coxinga, known as Zheng Chenggong in Chinese, the leader who won independence from Dutch colonial rule for the island of Formosa (Taiwan) in the mid-seventeenth century.

Zheng Chenggong was born of Japanese and Chinese parentage at Hirado, a city on the western coast of Kyushu. He was a Ming loyalist who studied at Nanjing, journeyed to Taiwan and at one point requested military assistance from Japan to overthrow the Qing invaders. From 1658 to 1659, Zheng Chenggong tried to attack Nanjing but failed; Shu Shunsui took part in that campaign and then, when it failed, fled to Japan. Chikamatsu, widely considered Japan's most famous playwright, penned a well-known puppet play about the event, which later was made into a successful Kabuki drama, entitled "The Battles of Coxinga."[10] Shu belonged to an era when all sorts of Chinese immigrants flooded into the west of Japan

---

[9] As quoted in Julia Ching, "Chu Shun-Shui, 1600–82: A Chinese Confucian Scholar in Tokugawa Japan," *Monumenta Nipponica*, Vol. 30, no. 2, Summer 1975, p. 182.

[10] Donald Keene, *The Battles of Coxinga: Chikamatsu's Puppet Play, Its Background and Importance*.

but it was not until the Japanese Confucian scholar Andō Seian intervened and personally invited him that Shu obtained legal status to reside permanently in Nagasaki. He became known for his profound erudition concerning Neo-Confucian thought. Andō asked him to teach classes in Nagasaki and from his own pocket paid Shu a handsome stipend.[11]

We can be reasonably sure that Mito Kōmon did not invent ramen, nor did he introduce ramen to Japan. In 1664, Mito's retainers traveled west to Nagasaki to invite Shu to the Mito fief to assist in spreading and strengthening Confucian learning. Shu became Mito Kōmon's political-cum-moral advisor. Shu enjoyed frequent audiences with his employer and traveled around Edo to lecture on Confucianism. In 1666, Mito Kōmon ordered many Buddhist shrines and temples to be destroyed because he favored a stricter interpretation of Confucian ideology.[12] Shu assisted in designing a Confucian temple in Mito and the same plans were used for a second Confucian temple in Edo, the Yushima Shrine, which still stands today.[13] Shu died in 1682 and is buried at the base of Mt. Zuiryū in Hitachi; Mito, his employer and disciple in Confucianism, is buried nearby. Shu never lived in Edo proper, however. His patron's "embassy" in the shogun's capital stood where Imperial Tokyo University, the first incarnation of the University of Tokyo, was later built. There was a memorial tablet honoring Shu on the university campus.

Mito Kōmon was a strict Confucianist known for his concern about the wellbeing of his peasants. A semi-apocryphal story about him illustrates the appreciation he felt toward his people for the rice they produced: apparently he used to fashion little figurines of peasants and place them on his altar, and every morning when he ate rice, he would offer (as if to a deity) a portion to the figurines as thanks. Supposedly, he even wrote a poem: "Each morning, each morning, every time I eat I do not forget that I owe my blessings to those less fortunate."[14] However, while he may have appreciated the produce of the fields that his peasants plowed, he was not a gourmet like the mythical Chinese Yellow Emperor, nor did he write tracts about culinary form and function in the same way as his Chinese contemporaries. One of the Mito chronicles recorded a conversation between the Mito lord and one of his vassals concerning how to make

---

[11] Nagasaki kyōikuīnkai, *Chūgoku bunka to Nagasakiken*, p. 115.
[12] Julia Ching, "Chu Shun-Shui, 1600–82: A Chinese Confucian Scholar in Tokugawa Japan," p. 187.
[13] Ibid., p. 188.
[14] Aoki Toshisaburō, *Edo jidai no shokuryō mondai*, p. 49.

Figure 21. The memorial stele to Shu Shunsui was tucked away just to the left of the main entrance to the University of Tokyo, in a shady and unused garden that was easy to miss. The inscription reads: "Memorial site in honor of Teacher Shu Shunsui." A new building now sits on this site and University of Tokyo authorities could not explain what happened to the monument because it is no longer there.

noodles. Mito Kōmon told his vassal how to mix the flour and water with a bit of salt and then roll the dough out into a noodle shape.[15] The retainer, astounded that his lord could know such mundane things, asked how he had attained such knowledge. Mito replied that he learned noodle-making by watching shop owners in Edo.[16] This is an entirely plausible explanation and certainly more believable than the myth of Shu Shunsui bringing *ramen* to Japan.

Edo – Feast and Famine

Depending on which records historians examine, it is possible to paint a relatively dismal picture of standards of living in early modern Japan. This is not a complete picture; according to one body of scholarship, there was growing wealth developing among a group of people at the top of Japanese society. Standards of living did improve across the Tokugawa domains, but daily life was still a struggle for most. In essence, the Tokugawa era was a period of extremes. Edo was not only a city of riches it was also the scene of daily tragedies for members of the upper classes who lacked the income appropriate to their stations. One story recounts the sobering tale of a masterless samurai, a *rōnin*, who traveled to Edo in search of employment. Masterless samurai were pretty much out of luck: they had pledged loyalty to one master, on whom their livelihood was dependent; if their lord died or was reduced in rank, which sometimes happened, or if a different ruling family took over by fiat, they were literally left out in the cold. A well-known Japanese saying, "A hawk, even when facing death is not going to grab at rice stalks," describes the difficulty of shifting allegiance. Hawks are carnivores: even when starving, a hawk will not suddenly eat something else. Like the hawk, the dutiful samurai will be true to his nature, unable to change even if it is to his detriment.

A common tale thought to date from the eighteenth century, and that exists in several versions, epitomizes this stoic behavior. One spring during the early 1780s, near the Ryōgoku Bridge in Edo, a raggedly dressed samurai carrying a sword and dragging along a child of six or seven came to a standstill in front of a store selling a huge pile of steamed Satsuma yams. The child, who clearly had not eaten for several days, cried out "I want to

---

[15] Aoki Naomi, "Mito Kōmon no teuchi udon," *Rekishi kōkishin*, NHK publishers, June, 2007, p. 49.
[16] Aoki Naomi, "Mito Kōmon no teuchi udon," p. 50.

eat! I want to eat!," whereupon a person standing nearby purchased a yam and gave it to the child who devoured it in seconds. The person was actually from the *eta* caste (literally "full of filth," sometimes also known as "hinin," or non-person) the lowest rung in Edo-period society. The look in the samurai's eyes, forced to accept charity from a member of society he should despise, is described at some length in the narrative. Having stared at his benefactor silently, able only to say "Thank you" in his heart, the samurai permitted his child to finish his last meal, then scooped him up into his arms and jumped off the bridge into the raging river and certain death. The suggestion is that the motive for taking his own life was his inability to bear the utter humiliation of having to accept assistance from someone so completely beneath him in the social order – an outcaste. One early modern author argued that this tale demonstrated the love of a father who wanted to allow his son at least to enjoy the yam before drowning, adding that the episode provided a true definition of "tragedy."[17]

Kansai versus Kantō Taste

The main groups in Japanese society did not eat a varied diet, but peasants often consumed at one sitting quantities of food that would seem vast in comparison with present-day meals.[18] Toward the end of the Muromachi era and into the beginning of the Edo period, wealthier classes began eating two and then three meals a day, increasing the proportion of white rice if they could afford it. As the upper classes became more dependent on white rice, there was a reported increase in cases of beriberi, which soon became known as the "Edo affliction," *Edo wazurai*. Like gout in nineteenth-century Europe, this problem mostly affected those who could afford a life of leisure.

Geographically, Japan has two regionally distinct seats of power: Kansai, the area around Kyoto and Osaka; and Kantō, the region to the east that surrounds and includes Tokyo. Historically, these regions developed different dialects, social attitudes and certainly divergent cuisines. Edo was the city of samurai and power politics, while Osaka was the urban center for merchants and money. Historically, and even today, people from Osaka are

---

[17] Miyagawa Masayasu wrote the story, entitled "Rōshichi o shi to su," published originally in 1862 in "Kyūsenshamanpitsu," Nihon zuihitsu zenshū, Vol. 10, p. 763. Koyanagi Kiichi mentions this as well in *Nihonjin no shokuseikatsu: kiga to hōyō no hentenshi*, pp. 7–8.

[18] Shinoda Osamu, "Shoku no fūzoku minzoku meicho shūsei," Vol. 2, *Kome to Nihonjin*, p. 61.

thought to dress ostentatiously (*hade*), while those in Tokyo are thought to be conservative in appearance (*jimi*). From the 1630s onward, Edo flourished as the shogun's metropolis and the seat of the Tokugawa clan in the Kantō region. Osaka was called the "nation's kitchen" because it was where most of the nation's rice was traded and where the account ledgers of many lords were balanced. When the lords and their extensive retinues returned to their home towns after fulfilling their alternate attendance duties in the capital, they invariably found their home regions poorer in comparison. They complained that they could no longer put up with wheat or millet mixed with their rice, having grown accustomed to meals of pure white rice in Edo.[19] Tokugawa wealth and the development of Edo as an urban metropolis began to affect and to help form a sense of national taste, or at least a desire for taste. Travel on the trunk roads and overnight stays in the post-station houses merely increased that tendency.

Edo set the standard for Japanese cuisine and in so doing set the stage for the arrival of ramen. The population of Edo enjoyed numerous restaurants years before either the French, whose first restaurant was established in 1765, or the English, who had none really until the early nineteenth-century. *Edokko* was the term used to label someone born and raised in Edo who was carefree and lived for pleasure. It was an expression of endearment first used during the late 1700s to describe a typical Edoite: loose with money, raised in a high-class manner, knowing all the ins and outs of the city and displaying refinement and character. The true *Edokko* was a connoisseur, or *tsū*, a term already in use in the 1760s. Connoisseurs emerged in the context of the pleasure quarters – in the theater, musical world and restaurants. Rules of behavior governing the exchange of money, formalities and specific phrases used in particular circumstances were codified and known only to the "in crowd." The opposite of a *tsū* was a boor, a country bumpkin, who tried to pass as a connoisseur but was ignorant of the values and behavior of the true and natural sophisticate.[20]

In the early years of the Tokugawa era, Kansai soy sauce manufacturers like Tatsuno had an edge because they produced sauce of a higher grade. This western region was also known as *kamigata*, the region of "higher ups." The imperial family lived in Kyoto and technology was more advanced there. As Kansai soy sauce was shipped from the imperial capital region to

---

[19] Hiraide Kojirō, *Tōkyō fūzokushi*, reprinted in 1985, p. 184.
[20] The 1996 French film *Ridicule* lavishly portrayed the court of Louis XVI and how witty put-downs curried favor with the monarch.

Edo, it was considered to travel "down" and was thus referred to as *kudari* soy sauce. This soy sauce, exported from the Kyoto basin, sold at twice the price of soy sauce made in the region around Edo.[21] If a superior product was imported to the shogun's capital from the *kamigata* region of Kyoto where the emperor lived, it was referred to as a *"kudaru"* product, or a product that went "down to Edo." Inferior or lower grade local products that were not suitable to bring to the shogun's capital were referred to as *"kudaranai,"* items of lesser quality that could not go down.[22] In contemporary Japan, when something is of poor quality or boring it is labeled *kudaranai*, a term first used to describe local products not suitable for export during the Edo period.

Along with flavors of thick and thin soy sauce and the *soba* noodles and similar delights that warmed diners' hearts throughout the capital, Edo also expanded the market for fish, developing the precursor to sushi. Not all fish was popular; only certain species were deemed appropriate to a high-class, discerning palate. *Sanma*, or mackerel pike, is a long, thin and silvery fish like an overgrown sardine. Nowadays, they are an autumn specialty, grilled out of doors with a pinch of salt and a squeeze of lemon and served with a chilled beer.[23] Edo's poorer laboring classes enjoyed *sanma*, but the elites considered it unpleasant, and did not really take to it until the late 1700s or early 1800s. The spread of *sanma* upward toward elite dining tables took time, demonstrating the extent to which Japanese dining has changed over the centuries.

The obvious divide between the food eaten by different social classes is illustrated in the *rakugo* skit *"Meguro Sanma,"* which satirizes ignorant lords and elites.[24] *Rakugo* is a form of traditional Japanese comedy where a lone performer sits on the stage and tells stories in the voices of many characters. *Rakugo* artists are only allowed two props, a fan and a handkerchief, and all stories are told while seated with legs folded beneath one in a formal seated position called *seiza*. Audiences enjoy the stories less for the punchlines and more for the performer's ability to mimic actions, create a mood, imitate accents and recount generally amusing tales.

---

[21] Tatsuno shōyu kyōdō kumiai edited, *Tatsuno shōyu kyōdō kumiai yōran*, p. 6.

[22] Hayashi Reiko, "Provisioning Edo in the Early Eighteenth Century," in James McClain et al., eds, *Edo and Paris: Urban Life and the State in the Early Modern Era*, pp. 213–215.

[23] Food tastes change with history and identity as much in Asia as elsewhere in the world. In New England in the early part of the nineteenth century until well after the dawn of the twentieth century lobster was also considered unfit for high cuisine and ground into fish bait or served at trough restaurants for the masses it was so loathed.

[24] Koyanagi Kiichi, *Nihonjin no shokuseikatsu; kiga to hōyō no hentenshi*, p. 15.

Rakugo is an irreverent form of humor that mocks traditional society – stupid samurai, bumbling young men from the countryside and virtually everyone and everything. This was the era when the elite ate different meals, dined on supposedly superior cuisine and lived completely separate existences from their servants and the common peasant.

In this fishy comedic skit, a lord is traveling with his servant from central Edo to the outskirts of town toward the village of Meguro, half a day's journey by foot (and now a twenty minute subway ride from central Tokyo).

> The two men stop by a village hut where they smell *sanma* being grilled and the servant says, "I am a bit famished, I think I will order a fish." To which the lord replies, "I am also hungry, I shall partake of the same."
>
> It was the first time the lord had eaten the fish and, not knowing what it was, he found it delicious. Returning to his estate the next day, the lord was disappointed that no fish like the one he had eaten with his servant was ever served up on his plate for dinner. One day, his relatives asked what his favorite dish was as they invited him to dine. To their astonishment he replied, "*sanma*." Surprised by his choice of a low quality peasant dish, the relative ordered the finest, most enormous specimen of the fish he could find from the most elite fishmonger in Edo. He cooked the massive fish, removed the bones and laid the glistening fat portion before his guest. The lord looked confused and said, "This isn't *sanma*. You've made a mistake." The uncle responded, "Well, to be sure it's a bit burnt on the edges, but...." The lord asked, "Where did you get it?" to which his uncle explained, "from the finest shop in Edo." The lord, demonstrating his complete lack of worldly knowledge and naiveté said, "That won't do, you need to get the kind they have in Meguro!"[25]

Meguro, of course, was not a fishing village, nor was it known to trade in *sanma*. The punch-line of the story demonstrated the foolishness of the lord, who clearly knows nothing about exactly what he is eating nor about its source, since he believes that a section of Edo not known for fish at all could produce the tastiest meal. The skit is probably best when it is performed live, but its real humor derives from the fact that it openly makes fun of supposedly superior members of society who actually understood far less about their surroundings and the real world than suggested by their rank.

From the 1770s, the variety of food offered by outdoor stalls increased in Edo: for example, a range of delicacies including tempura, broiled eel, dried squid, *dango* (small sticky rice balls covered in a tasty gelatinous

---

[25] Yano Seiichi, *Rakugo nagaya no shiki no aji*, pp. 176–180.

84   CHAPTER FOUR

sauce) and sushi.[26] By 1808, there were some six thousand restaurants in Edo alone, including stalls, establishments set up with a few basic tables on a street or a poorly lit alley, and a few shops that had an actual storefront. In the early half of the nineteenth century, fierce competition arose to attract the limited wealthy clientele and a few restaurants offered extra inducements such as hot baths with meals or an escort service with lanterns to take you home through the dark streets.[27] Not all cuisine was consumed by all classes, but the proliferation of noodles and the growing ease with which one could dine outside the home steadily increased the opportunities for diners to eat food above or beyond their station in life.

Edo and Meat Eating

One famous historian of Japan has used the term "container society" to describe the Tokugawa era.[28] The term refers to the strict social and political codes in which people were contained and that made social mobility for the most part utterly impossible, regardless of ambition or ability. If born into the peasant class, you basically stayed there and behaved accordingly, fulfilling a peasant's tasks, duties and obligations. Such restraints could make life unbearable for those with talent but no social position, preventing them from making money, traveling or making their mark. The Tokugawa social system stunted the dreams of many capable people. While Edo life might have been interesting and amusing for the wealthier kind of townsperson, this was not the case for everyone, especially those at the very lowest place in society.

The "untouchable classes," *eta*, were often relegated to the so-called dirty trades during the Tokugawa era. They were the leather craftsmen, butchers and disposers of the dead, and they lived on the very fringes of society. Some argue that before the Tokugawa period, the *eta* were treated with grudging respect; with Japan in a constant state of war for 150 years, leather goods like shields and armor were in great demand.[29] However,

---

[26] Watanabe Zenjirō, "Sekai o kakeru Nihongata shoku seikatsu no henbō," p. 12.
[27] Harada Nobuo, *Edo no shokuseikatsu*, p. 23.
[28] John W. Hall, "Rule by Status in Tokugawa Japan," *Journal of Japanese Studies*, Vol. 1, No. 1, Autumn, 1974, p. 48.
[29] Hugh Smythe, Yoshimasa Naitoh, "The Eta Caste in Japan," *Phylon*, Vol. 14, No. 1, 1953, p. 21. David Howell's work provides deeper historical insight into how these classes worked and interacted with the rest of Japanese society: David Howell, *Geographies of Identity in Nineteenth Century Japan*. Ian Neary describes how such discrimination has

they were always subject to a great many social restrictions, including not being allowed to eat with other Japanese because it was believed they would pollute the meal. Outcastes had to walk around barefoot and women could not use a sash for their kimono. It was not even truly a crime to kill them since they were not legally human.[30]

Edo history may help in unraveling the mystery of when exactly the Japanese started to eat meat. Eating meat was a defining step in the genesis of ramen: meat was essential both for the soup and the toppings. Certainly, upper-class Japanese considered meat in some respect unclean, or *kegare* in Japanese. However, for most people the social taboo against eating meat was probably economic in origin. Tokugawa society was founded on the production of rice. Rice was wealth and used as the basis of the monetary system, as gold was for many nations until the later twentieth century. Agricultural production determined whether lords and their vassals could match the economic power of competing fiefs, and funded the grandeur of the ten percent of the population who lived off peasant labor. In Aomori Prefecture in northern Japan, the peasants liked meat, in particular boar meat, which had a high fat content and supposedly medicinal qualities. By 1848, a farmer's cookbook noted that pork was fairly common in Edo and sold openly in various forms.[31] It seems safe to assume that while the law banning the consumption of meat was observed at official functions, it was often ignored by the lower classes.

What Edo city-dwellers considered appropriate to eat is the theme of another early modern comedy routine. *The Number Two Guard Station's Concoction* is a *rakugo* skit about city guards trying to keep warm during their rounds on a cold winter evening. There was a common saying that "fires and fights were the entertainment of Edo." The city was densely packed with small wooden-framed houses and a macho and easily-affronted male population so guards were hired to make the rounds, to keep a watch out for fires, and to maintain public order. The skit is usually performed as follows:

> A fire brigade leader separates his fire patrols into two groups. One stays to warm up around the stove, the other goes out on patrol. Upon returning, the two groups switch duties and survey the city in turns.

---

simultaneously persisted and transformed in modern Japan. See Ian Neary, *Political Protest and Social Control in Prewar Japan: The Origins of Burakumin Liberation.*

[30] Hugh Smythe, Yoshimasa Naitoh, "The Eta Caste in Japan," p. 21.

[31] Brett Walker, "Commercial Growth and Environmental Change in Early Modern Japan: Hachinohe's Wild Boar Famine of 1749," *Journal of Asian Studies*, Vol. 60, No. 2, May 2001, p. 342.

One of the guards pipes up and says, "Hey, my daughter didn't want me to catch cold so she made me take a flask of saké." The leader overhears him and says, "Are you crazy? What if the officials find out? What kind of image does this create for our younger guys?"

The leader pauses and then says, "Now listen." He continues slowly as if remonstrating but actually giving instructions, "Take the saké out of the flask, put it in that earthenware pot over there and place it on the stove."

The dumbfounded second-in-command says, "But I thought you said we couldn't have saké?"

"We can't but when you are drinking warm saké out of that container it's more like a medicinal drink isn't it," the leader responds.

Then another guard chirps in, "I brought some too."

A third guard meekly admits, "Actually, because I figured everyone was going to bring saké I brought along a little boar meat."

Guards keep chiming in around the group, reaching into their coats and pulling out various ingredients.

One also says, "I brought some onions." They keep discussing who brought what until they realize they do not have a pot. Luckily, one guy reaches around his back and says, "I just happen to be carrying one."

With all that they brought they neglect their guard duties that cold night and share in the warm meal of fresh meat stewing in alcohol.

The *rakugo* performer enacts all the eating and drinking of the hungry guards to the amusement of the audience but what is most telling is how each man only very cautiously reveals what food he is carrying.[32]

As the Tokugawa era ebbed into its last years during the mid-nineteenth century, Japan started to experience political unrest, which eventually culminated in a disturbing level of social upheaval. The shogun in Edo heard through his various *metsuke*, or spies, that the ruling Qing dynasty in China faced a massive internal rebellion led by a heterodox Christian convert named Hong Xiuquan who maintained that he was the Chinese Son of God. After the rebellion, Hong Xiuquan set up the "Heavenly Kingdom of Great Peace" (*Taiping Tianguo*) with a capital at Nanjing, controlling large sections of southern China, and also started to institute some quite radical social reforms, aiming to replace Confucian, Buddhist and folk religion with a version of Christianity. China was at this time reeling from British and French invasions in the southwest as well as a booming illegal trade in opium controlled and organized, in part, by the English company Jardine Matheson. Manchu administrators and Chinese officials worried day and night about how to expel the Europeans, with their superior military

---

[32] Tabi no bunka kenkyūjo, ed., *Rakugo ni miru edo no shokubunka*, pp. 18–22.

technology and disturbing new political ideas. All of these developments shocked the Japanese, who were themselves struggling to resist Western attempts to open Japan for trade and exchange. The scene was set for a clash between old and new ideas and Japanese cuisine was caught up in the struggle.

CHAPTER FIVE

THE MEIJI RESTORATION: MENU RENOVATION ON THE
ROAD TO RAMEN

Major shifts in the Japanese life-style occurred during what is called the Meiji Restoration, preceeded by a period of tremendous upheaval that lasted from 1854 to 1868 and later during the Meiji era (1868–1912). In this period, Japan was transformed from being an inward-looking society to one that opened its ports (beyond Nagasaki) and adopted international standards of law, military science and diplomacy, in the same way as it had adopted many things from China almost a thousand years before. After 1868, the Japanese shed their feudal system of lords, samurai, merchants and peasants. They re-instated the emperor as head of state, supported by a legion of bureaucrats and advisors eager to embrace new European concepts. This new elite trumpeted many novel ideas for modernization, including the establishment of newspapers, a telegraph system and the re-education of former samurai in such fields as maritime technology and navigation.

Japanese in the Meiji era had a very different relationship with China from their predecessors in the Tokugawa era (1600–1868). Japan after the Meiji Restoration turned away from most of what it had learned from China during the intense period of commercial and social exchange in the port city of Nagasaki from the seventeenth to mid-nineteenth centuries. Nevertheless, China was critical to the success of Japan's Meiji Restoration and the new imperial government's modernization plans, and equally crucial in the evolution of ramen. Without the presence and influence of the Chinese in Meiji-era Japan, ramen would never have developed as it did. Contrary to the conventional view that the West, represented by US Commodore Matthew Perry, forced open Japan's doors in the early 1850s, the reality was a little more complicated. The process of Japan's modernization cannot be explained without understanding what the Chinese were doing in Japan at the time.

The Chinese played a significant role in the opening of Japan because few Westerners understood the Japanese language. Japanese sailors who had been shipwrecked and ended up resident in the US, like John Manjirō (one of the first Japanese to live in America and learn English), contributed significantly as translators. But such men were rare, and when Perry first arrived on Japan's coastline in 1853, his "black ships" received Chinese assistance. Perry chose not to employ a Dutch interpreter for his journey to Japan, even though Dutch had been the lingua franca for Japanese communicating with foreigners during the Tokugawa era. Instead, he selected Samuel Wells Williams, who did not possess a good command of Japanese, but had lived in China since 1833. Williams could read and write Chinese and was an able enough translator even though, as many did at that time, he required the constant assistance of a native scribe and helper. Williams' first assistant on the mission was his old Chinese tutor, an incurable opium addict who died just before a high-level meeting between Perry and his Japanese counterparts was due to take place. This prompted a search for a more suitable and sober candidate.[1] Perry hired a Chinese assistant for Williams named Luo Sen for his second voyage to Japan in 1854 to gauge the Japanese response. Luo hailed from Guangdong and had lived in Hong Kong for several years conducting business with foreigners. He was classically educated but "open minded," and both the American and Japanese sides liked his demeanor and writing style.[2] The Japanese flocked to meet Luo. Japan's educated elites were well versed in Chinese poetry as well as the Confucian classics and were anxious to meet a real-life, breathing Chinese person who embodied their traditional view of the world. Japanese intellectuals would have read about ancient China but it was still rare in those days for a Japanese to be able to actually meet a Chinese traveler.

Not all Japanese were happy about their new relationship with Chinese civilization. Contact with the real thing sometimes stunned Japanese travelers in its difference from the idealized image they held in their minds. In 1862, one of the first passenger ships to carry Japanese travelers to China, the Senzai-maru, sailed from Nagasaki to Shanghai. During their two-month stay in the Chinese port, the Japanese recorded their shock at the grinding poverty and rampant opium usage in the city.[3] The fragrant and refined culture portrayed by the Tang master painters and Song era poets was nowhere to be seen.

---

[1] De-min Tao, "Negotiating Language in the Opening of Japan: Luo Sen's Journal of Perry's 1854 Expedition," *Japan Review*, 17, 2005, pp. 93–94.

[2] Ibid., p. 95.

[3] Tanaka Seiichi, *Ichii taisui – Chūgoku ryōri denraishi*, p. 187. See also Joshua Fogel, "A Decisive Turning Point in Sino-Japanese Relations: The *Senzaimaru* Voyage to Shanghai of 1862," *Late Imperial China*, Volume 29, Number 1 Supplement, June 2008, pp. 104–124.

The Qing Empire's first official ambassador to Japan, He Ruzhang, did not arrive until 1877. During his stay in Japan, he noted in his diary that married women still shaved off their eyebrows and blackened their teeth, as in olden times. Japan was making efforts to get rid of many of its Edo-period customs but some took a long time to disappear from the capital, not to mention the hinterland.[4] Rutherford Alcock, the first British diplomat to serve in Japan, made critical observations of the small loincloths worn by men, including boatmen, in the lower classes, and was quite unsparing in his comments on women. He recorded in the memoirs published soon after his return: "One must be brought up from infancy to the manner, to be able to look upon their large mouths full of black teeth and the lips thickly daubed with a brick-red color – and not turn away with a strong feeling of revulsion."[5]

Treaty Ports

Just as the Chinese in Nagasaki and elsewhere in Kyushu had given the Japanese a view of the wider world, new treaty ports in the mid-1850s through to the Meiji era widened Japanese horizons. The first such ports to be established were the cities of Hakodate in Hokkaido, Niigata on the western sea coast and Yokohama in the Kantō region. Treaty ports were later established in Kobe, near the merchant city of Osaka, and in Nagasaki, with its long history of international relations. On July 29, 1858, the US and Japan signed their first commercial treaty. From the start, the Chinese established themselves as necessary middlemen for doing business in Japan. They could communicate with the Japanese and were already familiar with the business practices of East Asia. Most of the Western delegations that came to Japan to trade already had offices in Hong Kong and Shanghai. These companies quickly dispatched Chinese assistants from their main offices in China to serve as liaisons for trade in Japan before entrepreneurs from the mother countries back in Europe had even left port.

The political environment in Japan in the late 1850s and early 1860s was far from stable, nor did the future look especially bright for international relations. Japan had not yet chosen whether to embrace Westernization or

---

[4] Bu Anryū, Yū Tatsuun, editors, *Chūgokujin no Nihon kenkyūshi*, p. 113. The more well known and inquisitive Huang Zunxian, who kept an extensive diary of his early years in Tokyo, was He Ruzhang's counsellor at the embassy.

[5] Rutherford Alcock, *The capital of the tycoon: a narrative of a three years' residence in Japan*, Vol. 1, p. 77.

throw out the foreign devils. The final outcome would take most of a decade to emerge. Japan did not change overnight and many of its more entrenched customs alienated foreign newcomers. Gangs of disgruntled samurai who resented the Western barbarians sullying Japan carried out a series of assassinations of Western diplomats and their attendants. The slogan of the day was *sonnō jōi*, "revere the emperor and expel the barbarian." The contemporary word for "foreigner," *gaikokujin*, was not widely used until the following century: the term "i," (*yi* in Chinese 夷) copied from the Chinese language, suggested something uncouth, unwanted and not quite human – a barbarian.

Even though some foreigners did roam through Edo, by 1860 restrictions were placed on their freedom. Non-Japanese required advance permission to go out, and regulations kept Japanese at least 300 meters away.[6] In a move designed to calm violence, reduce foreign influence and keep the foreigners isolated, Tokugawa-era leaders designed the new city of Yokohama as a foreign enclave, similar to the original Dutch trading enclave on Deshima, in Nagasaki. Construction of Yokohama began in 1858, and it opened for residences and business the following year. Like Nagasaki several centuries before, Yokohama quickly became the new hub for international trade and information. After March 1860, samurai were forbidden to carry their swords into Yokohama, as too many foreigners had already been murdered around Japan. (In 1876, the Meiji government passed a law prohibiting samurai from carrying any swords at all.) Some argued that the very existence of these foreign enclaves was a mistake, the barbarian should be kept out of Japan altogether; but the areas also had their supporters. One samurai in 1861 left a diary of his visit to Yokohama. The diarist wrote about meeting people and conducting "brush talk" conversations with the Chinese, in which they would communicate through writing down Chinese characters on paper and passing these sheets back and forth. The entire experience was akin to visiting "a cultural salon" and proved very satisfying, he wrote.[7]

In the early Meiji era, officially, Chinese were denied admission to Japan because China had not yet signed any new international treaties with Japan. This, of course, ignored the thousands of Chinese families who had lived in Nagasaki and other parts of Japan for the previous several centuries. In addition, many Chinese took advantage of a legal loophole and came to Japan accompanying their Western bosses.

---

[6] Nishikawa Takeomi and Itō Izumi, *Kaikoku Nihon to Yokohama chūkagai*, p. 40.
[7] Ibid., p. 89.

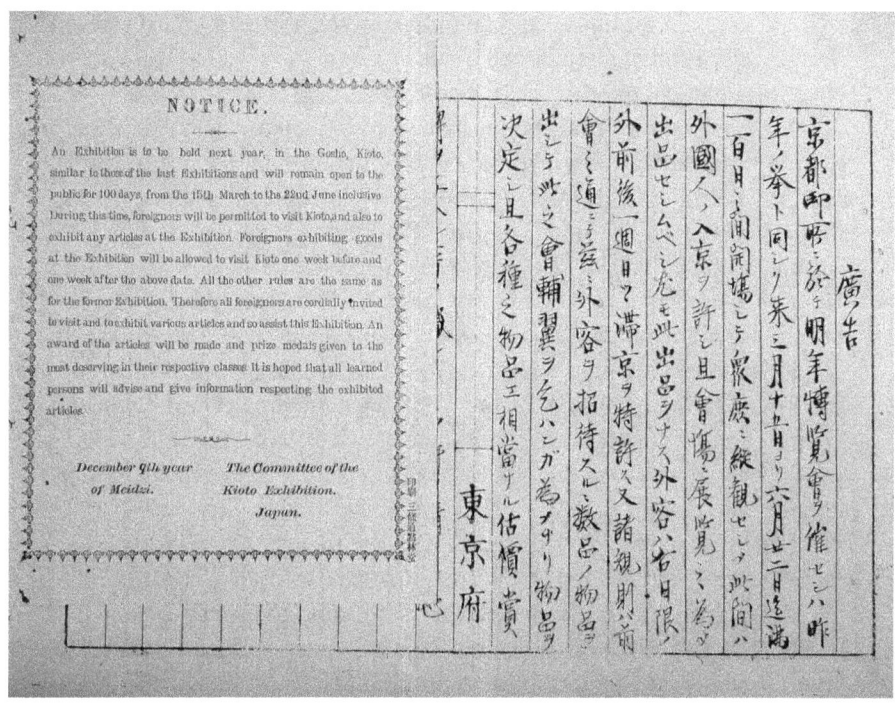

Figure 22. An official Meiji declaration with accompanying English translation outlining foreigners' rights to travel for a limited time to attend a cultural exhibition in Kyoto.[8]

Until the 1880s, the Chinese were in fact the dominant group in Yokohama. In 1874, approximately 2,411 foreigners lived within the boundaries of Yokohama and 1,290 of these were Chinese. Chinese traders, laborers, assistants and clerks made up 57.5% of the total foreign population in the city. In 1883 the Chinese made up almost three quarters of the foreign presence in town. Even in 1899, when Japan was on the verge of disbanding its unequal treaties with the West and had defeated the Qing Empire in the Sino-Japanese War of 1894–95, the Chinese population of Yokohama remained at 59%, with 3,003 people out of a total of 5,088 foreigners.[9] Inevitably, the Chinese market and numerous Chinese restaurants in

---

[8] Tōkyōto kobunshokan (Tokyo Metropolitan Archives).
[9] Itō Izumi, "Yokohama kakyō shakai no keisei," *Yokohama kaikō shiryōkan kiyō*, dai kyūgō, March 1991, p. 5. See also J.E. Hoare, "The Chinese in the Japanese Treaty Ports, 1858–1899: The Unknown Majority," *Proceedings of the British Association for Japanese Studies*, Vol. 2, 1977, part 1, pp. 18–33.

Yokohama had a formative impact on Japanese consumer choices, given the concentration of foreign food tastes in a single small area. This experience was mirrored in other treaty port cities around Japan.

John Black, one of the first journalists to launch a newspaper of any kind in Japan, keenly observed the radical transformations in the country from the moment of its opening to the West until the mid-1880s. During these crucial years, he noted that for a long time "two-sworded people" continued to act in an arrogant and rude manner to foreigners and Japanese peasants alike.[10] "Two-sworded people" was an oblique reference to samurai who traditionally holstered a long sword and a short dagger. Black's account reads like a laundry list of issues facing foreigners in the early opening years of new Japan, from constant threats and assassinations to simple verbal abuse from Japanese who taunted the foreigners with the aim of showing their reverence to the emperor by getting the barbarians out.

On the cusp of change in the mid-1860s, the Tokugawa *bakufu*, the traditional government headed by the shogun, did not sit idly by waiting to be overthrown but sent missions to the outside world to examine the source of the West's strength, investigate the political situation and gauge how Japan should best respond to the recent incursions on its soil. The problems they faced were twofold: Tokugawa officials had no realistic concept of what awaited them; and they held grandiose ideas about Japan's position in the world. They even did not seem to understand how diplomatic missions were supposed to eat. Fukuchi Genichirō, a young official in the 1860s and later founding editor of several prominent Meiji-era Japanese newspapers, recalled that as the *bakufu* prepared provisions for the officials to take on their long journeys abroad, bravado and arrogance masked a true understanding of conditions in the West. To travel to six European countries, Tokugawa officials packed hundreds of pounds of white rice, soy sauce and barrels of miso. Not only was it superfluous to bring such materials, Fukuchi argued, but asked: "How will the provisions be cooked in hotels?" Historically, international delegations from Korea or China to Japan had been housed in large estates and provided with servants and raw ingredients to cook for themselves. Unbeknownst to Japanese authorities in the 1860s, diplomatic travelers in Europe resided in hotels and did not need to requisition supplies but merely dined in restaurants or the hotel's own dining facilities. Fukuchi warned his superiors that the miso would spoil en route but he was told to stay quiet since he was of a very low

---

[10] John Black, *Young Japan, Yokohama & Yedo*, Vol. I, 1858–1879, p. 40.

rank. By the mid-point of the voyage the miso had turned so rank it had to be thrown overboard to avoid making the passengers nauseous. Fukuchi noted that "it was donated to Poseidon," thrown into the sea.[11]

Barbarians and Banquets

The fall of the *bakufu* government and the rise of the new Meiji imperial government in 1868 was not inevitable but it highlighted the rising importance of national identity and food. In fact, both the Tokugawa shogun and his opponents – the large fiefs of Satsuma and Chōshū in the west of Japan – believed that prowess in internationally acceptable diplomatic protocol would help Japan maintain its independence. Japan needed a national cuisine that could produce banquets capable of impressing international guests.[12] In 1854, the Perry mission had hosted *bakufu* officials aboard the USS *Powhatan* to a sumptuous feast. The Japanese reception reciprocating the favor, several weeks later, did not go down well: the Americans found most of the food inedible or "too fishy." According to the official nineteenth-century log of the trip, Perry's crew was "not impressed by the quantity of food served or with its taste."[13] In other words, Japan's first international banquet was a culinary disaster.

Nineteenth-century Japanese did not immediately take to foreign cuisine and dishes such as beef or pork roasts. Cheeses and sugary desserts were not well received either.[14] Several hundred years of gastronomic semi-isolation had placed the Japanese at a disadvantage when it came to formulating a strategy regarding the use of official dinners for international diplomacy. In the West, these had begun in earnest with Talleyrand in the mid-nineteenth century. Charles Maurice de Talleyrand-Périgord, Prince de Benevente, dominated the cuisine scene in France at the turn of the eighteenth and into the nineteenth century, when it became elevated into a symbol of the state and a formidable diplomatic tool. Talleyrand was an aristocrat and was later appointed minister of foreign affairs. He

---

[11] Fukuchi Genichirō, *Kaiō jidan*, reprinted in Bakumatsuhen, shinshiryō sōsho, Vol. 8, *Jinbutsu ōrai*, pp. 58–59.
[12] This was not only the case for Japan but also other cultures coming into close contact with the Western colonial powers developed similarly. See the fascinating situation in Iran, H.E. Chehabi, "The Westernization of Iranian Culinary Culture," *Iranian Studies*, Vol. 36, no.1, March 2003, pp. 43–61.
[13] William Steele, *Alternative Narratives in Modern Japanese History*, p. 115.
[14] The disgust that many Japanese felt toward Western food is well documented in research that has combed through many late Tokugawa and Meiji era diaries and official accounts. See Kumada Tadao, *Sessha wa kuen: samurai yōshoku kotohajime*.

orchestrated banquets and dinner parties as affairs of state. Japanese attempts at comparable revolutions in taste, as opposed to politics, did not appear to have impressed.

Meanwhile, the first Japanese envoys abroad described in their travel diaries the large feasts they were invited to attend. These meals were often apparently insufficiently salty and also far too oily. Some of the envoys tried to avoid eating altogether, eventually becoming so hungry that they had to cook in their rooms. The American press reported that the Japanese loved the gargantuan meals offered to the missions but the Japanese diplomatic record and diaries suggest that the reality was quite different: the Japanese disliked Western food and preferred making their own when they could.[15]

Meiji society was founded on a new structure and new ideals and food was an essential part of the nation-building process. Everything in Meiji was different. The social elite studied foreign languages and mingled with foreigners, but alien practices did not easily translate; nor were all new customs and ideas initially accepted. To modernize, Meiji had to reconfigure, reforge or shed all of the Tokugawa era's long-held traditions. As Japan became aware of its low international status, it also became eager to distinguish itself from China. As Katarzyna Cwiertka, a historian of Japanese cuisine, has observed: "Western-style dining became an integral part of the project" to build Japan's international profile.[16] The Meiji government hired foreign talent, including engineers, scientists and teachers, to educate the nation in the new learning and ideas. Ottmar von Mohl, a German diplomat and educator, arrived from Berlin on a two-year contract to teach the Japanese proper etiquette, reflective of the customs among European royalty.[17] Hiring foreign teachers to impart Western knowledge and customs was part and parcel of the "civilization and enlightenment movement," or *bunmei kaika* in Japanese.

Fukuzawa Yukichi, a famous Japanese educator of the period, was one of the first young Japanese officials to travel to the West, learn from his experiences and promote the modernization of Japan through wholesale Westernization. He traveled throughout the US and Europe several times in quick succession in the early 1860s, near the end of the Tokugawa era, and published a bestseller, *Conditions of the West*, in 1866. The following year, under a pseudonym, he published *Western Food, Clothing and Living*

---

[15] Harada Nobuo, *Washoku to Nihon bunka*, pp. 145–146.
[16] Katarzyna J. Cwiertka, *Modern Japanese Cuisine – Food, Power and National Identity*, p. 17.
[17] He was hired in 1887.

Habits. "Westerners do not use chopsticks," Fukuzawa wrote. "They take meat and other food and cut it carefully on a flat plate, then arrange it neatly. With their right hand they cut the meat and carefully with their knife place it on the end of the fork, which they are holding in their left hand and then they bring the food immediately up and put it in their mouths. Using the end of your knife and placing a bit of food onto the end is considered uncouth." Fukuzawa also explained simple manners. "When you are using your spoon to suck up some juice or drinking tea," he wrote, "it is considered impolite to make noise." The admonition not to slurp never really took hold in Japan. For a while, however, Fukuzawa's new terminology did: at the time there was no word in Japanese for fork, so Fukuzawa invented the word "meat skewer," *nikusashi*, for his readers.[18]

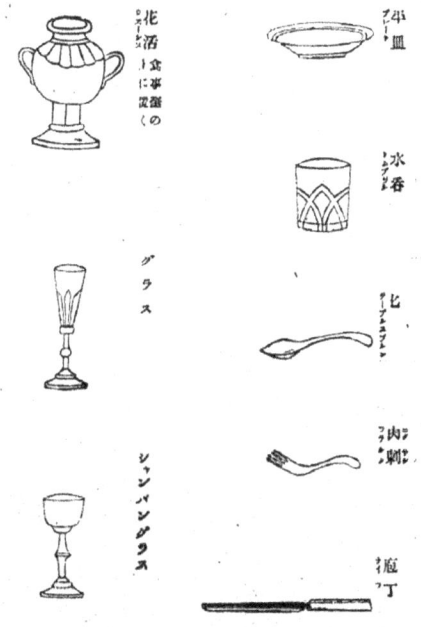

Figure 23. In his book, *Western Food, Clothing and Living Habits*, Fukuzawa explained and drew pictures of cutlery for Japanese readers: from the top right and reading downward, plate, cup, spoon, fork and knife. A Japanese word for knife already existed and he used the Chinese character for spoon, but a word for "fork" had to be invented. He also included a discussion of how to use these implements at the table.[19]

---

[18] Fukuzawa Yukichi, *Seiyō ishokujū*, in Fukuzawa zenshū, Vol. 2, p. 13.
[19] Ibid., p.13.

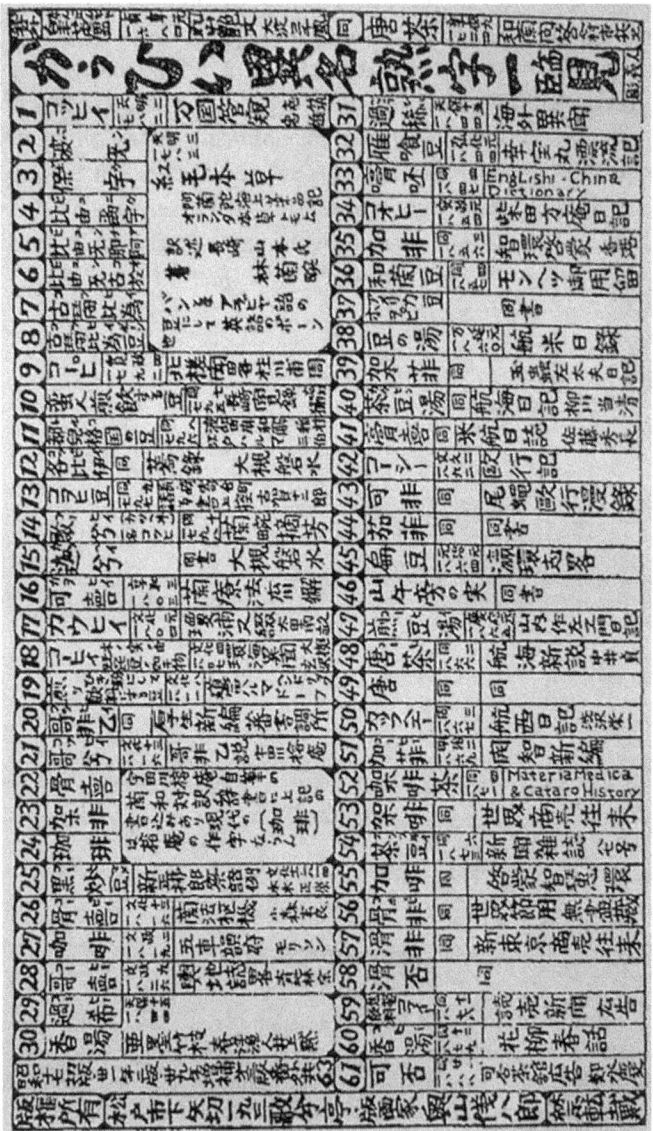

Figure 24. The words early Meiji Japanese chose as translations of Western food terms or implements sometimes bordered on the ridiculous. The image above demonstrates the complexity of translating the names of foreign food items into Japanese. This collage is a compilation of all the different ways in which the word for "coffee" has been translated into Japanese over the last several hundred years. There are more than sixty different ways of writing the word for "coffee," using the various Japanese alphabets, Chinese characters and assorted combinations.

In 1870, Fukuzawa published a famous treatise entitled "We Must Eat Meat!" in which he argued strongly that eating meat advanced civilization.[20] Fukuzawa's disquisition employed rather dramatic language. "At this moment the absence of meat eating in our country will lead to poorer health and the numbers of our weak will only increase. In the end," he wrote, "there will be one less country on this earth."[21] This dire prediction about the inadequacy of the nation's largely vegetarian diet reflects the tumultuous times, when many Japanese were worried about the future of the nation. Fukuzawa also recommended meat in the introduction to Takahashi Yoshio's book, "On Improving the Japanese Race." To be able to compete in the world, Takahashi believed that the nation needed strong bodies that could work ceaselessly. Key to promoting this muscularity and renewed vigor was a meat-centered, Western-oriented diet.[22]

The Meiji government did not lag far behind in putting changes in diet at the heart of becoming a strong and civilized nation. In 1872, at the behest of the government, Kondō Yoshiki penned a short pamphlet "A Consideration of Milk and Thoughts on Butchery," encouraging Meiji men and women to transform their eating habits. Kondō argued that the emperor had, during ancient times, consumed milk and beef (accurate in the case of the Nara emperors, although the practice dwindled in subsequent reigns) and adopting this practice in the Meiji era would make the Japanese strong once again. Kondō emphasized the fact that it was not "dirty" to eat beef or drink milk, but necessary for the health and survival of the nation.[23]

Eating "civilized" food in early Meiji took on political significance. In 1872, the Meiji leaders passed an edict to outlaw the serving of *fugu*, the poisonous fish so prized in some gourmet circles. (The ban fell mostly on deaf ears; *fugu* remained as popular as ever.) This edict was prompted by vigorous nutrition and hygiene campaigns launched to control the outbreaks of cholera and typhoid that rampaged through the newly opened country.[24] The government also launched a mass campaign to inform

---

[20] Fukuzawa Yukichi, *Nikushoku sezarubekarazu*, in Fukuzawa Yukichi zenshū, Vol. 8, pp. 452–456.
[21] Ōtsuka Shigeru, "Ryōri no kaikoku," *Gengo*, Vol. 23, no. 1, 1994, full text of Fukuzawa Yukichi, "Nikushoku no setsu," reproduced on p. 78.
[22] Takahashi Yoshio, *Nihonjinshu kairyōron* (originally published in 1884), republished in Meiji bunka shiryō sōsho, Vol. 6, p. 24.
[23] Kondō Yoshiki, *Gyūnyūkō tochikukō*.
[24] William Johnston, *The Modern Epidemic: A History of Tuberculosis in Japan*, and Ann Bowman Jannetta, *Epidemics and Mortality in Early Modern Japan*.

Figure 25. Article 7, at top left, reads, "It is forbidden to knowingly sell fake or spoiled foods and drinks."[25]

---

[25] Nishimura Kanebumi, *Kyōto ishiki kaii jōrei zukai*, no pagination.

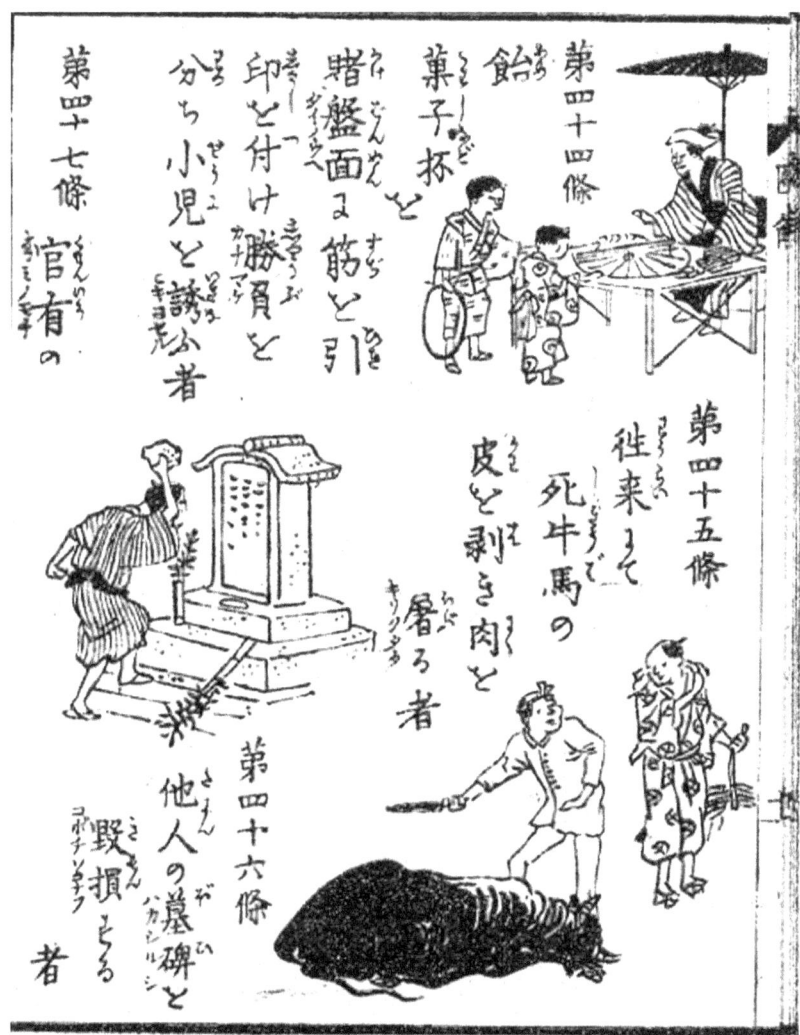

Figure 26. Article 45 at bottom right made it "illegal to butcher and skin a dead cow or horse in the street."[26]

people about behavior that would no longer be considered acceptable. As part of that campaign, the government produced a series of ordinances, called the "Petty and Misdemeanor Ordinances" (*Ishiki kaii jōrei*), persuading the populace to change how they acted in public, especially in front of foreigners. These ordinances were widely distributed around the country

---

[26] Ibid.

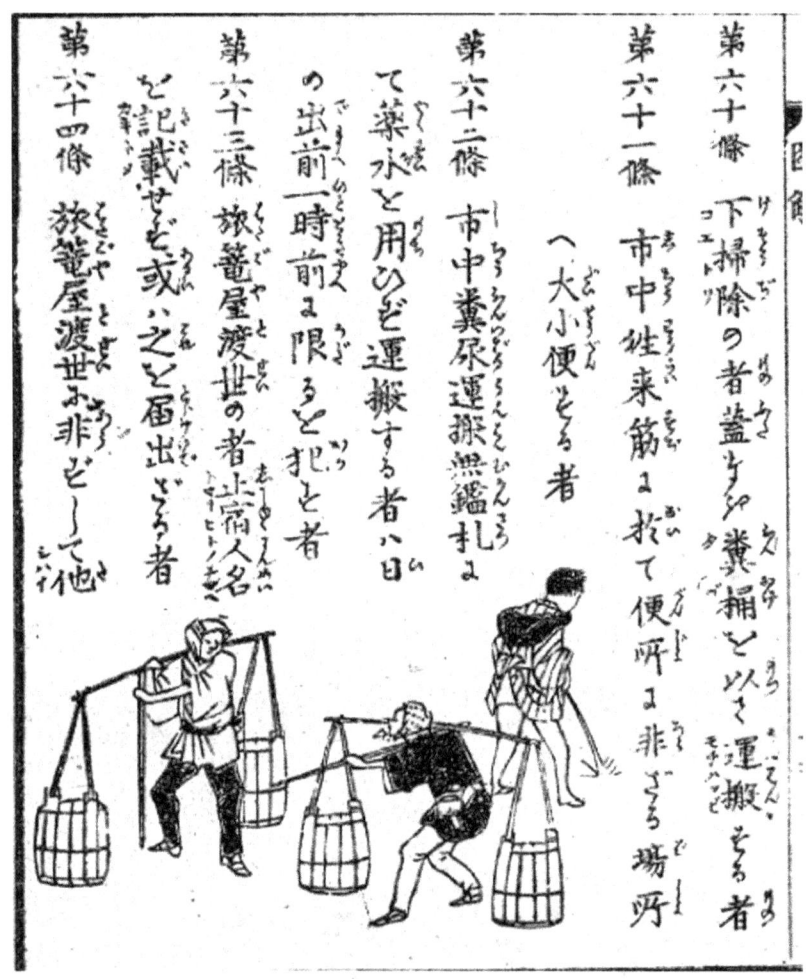

Figure 27. The government was also worried about how the country appeared to foreigners. Correct behavior in Meiji now meant you could no longer relieve yourself freely on the street. Article 61 stipulated: "It is forbidden to defecate or urinate on a city street where there is no bathroom." The cartoonist has dexterously depicted the man in the background on the right relieving himself in public.[27]

---

[27] Ibid.

in text and cartoon versions. Many of these new laws dealt with food and drink.

The option of eating new foods in order to rebuild the country in the Meiji era quickly became controversial. In January 1872, the Meiji Emperor's yearly greeting informed the public that he ate meat. In one fell swoop the imperial kitchen helped to revolutionize the nation's menu. That year the government also permitted Buddhist priests to consume animal flesh. However, the change in the emperor's diet did not please everyone. Some traditionalists were outraged. In February 1872, ten Buddhist hermits stormed the palace and tried to assassinate the emperor for his blasphemous act.[28] Contrary to popular belief, while meat was never truly out of fashion in pre-Meiji Japan, consumption of it mainly split along class lines. The literate classes who pushed for modernization probably had the most difficulty with the changes because, arguably, their diet had previously been the most meat-free. Commoners ate it when they could if they were not part of the legions of Japanese who believed it unwholesome. Unfortunately for them, however, the opportunity did not come often. Intellectuals keen to align themselves with Western practices enthusiastically adopted meat, perhaps forgetting that meat was also a favorite with Chinese.

Meat eating has occupied a shadowy existence throughout Japanese history; it was available here and there but existed at the periphery of society. It was certainly never a mainstay. The historian Katarzyna Cwiertka has written, echoing numerous Japanese historians of food, "… the Japanese did not raise or produce livestock, except chicken, and the commercialization of meat was absent."[29] Although the Emperor Tenmu's seventh-century decree did ban eating meat, as outlined in Chapter 1, the practice continued regardless. A constant tension remained between religious and government prohibitions on the one hand and consumption at different levels of society on the other. In 1612, the Tokugawa government had to announce a ban on the *slaughter* of cattle and the *sale* of any cattle that had died naturally. Many Japanese historians of gastronomy argue that not until the seventeenth century, as a consequence of these renewed bans, did a deep social antipathy toward the consumption of meat really take root across the entire population and transform into a strong taboo. The ebb and flow of efforts to keep Japan away from a meat-based diet

---

[28] Watanabe Zenjirō, "Sekai o kakeru Nihongata shoku seikatsu no henbō," p. 34.
[29] Katarzyna Cwiertka, "The Mıaking of Modern Culinary Tradition in Japan," PhD Thesis at Leiden University, Holland, 1999, p. 47.

were mainly successful by the middle of the Tokugawa era and a general public distaste for meat products had developed even though it continued to be consumed in various quarters.

Fukuzawa was monomaniacal about his message to save Japan from an ugly Darwinian demise at the bottom of the food chain. In a June 1886 article in his newspaper, he called for Japan to stop growing rice because it was a food historically imported from Southeast Asia and thus not truly culturally appropriate to Japan. He proposed, instead, that the Japanese focus on cash crops to be used as exports. Fukuzawa suggested that the Japanese grow mulberry bushes and breed silkworms for profit; this would gain Japan sorely needed hard currency from abroad, he argued. The public's negative response was immediate and harsh. Fukuzawa retracted some of his ideas and instead recommended growing abundant harvests of rice and exporting the crop, using the profits to feed industrial growth and promote Japan's further modernization.[30]

Japanese and Meat Eating

Whether or not to accept meat eating, associated with political and social modernity, was a crucial debate during the Meiji period, and the key to the subsequent growth of a national appetite for ramen. If meat had not been permitted to gain a following, there would have been no hope for a meat-based noodle soup. Japan's struggles with its newfound Meiji identity may explain why the shift from *soba* (buckwheat) noodles to ramen took several more decades, even after the opening of the country. In fact, Japanese society took about seven decades to expand the composition of its meals and change its attitude toward consuming products that were outside of the traditional palate. The country also required nearly half a century to change its view of Chinese cuisine.

Ironically, when Japan looked to the Western diet as a model, it focused on two countries that consumed gargantuan portions of meat on a daily basis – Germany and Great Britain. Had Japanese reformers set their sights on any similar country to theirs that was not that industrialized they would have realized that the Japanese diet was not that far off the international standard of the time. But Britain had a diet that was far from "average" in the early modern period. If we consider how much meat the English consumed, it quickly becomes clear. For example, in 1485, Henry VII

---

[30] Imai Saeko, "Mori Ōgai to Fukuzawa Yukichi no shokuseikatsuron," p. 18.

formed the Yeoman Guard. These permanent guards of the king ate prodigious amounts and under the Stuarts became known as "beefeaters" mainly for that very reason. In 1813, only a few decades before the Meiji Restoration in Japan, the daily rations of the thirty guards at St. James Palace comprised "24 pounds of beef, 18 pounds of mutton, 16 pounds of veal, 37 gallons of beer" and on Sundays, several extra large plum puddings. In other words, each guard every day ate an astounding 0.8 pounds of beef, 0.6 pounds of mutton and a half pound of veal, while glugging down 1.2 gallons of beer.[31] They were satiated and probably drunk as well. No wonder the Japanese felt their cuisine was unique in comparison to this kind of diet.

Meat was never completely off the menu in Japan, but it was limited, or at least kept out of view from most diners. As we saw in the *rakugo* comedy routine "The Number Two Guard Station's Concoction," discussed in Chapter 4, Japanese did sometimes eat and sell meat during the Tokugawa era. Those who peddled animal flesh called it by other names, since admitting you consumed meat would have contravened the spirit if not the actual law of the times. When it was found on sale, meat was often euphemistically referred to as "land whale," *yama kujira,* or tagged with other obscure references. Narushima Ryūhoku, a Japanese scholar of the Chinese classics and a journalist, walked around many of the "pleasure quarters" of Edo just before the Meiji Restoration. He kept a record of what people ate and graphically described the bloody meat stalls where butchered animals were displayed for eager customers.[32] Regardless of the distaste that many still felt in the early Meiji era, meat eating drew those Japanese who believed that changing their diets would make Japan a stronger, more civilized nation.

Against this backdrop, *gyūnabe*, a kind of watery stew with meat, suddenly became popular in the mid-nineteenth century. Kanagaki Robun, who wrote one of the first "novels" of the Meiji era, depicted meat eating in one of his early bestsellers. Kanagaki was originally a pulp fiction author and his writings are replete with word play in the peculiar style of the

---

[31] Ben Rogers, *Beef and Liberty. Roast Beef, John Bull and the English Nation*, pp. 17–18. The Yeoman of the Guard are not the same as the Tower Warders, more commonly known now as "beefeaters."

[32] Emanuel Pastreich, "The Pleasure Quarters of Edo and Nanjing as Metaphor," *Monumenta Nipponica*, Vol. 55, No. 2, Summer 2000, p. 209. For more see Narushima Ryūhoku (translated by Matthew Fraleigh), *New Chronicles of Yanagibashi and Diary of a Journey to the West: Narushima Ryūhoku Reports from Home and Abroad.*

late Tokugawa era. His first major popular work mocked the early academic Meiji books that published information from abroad. He was so successful that in 1873 the Meiji government commissioned Kanagaki to write a geography textbook. Although he continued to write novels sporadically, his greatest success lay in the traditional extended comic essay. One of Kanagaki's most well-known stories, though not his most popular at the time, was "Beef Stew," (*Aguranabe*).[33] The short story describes a meat restaurant where everything is topsy-turvy, reflecting the chaotic nature of early Meiji; the classes are mixing, men and women are no longer sitting separately and even the samurai are eating with peasants – the long-established strict social order of the Tokugawa era is in disarray. The range of customers seated together – old, young, men, women, merchant, peasant, samurai – reflected the new Japan where the traditional demarcation lines between classes no longer necessarily impeded social mobility. Kanagaki Robun's book, one of the first to satirize the practice of meat eating, brought the issue to the forefront. He parodied the new trend of consuming animal flesh, an act that Fukuzawa Yukichi, a staunch advocate of Westernization for Japan, believed aided Japan's progress. Early Japanese sightseers in Yokohama who ate at the food stalls complained about the smell of meat, and some businesses added soy sauce to tone down the smell and appeal more to traditional Japanese tastes. It is likely that such dishes were precursors to ramen. Hasegawa Shin, a popular writer of fiction and drama, wrote in his memoirs that when he used to go to Yokohama as a youth he ate delicious meals of noodles served with meat.[34]

The rise of meat eating also had implications for the religious-minded. Scholars began arguing that in contrast to Buddhism Japan's native religion Shinto had not banned meat and was therefore more suitable for a modern nation. In 1873, Katō Hiroshi published a book, *Civilization and Enlightenment*, which detailed among other things how the government was attempting to use the issue of meat eating to shed Buddhism and promote Shinto. Members of the older generation, in particular, felt that they were probably insulting their ancestors as they consumed meat. In 1881, Sugimoto Etsuko wrote in her autobiography "Daughter of a Samurai" that the first time her family had meat at the table, her grandmother went over

---

[33] Donald Keene has translated a small portion of the longer story under the title, "The Beefeater."
[34] Okada Tetsu, *Rāmen no tanjō*, pp. 86–87.

Figure 28. A drawing of beef stew restaurants and noodle shops (*soba-ya*) in Tokyo.[35]

to the family Buddhist altar and closed its shutters so that the spirits of their ancestors could not witness the tragic event.[36]

The Militarization of Food

In his work analyzing the radical shifts that took place in the Japanese lifestyle and mindset in the nineteenth century, the folklore scholar Yanagita Kunio noted that what people ate for meals became "warmer, softer and sweeter."[37] How these developments affected the growth of consumer preferences which helped lead to the rise of ramen had a lot to do with the ambivalence people felt about allowing foreign influences to

---

[35] Hiraide Kōjirō, *Tōkyō fūzokushi*, Vol. 2, p. 157.
[36] As quoted in Ōtsuka Tsutomu, editor, *Shokuseikatsu kindaishi*, p. 24.
[37] Yanagita Kunio, *Meiji Taishōshi sesōshi*, p. 60.

transform their supposedly traditional cuisine. We should remember that most commoners were eating something rather different from the pure white rice we see today: a bit of rice, perhaps, combined with millet and barley. In the contemporary West and historically in China, meals were eaten to be enjoyed rather than to participate in defining the national character. However, early Meiji Japan was different. As the nation started on its path of slow industrialization and international trade, it was neither rich nor necessarily willing to change drastically. Noodles were easily available from street stalls and small shops and Japanese from many walks of life enjoyed them in a variety of forms. And while the roots of consumer preferences for noodles existed, the notion of putting them into a rich meat broth as the Chinese started doing in Yokohama toward the end of the nineteenth century demonstrated how much Japan would actually have to change to be able to create a dish like ramen that was so different from inherited food preferences.

One major force that pushed along Japan's acclimatization to foreign cuisine was the establishment of a standing army based on conscription. In the military, soldiers were equal and thus ate the same food. This experience leveled regional disparities and more importantly exposed young men to a world of cuisine beyond their local village. The Meiji government, unlike the previous Tokugawa administration, did not focus on rice as a form of currency and measure of wealth, but rather on its place within a balanced diet. This diet included a variety of proteins, carbohydrates and vegetables, not just miso, as well as a portion of rice and some pickles. The emerging nation was anxious about the small physical stature of the Japanese in comparison with their larger Western counterparts, and a new diet was thought to offer a potential solution to this problem.

Despite numerous suggestions to do so from the educated elite, military leaders did not serve Western food to soldiers, leading to heated arguments about appropriate military diets. One camp argued that Japanese soldiers required Japanese food and that meant white rice and heaps of it. This was a partly successful argument. Most peasants, who comprised the majority of new conscripts (they could not afford to pay the fine to avoid being drafted), were enthusiastic about large meals of white rice. White rice, a rarity for the lower classes (90% of society), was usually reserved for *hare no hi* – the occasional holiday or wedding during the Tokugawa era. Harada Nobuo, a Japanese historian of food, has famously said the Japanese were not so much a people who ate white rice as a people who desired to eat white rice. Some modernizers in the military tried to promote bread but it never won mass support within the armed forces and so rice dominated until acceptable substitutes won over recruits.

The new Japanese imperial military – both the army and navy – faced severe disruption to its stability with increasing outbreaks of beriberi. Until the late nineteenth century, no one knew that the disease, which involved lameness and muscle atrophy, was caused by a vitamin deficiency. The symptoms were almost bearable if you were a physically inactive bureaucrat used to lounging around all day. For the military, this widespread sickness was disaster on a national scale, rendering its soldiers literally unable to move. The new Imperial Army might have appeared victorious in battle but it struggled with the problems of how to maintain its soldiers' health, what they should eat and how to ensure supplies. The navy, too, suffered from a great many expectations – as technology advanced, rice harvests also increased and Japan's leaders began believing that the nation was finally capable of feeding its soldiers the coveted dishes of white rice. The Meiji-era military diet pivoted on a key fallacy that the Japanese had somehow tricked themselves into believing: namely that Japanese by nature had to eat rice. Now that they could afford the rice they wanted, it was proving difficult to convince soldiers and officers to follow more nutritious or alternative diets. Excessive feasting on white rice to the exclusion of other foods caused health problems. In 1878, according to imperial navy statistics, 1,552 out of 6,366 sailors were struck by beriberi in the course of duty. In an insecure country bent on restructuring its international relations and terrified of Western colonialists, this was a calamitous turn of events.

By the 1880s, a debate ensued over the composition of military diets. Beriberi is caused by a deficiency of thiamine (vitamin B1). It can be easily avoided through a varied diet of fruits, vegetables, and other proteins, particularly meat. Although Chinese cuisine was present in Japan's treaty port cities and enjoying a slow growth in popularity, it remained too "exotic" to be included in the early military diet. The July 1882 Jingo incident, a riot in Seoul where a number of Japanese advisors were killed, brought the problem sharply into focus. The Japanese Imperial Navy, eager to subdue the uprising, quickly dispatched three vessels to Korea. However, of the 300 sailors on board, 180 had already been rendered inactive by beriberi. Beriberi became an unavoidable topic of concern for the military after this incident, when Japan lost half its force before the troops even set foot on Korean soil. At this juncture in the early 1880s, it became clear that the Japanese navy's unwillingness to diversify its meals was impeding the nation's further imperial expansion. Food was intimately tied to the nation's ability to protect and project its power and prestige abroad in a way that few government officials had recognized. The Japanese military diet would develop into an even more catastrophic problem during World War II.

Japan's military forces were far from unanimous in deciding how to resolve the problem of Meiji era military cuisine. While studying in Germany in October 1886, Mori Ōgai published "A General Treatise on Feeding the Japanese Soldier" in the army's military medical journal.[38] Mori was a multi-talented member of the Meiji elite who had earned his doctoral degree in Germany.[39] Novelist, doctor and chief medical surgeon to the Japanese Imperial Army, he embodied the new Meiji man who traveled abroad, gathered knowledge from the far ends of the earth and used his learning to help Japan modernize and expand its empire.

Mori claimed that Westerners were taller than the Japanese because their digestive tracts were different; he praised the nutritional benefits of rice and believed such a diet was not inferior to a Western diet. In December 1888, Mori published "Theories on Why a Non-Japanese Diet will be to the Detriment of Japan's Future."[40] The Japanese should keep rice as the central element of their cuisine, he argued, but add meat and a fuller complement of vegetables as side dishes. Fukuzawa Yukichi, on the other hand, championed a more Western diet. He saw the Japanese as physically pathetic in comparison to Westerners and argued that they should move to a fuller, meat-based and bread diet.[41] Mori Ōgai worried about Japan's ability to feed itself, something with which Fukuzawa, as a civilian, was not concerned. Mori calculated that introducing meat and bread into the Japanese diet on a large scale would force the country to be too reliant on imports – dangerous for reasons of national security.[42] The debate between white rice or no rice was more about political identity and national cuisine than science. The clash pitted two early modern Japanese intellectual giants against one another, and the solution would take years to implement due to the conflict of science versus culture. The

---

[38] Mori Rintarō (Ōgai), "Nihon heishokuron taiyi," in *Mori Ōgai zenshū*, Vol. 28, pp. 10–18.

[39] Richard Bowring, *Mori Ogai and the modernization of Japanese culture*, pp. 11–13.

[40] Mori Rintarō (Ōgai), "Hi Nihon shokuron wa shō ni sono konkyo o ushiwan to su," originally published in 1888, in *Mori Ōgai zenshū*, Vol. 28, pp. 78–88; "Zoku zoku hi Nihon shokuron shōshitsu sono konkyoron," originally published in 1889, in *Mori Ōgai zenshū*, Vol. 28, pp. 90–100.

[41] Imai Saeko, "Mori Ōgai to Fukuzawa Yukichi no shokuseikatsuron," p. 20.

[42] Ibid., p. 21.

fact that meat and an expanded range of ingredients were slowly gaining entry into Japanese cuisine created steady social pressure for the types of dishes that would lead to the development of ramen.

While the Imperial Army obstinately stuck to the rice tradition, the Imperial Navy began to change. Takagi Kanehiro, the Assistant Chief Medical Officer of the Navy, asserted that beriberi was somehow linked to a deficiency in sailors' diets, long before more traditional Japanese leaders accepted such a possibility. Many other – and much more distinguished – medical doctors, including the famous Mori Ōgai, disagreed. However, Takagi had had the benefit of unusual experience and training. In 1875, at the age of twenty-six, he had enrolled as a medical student in London's prestigious St. Thomas Hospital medical school and he had studied there for five years. Takagi was a top student, receiving several awards for superior grades and becoming a Fellow of the Royal College of Surgeons. At the still young age of thirty-one, he returned to Japan to face the national epidemic of beriberi. Japanese soldiers were dropping at alarming rates. This affliction struck the armed forces at a time when leaders believed that a beleaguered Imperial Navy was tantamount to a national emergency. No one knew whether the illness was caused by conditions in the ships, the climate, or a combination of several elements.

Takagi collected all the records of the deaths and cross-checked to see if beriberi affected different ranks of sailors. He then compared the data for British and Japanese sailors and was astonished to discover that beriberi was considered an East Asian disease – no British sailor fell ill in this way. This was important. Takagi suddenly hit upon the diagnosis that perhaps a lack of protein was the problem and suggested supplying sailors with more bread, meat and vegetables to prevent the disease.[43] At this point, he had a stroke of luck. The Navy ship *Ryūjō*, "Dragon Horse," conducting training maneuvers en route to New Zealand and South America encountered serious problems and returned early to port in September 1883. During nearly nine months of exercises, 169 out of the 376 sailors on board had suffered from beriberi. Twenty-five men had actually died from the disease, and the decimated crew was unable to sail the ship further. The *Ryūjō* stopped in Honolulu, dropped all its food and took on board meat and vegetables. Most of the stricken sailors recovered and the ship returned to Japan.[44]

---

[43] Matsuda Makoto, *Takagi Kanehiroden*, pp. 65–68.
[44] Ibid., pp. 68 -69.

This episode convinced Takagi that his theory was correct, although it did not immediately persuade his critics. Takagi's meetings with his naval superiors produced so few results that he appealed directly to the Meiji Emperor and senior statesman Itō Hirobumi, who had briefly studied in England. Again, fortune shone brightly on Takagi. Another naval vessel, the *Tsukuba*, was about to leave on training maneuvers. With the intervention of Itō and the emperor's permission, the ship incorporated the new diet designed by Takagi to guard against an outbreak of beriberi. The ship weighed anchor and sailed from Shinagawa port on February 3, 1884.[45] By the end of its half-year world tour, the vessel reported that there were just over a dozen cases of beriberi on board and no deaths. Of the few sailors who had succumbed to the disease, some had refused the condensed milk in the rations and eight had declined to eat meat because they said they found it revolting. Takagi's view should have completely confirmed his theory about the causes of beriberi but strong traditional voices and concern about proper "Japanese cuisine" for soldiers remained. Although the Navy quickly adopted a new menu, it was not necessarily popular with its personnel.

For most peasants, military service was the first time they encountered meat with any regularity and some never quite got used to it. Rice dressed up with meat and a brown sauce touted as "curry" proved little more appealing. One peasant, recalling his first few days in the military, said that he never really knew what they were feeding him. "It seemed to me like a mound of rice with a big pile of diarrheal shit dumped all over it," he recounted.[46] In fact, many Japanese would have preferred to have stayed in their village homes and to absent themselves from the military altogether. Young men tried every imaginable tactic to fail the physical exam through the Meiji and Taisho eras. The ways in which youths evaded service were inventive and often bordered on the extreme. According to military reports:

> Some placed harsh agents in their eyes to force them to become bloodshot; the night before the physical they would stay up all night and complain that they were infected with some eye disease; others would cram beans or such deep into their ears; some would shove feathers or similar items into their ear canal to impede their hearing and pretend they were handicapped; others would ingest extremely irritating foods and then claim their ears rang so they were incapable of service; others forcibly removed their own teeth;

---

[45] Ibid., pp. 73–74.
[46] Yoshida Yutaka, *Nihon no guntai: heishitachi no kindaishi*, p. 38.

some drank excess amounts of soy sauce or such products that raised their heart rate or they complained of various symptoms; some starved for two to three days prior to the physical to appear weak and unhealthy; some amputated a finger, or rubbed lacquer around their anus and complained of severe hemorrhoids.[47]

The Imperial Army did not prove as progressive as its naval counterpart but this at least enabled it to avoid the visceral reaction shown by the public to the fare offered to sailors. Mori Ōgai admitted that the Takagi diet lessened the outbreaks of beriberi but could not accept that it eliminated the disease completely. He still believed, as did many other prominent Japanese scientists, that a virus or bacteria might be the cause of the ailment. Satisfied with Mori's views, the army stuck to its rice-centered meals until years into the twentieth century, although it did provide meat to sick soldiers.

Sources of *Bunmei Kaika* – Civilization and Enlightenment

By the last decades of the nineteenth century, the Japanese could no longer afford to abstain from eating meat. The imperial Japanese army and navy realized the need to include meat and other proteins in soldiers' diets to make them stronger and larger. But Japan was attempting to modernize with a weak economy and that put a heavy strain on the country's coffers. It was not an era of great national wealth. During the first decades of the twentieth century, meat still represented only a small fraction of the national total food consumption. The cuisine remained vegetarian and largely fish-based. As Japan advanced toward establishing its own empire, Japanese food tastes slowly changed, while new products appeared on the market due to both internal demand and external influences. Even with mass conscription and a growing military force, the perception of Japanese cuisine did not change. A Ministry of Finance report from the middle years of Meiji discovered that, in Tottori Prefecture, most peasant farmers did not eat any rice all year, let alone meat.[48]

The Meiji restorationists' support for social and political change might have stemmed in part from their own hunger, historical and literal. Satisfying, flavorsome meals were in short supply. Ōkuma Shigenobu, statesman and prime minister of Meiji Japan, recalled his pangs of hunger

---

[47] Ibid., p. 4.
[48] Watanabe Minoru, *Nihon shokuseikatushi*, p. 303.

while studying at school at the age of sixteen in the heady years before the Meiji Restoration. The school provided students with seven hundred grams of rice a day with side dishes but this amount could not satisfy the growing young men's voracious appetites. Cafeteria servants cooked breakfast with pickled vegetables and lunch with black beans, seaweed, tofu and *konnyaku*. Konnyaku is a plant from which a firm, usually gelatinous paste is made that is then often molded into shapes to eat.[49] The main dish for dinner was again rice, relieved by side dishes such as boiled fish. These side offerings were dismal and so, on a fairly regular basis, the students would conduct what they called a "blitzkrieg for more board," *makanai seibatsu*. Several hundred students would rush into the cafeteria, smash open the rice containers and eat to their hearts' content. They would then place their chopsticks on top of their bowls and leave. One time, Ōkuma recalled, someone ate roughly twenty-eight bowls of rice.[50] Even long into the Meiji era, in 1900, one author recalled that, when he was at school, the upperclassmen grumbled about the poor state of food and planned a food blitzkrieg. "We descended like bolts of lighting," he reminisced, "and didn't leave one grain of rice or pickled vegetable." "You could hear the noise of people flipping tables over and running along the floor." After throwing the dishes out of the window and breaking them, "we sang the victory song."[51] Unfortunately, there is no record of the lyrics of this song but "blitzkriegs for board" were relatively common up through the Taisho era in the 1920s.[52]

The Meiji Restoration did not merely discard the old guard and introduce the new. The restoration threw out the old and, with it, all of the traditional institutions – almost every last one of them. Because Tokugawa society had been so stratified, lower-level samurai really had no concept of how the upper class lived, since the two remained physically and psychologically remote. The men who dominated the Meiji Restoration had grown up with high social status but little money, and as a result they had rather unsophisticated palates. They saw no need to raise the prestige of Japanese food culture, as this had not been an essential part of their pre-Meiji lives. Instead, they urged for a clean sweep of traditional customs that would pave the way for radical social change, including the

---

[49] It is known as Amorphophallus konjac and by various other names: devil's tongue, voodoo lily, snake palm, and elephant yam.
[50] Kodama Sadako, *Nihon no shokuji yōshiki: sono dentō o minaosu*, p. 24.
[51] Kobayashi Kazuo, *Kaikoroku*, p. 41.
[52] Deguchi Kisō, *Zenkoku kōtō gakō hyōbanki*, pp. 47–48.

development of a meatier diet and the growth of a population becoming gradually more amenable to foreign dishes. The development of ramen had begun. Attitudes to food and dining were transformed during the Meiji era and meat, as visitors to the foreign treaty ports noticed, went quite well with noodle dishes, which had already reached high levels of popularity during the Edo period. The stage was now completely set – a preference for noodle dishes had been in place since Edo, meat eating was now more acceptable to a growing portion of the population, and the restoration and concern with modernization had unleashed the possibility of further urbanization and travel. Foreigners, such as Chinese peddlers and Westerners, were arriving in Japan in ever increasing numbers bringing new tastes considered both desirable and "civilized."

Nagasaki and *Champon* Noodles

From early Meiji, new kinds of noodle soups appeared simultaneously in several regions in Japan, in part due to an influx of Chinese students keen to learn the secret of Japan's modernization. Chinese immigrants and newly arriving foreign traders were generally aghast at Japan's paltry cuisine, especially in light of the country's increasing prestige on the world stage. Nagasaki, the western city best known for funneling information and technology into Japan from China and Holland during the Tokugawa era, was home to *champon,* one of the first original noodle dishes to be invented by a Chinese immigrant. In 1887, an immigrant from Fujian province named Chen Pingjun opened a restaurant called the "Four Seas Tower" and started to develop dishes that in the Japanese parlance offered "stamina." His dishes were less fancy than the offerings at high-class restaurants where the newly wealthy or budding politicians entertained. Chen had unwittingly uncovered a market for what would later transform into ramen – Meiji era Japanese wanted a hearty and rich dish that was inexpensive, even if eaten in a shop. With a keen eye toward service and his customer base, Chen also concocted the dish that came to be known as *champon*, essentially a seasoned dish of leftovers into which he threw everything not used that day, usually with some kind of meat, and stirring in some noodles and soup mix.[53] *Champon* became a hit and not just among Japanese laborers looking for a filling meal. The 1907 Nagasaki prefectural history commented that Chinese exchange students frequently

---

[53] Okada Tetsu, *Rāmen no tanjō*, p. 88.

ate *champon*; a fan of the dish even penned a song about it.[54] In testament to its enduring popularity Chen's restaurant is now an enormous five-story edifice right on the edge of Nagasaki bay that also houses a small museum devoted to the founder's life and story.

Champon is only one example from a multitude of similar events around the turn of the century, where a Chinese immigrant utilized his cooking skills to develop a new product for the burgeoning Japanese food market. The popularity of Nagasaki *champon*, and similarly seasoned hearty noodle dishes from other cities, among overseas Chinese students (as well as the growing cadre of Japanese seeking work in the expanding urban areas), slowly promoted savory noodle-and-meat dishes. Chinese cooking was adapted to Japanese tastes, emerging as something new that appealed to Meiji youth. Nagasaki was one avenue through which Chinese cuisine and tastes entered Japan, but the Chinese community itself was key to the further spread of ramen.

Just a few years prior to the *champon* experiment in the far west of Japan, a similar food innovation had appeared in a port city in Japan's northern island of Hokkaido. "*Nanking soba*," as it was known, was first supposedly served at the well-known "Western restaurant" Yōwaken ("House of Recuperative Harmony") in Hakodate in 1884. It is not quite clear what the dish comprised but the fact that it mixed Japanese noodles, *soba*, with some form of "Chinese" taste that could only be expressed by a Chinese city name, suggests that the flavors and texture of the meal departed from the normal expectations diners had when they ordered regular *soba*.[55] Decades later, this forerunner of ramen was known in equal parts as "*Nanking soba*" and later "*Chūka soba*," or Chinese noodles. Toward the end of the nineteenth century the Japanese love of noodles was climbing toward a crescendo of consumer interest. The interesting thing about this Nanking version of the noodle dish was that it was not served in a Chinese shop or by Chinese cooks but in a restaurant that specialized in Western food. During the Meiji era such hybrid dishes were sold in a variety of shops and under numerous names, causing one to wonder if ever any clear distinction was made between cuisine from the West or East. It is entirely probable that the term "Western food" referred to any previously unknown cuisine, even if it was distinctly Chinese in origin.

---

[54] Ibid., p. 90.
[55] Miyachi Masato et al., eds., *Bijuaru waido Meiji jidaikan*, p. 92.

Figure 29. Image of Yōwaken restaurant where "*Nanking soba*" was supposedly first served in 1884.[56]

---

[56] Kakinuki Ichiemon and Kojima Torajirō, *Shōkō Hakodate no sakigake: Hokkaidō hitori annai*, unpaginated.

CHAPTER SIX

DIPLOMACY AND THE DESIRE TO IMPRESS

Fukuzawa Yukichi and other Meiji-era statesmen understood that for Japan to appear enlightened it had to adopt the diplomatic protocol and the visual splendor at which the West – particularly Victorian England, arguably the richest nation at the time – excelled.[1] Fukuzawa captured the essence of why such pomp and ceremony were necessary: "If you stand at someone's door in tattered rags and beg for a little money the world calls you a beggar, *but* if you wear silken cloth and enter a fancy room asking to borrow a little, people will call you a gentleman." He noted: "A beggar and a gentleman are only a hair's breadth apart."[2] To avoid being seen as a beggar at the international banquet table was of such importance to nineteenth-century Japanese rulers that the government that emerged after the Meiji Restoration published an extensive internal guidebook on how to host parties and observe proper imperial protocol. The instructions included directions for crafting menus and deciding where servants and guests should stand, as well as who should take coats and hats and the order of seating arrangements, covering the minutest details of hosting an international banquet. One initial problem was to find an appropriate venue. The preferred site was the Enryōkan, a former Tokugawa residence converted for use as a hotel-cum-early-modern-convention-center to house and entertain foreign dignitaries. Later, at great expense, the Meiji government built the larger and more palatial Rokumeikan, the Deer Park Pavilion, to serve as a Western-style diplomatic entertainment hall.

The various dishes and their accompaniments at these international gatherings were so confusing to most diners and guests that these sorts of menus had to include three sections of explanations. The top section listed each dish's basic ingredients. Underneath, a guide in *katakana*, the phonetic Japanese syllabary for foreign words, explained pronunciation of the name of the dish. The bottom section gave a detailed description

---

[1] Takashi Fujitani details the gradual process to fit the Japanese emperor with such frills in *Splendid monarchy: power and pageantry in modern Japan*.
[2] Watanabe Shōyō, *Meiryū hyakuwa*, p. 92.

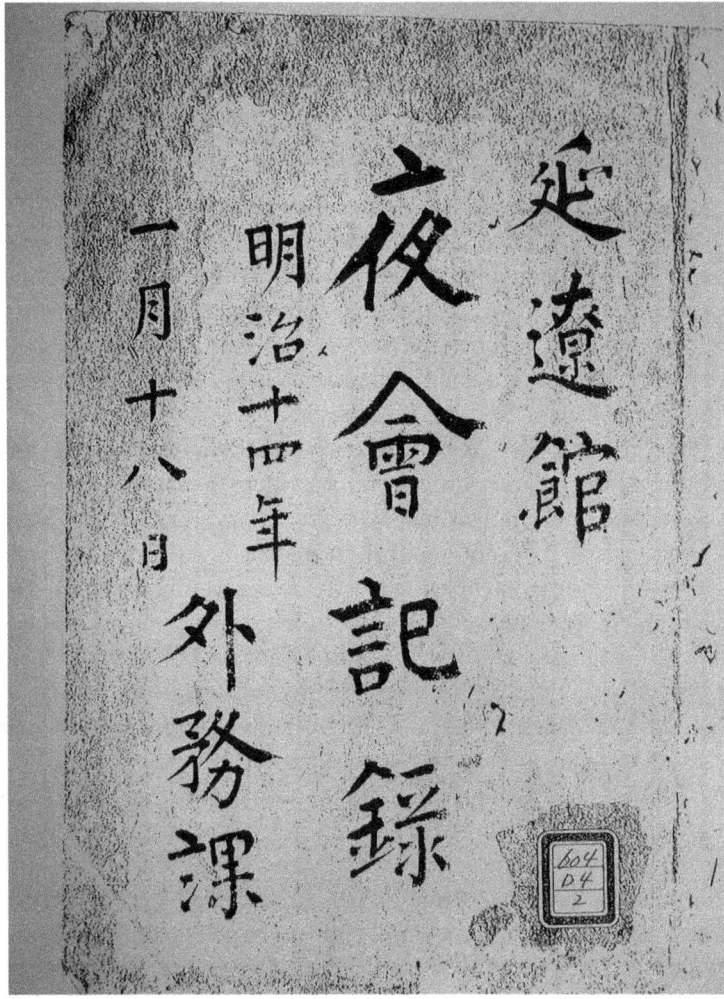

Figures 30 and 31. The first image is of the cover of the instruction manual for evening events. The second image is of a partial menu, showing the foreign dishes spelled out in *katakana*, with a Japanese explanation below. The menu is read right to left and top to bottom. The word soup, written phonetically as the French term *potage*, is translated as *"geng,"* the Chinese word historically used for a thick soup. *Poisson*, the French term for fish, is explained as "fish meat," and the delicacy *foie gras* simply as "chicken meat."[3]

---

[3] "Enryōkan yakai kiroku," 604. D4. 2, Tōkyōto kobunshokan (Tokyo Metropolitan Archives).

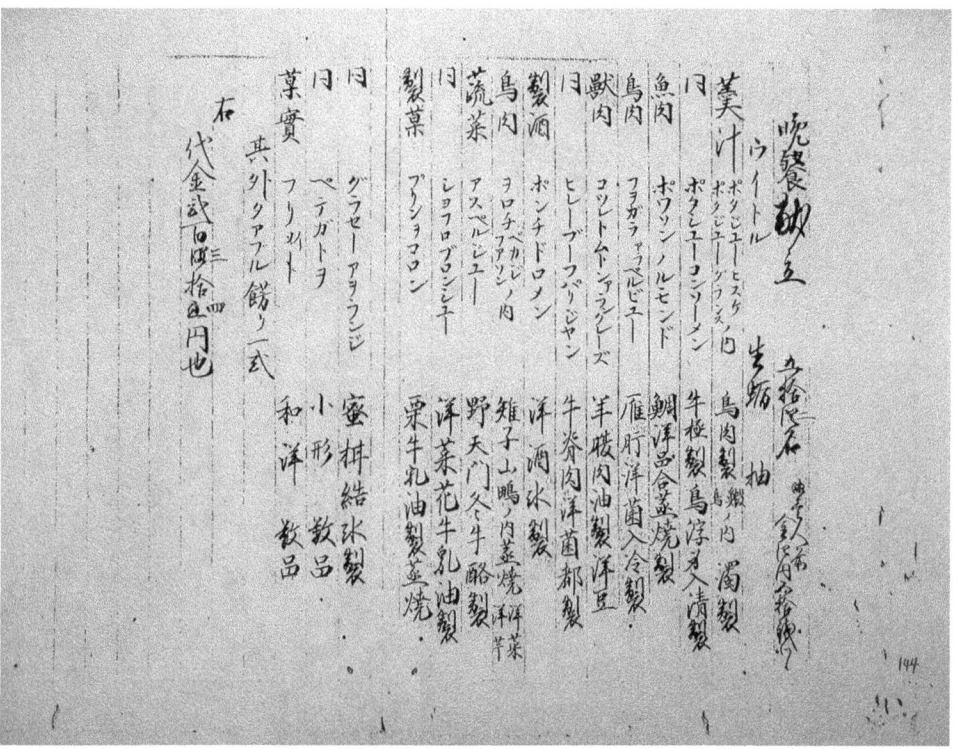

Figures 30 and 31. (*Continued*)

in semi-classical Chinese of what kind of food the diners were consuming. In early Meiji Japan, dining was a tricky business and quite linguistically cumbersome.

Not only did the names of new dishes confound Japanese chefs and menu writers, but the implements of dining were also a concern. The question of what kind of cutlery, in particular, should be supplied to foreign guests continued to be a problem throughout the Meiji era as more and more non-Japanese became interested in the nation, especially at the official level. The Ministry of the Imperial Household pulled out all budgetary stops for former US President Ulysses S. Grant's 1879 tour of Japan (in the midst of a severe cholera epidemic and national panic, when authorities suddenly became cognizant of the comparatively low standards of the nation's hygiene). The Ministry decided that only the very grandest Western-style table settings would be satisfactory and ordered

Figure 32. A drawing of life at Enryōkan and a glimpse of former US President Ulysses S. Grant's tour of Japan in 1879. Grant was one of the first important Western visitors to Japan and raised the profile of diplomatic protocol and dining in the new nation. The Meiji government accommodated the president and his retinue at Enryōkan during his highly publicized visit. The transliteration of Japanese into English was still in its infancy so the place name was romanized differently, as Enriokwan.[4]

---

[4] John Russell Young, *Around the world with General Grant: a narrative of the visit of General U.S. Grant, ex-President of the United States, to various countries in Europe, Asia and Africa, in 1877, 1878, 1879; to which are added certain conversations with General Grant on questions connected with American politics and history*, Vol. 2, p. 550.

sets of "sterling silver, engraved in ivory with the Imperial crest of the chrysanthemum" specifically for the banquets.[5] On July 8, 1879 the famed industrialist Shibusawa Eichi's daughter Utako sat next to the victorious general of the US Civil War at a state dinner held in his honor. She was surprised that the former president did not act as Japanese expected Westerners to behave, all blustery and wordy; and was also completely puzzled by what appeared to be a form of butter that kept melting off her spoon before she could bring it to her plate. "All I could think was 'What an odd food'?" she reflected. It was ice cream.[6]

Imperial Dining

In the last three decades of the nineteenth century and beyond, as Japan started to flex its imperializing muscles, the concept of dining and national cuisine changed, with consequences for the further development of ramen. The conquest of Taiwan, an island off the southeast coast of China, began in 1874 with a military incursion, and accelerated in 1895 when Tokyo acquired the land as part of the Qing Empire's indemnity payments for defeat. Korea, an object of Japanese management and intrigue since the early 1880s, also moved slowly into Japan's colonial orbit, and was annexed in 1910. Japan's new stature as a colonial power was reflected in its cuisine, which absorbed influences from West and East, both of which had impressive culinary cultures. Soldiers conquered foreign lands and housewives slowly incorporated new tastes into dishes at home. The colonization of cuisine had begun.[7] By the 1920s one could taste Japan's geographic conquest of other lands on the tip of one's chopsticks. Ramen evolved out of this hybrid collection of new tastes that entered Japan as part of its expanding empire.

On the heels of the Tokugawa-era boom in noodle production and numbers of restaurants, Meiji era Japanese ate new noodle dishes, topped with meat and frequently seasoned with a heavier soy sauce for flavor. But further adaptations and transformations of the national cuisine and dietary changes at the family level required renovating the kitchen as well

---

[5] Richard T. Chang, "General Grant's 1879 Visit to Japan," *Monumental Nipponica*, Vol. 24, No. 4, 1969, p. 376.
[6] Ibid., p. 387.
[7] In British homes during the mid-1800s, former colonial officers and families brought Indian food into the national British diet and made it culturally British. War may forcibly alter the landscape of what people eat, but the person who cooks it is still Mom.

as the household. Cookbooks had been published during the Tokugawa era, but they only became a home staple, part of the arsenal of the mother of the household, when the Meiji era's new idea of the family took root. A proliferation of these recipe collections, aimed more and more at the female head of the household, suggests that literacy rates among women were rising, together with social expectations. A similar change during a similar time can also be seen in Africa, Europe and India when the idea grew that national cuisine was something that emanated from the home and was thus the woman's domain. Civilized food made Japan look strong and prosperous internationally, while bringing personal glory to the man whose wife produced it in his home.

One important aspect of the translation of foreign tastes into a new Japanese cuisine was the multiplicity of fresh words used to label national dishes. Meiji terms for cuisine did not sort themselves out for over half a century. The process of choosing vocabulary to label a national cuisine mirrored a parallel national movement to establish a national Japanese language, *kokugo*. As historian Lee Yeonsuk illustrates in her provocative analysis of this phenomenon in early Meiji Japan, Japanese elites and leaders continually anguished over how to write Japanese in a modern way that could be taught to all members of society. Should they abandon Chinese characters and employ the English alphabet? What would this entail and what did it say about the nature of the Japanese language?[8] Anxiety about teaching and codifying the language of "new" Japan spilled out of the confines of academia and government into daily life. Not only was the nature of society and history being questioned, but an influx of new food items from abroad left people unsure even of what to call the food they were eating.

Strong links exist between cuisine and identity – a geographic version of "you are what you eat." The protective mindset toward local food is similar to the French concept of *terroir*, which "evokes issues of roots and identity at once national and regional."[9] However, as noted in previous

---

[8] Lee Yeounsuk, *Kokugo to iu shisō*, p. 29.

[9] Timothy J. Tomasik, "Certeau à la Carte: Translating Discursive Terroir in the Practice of Everyday Life: Living and Cooking," *The South Atlantic Quarterly*, 100:2, Spring 2001, p. 524. See also Arjun Appadurai, "How to Make a National Cuisine: Cookbooks in Contemporary India," *Comparative Studies in Society and History*, Vol. 30, No. 1, 1988, pp. 3–24; Raymond Grew, ed., *Food in Global History*; Sidney W. Mintz, *Tasting Food, Tasting Freedom: Excursions into Eating, Culture and the Past*; Massimo Montanari disputes the idea that cuisine was ever truly regional in the early modern era, *Food is culture*, (translated by Aine O'Healy), pp. 75–79.

chapters, these "traditions" are not usually as longstanding as they are made out to be, and of course rarely natural or inherent. Fuchsia Dunlop, the well-known Chinese food critic and writer, notes in her discussions of the history of Chinese cuisine that "culinary communities" usually bear "little relation to geographical or even culinary boundaries." These concepts are symbolic, she argues, "drawing selectively on the resources of the past and the eating practices of the present to create the idea of community."[10] Newly created linguistic labels for national cuisine created a more forceful perception that food was either Japanese or Chinese; cuisine was no longer just what one ate, it had a national brand attached to it.

During the nineteenth century, it became important to believe that Japanese cuisine was not interactive but static, arising naturally out of the single geographic entity of the nation. This concept promoted the myth of a national cuisine as something members of the nation all consumed in common. One might speculate that before the birth of a national media, the idea of a national cuisine was the original fabric that bound the nation together.[11] From Meiji to the present, there has never been a single accepted term for Japan's national cuisine. *Nihonshoku, washoku* and *Nihon ryōri* are somewhat interchangeable terms. It is probable, though far from definite, that *washoku*, the idiom most commonly used to identify traditional and light Japanese cuisine, developed as the opposite of *yōshoku* or "Western food," the term used in Japan to discuss any cuisine that was not Asian in origin.[12]

Once Chinese food became an item, acknowledged as such, on Japanese menus, there was the question of the terms to describe it: should it be *Chūka ryōri*, or *Shina ryōri*?[13] These terms are loaded with historical significance because they create a geographical space in which the Japanese labeled a certain cuisine as Chinese. *Chūka ryōri*, "Chinese food" uses a more politically neutral term for modern China that avoids using the term "middle kingdom." *Shina ryōri* (the same meaning but with a more politically loaded label for China) grew in usage from the start of the twentieth

---

[10] Fuchsia Dunlop, *Gastronomically Chinese: Culinary identities and Chinese modernity*, MA Area Studies (China) of the University of London, September 1997, p. 7.

[11] In *Imagined Communities: Reflections on the origin and spread of nationalism*, Benedict Anderson postulated that it was a national language and media that assisted in the creation and formation of a shared "national" experience that served as a foundation to the rise of a national community.

[12] Harada Nobuo, *Washoku to Nihon bunka*, p. 10.

[13] Eric Rath questions whether these terms are completely modern constructs in his article, "Banquets Against Boredom: Towards Understanding (Samurai) Cuisine in Early Modern Japan," *Early Modern Japan*, Vol. 16, 2008, pp. 43–44.

century but even then the two terms were often used interchangeably.¹⁴ Two common modern terms in the Chinese language, *Zhongcai* and *Zhongguocai*, mean Chinese food but retain some political baggage by referring to China as the "middle kingdom."¹⁵ All of these translations lose their nuance in English, where there are just two terms that are essentially devoid of historical or political baggage – "Japanese food" and "Chinese food" – without any colonial or nationalist overtones.¹⁶ The issue of what term to use to refer to the new idea of national cuisine is the connective tissue that links language, identity and cuisine, and runs deep in East Asia.

Regardless of what you called it, cooking in Japan was still normally learned and consumed at home, with family and friends. Manners were likewise taught in private but efforts to raise the position of women created a new category, *ryōsai kenbo* or "good wife, wise mother." During the Meiji era, the state tried to give women a more central position in the home, with home economics as their domain. Women were expected to raise healthy, smart and productive imperial subjects to make Japan strong and great. It was an awesome responsibility and social concern with the new sciences of nutrition and hygiene began to dominate public discourse as never before. If your "meat spear," the newly-minted word for fork, "drops and gets dirty, pick it up and wipe it with your napkin," counseled a Meiji volume on etiquette.¹⁷ At the same time, Japanese began to travel more – liberated by the new railways – and eating was even less only conducted in the home. Before long, station lunches, *ekiben*, materialized.

---

¹⁴ These terms in Chinese characters are 中華料理 and 支那料理. The historian Joshua Fogel holds that *Shina* was not a word that was used as a derogatory term in imperial Japan to label China. While agreeing that it was not always so, I am inclined to think that it is fairly clear that at least in areas such as wartime propaganda pamphlets and other such media that mocked China, *Shina* was employed more as a derogatory word in such tones. See Joshua A. Fogel review of Stefan Tanaka, *Japan's Orient: Rendering Pasts into History*, Monumenta Nipponica, Vol. 49, No. 1, Spring, 1994, pp. 108–112.

¹⁵ See Frederico Masini, *The Formation of Modern Chinese Lexicon and Its Evolution Toward a National Language: The Period from 1840 to 1898*, Special Issue of the *Journal of Chinese Linguistics*, Monograph Series Number 6, 1993 and David Pollack, *The Fracture of Meaning: Japan's Synthesis of China from the Eighth through the Eighteenth Centuries*.

¹⁶ Lydia Liu discusses translation, power and colonialism in *Translingual Practice: Literature, National Culture and Translated Modernity – China, 1900–1937*; and her edited volume *Tokens of Exchange: The Problem of Translation in Global Circulations*. See Joshua Fogel for a critique of translation theory concerning her edited volume in "'Like Kissing through a Handkerchief:' *Traduttore Traditore*," *China Review International* 8.1, Spring 2001, pp. 1–15.

¹⁷ Shōwa joshi daigaku shokumotsu kenkyūshitsu, editors, *Kindai Nihon shokumotsu-shi*, p. 85.

The first train line to sell these boxed lunches was the line between Tokyo and Utsunomiya which, in July 1885, offered a meal of black sesame *ume boshi* rice balls and *takuan* pickles wrapped in bamboo leaves.

Japan also began to mark its colonial territories through its national cuisine. When Japan colonized Taiwan and Korea, businessmen quickly transplanted the *ryōtei* from Japan. *Ryōtei* were upper-class restaurants where statesmen and political figures would gather in the evening for drinks and dinner, mainly to discuss politics, away from the public fray. The elite made such establishments a fixture of the new imperial political and capital culture. In 1887, long before the official annexation of Korea, one such salon, Imonrō, opened in Seoul. In 1910, more stores catering for the Japanese living in colonial Korea opened and flourished.[18]

Japanese people traveling to or writing about China held contradictory attitudes about Chinese cuisine.[19] While admitting that Chinese food was delicious Japanese authors often wanted to prove that Chinese culture was at the same time decaying, and that Japan should step into the vacuum and assume the position of standard-bearer in East Asia. Andō Fujio, a well-known Japanese writer, journeyed to the Chinese mainland in the late nineteenth century and wrote a book about his travels. He grudgingly accepted that, even though China was culturally deficient, an ossifying empire no longer at the center of East Asia, in food culture it was more advanced than Japan. Andō argued that Cantonese-style food was best suited to the Japanese palate.[20] He was more complimentary than most.

By the end of the nineteenth century, national cuisine had become important not only because it defined Japan and was important diplomatically, but also as a means of differentiating Japan from China and the rest of East Asia. A late-nineteenth century history exam primer instructed the burgeoning populations of newly literate citizens as follows:

> In our country, from the time of the gods, we were already planting rice and most of the people ate rice. This rice was usually *genmai*, or steamed to make *kowameshi* and on festival days people would eat white rice. Following Emperor Nintoku most people ate rice and usually fish, fowl or animal meat

---

[18] Harada Nobuo, *Washoku to Nihon bunka*, p. 196.
[19] I detail this love/hate relationship among the Japanese intellectuals, the public and Chinese culture more fully in Barak Kushner, "Imperial Cuisines in Taishō Foodways." In the field of Japanese literature this mindset is explained more eloquently in Kawamoto Saburō, *Taishō genei*.
[20] Andō Fujio, *Shina manyū jikki*, p. 33.

in the olden days, but after the arrival of Buddhism and the punishment for killing live things, eating meat dwindled and people began eating two meals a day.[21]

Health, Hygiene and Food

Empire, modernization and urbanization altered the way in which the Japanese conceived of themselves within East Asia, but the new economic situation exacerbated many of the problems that an agricultural and rural life-style had previously hidden – unemployment, an eroding family structure and the unraveling of traditional village life. In his 1899 book, *Japan's Underclass*, Yokoyama Gennosuke, a late Meiji social commentator and journalist, exposed grinding levels of urban poverty across Japan. On page after page, Yokoyama detailed the extreme deprivation in which whole families subsisted. As he observed in one instance, "In one ugly room about six tatami mats wide and one hallway about four tatami mats across a couple resided with children, totaling about five to six people on a given day."[22]

The strange foods one ate in the countryside, the rank stench pouring from these small, stifling abodes and the pockets of poverty that existed around the country were not lost on foreign travelers. This worried the Japanese government, which was fervently trying to maintain a strong international posture. Basil Hall Chamberlain, an early foreign resident of Japan and professor of Japanese philology at the Imperial University of Tokyo, counseled travellers to bring carbolic acid with them in his 1891 *A Handbook for Travellers in Japan*, since Japanese inns gave off offensive smells. Both Chamberlain and famed world traveler Isabella Bird commented on the pestilent bugs and bed lice. Edward Morse, an early Meiji era American educator hired to teach in Japan, experienced unusual gustatory delights with aplomb. In his memoir of travel during those years Morse recalled that: "In one place a man had grasshoppers for sale as articles of food, the insects having been boiled or baked. I ate one and found it very good, tasting like a dried shrimp."[23] He also carefully catalogued dining habits on his travels outside of Tokyo, where the Meiji transformation was progressing more slowly, and in Hakodate in the north, where he

---

[21] Matsumoto Kendō, ed., *Nihon rekishi shiken mondai tōan*, p. 18.
[22] Maruoka Hideko and Yamaguchi Mieko, eds., *Nihon fujin mondai shiryō shūsei*, Vol. 7, *seikatsu*, (reprinted from the 1899 book), pp. 127–133.
[23] Edward Morse, *Japan Day by Day*, pp. 344–345.

did not enjoy the food as much as he had in the capital. Morse wrote that in the north he ate marine worms resembling angleworms, which were eaten raw "and the taste was precisely as seaweed smells at low tide." Tenaciously adventurous, but with the quiet disdain of one who considered himself civilized and modern, he wrote in his diary of daily adventures: "On the whole, I am keeping body and its animating principle together, but long for a cup of coffee and a slice of bread-and-butter."[24]

At the turn of the nineteenth century, Japan was not as clean and germ-free as we modern readers might assume.[25] From the early to mid-Meiji period, a very large underclass in a growing number of cities ate cheaply at shops called *zanpanya* (leftover food stalls), which collected leftover food and resold it cheaply to the poorer masses.[26] In some cases, this food had not yet been cooked, in other cases it was actual leftovers, half-eaten meals that were then stirred into new dishes. Social pundits publicly commented that these shops sold victuals of such a low and vile quality that "it was even something dogs wouldn't eat." Beggars often scavenged among the discarded remnants of tossed away or unfinished meals thrown away behind small eateries, referring to this type of leftover food as *zuke*.[27]

The existence of these "leftover food stalls," or eating *zuke*, demonstrates how hungry the Japanese were for cheap and tasty meals. The market was ripe for entrepreneurs who could deliver food that would be nutritious, tasty, and most importantly, inexpensive.

The debate about what the best food was for Japanese society in general and for soldiers in particular continued during Japan's second imperial war of conquest, with Russia, from 1904 to 1905. At this point, Chinese cuisine began slowly to appear in military rations but the navy was still better provisioned than the army, having previously accepted Takagi Kanehiro's theory on the origins of beriberi. Men on ships received rations of eggs, oatmeal, coffee, fish, meat and alcohol. The era of the Russo-Japanese War also witnessed a new phase in the publication of cookbooks and food appreciation manuals – guides for late Meiji connoisseurs. Murai Gensai's fictional accounts of fine dining in "The Gourmand" (*Kuidōraku*), became a runaway bestseller and sold over 100,000 copies. The author

[24] Ibid., pp. 339–441.
[25] Kimura, *Nihon no hoteru sangyōshi*, p. 19.
[26] Onishi Shirō, et al., eds. *Seikatsushi II*, Taikei Nihonshi sōsho 17, p. 78.
[27] Onishi Shirō, et al., eds. *Seikatsushi II*, p. 203. Miriam Silverberg details how beggars and the lower classes often scrounged for food in parts of Tokyo. See Miriam Silverberg, *Erotic, Grotesque Nonsense: The Mass Culture of Japanese Modern Times*, pp. 206–212.

Figure 33. Picture of a "leftovers stand" in Tokyo with the proprietor weighing out food that was collected, mixed and then sold back in bulk form. Illustration from the book *Darkest Parts of Tokyo*, 1893.[28]

wrote that he intended to introduce Western cuisine to Japan because it was "more nutritious, hygienic, practical, modern and democratic than traditional Japanese fare."[29] Originally, the book had been presented as a series of newspaper columns but the published book arrived in stores around the time of Japan's victory over Russia. The effect was electric. Murai described his new dishes as a "victory cuisine," using the language of military conquest for such offerings as "Hōten Soup," "Port Arthur Fry" and "Karafuto Cake."[30] The dishes were all named after key battle sites in celebration of Japan's conquest of Manchuria and defeat of the Russians. "The Hōten soup is a peace (dove) base, Port Arthur Fry

---

[28] Matsuhara Iwagorō, *Saiankoku no Tokyo*.
[29] Tomoko Aoyama, "Romancing Food: The Gastronmic Quest in Early Twentieth-Century Japanese Literature," *Japanese Studies*, December 2003, p. 253. See also her *Reading Food in Modern Japanese Literature*.
[30] Harada Nobuo, *Washoku to Nihon bunka*, p. 278.

uses arrowroot... and the Karafuto cake is a long dessert cut in half, just like the island," Murai explained.[31] The southern half of Karafuto (also known as Sakhalin) was acquired by the Japanese in 1905 after their defeat of Russia and thus the island was split in half to share between the two imperial governments. Another popular food product at the time was the mellifluously labeled "Smash the Baltic Fleet Memorial Tōgō Marshmallow," probably a children's favorite, commemorating Admiral Tōgō Heihachirō's victory in the stupendous naval Battle of Tsūshima in 1905, when his forces sank virtually the entire Russian fleet.[32] Supposedly, Japanese victory encouraged even foreigners to eat in the Japanese style. According to one newspaper, British celebrated the Japanese victory over Russia (a mutual enemy after the Crimean War) by eating rice meals in celebration.[33] Britain entered a formal naval alliance with Japan in 1902: its partner's victory meant that Russia could be controlled and would pose less of a threat to Britain's extensive colonial holdings in the Middle East and India.[34]

The Russo-Japanese War further promoted the pivotal linkage between eating correctly and nutrition in Japanese cuisine. Kawashima Shirō, an army medical officer and famed nutritionist to the military, asserted that Russia surrendered Port Arthur to General Nogi because its forces were ignorant of the importance of proper nutrition. According to Kawashima, nothing could grow on the fortress of Port Arthur. As there were no vegetables, many Russians succumbed to scurvy, a Vitamin C deficiency that causes, among other symptoms, massive fatigue and the slow decomposition of the skin. Ironically, the Tsar's army was sitting on a mountain of vitamins, acres of soy bean fields. Kawashima suggested that the Russians knew little about soy bean food technology but once the soy beans are collected they can be easily processed to bud shoots. This little vegetable, known as "bean sprouts," contains Vitamin C and other crucial nutrients. The Russian army could not have known much about nutritional balance or the risk of illness: a bit of science applied to military cuisine might have

---

[31] Murai Gensai, *Kuidōraku*, section five, "zokuhen haru no kan," p. 9.
[32] Shōwa joshi daigaku shokumotsu kenkyūshitsu, editors, *Kindai Nihon shokumotsu-shi*, p. 278.
[33] Ibid., p. 298.
[34] Colin Holmes and A.H. Ion discuss the British affinity for Japanese style and culture during this period in "Bushido and the Samurai: Images in British Public Opinion, 1894–1914," *Modern Asian Studies*, Vol. 14, No. 2, 1980, pp. 309–329.

saved them from so easily surrendering in that key battle and hence blocked Japan's 1905 victory.[35]

Demobilized soldiers from Japan's wars provided another important intersection between imperialism and food. In 1906, the Returning Reservists Association published a guidebook for repatriating soldiers following the end of the Russo-Japanese War. Notwithstanding the victory, the war had brought Japan to the brink of economic ruin and the deaths of thousands of breadwinners had left thousands of families in economic hardship. Tens of thousands of civilians in Tokyo and elsewhere rioted *en masse* upon hearing that Japan would not receive an indemnity from Russia; it had after all received a hefty indemnity from the Qing Empire in 1895. Soldiers felt particularly disgruntled and betrayed by the peace treaty terms. "To prosecute the war many [soldiers] discarded important careers and answered the call of duty," the guidebook noted. "Following victory, these men wanted to return to their former professions but they couldn't. With families at their wits end, there are probably many like them...." The author declared: "It is for these men that I put pen to paper."[36] His recommendation was that these men should open a cantina for laborers. "Even an amateur can do this work. Open a high- or mid-level eating and drinking establishment and capital will flow in fairly easily." However, he cautioned, "there is a kind of knack to the business, so people who are not really outgoing shouldn't try their hand at it." "Welcome" and "Thank you" were phrases of the utmost necessity, the guidebook reminded demobilized imperial Japanese forces.[37] A variety of other jobs were detailed, but short-order cook as a temporary means of gaining employment for repatriating soldiers would continue to hold appeal for later generations. Post World War II Japanese repatriates to the home islands opened thousands of similar canteens after 1945, transforming postwar Japanese cuisine. The idea of starting a career in catering after military service dates from the beginning of the century and appears to have been government sponsored, in part.

One of the other important hygiene-promoting functions assumed by the Meiji state was the certifying of whether food or drink was safe. Britain enacted similar measures in the 1870s to stem a tide of unsafe foods and unscrupulous marketers, and the move on Japan's part helped to establish

---

[35] Yamashita Tamiki, *Kawashima Shirō kyūjissai no kaiseinen*, pp. 141–142.
[36] Senryūdō Kobayashihen, *Kikyō gunjin shūshoku annai*, introduction.
[37] Ibid., p. 131.

it as an international equal. The authorities implemented these measures because food and drink had become much more complex products, containing more and more ingredients shipped across numerous regions or countries; a single person could no longer determine the specific provenance of something on sale. In February 1900, the Japanese government passed "laws pertaining to beverages and foodstuffs." Government oversight continued to increase in the ensuing years.

The Meiji era not only changed the Japanese palate, it began a process of judging civilizations by their diet. By the 1910s, the Japanese began to use their own verbs to discuss cooking, moving away from classical Chinese words previously employed. (Historically, the Japanese language borrowed heavily from the Chinese language.)[38] Yamagata Kōhō, a Japanese social commentator writing in 1907, openly admitted that Western food was more popular than Chinese cuisine mainly because Japan was now learning from the West and sending its students there. "Previously, there was a period when we learned from China but that relationship has now reversed and currently what we need to learn from them has reduced to virtually nothing."[39] Yamagata noted that Chinese cuisine had 4,000 years of history behind it and had obviously contributed to world cooking; nevertheless, he wrote, it was now unworthy of imitation. It was too heavy, Yamagata complained; it never changed, there were too many dishes, the selection of ingredients was too varied and the food was not hygienic.[40] His was not a very analytical or objective argument but it underscored the influence of politics on Japanese notions of taste and food culture. As much as Japanese society yearned for meatier, flavorful dishes that offered the cherished "stamina" of *champon* noodles, the acceptance of such meals among the upper classes would take time.

Japan saw imperialism and Great Britain's possession of colonies not merely as a symbol of international prestige but also as a steady pipeline of food for the mother country. A Japanese treatise on opening up China for trade, published in 1903, noted: "Even during times of peace, it is of the utmost importance to maintain a strong national supply of food (*minshoku no jūjitsu*) to serve as the base in supporting flourishing commerce and industry." Furthermore, "by opening sea lanes between the Qing Empire and Japan, within a few days it is not difficult to ship enormous

---

[38] The Chinese language term used in Japanese was previously 割烹, (kappō). Later, a Japanese verb, 料理する (ryōri suru), was used in place of the borrowed Chinese word.
[39] Yamagata Kōhō, *Ishokujū*, p. 440.
[40] Yamagata Kōhō, *Ishokujū*, p. 441.

amounts of foodstuffs." The book concluded: "We must work toward the development of *Shina* [a term for China] to assiduously meet this end."[41]

Early twentieth-century changes in food culture prompted the Japanese government to be concerned not only about its own food culture but those of its colonies as well. The authorities began to investigate what exactly everyone around the empire was eating and a by-product of this inquiry was a two-year study of Korean cuisine. The study concluded that "Overall Korean living standards are extremely low, especially among the lower classes who eat a most tasteless and rough cuisine. One would be surprised at how basic their personal income is."[42] The report concluded that Koreans mostly ate rice mixed with some grain or cereal and that once in the countryside, away from urban areas, people who dined on rice were few. The report was especially condemning of Korean kitchens: "Calling a room such as that a kitchen," it noted, "is a misnomer: it is usually just a dark and filthy place to cook."[43]

One goal of this government initiative was to determine if the colonial subjects were receiving proper nutrition that would allow them to grow healthier and stronger, so that they could follow the lead of Japan and modernize in its shadow. Such concerns were not limited to Korea but extended to the Chinese areas in Japan's imperial holdings as well. These investigations and colonial exchanges invariably influenced the development of new Japanese tastes and preferences, although not all the changes were welcomed.

Chinese in Meiji Japan

The Meiji era witnessed the internationalization of the Japanese population. The city of Nagasaki, on the western island of Kyushu, already had a sizeable population of Chinese residents and travelers consisting of several thousand, but after 1895 many more Chinese emigrated from China to Japan to work, often with the idea to study Japan's success at modernizing. China's defeat at the hands of Japan in 1895 had surprised Chinese leaders and intellectuals. Foreign students as well as workers from around Japan's growing sphere of influence flocked to new communities in Yokohama, parts of Tokyo, Kobe, and Sapporo. Japan had already become a haven for

---

[41] Satō Torajirō, *Shina keihatsuron*, p. 81.
[42] Murakami Tadakichi, *Chōsenjin no ishokujū*, p. 27.
[43] Ibid., p. 88.

Figure 34. The front page of the Japanese government study of its colony, "How Koreans Dress, Eat and Live."

reform-minded Chinese such as Sun Yat Sen, founding father of the Republic of China, and late Qing intellectuals Kang Youwei and his disciple Liang Qichao. The latter two sought exile in Japan after suggesting that only military and political reform could save the ailing Qing Empire, which earned them imperial wrath. It seems from the Japanese newspapers and journals at the turn of the century that there were several kinds of Chinese students studying in Japan, ranging from privately funded individuals to others on scholarship from their local councils or provinces. In the common parlance of the day, however, there were really only four categories of overseas student, the ones interested in "whoring, gambling, eating and drinking."[44] The Japanese had changed their diet but not changed their new, rather arrogant Meiji attitudes and this friction sometimes made itself felt in quite unpleasant ways. Many reform-minded Chinese students were keen to discover the secret of Japan's success but attitudes toward national cuisine and taste on both sides of the sea often impeded this exchange. In March 1896, during the first post Sino-Japanese War wave of exchange students, four of the original thirteen pupils returned to China from Japan. There were probably many reasons but one primary issue they mentioned was that they could not tolerate the food.[45]

Earlier Chinese diplomatic musings on Japanese cuisine had been much more sympathetic. Huang Zunxian, one of the Qing dynasty's first diplomatic officers posted to Japan, waxed poetic about the epicurean delights of sushi, writing that it "melts in your mouth like ice and has an absolutely wonderful flavor!"[46] Late-nineteenth century Chinese students were less impressed. Their second reason for abandoning their studies was that many could not endure the incessant taunts of Japanese children constantly shouting "Chink! Chink!" at them wherever they went.[47] Many of these early Chinese students still maintained the imperial Qing hairstyle of the queue, a long ponytail of hair, and complained that they were treated as second-class citizens in Japan. However, even the growing racial divide, insults, poor Japanese cuisine and a fairly unwelcoming Japanese attitude did not stem the tide of Chinese students seeking a "modern" education and a window to the wider world, still unavailable in China.[48] As Chinese student numbers increased, more restaurants in Japanese urban areas opened to serve them, seeking to profit from the

---

[44] Son Ansoku, "Keihi wa yūgaku no haha de ari," in Kanagawa daigaku jinbun gakkai ed., *Chūgokujin Nihon ryūgakushi kenkyū no gendankai*, p. 177.

[45] Sanetō Keishū, *Chūgokujin Nihon ryūgakushi*, p. 15. Fascinatingly, this small historical episode is also commented on in a 2006 CCTV production of *Daguo Jueqi*, a multi-part Chinese television TV series analyzing the rise and fall of nations.

[46] Richard John Lynn, "'This Culture of Ours' and Huang Zunxian's Literary Experiences in Japan (1877–82)," *Chinese Literature: Essays, Articles, Reviews* (CLEAR), Vol. 19, December 1997, p. 137.

[47] Sanetō Keishū, *Chūgokujin Nihon ryūgakushi*, p. 38.

[48] See Steve Platt, *Provincial patriots: the Hunanese and modern China*; and Paula Harrel, *Sowing the seeds of change: Chinese students, Japanese teachers, 1895–1905*.

expanding educational exchange market. This step had an impact on the future of noodle-eating and helped to create a future market for ramen.

Bitter feelings, perhaps tinged with a certain nationalism, remained. One Chinese student who had lived in Japan wrote in his diary that, while the Chinese had much to learn from Japan's modernizing Meiji ways, the Japanese were arrogant. "Japanese, Japanese," he lamented, "you have forgotten your debts." He implied, of course, that the Japanese had forgotten their great cultural debt to China. "Japanese," he continued, "your imperialism has succeeded but your conscience has perished."[49] It was a prescient statement: Japan would soon move toward a more stridently military path of imperialism.

The number of Chinese students living in Japan was not insignificant; they were one of the largest foreign groups. From 1896 to just before 1938, over one hundred thousand Chinese students pursued some form of study in Japan, creating a large and new class of lower- and middle-class restaurant customers eager to dine on something other than traditional Japanese

Figure 35. From 1894 onward Japanese caricatures of Chinese frequently depicted them as pigs. This cartoon is taken from the 1894 Japanese book offensively entitled, "Humorous Military Songs about the Chinks."[50]

---

[49] Sanetō Keishū, *Chūgokujin Nihon ryūgakushi*, p. 215.
[50] Yamazaki Kanei, *Chanchan kokkeigunka*.

cooking. Many of these students kept diaries in which they complained about Japanese food. In 1905, one of these exchange students, Huang Zunsan, wrote about ordering food on his first day in Japan: "Japanese food is truly quite simple," he noted. Later meals were not much of an improvement and he wrote: "I do not think I'm going to get used to this." Dinner was often one small soup and some pickled vegetables served with a bowl of rice.[51] Zhou Zuoren, brother of China's famed modern novelist, Lu Xun, and long-time resident and observer of Japanese culture, did not hold Japanese food in high regard (though he cherished other aspects of the country). Reminiscing about Japanese *bentō*, boxed lunches, Zhou observed that the Japanese did not mind cold food or rice; the Chinese on the other hand preferred hot food and shunned chilled rice.[52]

Guides to Japanese language and customs could be purchased in most major cities in China, offering students tips on how to get by in Japan. Of the long list of "do's and do nots," a few stood out. Students needed to curb their Chinese scholar/official behavior, and were advised to "only spit in a spittoon" and to "urinate into the toilet correctly." "If you are eating on a tatami mat and drop some food, pick it up and put it to the side of your setting, do not eat it," the guides recommended. "Japanese rice digests poorly so be careful not to over eat."[53] Publishing companies that produced social guides to correct etiquette were not the only institutions concerned with Chinese exchange students in Japan. An argumentative essay in the 1905 "Central Review" (*Chūō kōron*), a respected and highbrow Japanese journal, explained to readers why it was in Japan's interest to offer these overseas exchange students a positive experience, rather than bullying them. The article cogently reasoned that Japan benefitted economically from Chinese students who spent money and then returned to China, having acquired the accoutrements of Japanese civilization during their studies. The author noted that Chinese students did not mingle with others and tended to "travel en masse even in town, like schools of fish in the ocean."[54] Although he supported policies to recruit and retain Chinese students, the author commented that they were often dirty – not washing, and spitting from their windows. They also got into constant arguments.[55]

---

[51] Sanetō Keishū, *Chūgokujin Nihon ryūgakushi*, p. 155.
[52] "Riben guankui," originally published in May 1935, reprinted in Zhong Shuhe, ed., *Zhou Zuoren wenleibian*, Vol. 7, pp. 32–33.
[53] Sanetō Keishū, *Chūgokujin Nihon ryūgakushi*, pp. 194–195.
[54] Terada Yūkichi, "Shinkoku ryūgakusei mondai," *Chūō kōron*, January 1905, p. 18.
[55] Ibid., p. 19.

Clearly there was cultural friction on both sides. However, the writer did grasp the need for Japanese government plans to mitigate the situation, because these Chinese students would repatriate to China with a Japanese education. Exchange students tend to think of their host country in positive terms, the writer argued – "our students who went to England believe in England and those who went to Germany love that country."[56] If Japan wanted good press in China from its former exchange students, the government needed to appreciate the urgency of the situation. Surely they did not want the Chinese to stop sending students and send them to Europe instead. In 1924, a secret Japanese Ministry of Foreign Affairs document described the conditions of interaction between Chinese students and the Japanese public in the west of Japan. It reported: "Average people look down on Chinese students and use derogatory language toward them. This is impeding the development of good relations between the two countries."[57]

Notwithstanding the difficult social relationship between Chinese students and their Japanese landlords, Chinese cooks in small restaurants all over Japan had an eager clientele for what would develop into the new dish of ramen. Foreign students needed an alternative type of dish because, for the most part, they did not take to Japanese cuisine. Rising Chinese student numbers and solid market demographics serendipitously coincided with Japan's industrialization, which thrust another eager group of eaters into the market – factory workers and the new urban working class.

Imperialism and Food

At the turn of the century, Japan's national cuisine was in a constant state of revolution. The situation had been in flux from the Tokugawa era; Meiji social and political transformations helped to continue the change. The Japanese had left their previous taste buds behind but had not yet switched to the hybrid diet that would sweep the country by storm during the 1920s. Cookbooks and recipes in magazines were more prevalent, showing not only that more women were literate but also that they spent time in the kitchen and controlled the daily menu. These women did not necessarily

---

[56] Ibid., p. 20.
[57] "Zaihonna ryūgakusei kankei zakken," H5-0-0.1, letter from the governor of Fukuoka Prefecture in Kyushu to the Home Minister on October 27, 1924, (Ministry of Foreign Affairs Archives, Tokyo.)

do the cooking or cook alone – many families had maids, on whose treatment the early household budget books gave advice to their readers. Despite these changes and the ongoing discussions of food culture, no Japanese "national cuisine" would truly form until after World War II. National preferences may have changed but the market necessary for the creation of ramen required what one well-known anthropologist of food, Arjun Appadurai, labels "a postindustrial, postcolonial process."[58] Japan had to undergo yet another revolution after World War II that would divide it further from its traditional food roots, following modernization and the loss of empire.

Ramen could not have become a symbol of Japanese national cuisine without the modern media, who were instrumental in the construction of the concept of a national cuisine. At the turn of the century, various stores were offering similar noodle soups with meat and soy sauce to an expanding clientele. These stores served Chinese students and industrial workers in regions around Japan. Over time, eager Japanese media outlets, newspapers and magazines noted each local dish and dressed it up as something that represented the nation. Although changes in dining started as local transformations, regions wanting to increase tourism and investment in their communities competed for diners, and slowly constructed a concept of a "national" cuisine. In actuality, any national cuisine is merely a deeply held set of assumptions about what a meal is. In a divided nation of fiefs and competing domains there had been little chance for such uniformity, but as Edo slipped into Meiji and the Meiji into Taisho, Japan transformed as a nation and its cuisine slowly homogenized. On the cusp of this change, consumers (both foreign and domestic) wanted not only more food and more nutritious food, but also improved taste. A few more years were needed to locate the final ingredient necessary to create a market that would accept the arrival of ramen; by the end of that era the search for "delicious" was possible.

The quest for delicious food mirrored the social and political changes Japan underwent during the final decade of the nineteenth century and first few decades of the twentieth. These shifts set the stage, in the evolution of Sino-Japanese cultural exchange, for a monumental set of events that would alter Japanese national cuisine forever. The Japanese were now, generally speaking, wealthier and eating a larger variety of foods including

---

[58] Arjun Appadurai, "How to Make a National Cuisine: Cookbooks in Contemporary India," *Comparative Studies in Society and History*, Vol. 30, No. 1, January 1988, p. 5.

meats, oils and vegetables from all over the world. Japan was becoming more multi-ethnic, with large East Asian populations joining masses of day laborers and the urban poor to create a new public demand for cheap eateries. A multitude of new shops, combined with new habits of eating out and a social quest for delicious, spurred this transformation. An additional factor was the new role of women in producing nutritious and healthy meals that their families could enjoy around the dinner table at home – replacing the rural cottage industry setting where family took second place to the daily demands of making a living. These factors all began to play out and expand into the ensuing century. Ramen was just around the corner and the Japanese, it seemed, could almost taste it.

CHAPTER SEVEN

EMPIRE AND JAPANESE CUISINE

In the early twentieth century, Japan was still a hungry nation. The country and its leadership were not just hungry for power, they were literally hungry. Japan was wealthier and gaining international economic power but, as Murai Gensai described in his bestselling guide "The Gourmand," its expanding population lusted after taste and ached to be gourmands. The late-Meiji and Taisho eras were periods of dramatic transformation in Japan and not just in the kitchen. Labor unions raised their profile and attempted to secure better wages and a reasonable workday, breaking traditional patterns of employment exploitation and raising the political consciousness of the working poor.

After Japan defeated Russia in the Russo-Japanese War of 1904–5, Indians – especially those bent on proclaiming independence from Britain – flocked to Japan. Millions of colonial subjects throughout the world and especially in the southeast and far east of Asia thought of Japan as the first "colored" nation to have defeated a "white" nation. During Japan's historic war, an article in the *New York Times* in April 1905 went so far as to criticize the idea that Japan represented a "yellow peril," arguing instead that it represented modernity and Westernization in Asia.[1] As the twentieth century opened, Japan stood as a beacon of what a non-white, modernizing nation could achieve and attracted many Asian revolutionaries.

The influence of refugees from the subcontinent was not always limited to the political. Indian revolutionary Rash Behari Bose, for example, sought shelter in Japan in the years around World War I. Bose found protection under Toyama Mitsuru, a shadowy pan-Asianist who collaborated with other like-minded nationalists to promote the idea of "Asia for the Asiatics." Toyoma proclaimed that Japan should lead the new order in the East, supported imperial expansion and had ties to Sun Yat Sen, the early leader of Chinese nationalism. While Bose remained an active revolutionary, he also had to make a living and did so by concocting a light, zesty curry sauce designed specially to suit the Japanese palate and that sat atop

---

[1] "Yellow Peril," *New York Times*, April 18, 1905.

a mound of rice. His creations led to a curry rice boom that enveloped the nation in the 1920s, accompanying the rise in popularity of Chinese food.[2]

As the working classes struggled for money and access to previously denied social and political privileges, Japan's empire spread its wings and in addition to Taiwan, encompassed Korea and parts of China, as well as several islands in the South Pacific. The transition to the Taisho imperial reign in 1912 saw more changes in the national diet and attitudes toward foreign cuisines. China underwent a revolution and declared the country a republic. In Japan, Chinese cooking began to be seen as tasty and worthy of emulation. Japan's first modern book about Chinese cooking was published in 1886, and it was followed by eight more (a small number when compared with the one hundred and thirty cookbooks published on Western food). However, it is a remarkable fact that Chinese food was not served once at the imperial palace during the entire Meiji reign. The Japanese Imperial Army also avoided Chinese food until the early Taisho era, although its soldiers fought several major battles in and around the Chinese continent.[3] This changed abruptly during the early Taisho era, when Japanese Army Quartermaster Marumoto Shōzō invited Chinese chefs to Japan and included their recipes in the military menu. Two decades later he wrote a book about Chinese cuisine. For the first time, Chinese recipes began showing up in navy cookbooks.[4]

Time is the Meter of Civilization – the Birth of Delicious

In the Japanese language, as with other languages, speakers can choose numerous adjectives to describe something that tastes good. The most common is *oishī*, a term that you should employ when you eat at a friend's house. He or she, but usually she, will respond in a self-deprecating manner, saying that she is sorry the taste might not be to your liking or that it did not turn out the way she had hoped. Do not worry, this is all polite conversation, a minor part of the scripted dialogue that takes place when you are offered the rare chance to enter someone's home in Japan. If you fail to say that the dishes are *oishī*, then you have not fulfilled your part of the bargain, and your hostess will not have a chance to say how small her kitchen is or how poor her supplies – the prescribed etiquette of host and

---

[2] Kosuge Keiko, *Karē raisu no tanjō*, pp. 156–158.
[3] Tanaka Seiichi, *Ichii taisui – Chūgoku ryōri denraishi*, pp. 182–185.
[4] Ibid., p. 203.

guest. Saying that something is delicious in Japanese means more than "This food tastes good, thanks," and involves a conversation that is more about your mutual obligations as host and guest.

There are other ways of remarking that food is delicious – for example, *sugoku oishī*, which emphasizes something as truly delicious. *Taihen* or *totemo* or *monosugoku oishī* means really, truly and marvelously delicious. The other term that is frequently heard is *umai*. *Umai* means delicious and historically it was the preferred term, employed more by men than women to describe food that tasted very good. However, there is another side to this rather complex word even more difficult to translate – *umami*. The Umami Information Center in Tokyo defines *umami* as "the fifth taste," the anchor in the relay race of the first four tastes of sweet, sour, salty and bitter. In the late nineteenth century, German scientists hypothesized that four major tastes dominated the mouth and that all other tastes sprang from them. Many theorists of taste disagreed and criticized this myopic belief by pointing out that other flavors abounded: putrid, watery, alkaline, harsh, etc. Nonetheless, the theory that the food world consisted of four tastes reigned supreme until the early part of the twentieth century when the Japanese idea of *umami*, or savory, would slowly make a grand entrance.

Over the centuries Japanese cuisine had employed two main ingredients to make food more palatable: *konbu* and *katsuobushi*, both of which made meals more savory or heartier – bringing out the embedded natural taste and making it more easily recognized by the tongue. These ingredients are filled with an amino acid called glutamine which adds a richness to flavor. *Konbu* is kelp, a thick, leafy type of seaweed with a distinctive taste – the product the hapless itinerant salesman was trying to sell before being overtaken by the bumbling samurai in the *kyōgen* play discussed in a previous chapter. Kelp is rarely eaten on its own. It is boiled in water to make a stock that is then used for seasoning. *Katsuobushi* is the flesh of the bonito fish, first boiled or steamed, then dried in the sun, or smoked and flaked. It is frequently added to create a savory broth or to "thicken" foods, to give the flavor some depth.

The best way to explain *umami* as a taste is to think about the four tastes in a kind of three-dimensional pyramid with flavors along the bottom axes and one at the top point. *Umami*, is the culmination or the pinnacle along these flavor axes – neither sweet nor salty but a bit of both, and halfway between bitter and sour. It thus sits exactly in the middle of the three dimensional pyramid. *Umami* is, in a sense, all flavors combined at the same time and that makes it an extremely savory taste. And yet the flavor does not really have a taste in itself. *Umami* enhances naturally occurring flavors.[5]

Ajinomoto, "the essence of taste," was the first company to produce monosodium glutamate (MSG), the food additive that creates the flavor of *umami*, invented by Professor Ikeda Kikunae from Tokyo University. The company began operations in 1908 and soon produced the additive on an industrial scale. The patent holders intended the MSG additive to be mixed into food to enhance its natural flavor. It could be made into a broth, or *dashi* in Japanese, and served as soup, or added as gravy to create a savory taste. In short, MSG makes food more pleasant tasting and adds richness to the natural taste. Contrary to popular belief, however, MSG has no taste nor is it salty even though its scientific name sounds as if it should be. The additive creates the sensation of *umami*, that fifth taste. The seasoning was not initially used in the making of ramen but its arrival on the market altered the taste that Japanese consumers demanded.

What is fascinating is why people crave the *umami* flavor. Ikeda hypothesized that "the taste of glutamate is closely associated with animal food" with the result that people are drawn to the flavor almost physically because it leads to an intake of "nutritive foods."[6] American chemists and food industry leaders were impressed. Their tests revealed that when glutamate was added to foods it stimulated a "tingling feeling in the mouth and the taste sensation persists." American researchers added that "this glutamate sensation, independent of true taste, has been described as a 'feeling of satisfaction.'"[7] It is hard now to imagine the dramatic impact this invention had on the market, with our gourmet television shows and manufactured food products available in local stores, but the appearance of MSG was an epoch-making moment for the food industry. The additive held the power to make bland and not necessarily pleasant food palatable and tasty.

Ikeda was an excellent chemist who had completed advanced research in Germany, like many of his academically gifted Japanese counterparts; but he was not a businessman. The "essence of taste" product succeeded only because of Ikeda's association with Suzuki Saburō. They took out a

---

[5] Kawamura Yōjirō, *Umami mikaku to shoku kōdō*, p. 5.

[6] Kikunae Ikeda, "New Seasonings," (translated by Yoko Ogiwara and Yuzo Ninomiya) *Journal of the Chemical Society of Tokyo*, no. 30, pp. 820–836, 1909) in *Chemical Senses* 27, 2002, pp. 847–849. See also Jordan Sand, "A short history of MSG: Good science, bad science and taste cultures," *Gastronomica* 5, no. 4, 2005, pp. 38–49.

[7] Daniel Melnick, "Monosodium Glutamate – Improver of Natural Food Flavors," *The Scientific Monthly*, Vol. 70, No. 3., March, 1950, p. 202.

patent together and started to produce MSG on a large scale by isolating glutamine acid from wheat. It had previously been expensive and time-consuming for chefs to make their own *dashi*, or soup stock. With MSG, what used to take hours of preparation could be achieved quickly with a few sprinkles and this had serious implications for small, family-run food-stands and the home kitchen. MSG was an industrial-sized revolution in cuisine. Ajinomoto would also prove itself a prescient company in terms of advertising.

Most people today, and perhaps especially in contemporary Japan, use a variety of spices and industrially produced flavors in our kitchens, but this was not the case in the early twentieth century. The Japanese were not convinced that such products were necessary, nor did they quite understand their use. The infant Ajinomoto Company had to teach the public to appreciate the idea of convenience and how to make use of the new product. Several anti-seasoning campaigns at the time spread rumors that hinted the additive was made from snake and at first people avoided using it.[8] To attract customers, Ajinomoto placed an advertisement in the *Asahi Newspaper* in May 1909, using a geisha posed in an apron as the model. The company also handed out thousands of leaflets on the street. When this campaign failed the company resorted to public tastings and paying *chindon* performers to march around the country praising the new product. *Chindon* performers were elaborately costumed street musicians in the late Taisho and early Showa reigns paid to parade around towns drawing attention to a particular brand or object.[9] These activities helped to raise awareness of the seasoning, and sales rose – but only slowly at first, because pharmacies stocked the product in a glass bottle that looked like it should contain medicine.[10] Sales increased rapidly once Ajinomoto marketed MSG as a spice and additive for cooking. The company concentrated its efforts in Osaka, where a *konbu*-heavy cuisine was favored. Initially, seventy percent of its sales were in the central Kansai region. The media appeared to understand the fantastic potential of MSG. One Japanese magazine in July 1909 unapologetically announced that the arrival of MSG "provided a huge thunderclap of good fortune to our world of Japanese cooking."[11] A savory flavor also complemented the noodle and

---

[8] Ema Tsutomu, *Tabemono no konjaku*, p. 210.
[9] Ingrid Fritsch, "Chindonya Today – Japanese Street Performers in Commercial Advertising," *Asian Folklore Studies*, Vol. 60, No. 1, 2001, pp. 51–54.
[10] Ōtsuka Tsutomu, editor, *Shokuseikatsu kindaishi*, p. 111.
[11] *Meiji nyūsu jiten*, Vol. 8, July 22, 1909, p. 6.

wheat dishes slowly being imported from China and adapted for the tastes of Japanese consumers during the 1910s and 1920s. The newly-born clamor for a savory taste was an essential consumer demand that helped initiate the birth of ramen and formed a large basis for its popularity.

Ikeda and Suzuki were not the first to discover the essence of taste. The German scientist Karl Ritthausen had already managed to isolate the savory constituent within a protein but he was not able to mass-produce the essence, as technology had enabled the Japanese to do. The Chinese had also tried to discover the chemical composition of savory flavors and many entrepreneurs and chemists spent countless hours trying to match Japanese industrial know-how. Wu Yunchu succeeded. Wu was born in the 1890s outside Shanghai and studied at a school attached to the Jiangnan Arsenal. In the 1920s, he managed through experimentation to manufacture the Japanese product MSG that was proving so popular with Shanghai restaurants and patrons. He labeled his product *"weijing,"* a Chinese term similar to the Japanese label of "the essential taste," and applied for a patent. By the mid-1920s, Chinese in Shanghai and other modernized cities in China spent one million US dollars annually to enjoy the extra flavor MSG brought out in food.[12] Ajinomoto accused Wu of patent infringement but the plants kept producing and by 1928 domestically produced Chinese MSG had outstripped imports from Japan.

In many ways MSG was the archetypal colonial food product. Japan required massive amounts of soy, rice and other cereals to feed the nation and imported a larger quantity each year from China and its colonies of Taiwan and Korea. The Ajinomoto company conducted intensive research into the Korean food market, giving away samples as a marketing incentive at cold noodle shops. MSG was also used in *seolleongtang*, a thick soup made with beef stock. Korean cold noodle shop-owners formed an association in Seoul to link up with Ajinomoto and receive direct distribution. Cold noodle associations formed in other urban centers like Pusan in the south, Pyongyang in the north and Inchon and Wonsan toward the west. It is not clear if the Japanese Governor General of Korea Yamanashi Hanzō formally supported Ajinomoto but the company president of Ajinomoto was one of his school friends.[13]

---

[12] James Reardon-Anderson, "Chemical Industry in China, 1860–1949," *Osiris*, 2nd Series, Vol. 2, 1986, pp. 188–189.

[13] Keun-Sik Jung, "Colonial Modernity and the Social History of Chemical Seasoning in Korea," *Korean Journal*, Vol. 45, no. 2, Summer, 2005, p. 32.

As the famous Japanese novelist Natsume Sōseki wrote in his novel *Sore kara* (*And then*), the speed with which Japan was changing was flabbergasting to the older generation still accustomed to the patterns of life in rural Meiji. But "to live by the ethic of the past among the hourly demands of the modern life was to 'wage war against oneself'," Sōseki keenly observed.[14] As Japan continued to industrialize during the 1910s those hourly demands on life and labor would only increase, as did consumer demand for convenience and nutrition, all at a reasonable price of course. Sōseki was probably one of a very few sounding a note of caution about the breakneck speed of modernization; most Japanese eagerly championed the new and convenient. The biggest issue in improving life-style was that of time, one author wrote in a women's magazine. Japanese daily life required systemic change to advance, which meant people needed "to calibrate all the clocks of the house so that they tell the same time," he recommended. After all, he wrote, "Westerners observe time" – the implication being that Japanese did not and this was to their own detriment.[15] The new mass media developing during the Meiji and Taisho eras, with more consumer magazines and aggressively marketed advertising campaigns, also led to many changes in concepts and expectations concerning Japanese cuisine.

Food and Excrement

Even as the Japanese were adapting to new food products and trying new additives that improved taste, searching for more nutritious and tasty ways to modernize, prejudices about smell and hygiene still caused some people to avoid Chinese cuisine. The laboring classes slowly adopted cuisines from countries within Japan's growing empire but the intelligentsia and elites initially hesitated to try Chinese cooking. Through the 1910s, they still associated Chinese cuisine with a backward culture, quite different to the West, with which Japan was trying to identify. National cuisine and hygiene were markers of civilization. In the words of one historian of medical science, advanced nations became obsessed with what he terms

---

[14] As quoted in Fred Notehelfer, "On Idealism and Realism in the Thought of Okakura Tenshin," *Journal of Japanese Studies*, Vol. 16, No. 2, Summer 1990, p. 346.
[15] Tamura Kikujirō, "Seikatsu kaizen no dai ippo wa nani zoya," pp. 218–221, originally published in 1920, reprinted in Maruoka Hideko and Yamaguchi Mieko, eds., Nihon fujin mondai shiryō shūsei, Vol. 7, *Seikatsu*, p. 219.

"excremental colonialism."[16] Colonized areas were not seen as just socially and politically backward: what they ate was bad and their methods of sewage disposal were even worse.

During late Meiji, at the turn of the nineteenth century, many Japanese experienced China and Korea directly for the first time through travel, and their findings proved enlightening and shocking. Their negative experiences increased their regard for Japan and denigration of their Asian brothers across the sea. Japanese travel books, which appeared in great numbers during the early years of the twentieth century, frequently described the backwardness of Korean society. One book, Okita Kinjō's "The Backside of Korea," lambasted the small huts Koreans lived in as pigsties and said that the Korean way of defecating everywhere made Seoul the "shit capital" of the world, with a corresponding stench.[17] Okita held an even lower opinion of Korean cuisine. "There are people who imagine pig, dog, it's all the same in Korean food...it more or less seems like you are picking up horse dung and eating it, but that would be judging it too quickly because we know they are, after all, a rice-eating people."[18] Arakawa Gorō, in his travelogue "Contemporary Korea," was similarly denigrating: everything was so dirty, he complained, that Koreans could not distinguish *miso* (a fermented paste used to make Japanese soup) from *kuso*, or *miso* from shit.[19]

Japanese obsession with the relationship of bowel movements and the food of East Asia did not necessarily mean that their general perceptions of these countries were all negative. Japan was, after all, still largely agricultural and night soil (human waste) as a fertilizer was a topic of great concern to most farmers. In addition, the topic of toilet activity ranked very highly in all sorts of intellectual and popular literature. A 1908 newspaper article entitled "A Consideration of Urine" castigated Tokyo women for no longer peeing as they had used to – an obvious sign of urban decline. The anonymous article noted that in previous times women urinated by standing and sort of leaning back a little. (How this was accomplished was not explained in the article, nor were diagrams provided.) "Now, they

---

[16] Warwick Anderson, "Excremental Colonialism: Public Health and the Poetics of Pollution, *Critical Inquiry*, Vol. 21, No. 3., Spring 1995, pp. 640–669.

[17] As quoted in Peter Duus, *The Abacus and the Sword: The Japanese Penetration of Korea, 1895–1912*, pp. 401–403.

[18] Orita Kinjō, *Rimen no kankoku*, p. 76.

[19] As quoted in Peter Duus, *The Abacus and the Sword: The Japanese Penetration of Korea, 1895–1912*, p. 403; Arakawa Gorō, *Saikin Chosen jijō*, p. 89.

squat," the anonymous writer bemoaned, considering this unladylike.[20] One early-twentieth century article on bowel movements demonstrated the extent to which Japan looked down on other East Asian nations, since even Western excrement was considered higher class. This article, penned by an aristocrat and art history professor, explained that the Japanese consumed a lot of indigestible food, so when they defecated they expelled a lot of gas. Westerners ate more easily digestible foods so they excreted less, and the professor waxed poetic about the quality. Western excrement "comes out 'phew' like the stroke of a paint brush, long and thin with both ends tapered, similar to a piece of rope," he elegantly described.[21]

The Japanese were not alone in their obsession with hygiene as a marker of the level of the civilization; it was a common colonial trait. The finicky French in the Indochinese colonies were perturbed to have natives cooking food for their meals; supposedly this rendered the process unclean and threatened colonial health and welfare. Bakers in the French colonies advertised the "cleanliness" of their products, intending to assure customers that they were prepared by French hands. This mark of hygiene meant that, although the ingredients might not have French provenance, the artisan was French and his product was of French quality, not cooked by someone presumed to be racially inferior and hygienically questionable.[22]

Raising the Standard

The real sticking point for bureaucrats bent on modernizing Japan and rendering it the most advanced country in Asia remained kitchen hygiene. Since Japan was the modernizer of Asia, it needed to look the part. Many authorities felt that traditional kitchens were symptomatic of a larger national problem. The Taisho population obsessed over what it termed "cultured living," or *bunka seikatsu*, a kind of forerunner to the Martha

---

[20] March 20, 1908, *Kokkei shinbun*, reprinted in Koishikawa Zenji, ed., *Kawaya to haisetu no minzokugaku*, pp. 36–37.
[21] Iwamura Tōru, "Nihon no fun to seiyō no fun," in December 1911 *Niko Niko*, reprinted in Koishikawa Zenji, ed., *Kawaya to haisetu no minzokugaku*, pp. 64–66. See also David Howell, "Fecal Matters: Prolegomenon to a History of Shit in Japan," in Ian J. Miller, Julia Adney Thomas, and Brett L. Walker, eds., *Japan at Nature's Edge: The Environment of a Global Power*.
[22] Erica Peters, "National Preferences and Colonial Cuisine: Seeking the Familiar in French Vietnam," *Proceedings of the Western Society for French History*, Vol. 27, 1999, pp. 152–153.

Stewart movement in the United States during the early twenty-first century. Cultured living required hygiene and convenience. During the pre-World War I era, a mix of rice and other grains was often the mainstay of the Japanese diet, but bread offered an easier and quicker way to prepare and eat breakfast for the growing urban sectors of society. This idea of convenience would contribute to the later appeal of ramen – eating without the long preparation necessary for most Japanese dining. The *jochū*, maid, or matron of the home if there were no servants, had to get up two hours before breakfast to cook rice and make miso soup. Bread was a massive time-saver: you just cut a slice, slapped butter on it, drank some coffee and walked out the door to work. One woman wrote in an April 1913 women's magazine, "Housewife's Companion" (*Shufu no tomo*), that in her kitchen she only had a frying pan and one pot – having bread at her disposal reduced the hours she had to spend in the kitchen because she only had to cook rice once a day.[23] There were no electric kettles or rice-cookers in those days so rice was made by boiling water over a small coal stove that required repeated fueling, constant attention while cooking and then maintenance while cooling down.[24] If rice were eaten at night as well, the same time-consuming processes had to be repeated, new fuel for the fire collected and the old ashes disposed of.

Maids were an indispensable part of nineteenth and early-twentieth-century cooking. Cheap labor in urban areas was readily available and food preparation took an inordinate amount of time when one had to make everything from scratch. One Japanese manual, entitled "Renovating Kitchens," explained in great detail how to extract the most work from your maid for the smallest amount of money. Clearly, treating one's servants with respect and on equal terms with other laborers was not foremost on readers' minds. The chapter on hiring maids suggested that you ask them straight out: "Do you have any kitchen experience?" If the answer was "No," the manual recommended that you paid them less. The book also suggested that if they claimed that they had experience you could then make them produce written proof from a previous employer and use it as the basis for their hourly wage.[25]

---

[23] Shōwa joshi daigaku shokumotsu kenkyūshitsu, editors, *Kindai Nihon shokumotsu-shi*, p. 443.

[24] A full description of the social impact of the change in how rice was cooked and how such appliances spread in Asia can be seen in Nakano Yoshiko and Ō Kōka, *Onaji kama no meshi: nashonaru suihanki wa jinkō roppyaku hachijūman no honkon de naze happyaku-mandai ureta ka.*

[25] Amano Seisei, *Daidokoro kairyō*, p. 177. Domestic servants were a constant issue in letters to the editor as well. One such letter from 1919 typified housewife complaints

Figure 36. Picture of a housewife and maid discussing kitchen tasks from *Renovating Kitchens.*[26]

Not only were ways of cooking Japanese food changing in the kitchen but new tools and new products were coming onto the market. The late-Meiji and early-Taisho eras were characterized by advances in Japanese food science and tremendous progress in general science as well. New inventions, such as the production of MSG, allowed tastes to reach a much wider audience than ever before and food science products changed the

---

concerning how to deal with uncooperative servants; letter to the editor, "I do not like maids that are hard to use," from January 14, 1919 in Catalogue House, editors, *Taishō jidai no mi no ue sōdan*, pp. 298–299.

[26] Amano Seisei, *Daidokoro kairyō*.

face of East Asian food. The Meiji Restoration was more than just a political reconstruction of Japan; it reformed deep social structures encompassing science, technology and popular attitudes. The new science of food also introduced exciting new treats to Taisho Japan, such as milk chocolate bars that proved immediately popular, fermented yoghurt drinks sold as health tonics (the soft drink *Calpis*), sweet lemonade drinks known as *ramune*, chewy caramels and other sugary snacks.[27] The public's desire for the exotic and the new was met with a deluge of products, initially tied to the West but later derived or sourced from China and East Asia. The Japanese mass media played a fundamental role in changing the way people cooked. Women's magazines such as "Ladies' Companion" (*Fujin no tomo*) now focused on food and cooking with renewed attention to hygiene, nutrition, economy, convenience and novelty.[28] Chinese food was gaining ground in restaurants and slowly proving popular in the home as well. Tastes had changed in a fundamental way.

The kitchen, hygiene, personal health and the stability of the family were all tied together around the time of World War I (1914–1918) into an important symbol of a modern, civilized and advanced country. One male writer in a Japanese women's magazine, "Housewife's Companion," explained the situation in the following way. "Currently in this war," he said, "Germany is fighting many other countries – England, the US, France and Russia. The men have left for the front and the women are taking care of the house and working away from home." He explained: "The home is the center of a nation's society. An orderly home with no waste assists national security. The first priority of business is to improve the economy of the home and the structure itself. We need to do away with rooms we do not need and put in Western-style doors so we are safe when we leave." "Of second order are Japanese kitchens: they are dark and very unhygienic. We really must improve this situation. Kitchens are like people's stomachs, the place for providing nutrition and thus a most important space," he said.[29]

To many Japanese in the early twentieth century, Chinese kitchens were equally abhorrent and the country itself was like a museum of Asian history. Japanese were ambivalent about Chinese cuisine but happy to import

---

[27] For more on the growth of sweets in Japanese food culture see Barak Kushner, "Sweetness and Empire: Sugar Consumption in Imperial Japan."

[28] Katarzyna J. Cwiertka, *Modern Japanese Cuisine – Food, Power and National Identity*, pp. 99–100.

[29] Yamawaki Gen, "Katei seikatsu no keizaitekini kairyō seyo," pp. 179–181, reprinted in Maruoka Hideko and Yamaguchi Mieko, eds., Nihon fujin mondai shiryō shūsei, Vol. 7, *Seikatsu*.

ingredients. China, or *Shina* as it was then frequently referred to in Japan, was seen as backward, embodying the repellent corruption typified by the Empress Dowager Cixi and President Yuan Shikai, a former Qing official who helped govern China when it first became a republic. Kodama Kagai expressed this disdain in a 1911 Tokyo guide when he wrote about the cramped housing and small entertainment venues and restaurants squashed together in the Chinese quarters in the city. "There were many Chinese restaurants – *Shina ryōri*," he wrote. "They are covered in a kind of great rodent-colored film of dirt. When you opened the door smoke billowed out with the stench of pig fat and you got the feeling it was a sad and decrepit place. Pork is tasty but it's the food of an indolent and withering people."[30]

Despite its sense of superiority, Japan was far from a utopia for the majority of its population. The working conditions for laborers, even after the passage of The Factory Act in 1916, were not ideal. The legal working day was twelve hours long in organizations that employed more than fifteen persons. Women and children were guaranteed two holidays a month and a half hour's rest after a half day of labor.[31] In 1917, Suzuki Bunji, a leader of Japan's labor rights movement, described mines that employed 70,000 women where "they work in the bowels of the earth, naked like the men, wearing only a little breech-clout.... They are so like animals they can hardly be called human."[32] The 1918 rice riots, led mostly by women, "stand out as a sign of women's frustration and rage in the economic and political realms, capitalism, which made leaps during the war, and changed the face of urban life...."[33] Even by 1921, only 10% of the population could be classified as middle class.

Ramen Debuts on the Japanese Stage

It was amidst this swirling vortex of new food technology, a growing Chinese presence, and the gap between extreme wealth and downtrodden penury, that ramen emerged into the Japanese food market – albeit in a

---

[30] Kodama Kagai, *Tōkyō inshōki*, p. 80.
[31] Herbert H. Gowen, "Living Conditions in Japan," *Annals of the American Academy of Political and Social Science*, Vol. 122, The Far East, November 1925, pp. 161–162.
[32] Herbert H. Gowen, "Living Conditions in Japan," pp. 162–163. See also Iwaya Saori, "Work and Life as a Coal Miner: the life history of a woman miner," in Wakita Haruko, Anne Bouchy and Ueno Chizuko, eds., *Gender and Japanese History*, Vol. 2: The Subject and Expression/Work and Life, pp. 413–448.
[33] Barbara Sato, *The New Japanese Woman*, p. 30.

still less than complete form. Ramen was not immediately chic; it did not sell hundreds of thousands of bowls per day as it does now; nor did it necessarily represent Japanese cuisine. This was, after all, only the beginning. What ramen did offer was a full stomach and a cheap, nutritious alternative to a rice-based diet. What is more, ramen was a national phenomenon, sold not just in Tokyo or the international city of Yokohama, as so many products were. Ramen was not a *kudaru* or *kudaranai* food – it had neither royal nor common provenance. It was so new that no one could be sure how the savory noodle soup had come about. As we have seen in the previous chapters, the conditions that helped ramen arrive on the market appeared in different forms all over the country.

Kanagaki Robun had described a rapidly changing Japan in late-Edo and early-Meiji times, and the first decades of the twentieth century saw a Japan that was equally restless. The nation was becoming an empire and home to more and more non-native Japanese. The growing heterogeneity of the Japanese population and the consequent merging of food preferences, combined with a changing landscape of consumer demands, produced some unusual results. In 1911, the Takeya Cafeteria in Sapporo began offering a small amount of Chinese food to its mixed clientele. The cafeteria served many of the students flooding into the newly established imperial Hokkaido University, which had one hundred and eighty Chinese exchange students. One day a Chinese worker, Wang Wencai, who had worked in the Soviet Far East, stopped in to eat. The proprietor Ōhisa Masaji soon hired Wang as a short-order cook, changing his menu to feature "Chinese food." This may have been for economic reasons; it is possible that Ōhisa had heard of restaurants in other regions attracting customers in this way. Wang made numerous meat noodle dishes and a particularly popular one was called "*Shina soba*," Chinese noodles. The noodles were not like any other noodles with which the Japanese were familiar. Unlike *soba* noodles, which break easily and *udon* noodles, which are thick and slippery, Wang's noodles had a springy consistency and he bathed them in a meaty broth. The springy noodles he crafted were made with alkaline water because he used a bit of carbonate of soda in the dough.[34] Wang made several varieties of meat soup with a chicken base, vegetables and salt broth. They were an instant hit.

The exact geographical provenance of the ramen noodle soup and how it gained the name *ramen* remain unclear. There are various theories but

---

[34] Okuyama Tadamasa, *Bunka menruigaku rāmenhen*, p. 56.

many just called it "Chinese noodles" or *Shina soba*. Until just after World War II, peddlers on carts around urban and rural areas would call out in the late afternoons and early evenings, announcing their arrival with a mournful toot on a tiny trumpet and a tuneful refrain referring to *Shina soba* or Chinese noodles: "Chinese Noodles! Hey There, Chinese Noodles for Sale!" Many of the peddlers were Chinese, and "Chinese noodles" implied something different from ordinary Japanese noodles. Takeya Cafeteria customers rarely asked for "Chinese noodles," though, but merely barked, "Gimme some of that chinky soup." One theory suggests that Ōhisa's wife had the idea of calling the noodle dish *ryūmen*, after the willow trees across the street from their shop; *ryū* is a Japanese reading for the Chinese character for willow and *men* means noodles in Japanese. Noodle stalls in late-nineteenth-century Yokohama had been called *ryūmen* stalls (written with different characters but the same pronunciation) so it is possible that the label just traveled north to Hokkaido. Another possibility often considered is that, when Wang was done making his dish he would yell to the front in Chinese, "*hao le!*" ("Ready!") but with his northeastern Chinese pronunciation it sounded more like "*hao la!*" Wang had an accent that was perceived as harsh by the Japanese, who would have focused on the harder "*la*" sound, which could also have been heard as "*ra*." The term for noodle in the Chinese and Japanese languages uses a similar reading for the same character, *mian* in Chinese and *men* in Japanese. So, uncouth customers might joke and demand some of the "*la – men*," or "*la* noodles." This term, combined with the fact that in Chinese the actual word for pulled noodles is "*la-mian*," might have led to the term being written as "*la men*" on the Sapporo menu. The storeowners used katakana instead of the Chinese characters on the menu and gradually over time clients began to order the noodle dish by name.[35] Thus it was that a new dish was born: "*ra-men*," since the Japanese language does not distinguish between the pronunciation of "l" and "r."

Other Theories

In addition to the establishment described above, there are quite a few other shops that vie for the position of the birthplace of ramen, owing perhaps to the startling simultaneity with which ramen appeared, suddenly, all over the country. In 1910, in the Asakusa section of Tokyo, a new

---

[35] Ibid., p. 57.

store opened called *Rairaiken*, which might translate best as the "C'mon Shop." The shop served "Chinese noodles," *wontons* and *shūmai*, a Japanese style of wrapped and steamed Chinese pork dumpling. Dining was cheap and you could fill your stomach with a single serving. The man who started this new venture was Ozaki Kanichi, a former tax bureaucrat in Yokohama who retired at fifty-two and opened a Chinese restaurant.[36] It is important that Ozaki came from Yokohama because he would have experienced Chinese food there and seen the popularity of Chinese noodles in a city built specifically for foreigners to reside in. The sign above the store, which remained in business until 1943, announced "Nutritious Chinese Cooking – Noodles and Dumplings 7 sen." (A *sen* was a small unit of Japanese currency and until just after World War II one yen equaled 100 sen.)[37]

A few years later in 1925, in the city of Kitakata in Fukushima Prefecture in northeastern Honshu, another ramen shop appeared. Kitakata is not a populous city but it currently boasts eighty ramen establishments, the largest number per capita in Japan. The story of how Kitakata became the nation's ramen capital is intriguing and it illustrates the way in which regional identity and marketing played a role in the explosion of ramen shops. As will be explained in a later chapter, the Kitakata tale is both similar to the early-twentieth century Sapporo and Tokyo ramen shop origin stories, and unique. In 1925 a Chinese traveler from Zhejiang province, named Ban Kinsei in Japanese or Fan Qinxing in Chinese, arrived in Kitakata and opened a noodle shop. Unlike Japanese merchants, Ban managed his own shop, which he called *Genraiken*, or "The Original Come and Get it Shop," an obvious homage to the *Rairaiken* in Tokyo and a play on the popular name.[38] He located his shop in the rougher area of town near the railway station and his business flourished. But Ban's ramen success does not explain the postwar proliferation of ramen shops in the city of Kitakata. For that, readers need to wait until the postwar and a fuller understanding of the intersection between local identity and food tourism.

All of these theories sound plausible and make sense, so it is possible that they are all, in some way, true; or that a combination of them reveals the truth. It is virtually impossible to peg down one single explanation that substantiates the appearance and naming of similar dishes all over the country at almost the same time.

---

[36] Okada Tetsu, *Rāmen no tanjō*, pp. 91–92.
[37] Ibid., p. 93.
[38] Ibid., p. 97.

While Japanese urban areas modernized and Tokyo became one of the most advanced cities in East Asia, most people in Japan continued to eat a fairly poor diet. The Ministry of Home Affair's Bureau of Hygiene completed a survey in 1918 examining the constituents of the people's daily diet. In rural areas, people still did not consume very much rice, or indeed very much of anything.[39] The reason a majority of farmers ate such crude meals was purely economic; it made sense to produce millet to eat at home and sell the more expensive rice crop for cash. Traditional farmers before World War II ate pure white rice and *mochi* (sticky rice cakes) only a couple of times a year, if at all.[40] In early Taisho, Japan started having to import more to provide enough food for its people; during the same period, prices for most goods began to rise. Between 1903 and 1933, the amount of rice imported from Taiwan quadrupled and that from Korea rose about twenty-one times. Laborers, an important element in the transformation of urban cuisine due to their demand for cheap and filling meals, started to clamor for better wages and a greater share of the economic pie. This was not a full-fledged political revolution but a social campaign for equality and a higher standard of living.

The numbers of workers who earned money as day laborers in urban areas grew enormously throughout the 1910s and 1920s and these individuals often experienced economically rough times. Restaurants aimed specifically at the working poor, called "one-meal stands," *ichizen meshiya*, began to proliferate in areas where these people congregated. They were a slight improvement over the mid-Meiji "leftover food stalls," *zanpanya*, because the food was made fresh to order. At these stands you could order a bowl of rice topped with a sprinkling of vegetables or some other topping for a slightly higher price. On the days when it rained and there was no work, people would buy cheap bottles of alcohol or make do with water, abstaining from food as they waited for the next opportunity to work, earn a wage and eat. These "one-meal stands," combined with Tokyo's history as a Mecca for noodles and an urban population clamoring for inexpensive and tasty meals, were fundamental factors in the Japanese push toward ramen. Noodle stands, *soba-ya*, were also cheap places to eat.[41] Ex-colonials and former soldiers, many of whom had become culinary entrepreneurs on their return to Japan, had eaten a wide variety of foods and meat on the

---

[39] Segawa Kiyoko, Nihon no shokubunka taikei, Vol. 1, *Shokuseikatsushi*, p. 18.
[40] Ibid., pp. 24–26.
[41] Shōwa joshi daigaku shokumotsu kenkyūshitsu, editors, *Kindai Nihon shokumotsushi*, pp. 391–392.

Chinese continent. Noodle stands gradually expanded their repertoire to serve up varied offerings.

Nighttime Dining, Students and Erotic, Grotesque Nonsense

With an increasing population pouring into the cities and more avenues for pleasure and entertainment opening up in urban areas, the popularity of noodle dishes rose. Rickshaw-pullers, laborers going to work, playboys coming home after late nights – they all ate at the expanding number of food stalls. For those who could afford to eat well noodles were not usually a main meal; ramen was a snack to consume after carousing, or as a way to relax on the way home. For those who lived on the streets, toiled in day jobs or were factory or manual workers, ramen might sometimes serve as the main meal, like a form of fast food. Students increasingly also met their economic and nutritional needs with ramen. In the early 1920s, ramen became a symbol of the nocturnal passions of the evening as well as the meals of students and the working classes. The dish served many purposes.

But who staffed the noodle carts? Judging from advertisements, many companies looked for staff among impoverished customers, the unemployed and students from the hinterland known as the *"kugakusei"* or "hardship students." *Kugaku* was a late-Meiji era term used to describe students who wanted passionately to move up in the world, and who had to work to pay for this social advancement. Publishing consortiums produced numerous guides explaining in detail how students could acquire skills to succeed, a keen goal during the 1920s. One manual offered suggestions for possible jobs to pay for a student's studies: running an *oden* stand (selling seasoned boiled vegetables and tofu), running an *udon* noodle stand and being a rickshaw-puller were all listed as lucrative employment opportunities.[42]

The rapid proliferation of ramen during the prewar era suggests that the popularity of instant ramen today draws on a historical accretion of "noodle traditions" dating back to the Meiji era and before. One factor that enabled ramen to infiltrate daily life was its link to the entertainment districts, known as *sakariba* in Japanese. Ramen was the repast of choice for those enjoying themselves in bawdy districts of the city, which grew

---

[42] Chikamori Takaaki, "Roji ura no yashokushi," in Nishimura Hiroshi, ed., *Yashoku no bunkashi*, p. 79–90. On the *kugaku* phenomenon see Shimanuki Hyōdayū, *Shinkugakuhō*.

during this period. Ramen grew in popularity in parallel with an increase in transport, bars, brothels and movie theaters. In 1929, the international sociologist Isomura Eiichi conducted a survey of working hours in Tokyo and found that for those who worked in the food industry (in restaurants, servicing food stalls and transporting food) it was normal to work from dawn until midnight. This meant that transport had to be available and places of business open during the dark hours. Ramen or noodle shops that offered ramen-like products proliferated in Asakusa, the party center of Tokyo and home of *Rairaiken*. It was said that the smell of Chinese food wafted through the area. Chinese cuisine, especially dishes like "Chinese noodles," gradually started to be sold in these amusement quarters, to be eaten in the late evening or even early morning. Eating ramen itself became an act of pleasure or entertainment, part of the evening's fun. Whether working late or going to a play, movie or vaudeville cabaret, finishing the evening off with a bowl of ramen became *de rigueur* for a night out.

So what kind of image did people have of "*Shina soba*," what ramen was still being called up through the late 1940s? Mostly it was considered *ikagawashī*, or unseemly, a bit dirty perhaps. And precisely because it was a bit low-class, it was the perfect meal to enjoy in the entertainment districts. For youth, it was also a way of rebelling, as famed Japanese postwar novelist Ōoka Shōhei described. For him, sneaking out to eat forbidden Chinese noodles in an off-limits area of town provided a thrill in an otherwise staid adolescent life.[43] Japanese attitudes toward Chinese culture were still disparaging, mixing superiority, myth and perhaps a sneaking feeling of inferiority. It was not uncommon for ruffians, hoodlums and youths to eat at Chinese late-night establishments and then run away or start fights; both the cuisine and the shops were always a bit away from the mainstream and off the radar of the authorities.[44] However, the most important point about ramen was that it was eaten away from home – you specifically ate it at a stall or restaurant, or ordered it to be delivered. By the late 1920s, the noodle soup had become a meal for the lower classes and laborers as an addition to their regular three meals a day, as well as a late-night or other form of treat. Ramen had thoroughly infiltrated daily life.

---

[43] As cited in Migita Hiroki, "Rāmenshi o yoru kara yomu – sakariba demae charume to senzen no Tōkyōjin," in Nishimura Hiroshi, ed., *Yashoku no bunkashi*, p. 127.

[44] Migita Hiroki, "Rāmenshi o yoru kara yomu – sakariba demae charume to senzen no Tōkyōjin," pp. 110–160.

In his book *Taisho Illusions*, Kawamoto Saburō demonstrates the love/hate relationship that Japanese in the 1920s and 1930s had with Chinese culture and cuisine. In analyzing trends in Taisho era Japanese literature through the works of Nagai Kafū, Tanizaki Junichirō and Satō Haruo (among others), Kawamoto detects a subconscious psychological split. The Meiji reforms, growing military prestige and inclusion in the Allied camp during World War I had produced a superficially more confident and prosperous Japanese society. But anxiety lurked beneath the façade of Westernization. Though ramen was growing in popularity, a disdain toward China lingered.

Venerated novelist of prewar Japan, Tanizaki Junichirō praised Chinese food long before it became socially acceptable to do so. In a 1919 newspaper article in the *Asahi Newspaper,* Tanizaki said that since childhood he had always felt that Chinese cuisine was tastier than Western food and that his favorite restaurant in Shenyang (a city in the northern China region) was better than anything Tokyo could offer.[45] Tanizaki did not, however, appreciate all aspects of Chinese cuisine. "I like Chinese food and garlic is ok," he wrote, "but I do not appreciate the way the day after I eat it, it makes my piss stink. It's a bit annoying."[46] Even by the 1920s, with a prosperous Taisho life-style, the Japanese still ate a fairly bland diet and were disturbed by the pungent scent of garlic. Many Japanese intellectuals during the 1920s began to feel that Japan had turned its collective head away from its past and lost its true nature.[47] These intellectuals (and consumers) sought to replace what they believed lost with exotic Chinese or other foreign products. This is one explanation for the China boom of the late 1920s and early 1930s when Japanese consumers began to exoticize and favor Chinese-themed goods. This rise in Japanese consumption of "foreign" products included goods from the southern islands, including Taiwan; it was a way to return to a mythical but cherished "Asian" past. Kawamoto labeled this social and consumer phenomenon the "adoration for foreign lands." Eating ramen was part of this pattern. Did Japanese acceptance of Chinese cuisine reflect a more general interest in Chinese

---

[45] Tanizaki Junichirō, "Shina no ryōri," *Tanizaki Junichirō zenshū*, Vol. 22, pp. 78–83. This is in the Osaka edition of the newspaper.

[46] Chinba Junji, ed., *Tanizaki Junichirō, Shanhai kōyūki*, p. 43.

[47] Kawamoto Saburō, *Taishō genei*, p. 175 and p. 196. Many of these issues concerning the split between Meiji and Taisho generations are also detailed in J. Thomas Rimer, ed., *Culture and Identity: Japanese Intellectuals during the Interwar Years*.

songs, movies, and clothing during the era of the China boom?[48] It is hard to say definitively but the overlap is striking.

The evolution of this hybrid Japanese society that was churning up tradition and incorporating Chinese elements was loathed by some and welcomed by others. It was a mixing and matching of styles, high and low, which melded into something historian Miriam Silverberg has labeled the "grotesquerie" of Japan's mass culture by the late 1920s. The carnival atmosphere of theater, cinema, shopping and temple worship, as depicted at the playground of Asakusa, Tokyo, included "the celebration of food, the peep shows… where tourists 'up from the country' prayed and bought trinkets at the Asakusa Kannon, factory workers on their days off went to the moving pictures and where everyone, including the beggars, ate a panoply of foods from East and West."[49]

The Rise of "Nutrition"

With the rise of the consumption of Chinese noodle soups in shops, stalls and markets, the Taisho era witnessed a rise in awareness of the importance of nutrition; it was now more than merely a military matter. During the late Taisho era, the nation established its first national nutrition research center, the Imperial Government Institute for Nutrition, headed by Saeki Tadasu. Saeki, a noted scientist and founding father of Japanese diet research, had received his doctorate from Yale University. He wrote a book about the role that nutrition played in society and offered charts and diagrams explaining how the body acquired vitamins that allowed humans to thrive. The first page of his book displayed the music and lyrics to the *Nutrition Anthem*. The song explained, to a rather monotonous and marching rhythm, how nutrition kept one healthy and free of illness, provided strength and assisted in keeping one warm and cool as necessary during the year.[50] Saeki repeated what had come to be common knowledge by the mid-1920s, that "people and nations are built on food."[51] Following World War I, the military even made an effort to introduce Chinese food

---

[48] Michael Baskett discusses these images in film and entertainment in *The Attractive Empire: Transnational Film Culture in Imperial Japan*, pp. 72–84.
[49] Miriam Silverberg, *Erotic, Grotesque Nonsense: The Mass Culture of Japanese Modern Times*, p. 205.
[50] Saeki Tadasu, *Eiyō*, p. 1.
[51] Ibid., p. 215. Such a belief was mirrored in Japanese internal military and government reports. See Rikugun chōsa, "Heishoku oyobi sono heisotsu no nōritsu," January 30, 1922, (2A-036-00 委 137-100, Reel 008100), (National Archives, Tokyo, Japan).

dishes, popular because they were flavored with soy sauce and even sugar.[52] War and the expanding knowledge of science all had an impact on the development of Japanese consumer preferences and the rise of ramen.

As Japanese preferences for heartier tastes evolved and began to incorporate Chinese cuisine, Japanese scientific and political colonial projects in Korea and Taiwan began to receive Western acclaim. As an extension of these results and as a small effort against the German outpost on the Shandong peninsula in China during World War I, Japan took over the mandate of the Marshall Islands (Micronesia). During an exchange of League of Nations officers, a British Foreign Affairs official noted in his report on hygiene conditions in the Far East, that Koreans "as a race are fine in physique and have capable brains but they are indolent people and require rousing to action."[53] "Until the country came under Japanese influence," he added, "there was practically no sanitation."[54] The glossy magazine *Trans-Pacific* applauded Japan's colonial regime in Taiwan and its accomplishments in what was considered by most to be a malarial swampland. The article quoted Mr. Poultney Bigelow, a well-known American publicist: "Japan is now a competitor in the colonial race.... if Japan can succeed here [Taiwan], she can succeed anywhere. And in my opinion, Japan has achieved in Taiwan a brilliant Colonial triumph."[55] Japan was urbanizing and growing stronger in its stance toward China, but in fact, it still struggled in the shadow of the Western powers.

As it had done years earlier in Korea, in 1925 the Japanese government investigated the food situation in Taiwan. The investigation noted that the food situation in Taiwan was not totally dire, unlike Korea. Rice was found in abundance in numerous markets, as were fresh vegetables and fruit not previously obtainable in the home islands of Japan.[56] Nowadays, we tend to think of bananas as a common fruit but during the Edo period, bananas were occasionally available to the upper echelons of society: wealthy people would present them as special gifts to the shogun. In the modern era bananas first became available to the average consumer in 1903 – imported from Taiwan, Japan's new colony.[57]

---

[52] Katarzyna J. Cwiertka, *Modern Japanese Cuisine – Food, Power and National Identity*, p. 79.
[53] A.R. Wellington, *Hygiene and Public Health in Japan, Chosen and Manchuria*, p. 39.
[54] A.R. Wellington. *Hygiene and Public Health in Japan, Chosen and Manchuria*, p. 40.
[55] February-March 1923, special issue on Taiwan, Sagataro Kaku, superintendent of General Affairs of Governor general of Taiwan, "Taiwan Vastly Benefited by Japanese Rule," *The Trans-Pacific*, p. 77.
[56] Aiai Ryō, Shi Qian, *Kojiki shakai no seikatsu*, pp. 157–158.
[57] Tsurumi Yoshiyuki, *Banana to Nihonjin Firipin nōen to shokutaku no aida*, p. 1.

The experiences of a young Japanese who elected to go and work in Taiwan as a policeman in the mid-1920s illustrate the seemingly contradictory state of Japanese public opinion toward colonial cuisine. Before he went to Taiwan, while Aoki Setsuzō was serving his mandatory military service in the Japanese imperial military, a fellow soldier performed a skit about life on the island where he had grown up. "Taiwan is warm, rice is harvested twice a year and there is lots of food," his friend explained. And, he added, one can wear summer clothes all year round. The young Aoki recalled that his friend's comments were persuasive – prospects for employment sounded better in Taiwan than in Japan. Things were tough once you left the army; his friends were applying for simple patrol jobs and other low wage positions. Somehow it seemed like a good idea to go to Taiwan but the difference in food culture proved a difficult obstacle to overcome. In his recollections about early colonial life in Taiwan, Aoki obsessed about odor and food. He admitted that garlic was healthy and full of vitamins but wrote, "I can't stand the smell but the people who eat it can't smell themselves." "Because of that," he added, "when you enter a Taiwanese house here there is some indescribable stench. It's really a huge problem." The first time he entered a villager's house and was assailed by the smell of garlic he thought he was going to vomit.[58]

Edo Started the Process, Meiji Promoted and Taisho Finalized

While the Edo era laid the foundation for Japanese cuisine, the late Meiji and early Taisho eras helped to create modern Japanese taste and diet by embracing Chinese cuisine. The culmination of this was a product that we now recognize as ramen. One important ingredient in this process was the new urban working class, which demanded fattier foods. The Chinese food boom of the 1920s was due in part to increased numbers of wage earners living in urban areas. This ethnically mixed, blue-collar population accepted the more proletarian ideal of Chinese food, which emphasized taste over presentation, in contrast to "traditional" Japanese cuisine. We should remember that as late as 1915 Chinese laborers made up the largest foreign population in Japan.[59] By the 1920s, some Japanese appreciated Western food but many more enjoyed Chinese food, which was eaten

---

[58] Aoki Setsuzō, *Harukanaru toki Taiwan: senjūmin shakai ni ikita aru Nihonjin keisatsukan no kiroku*, p. 84.
[59] Andrea Vasishth, "A model Minority – Chinese community in Japan," in Michael Weiner, ed., *Japan's Minorities – The illusion of homogeneity*, p. 108

with rice like Japanese cuisine and provided a more easily digestible combination. Ichinohe Iseko, a professor at a women's college and a noted food researcher, traveled to Manchuria and Beijing to research Chinese food. In 1922, the Imperial Ministry Agency sent one of its food stewards, Akiyama Tokuzō, to study Chinese food at the former Qing palace.[60] By 1923, there were about 20,000 eating and drinking establishments in Tokyo, including maybe 1,000 Chinese restaurants.[61] In 1926, Yamada Masahei's book of recipes for simple Chinese dishes was published to popular acclaim.

Twentieth-century Tokyo witnessed three distinct eras of urban landscape and most existed in a garlic-free zone. There was the pre-1923 traditional Tokyo, which had arisen in a higgledy-piggledy, organic fashion out of Edo and Meiji times, densely packed with premodern and modern features that competed with each other until the Great Kantō Earthquake in 1923 reduced the city to rubble. Then there was the post-1923 city, an imperial capital struggling to rebuild itself, where a new cuisine for workers and the wealthy emerged as the city worked to prepare itself for the planned 1940 Olympics. Finally, there was post-World War II Tokyo, as we know it today.

In the versions of Tokyo before the great 1923 earthquake, noodle-sellers could be found not just in major cities but all around the country, in every region and town. They were mostly Chinese (or assumed to be) and they announced their wares by blowing melancholy little tunes on a *charumela*, or "little trumpet" (the word is a Portuguese loan word).[62] Chinese food, as the military discovered when it delighted soldiers by incorporating Chinese dishes into the official menu, was growing in acceptability. Japan's empire increased in parallel with its interest in Chinese continental culture as is revealed in the 1930 diary of Matsuzaki Tenmin, a journalist and later publisher of a well-known epicurean magazine. Like many other urban intellectuals, he appreciated Chinese cuisine because "it gave off the hybrid character of an acculturated mix of Eastern and Western."[63] Li Hong-en, a former imperial cook at the forbidden palace of the Qing court wrote a book on Chinese cooking with a military translator Honda

---

[60] Shōwa joshi daigaku shokumotsu kenkyūshitsu, editors, *Kindai Nihon shokumotsushi*, p. 636.
[61] Ibid., p. 643.
[62] Yonezawa mengyō kumiai kyūjūnenshi kankō īnkai edited, *Yonezawa mengyōshi*, p. 86. Ujima Eishun, *Ame to ame uri no bunkashi*, p. 55.
[63] Minami Hiroshi, ed., *Kindai shomin seikatsushi*, Vol. 6, p. 174.

Kiyohito, entitled "Easy Dishes for Chinese Cooking." Yamada Masahei's newspaper columns on Chinese food in the magazine "Housewife's Companion" also became a book and bestseller between 1931 and 1932.[64]

From the ashes of the Great Kantō Earthquake arose new department stores, complete with mass-market restaurants for eating and drinking, *taishū inshokuten*. At these establishments you could shop and eat, all under one roof. In a sense, the 1923 Great Earthquake eradicated so much of old Tokyo that businessmen and stores could break free from the past and invent new tastes and places for consumption. Rail transport was on the move and taste was no longer locally confined. Kansai tastes, the flavor of Osaka and the Kyoto basin, began to float upriver and ride north on steel tracks to compete in the new and open market in flourishing Tokyo, creating an entirely different, more homogenized national taste.[65]

Radio, introduced in 1925, also helped to advance cuisine. In 1926 in Nagoya, a home cooking show was launched, creating a new image of the family. These broadcasts were later published as a book, "'Four Seasons of Cooking' Radio Broadcasts." Efforts to render daily life more hygienic and cultural were part of the larger "Life Improvement Campaign" that rationalized and scientifically calculated values for women's household chores. This focus on women's domestic industry spurred a market in *sokuseki* (instant) foods, including curry and instant seasoning with MSG. By the middle to late 1920s, instant food products and ingredients were on sale, allowing some housewives or those servants who normally did the cooking to make tasty and nutritious meals for their families without spending hours in a hot, dark kitchen.[66]

The prewar Showa era introduced less change to Japan than did the Meiji era or postwar period. In 1926, at the start of the new imperial Showa reign, many household activities remained the same as they had been since traditional times. You still made your own fire in the kitchen and hauled your own water into the same area to cook. Around 1930, some sinks started to have faucets, but plumbing in Japan spread slowly – only 29.1% of the population had installed indoor plumbing in kitchens by 1935.[67] People were also starting to dine out more, especially those who lived near expanding urban markets. By the 1930s, there were 800 cafes

---

[64] Shōwa joshi daigaku shokumotsu kenkyūshitsu, editors, *Kindai Nihon shokumotsu-shi*, pp. 782–783.
[65] Ibid., p. 711.
[66] Ibid., pp. 713–715.
[67] Nihon shokuryō shinbunsha, *Shōwa to Nihonjin no ibukuro*, pp. 194–195.

and 10,000 waitresses in Osaka alone; in 1936, there were 12,000 young ladies offering hot beverages. At first, these new dining and socializing facilities served mainly middle class and intellectual men. The waitresses wore kimono with an apron and chatted with customers as they served. These women were an enormous social phenomenon, simultaneously lauded and demonized in the press and tabloid magazines, as well as novels.[68] The women worked mostly for tips at the cafes and so were beholden to their male customers.[69] They frequently accompanied men after hours to sweet shops and noodle restaurants. It was not just female employment that expanded into the food business. By the 1930s, people in the urban areas were eating out more in restaurants or at simple street side stalls often run by fringe members of the Japanese imperial expansion – Chinese, Manchurians, Koreans, or Taiwanese.

By the time Japan began to mobilize for war in China, the Chinese had been working in the country for years and Japanese cuisine was already a hybrid. In September 1931, the Japanese Kwantung Army initiated a strategy outside the city of Shenyang and used an exchange of gunfire with the Chinese military as the pretext to mobilize thousands more troops to subjugate large parts of Manchuria. Within a year, Japanese airplanes would be bombing Shanghai and Japan's aggressive inroads into China would begin full-scale. Japan's preparation for war and empire stunted the spread of Chinese cuisine and the full effect of prewar culinary exchange would not be felt until the close of the American occupation in 1952. The Taisho reign had set the stage for a real food revolution in the Japanese diet but this was obstructed by the militarism of the 1940s. Not until the mid-1950s would hybrid foods like ramen return to any significant extent. For the immediate future, what worried most inhabitants of the empire was less where they could get a good bowl of noodle soup and more the increasing likelihood of being called up to fight in a distant land and die for one's country.

---

[68] Miriam Silverberg, "The Café Waitress Serving Modern Japan," in Stephen Vlastos, edited, *Mirror of modernity: invented traditions of modern Japan*, p. 213.
[69] Ibid., p. 221.

CHAPTER EIGHT

WORLD WAR II CUISINE: A WORLD ADRIFT

Before ramen; before the advent of *pachinko* with its rattling, silver shiny balls; before the most famous Japanese professional wrestler of all time Rikidōzan beat the Sharpe brothers (touted as great American wrestlers even though they were born Canadian) in one of the biggest televised sporting events in Japanese postwar history; before Japanese traveled on holiday to exotic destinations, touring Guam and honeymooning in Hawaii. Before the economic boom of the late 1950s and the 1964 Olympics in Tokyo; before American imports of postwar wheat and forced distribution of farmers' produce in the cities – before all of that. And before Japan's surrender in 1945 after a devastating war of fifteen years (1931–1945) that brought economic and personal blight to half the globe, ending European colonialism but subjugating millions and killing as many. Before the introduction of bread, oil and piles of pork, beef and curry; before Tokyo with its gleaming convenience stores replete with shelves of fresh *onigiri*, boxed lunches, noodle soups, *oden*, hot *and* cold cans of coffee and soda.

Before all of these things appeared, wartime Japan was hungry.

Years ago, I joined a group from my friend's Buddhist congregation on its annual autumn pilgrimage to the Eihei Temple, the main temple for Sōtō Zen Buddhism located in southeastern Fukui Prefecture. The Eihei Temple was originally founded in the thirteenth century and like many monasteries it retains an aura of austerity and majesty. Zen Buddhism requires hours of unforgiving meditation. As my friend was the head priest in his village, I set out to try to fathom his devotion by attending the early morning Buddhist sermon. When you say "early morning" at a Buddhist temple you really mean the middle of the night. Leaving the pleasant confines of a fluffy futon at 3:45 am to stumble half awake into pitch black is the true mark of a believer. Fortunately, in my case, it was early autumn and not yet freezing cold. The halls are not equipped with air conditioning or heating so you are aware of your natural surroundings. Buddhists who make this pilgrimage really do believe in mind over matter, or at least over climate. In the very early morning it is often chilly, it is certainly dark and you are half asleep. Younger monks-in-training escort pilgrims to the inner rooms of the main hall where the senior monks are already kneeling in the formal sitting position in their black robes, silently meditating.

We pilgrims were led off to a side room by an assistant to the head of the temple and allowed to sit in relaxed, cross-legged fashion for a while. The head priest arrived dressed in a resplendent red silk robe and because he was quite elderly was allowed a small chair on which to sit while he chatted with us. He explained that the theme of the morning's sermon would be "abundance" and the concept of appreciating what one had in life. The subtext was essentially, "do not covet others' possessions too much and life will be easier." He then recounted a story from his childhood, near the end of World War II, to make his point.

Like many of his generation, the head priest's parents could not clothe and feed him so he was fostered out to a temple where he grew up. The temple housed and educated him; in return he helped out with chores and served as an assistant acolyte. He was around elementary school age at this time and conscious of his rank as the lowest in the strict pecking order of a prewar Japanese temple. One day, the wife of the then head priest made a meal of white rice and the acolyte was invited to eat with the family. "I couldn't believe my luck," the monk recounted to us. He was ecstatic because white rice was *the* delicacy – in wartime, especially, one could only dream of such a thing, given the strict rationing and general unavailability. The wife placed the lidded pot with the rice down on the tatami mat next to the low table and said she'd be right back, popping back to the kitchen to get some other items, the head priest told us as he warmed to his story. In traditional Japanese dining, the rice bucket is placed next to the head of the house, on the floor at the end of the table and doled out in order of seniority.

In the meantime the young monk sat there not believing his good fortune. "Suddenly," he continued, "in waddled the head priest's young infant, swaddled in diapers and little else. The kid picked up the spoon for scooping rice, [the *shamoji*] popped the lid off of the covered rice tub, stuck the paddle in and swirled it around." The priest demonstrated as if he had told this story before. "I wasn't sure if I should grab the spoon away, but before I could make a move the baby decided it was a good idea to stick the spoon in his diaper. He jammed the rice paddle into his diapers, rubbed it around a bit and then returned it to the pot of rice. Then he shuffled off," he told us.

The elder monk paused for our laughter in the style of a professional storyteller, and then asked, "What would you all have done in my place?

Could the family afford to waste this meal? Certainly not. Whom would it hurt to tell and what would the benefit be?" he asked of us though we never learned if the family ate the meal or not. As with many Buddhist anecdotes, this one had no right answer.

Starving Japan and Bountiful America

The story above reveals two facets of wartime Japanese life, as well as the fact that Buddhist monks often use humorous stories to frame their religious sermons.[1] First, for all of its technological advances and military might, wartime Japan was materially and economically deprived. The war against China, which exploded in 1931, began auspiciously. Second, for close to a decade, from 1931 to 1941, Japan's population celebrated victory on top of victory. But conditions deteriorated quickly after opening up the second front against the Allies in 1941 and by 1943 most of the population subsisted on an extremely poor diet. These meager living standards did little to sustain the average worker in ordinary times, let alone during a war. In wartime Japan, as in Britain, Europe and most of the world with the exception perhaps of America, food was scarce. The Japanese government and military exhorted the people to tighten their belts, plow up their front yards and make do with potatoes and other vegetables, saving white rice for the soldiers. In fact, the government crafted a slogan, "Luxury is the Enemy," to drive home the message about scraping and saving.

Food consumption outside the home is taken for granted in wealthier societies now, where copious choices are available at all hours of the day. For the vast majority of Japanese wartime consumers, this was not the case. The war brought about two drastic changes that set the stage for major transformations in Japanese cuisine. First, it set the stage for the immediate postwar economic catastrophe that forced people to look for alternatives to a rice-based cuisine. Second, it removed many of the social divisions that had still divided prewar society, creating a mass public defined by a sense of consumerism that modeled itself on the United States. The military was a great equalizer in that it continued what previous wars had started – it brought men in from the countryside and acquainted them with the new foods of the city, including noodle dishes.

---

[1] The extent to which the state hired performers and others as part of a national campaign to teach the inhabitants about Shinto is richly detailed in Helen Hardacre, "Creating State Shinto: The Great Promulgation Campaign and the New Religions," *Journal of Japanese Studies*, 12, Winter 1986, pp. 29–64.

In the *shuho*, or military base canteen, soldiers could supplement their meager meals with cheap beer, as well as *soba* or *udon* noodle dishes that were considered delicious snacks. Sometimes even Chinese noodles (*Shina soba*) were for sale.[2] When the war was over, soldiers would return home with these tastes and memories of meals.

The Path to War

Like Germany in World War I, Japan during World War II faced many logistical problems for supplies and had to find other ways and methods to supplement soldiers' caloric intake.[3] Japanese nutritionists devised a theory that the Japanese spirit, *yamato damashī*, could actually overcome physical deficiencies and a lack of food. Many pundits and even intellectuals may have believed such fantasies, but, as the Chinese learned during the disastrous Great Leap Forward in the late 1950s, the mind cannot in fact overcome a severe deficiency of nutrients and calories. Before 1945, most Japanese families had scarce personal savings to spend on luxury items. Food accounted for roughly thirty percent of the average Japanese laborer's income, where in America, it was only twenty percent. The average peasant family was worse off, spending sixty percent of income on living expenses alone. Poverty was widespread and unavoidable for both urban and rural inhabitants. Well into the 1930s, the average life expectancy of males in Japan was only forty-six![4] The war did little to improve such statistics. Families remained strictly patriarchal.

For the underclass and rural populations, eating, even at home, was undertaken more to stuff calories into the body than as any sort of pleasure. One woman who grew up in Yamagata city in the central north of Japan in 1933 detailed in her memoirs how her childhood meals did not occupy a high point of the day. In our "daily meals," the woman recalled, "there was not much of a change through breakfast, lunch and dinner." Meals tended to center on starchy foodstuffs, rice supplemented with other grains, miso soup and pickles. There were some vegetables for dinner, sometimes boiled items. "Fish, [was served] about once a week," if at all.[5] But it was not only the scarcity and lack of variety in the food that

---

[2] Masuda Yutaka, *Jūgun to senchū sengo*, pp. 33, 38.
[3] Lizzie Collingham talks about this phenomenon in her *Taste of War: World War Two and the Battle For Food*.
[4] Gary Allinson, *Japan's Postwar History*, p. 16.
[5] Ishige Naomichi, et al., eds., *Shōwa no shoku*, pp. 11–12.

made meals dour occasions. Everyone sat around the central fire pit in the middle of the traditional village home, the *irori*, in formal *seiza* position. Only the patriarch of the family was permitted to sit in the more relaxed cross-legged style. Members of the house were arranged in a circle from eldest to youngest and each was served his or her portion of rice mixture, in order of seniority, by the patriarch. The dinner was strictly regulated in other ways as well. "There might be some talk of the fields among the adults. But otherwise there was hardly any conversation. Everyone ate silently. If the children started to chat my father would shout out with a roar, 'What are you doing!'" she recalled.[6] At the end of the silent meal each person would pour some hot water into his or her bowl and swish around the water with a slice of pickled radish, *takuan*. They would then dry their utensils with their own handkerchiefs and place the dishes back in the cupboard. (A more thoroughgoing dish-wash with soap and water was completed once a month.[7]) This mute family dinner is a far cry from the international banquets and dances hosted by the Meiji state in its efforts to advance Japan's international diplomatic prestige, and from the traditional Chinese banquets filled with song and boisterous discussion, as occurred in Nagasaki during the Tokugawa period.

Wartime Cuisine and the Nation

During Japan's fifteen-year war in Asia, patriots hailed the Japanese diet as a point of national pride and the source of the superior health of the Japanese people. Such convictions stretched the truth a bit – Japanese people were not particularly healthy – but it was best not to admit this: nor the fact that even though Japan started the war with a food surplus, by the late 1930s it had instituted rations for many daily needs. Everyone ate rice and miso soup to demonstrate that they were Japanese; and in a self-fulfilling prophecy, these dishes became the markers of Japanese identity throughout the colonies and empire. By 1910, Japan's empire already stretched from Taiwan to Korea and in the 1930s Japan absorbed large portions of Manchuria and northern China, culminating in the occupation of Indochina and later Southeast Asia in the early 1940s. During the long war, the term *kokuminshoku*, "national food," acquired a different meaning, moving away from a more general idea of "food eaten in Japan," to

---

[6] Ibid., pp. 11–12.
[7] Ibid., p. 12.

something more like "the people's national food." A national magazine on nutrition explained the implications of *kokuminshoku* in 1941:

> Our bodies are not ours to live with as we please: we must use them in the assistance of the nation. To get ill by abandoning ourselves to gluttony and excess, to not plan our meals and make sure that our bodies are sustained with sufficient nutrition, is to be disloyal. We must create policies to develop appropriate *kokuminshoku*, "the people's national food."

"This 'national food' should accord with the appropriate age and degree of labor," the article explained.[8] The distinction between Chinese food, *Shina ryōri*, and the more refined, healthy and supposedly superior Japanese *kokuminshoku* affected prewar and wartime attitudes toward food from the colonies, though this attitude improved marginally through the 1930s, with a "China boom," a rise in the interest in Japan in Chinese-themed movies, songs, Chinese-inspired clothing and other products. By the end, the Japanese empire contained many disparate regions, including Korean, Taiwanese, Chinese, Polynesian, Okinawan and Indochinese, all of which inevitably had repercussions on Japanese cuisine, both in expatriate communities in the colonies and back at home. The reverberations continued after the war, pushing out the borders of the national cuisine so that in today's Japan, dumplings, noodle soup, stir fry, *okonomiyaki* (an egg and noodle omelette), fried pork cutlet, rice omelettes and beer are not considered alien dishes but truly Japanese.

Rice remained central during the war years but substitutes were necessary, as Army General and State Planning Board official (and war criminal) Suzuki Teiichi proclaimed at a November 5, 1941, Imperial Conference one month before the attack on Pearl Harbor:

> I think it will be necessary to consider substitute foods for rice, such as soybeans, minor cereals and sweet potatoes. We also need to exercise some control over food in case the expected imports of rice from Thailand and French Indochina called for in the Food Supply Plan for the 1942 rice year are reduced owing to operations in the South.[9]

The army may have realized the potential for disaster. Rather than make sacrifices, however, it attempted to requisition as much white rice as possible, notwithstanding the consideration of substitute forms of nutrition. Such head-in-the-sand behavior suggests that the imperializing project was doomed from the outset.

---

[8] "Kokuminshoku to wa," *Eiyō to ryōri*, Vol. 7, no. 4, 1941, p. 4.
[9] David Lu, *Japan: A documentary history*, p. 429.

Japanese Soldiers and Food

In the popular Japanese postwar comedy film *Letters to the Emperor*, the lead character, portrayed by Atsumi Kiyoshi (who also starred in the acclaimed postwar *Tora-san* series), is a peasant who enjoys being in the military because it allows him to eat white rice for three meals a day.[10] The film demonstrates in a tongue-in-cheek manner that for many poor Japanese peasants the military was actually an escape from grinding agricultural poverty; in the military, a man could receive clothing, wear shoes and eat nutritious meals.

This image of soldiers eating white rice was echoed in the film on wartime Japan in American director Frank Capra's series of propaganda "documentaries" *Why We Fight*. In one scene in *Know your enemy Japan* Japanese soldiers are seen sitting and eating a meal. In a stentorian voice the narrator explains to Western viewers: "They eat rice, sometimes with a bit of fish but mostly rice."[11] The camera is then panned to stacks of metal canteen boxes filled with white rice. Ironically, US and Japanese wartime propaganda perpetuated an identical myth – to be Japanese meant to eat meals of white rice. Prewar Japanese food consumption of fats and oils was already at a very low level, about two percent of total caloric intake. According to one postwar assessment, the total caloric intake "was on the average a good deal lower than in Western nations like the United States and Canada, but was nevertheless what would be expected, especially in view of the smaller bodies of adults and the high proportion of young children in the population."[12] The extreme focus on rice caused severe shortages both during the war and in the postwar period, one reason why noodles reclaimed some dominance. Alternatives for daily caloric consumption had to be developed and to be made socially acceptable.

The reasons why Japan went to war with most of the world are ably discussed elsewhere, but when we look at the food situation and Japan's assessment of the situation, the pointlessness of it all screams out even louder. The Japanese empire, like Britain in its imperial project but far less successfully, for a variety of reasons followed no master plan. Japanese imperialism was opportunistic and thus jumbled and contradictory.

---

[10] The Japanese title is *Haikei tennō heikasama*, Shōchiku Studios, 1963. A sequel followed in 1964.
[11] This film was never released publicly but is available now on DVD, Elstree Hill Entertainment, 2004.
[12] Bruce Johnston, *Japanese Food Management in World War II*, p. 90.

Figure 37. A US World War II poster demonstrating the disparity between what wartime Americans were expected to eat and what the Japanese government beseeched its people to consume. A diet of meat, fruit, potatoes, eggs and bread every day would have been unthinkable for Japanese people in wartime.

By 1942, Japanese rule extended to 350 million or so people, stretching from the Aleutian Islands to India. This bloc held five to six times the population of the French and Dutch empires and reached three quarters the size of the British but was acquired with much more speed.

Food and Victory

Why the Japanese military ignored prescient warnings about the strategic importance of food is significant in how Japanese cuisine was shaped postwar. Knowledge about the intimate relation between war and food did not suddenly appear after the war against the Allies began. In fact, the Japanese military and authorities had been talking about this linkage for decades. Prewar Japanese strategists and pundits were well aware of the dangers of a poorly supplied military and country. During the 1920s and 1930s, the Japanese spent precious financial resources and expertise on translating German and British treatises analyzing World War I from all angles. The Japanese government had been concerned about the health of its people and what they were eating long before World War II. The Japanese Prime Minister's office proposed the establishment of a National Bureau of Nutrition Research on August 28, 1919, just after World War I had ended. The motion declared that Japan "needs to investigate nutrition to learn how to maintain and advance the health of the people."[13] A few months later, on December 16, 1919, Prime Minister Hara Kei penned a memo, "Matters relating to the promotion of national strength, nutrition and substitute foods." The plan suggested that investing in the health and strength of the nation at the home front required dispatching officials to give talks and to conduct investigations into the health of people in the hinterland. To talk about substitute foods and encourage their consumption "is the most important way in which we will solve the food supply crisis in our country," the report concluded.[14] This interest continued well into the 1940s. Japan was far from ignorant about the need for military supply lines, nutrition and the effects of food shortages on the population in times of crisis.

One Japanese book published in 1942, "Emergency Food," while building on this knowledge also clearly adhered to the flawed belief that the

---

[13] The Prime Minister's proposal to create a national bureau of nutrition research, August 28 1919, (纂 01462-100, Reel 034700), (National Archives, Tokyo, Japan.)
[14] "Minryoku kanyō narabi konshoku daiyōshoku shōrei jimu kankei," (単 02247-100; Reel 020400), (National Archives, Tokyo, Japan.)

Japanese psyche could overcome physical demands through sheer spirit. The tome detailed how Japan dealt with famines and agricultural misfortunes through history. It cited the World War I case of Germany simultaneously overcoming five nations but ultimately losing the war due to food-supply issues caused by the neglect of its internal distribution infrastructure. Another wartime Japanese author drew parallels between that situation and the present situation of Japan, and wrote: "Currently the ABCD [American, British, Chinese and Dutch] blockade is doing the same to us, trying to strangle our country. Our soldiers are stacking up great victories but we are not blessed with a great climate or crops, so what can we do?"[15] The need to quickly search for substitutes was echoed within the halls of the government administration. A memo from the Minister of Agriculture and Forestry, Ino Hiroya, to the Osaka merchants association on October 21, 1941, suggested using soy as a substitute for rice and wheat and importing it from Manchuria. Whether this move was feasible and what impact it would have on the soy sauce, miso and fertilizing industries was considered an important enough topic for debate. The report was based on production issues in Manchuria and Korea before war with the US had even began.[16]

Another fascinating problem that caught the attention of military planners concerned a 1936–1937 study on nutrition and the military, regarding the fact that Japanese taste preferences were not as homogeneous as most people thought. Today, we take for granted the variety of ramen in Japan – reflecting local tastes, available ingredients and regional cuisine history. This pattern seemed to surprise the wartime Japanese military. Military food planners noted that, contrary to their own belief that Japanese all ate alike, each soldier who took part in these questionnaires or investigations offered different, deeply-held views on how rice should be cooked, whether miso should be salty or sweet and other fundamental aspects of Japanese cuisine. Japanese Army Major General Kawashima Shirō, a military nutritionist, began to look into these issues. Kawashima was first hired during the 1930s in Tokyo in the army provisions depot and in 1942 received his doctorate from Tokyo Imperial University after conducting research on portable rations for Japanese soldiers. His comments reflected a larger national issue: there was a serious split in food preferences between the

---

[15] Higashikata Hakaru, *Hijōshokuryō no kenkyū*, pp. 1–2.
[16] Memo from the Minister of Agriculure and Forestry, Ino Hiroya, to the Osaka merchants association on October 21, 1941, (纂 02657-100; Reel 070900), (National Archives, Tokyo, Japan.)

Kansai (western) and Kantō (central) regions and the differences became even more pronounced beyond the urban centers. Most Japanese during the Meiji era had taken such differences as a fait accompli, firm in the historical knowledge that some inhabitants preferred, for example, *soba* to *udon*, depending on their prefecture of origin. The Japanese militarization had to re-orient soldiers and society at large to believe that the nation was much more homogeneous than it truly was and this drive was reflected in the military's plans to feed the armed forces. Ironically, the decision to introduce Western and Chinese mixed food into the military menu was a policy designed to thwart discontent since few soldiers could harbor preconceptions – the cuisine was equally foreign to everyone and therefore useful as a means to create a more homogeneous "national taste."[17] Otherwise, just as during the early Meiji years, "military menus in Japan reinforced the nationwide spread of the ideal of rice as the centerpiece around which a meal was constructed and of soy sauce as a crucial flavoring agent."[18]

As Japanese society militarized, so did the cuisine; in many crucial ways, ramen is a direct outgrowth of that transformation. The imperial military from 1940 to 1945 augmented its requisition of rice from 161,000 to over 744,000 tons by the end of the war. Throughout the war years the military ate its fair share of the populace's dinner. When military privileges did not work to procure food, black marketeering skills very often could.[19] Obviously, more austerity was required at the home front to support this excess and frequent military requisitioning occurred. Somewhat paradoxically, this situation forced consumers and the government to look for substitutes, opening up opportunities for noodle dishes, like ramen and *soba*, to find space on Japanese wartime menus.[20] The Hoshi Pharmaceuticals Company invented a heroin-based pill to stimulate digestion, advertising it as an activator that improved the taste of food.[21] Looking for substitutes was not an easy task given the Japanese wartime obsession with rice as the centerpiece of every meal and main component of the national diet. The food management law of 1942 turned theory into policy – declaring that all

---

[17] Katarzyna J. Cwiertka, *Modern Japanese Cuisine – Food, Power and National Identity*, pp. 82–83.
[18] Ibid., p. 84.
[19] Tamura Shinpachirō, "Sengo – heisei no shoku," *Gengo* (gekkan), Vol. 23, no. 1, 1994, p. 81.
[20] Katarzyna J. Cwiertka, *Modern Japanese Cuisine – Food, Power and National Identity*, p. 129.
[21] Ibid., pp. 131–132.

Japanese should have access to rice as a staple, although this obviously could not be implemented in practice. Regardless of the military's concern for supplies and logistics, over half of the mobilized Japanese soldiers died of starvation and disease caused by poor planning. According to imperial Japanese government statistics and postwar investigations, a startling number of soldiers never even saw battle. It was a tragic irony that "wartime mobilization created the basis for sound nutritional policies in postwar Japan that encompassed the entire population," because that impact was not felt until the years following surrender.[22]

In short, the military, authorities and even intellectuals colluded in a bid to convince the population that it could survive on less. Kawashima went to great lengths to persuade the Japanese people that they were not really experiencing a food shortage. His book mocked reality but was written in all seriousness. In his 1943 volume, "The Decisive Battle and the Food Supply," Kawashima explained that Japan was actually on track in chapters with titles such as, "In Japan there is no food supply shortage," "Rice must be the center of our diet," and "Alcohol should wait until we have won the war." The preface declared that Japan was not deprived of food supplies at all. Kawashima blamed apparent shortages on poor harvests in western Japan and Korea, and rejected reports of Japan's food problems as foreign propaganda designed to damage Japan's imperial prestige.[23] Of course Kawashima and other authorities grossly misled the public and themselves. The government, and more importantly the military, did not care about food shortages. It was an egregious oversight that had immense military and social ramifications both during the war and after.

Japanese Identity and Rice

Rice, according to the logic of the time, was perfect for a small island with a big population – supposedly, no other foodstuff was as appropriate to Japan's conditions. Kawashima spent pages detailing how rice was perfect for Japan's geography and climate. Rice was economical because it did not have to be milled to make flour and it could be used just as it grew.[24]

---

[22] Ibid., p. 135.
[23] Kawashima Shirō, *Kessenka no Nihon shokuryō*, p. 2.
[24] Ibid., p. 27.

This argument completely ignores the husking and polishing process required to produce white rice but Kawashima was promoting an ideology.

Kawashima championed Japanese food quality and nutrition policies that had supposedly proven their mettle during the 1936 Olympics in Berlin. At the Nazi Olympics, Japanese runner Son Kitei won the marathon, while a fellow Japanese athlete came third. The event was not broadcast live but the results were published as front-page news in Japan and throughout the empire as proof of Japan's rising stature in sports and international games. The victory also highlighted, for the Japanese authorities, Japan's strong showing as a physical presence on the international stage. The problem was that Son, who sported the Japanese flag on his jersey when he participated in the Olympics and later attended university in Tokyo, was not actually Japanese: he was Korean, as was the third place winner.[25] Nevertheless, he was portrayed as a Japanese national and recognized as such by the international community. Koreans rejoiced over Son's victory and believed that his victory proved that Korea had not yet been physically subdued by Japan. One of the major dailies in Korea, *Toa Nippō*, printed a picture of Son without the Japanese flag on his shirt. This incensed the Japanese Governor General of Korea who ordered the paper suspended for six months.[26]

Kawashima, the military nutritionist, perhaps unaware of the true state of affairs, was ecstatic that Japanese runners won first and third prizes in the Nazi Olympics marathon. The military scientist attributed the first and third place victories to the Japanese diet, arguing that because both runners relied on a rice-based diet they supplied themselves with longer-lasting energy through a better replenishment of blood sugar.[27] The sole downside of a monocultural cuisine, admitted Kawashima, was that if the climate changed for the worse – did not offer enough rain, or was too

---

[25] Son, who later used the Korean spelling for his name as Sohn Kee-chung, carried the Olympic torch at the opening ceremony of the 1988 Seoul Olympics. William Tsutsui, "Introduction," in William Tsutsui and Michael Baskett, eds., *The East Asian Olympiads, 1934–2008: Building Bodies and Nations in Japan, Korea, and China*, p. 7.

[26] Sawaki Kotarō, "Nachisu orinpikku," *Bungei Shunjū*, August 1976, p. 244. The author also claims that in 1936, when asked by a foreigner for his autograph, Son wrote "Korea" by his name. For more on wartime Japanese Olympic fervor and the sports war connection in East Asia see Xu Guoqi, *Olympic Dreams: China and Sports, 1895–2008*; Sandra Collins, *The 1940 Tokyo Games: The Missing Olympics: Japan, the Asian Olympics and the Olympic Movement*, and Barak Kushner, "Going for the Gold – Health and Sports in Japan's Quest for Modernity."

[27] Kawashima Shirō, *Kessenka no Nihon shokuryō*, pp. 32–33.

cold – the harvest would fail.[28] During the war, all the Meiji-era debates about cuisine, civilization and eating meat seemed to evaporate. Replacing them was a cacophony of nutritional gibberish based on jingoistic pipe dreams. At one point near the end of the war, for example, Kawashima went on national radio and suggested to people that to stay healthy they should consume egg shells to get all the nutrients they could out of food. The imperial chef, Akiyama Tokuzō, got in touch with Kawashima because he worried about the emperor's health near the war's end. Akiyama was anxious because he believed the imperial family might have to eat grass and he wanted to find out if that would be nutritionally advisable for royalty.[29]

Of course, not everything that the wartime nutritionist claimed was wrong; it is still possible to appreciate why Kawashima's expertise was well regarded. Another thing that concerned nutrition and science researchers was the well-being of fighter pilots. Prewar and wartime fighter planes were not pressurized. Planes at high altitude experience about one quarter of the pressure that would be normal at sea level and Japanese fighters had to climb very high to engage with the American B-29 "Superfortress" bombers. Less pressure at high altitudes causes the stomach to fill with gas as it expands to equalize with the atmosphere. The same thing happens to the urinary tract; as it expands, g-forces while flying also put more pressure on the bladder. Kawashima Shirō, the nutritionist, remembered seeing pilots descending from their fighter planes after a mission, trousers stained with urine. Given the physics of the situation, pilots could not avoid wetting themselves at certain altitudes. Kawashima had an idea how to alleviate this problem. He gave pilots a small amount of salty water before their flights. The intestines absorbed the table salt, released it into the blood, which raised the salt levels; the brain then told the body to deliver more liquid to that area. Since the body was thirsty but not receiving sufficient liquids the body automatically thinned the blood to send it to where more was needed. The body, always looking to balance its situation internally, excreted less urine, and pilots were saved the uncomfortable and unpleasant mess of sodden flight suits.[30]

While officers may have found a solution to keep pilots from turning flight suits into wet suits, in other areas of nutrition the Japanese military consistently and criminally neglected the issue of supply lines for its

---

[28] Ibid., pp. 33–34.
[29] Yamashita Tamiki, *Kawashima Shirō kyūjissai no kaiseinen*, p. 18.
[30] Ibid., p. 22.

troops. As a result, military planners focused on invasion strategies and never even considered logistical issues of distribution and delivery.[31] For years, the Japanese military had both planned and experienced fighting in China and the northern regions of East Asia, but they were ignorant about battlefield conditions in the South Pacific once a new front opened against the Allies in December 1941. Military planners and strategists (if we can label them as such) did not conduct even cursory investigations or prepare reports about these zones.[32] The belief in mind over matter, "spiritualism over materialism," contributed to Japan's downfall. Japan's military strategy was poor from the outset, relying on unsubstantiated belief rather than military intelligence; but food was also a decisive factor. Soldiers were told not to fear death because they were dying in the service of a divine being – but this did not actually comprise an effective military tactic.[33]

Battle Zones and Prisoners of War

Japan's imperial advance created immense hardships in all sorts of ways, but the personal misery at the battlefront and in the POW camps could also be horrific. A Japanese survivor from Guadalcanal recalled the hunger and malnutrition. He would recook his rice ball about four times and then just drink the water. Other survivors recalled that maggots would feast on half-alive soldiers, the men too weak with malnutrition to fight them off as they rotted, breathing and dying a terrible, preventable death.[34] While the standards of eating for Japanese both at home and abroad worsened over the fifteen-year war, many seemed less obsessed with food than with toilet activity. Fukushima Kikujirō wrote in his diary how brutal life was in the military, despite having been jingoistic at the start. "Extreme diarrhea persisted," he wrote and "what I ate came out in its original shape – I let it go in my pants while I was in training sessions." He then revealed that unfit soldiers received more regular beatings in platoons.[35] Kurumizawa Kōshi

---

[31] Fujiwara Akira, *Uejinishita eireitachi*, p. 143.
[32] Ibid., p. 155.
[33] Edward J. Drea details how US military strategy was superior to that of Japan and how that affected the evolution of the war, in *In the service of the Emperor: essays on the Imperial Japanese Army*. Fujiwara Akira, *Uejinishita eireitachi*, p. 178.
[34] As quoted in Simon Partner, *Toshie: A story of village life in Twentieth-Century Japan*, p. 95.
[35] Yoshikuni Igarashi, *Bodies of Memory: narratives of war in postwar Japanese culture, 1945–1970*, p. 51.

was a POW in Mongolia during the war and recollects the extreme lack of food there as well. All the POWS dreamed of food all the time. Kurumizawa says that he actually taught himself to masturbate while dreaming of the dishes he had eaten in Japan.[36]

One of the few Japanese books to analyze the problem of starvation in the army sheds light on the dubious value of Japan's imperial expansion, both theoretically and practically. To be sure, Japan may have grown in power in the war, but really only in relation to weaker nations. Fujiwara Akira's analysis of the starvation rates of World War II Japanese soldiers in the field, sober reading as it is, is exceedingly important because his data helps to debunk the claim of Japan's "great" war to liberate East Asia. If Japan's *casus belli* was so liberating, why did it starve so many people?[37] Fujiwara's work should make the Japanese themselves angrier. The war was not a case of, "Well, it's too late now to stop it so we might as well go ahead," embodied by the Japanese phrase, *shikata ga nai*, which signals a resignation to a situation, but a case of "We do not care about our soldiers at all." Complete indifference. How could such indifference help win the war?

World War II-era Japan developed an overarching belief that the Japanese spirit was invincible and would enable Japan to overcome its limitations to defeat the more technologically advanced but less spiritually aware West. Fujiwara examines the issue of food and supplies to demonstrate that the lack of planning was not limited only to the home islands or islands in the Pacific: Guadalcanal, Port Morseby, New Guinea and Wake Island. Food and supplies were lacking on the China battlefront and in eastern India and Thailand. There was an overall absence of any planning. Fujiwara's conclusions are shocking: "Over half of the war casualties for Japanese military were from starvation." He elaborated, "This was not some noble death resulting from a valiant struggle in the midst of battle. It was a tortuous death through sickness and starvation, dying in the thick of the jungle holding back tears in vain while getting thinner and weaker. That was the kind of death it was."[38]

---

[36] Ibid., p. 55.

[37] This question, while exceedingly important, cannot be fully dealt with here but insight into the cause of starvation and Japan's imperial rule has been examined elsewhere. See Bùi Minh Dung, "Japan's Role in the Vietnamese Starvation of 1944–45," *Modern Asian Studies*, Vol. 29, No. 3., July 1995, pp. 573–618.

[38] Fujiwara Akira, *Uejinishita eireitachi*, p. 142. Also see Kano Masanao, *Heishi de aru koto – dōin to jūgun seishinshi*, pp. 230–233.

With their own soldiers already undernourished by the early 1940s, the problem of feeding Allied POWs unexpectedly taken in astonishing mass surrenders exacerbated an already tense food supply situation. Domestic attitudes about Japanese food had quickly reverted to the traditional "nutritious" diet promoted by Mori Ōgai and the Meiji intellectuals – rice, miso and fish – in place of the more expansive Taisho era definition of Japanese cuisine which included meaty noodle soups, curries and Chinese food. Virtually none of the Allied POWs had experience of this sort of poor and "fishy" Japanese meal and most did not like it at all.

One American soldier taken prisoner was a nutrition expert and kept careful records, which he wrote up after the war. He calculated that the average POW consumed around 2,000 calories a day – far less than the recommended 3,000 calories for a seventy-kilo soldier doing hard labor. Japan had always maintained a lower daily caloric standard than the West, even after the war, and Allied POWs suffered even more as a result of this gap.[39] A Japanese military doctor, Nagao Goichi, inspected the nation's POW camps in the early 1940s and tabulated the nutritional problems. One copy of his report survived postwar. Nagao was frequently called on during the Yokohama war crimes trials as a witness for issues relating to starvation and abuse. In 1943, the army was worried enough about the high rate of mortality among Allied POWs that Nagao was sent to the POW camps to investigate. He recommended providing POWs with more cartilage and animal innards because he realized they needed more meat, which is what they clamored for. Unfortunately, given the state of the market and economy in Japan, this was not possible.[40] Allied POWs and Nagao both commented on a common ailment referred to by the POWs as the "rice itch." Eating only rice, without the essential fats they were used to, made their skin dry and flaky, and thus itchy.[41]

At some POW camps, such as one of the first in Shikoku, the commanding Japanese officers saw that the POWs were asking for wheat instead of white rice, which in their minds signified poor nutritional planning. Rice was the cuisine of the victor, as demonstrated during the 1936 Olympics; it offered superior health, which explained why the Western Allies had surrendered early in mass numbers. How could the POWs not want to eat this

---

[39] Nakao Tomoyo, "Sensō horyo mondai no hikaku bunkateki kōsatsu, (ge)" [there are three articles by Nakao on this topic] *Kikan sensō sekinin kenkyū*, dai 23gō, Winter issue 1999, pp. 77–78.
[40] Nakao Tomoyo, "Sensō horyo mondai no hikaku bunkateki kōsatsu, (ge)," p. 80.
[41] Ibid., p. 81.

cuisine, the Japanese military authorities wondered? Showing the natives in the colonies that white POWs were working for the Japanese was also a form of propaganda designed to counter any residual worship of the West.[42] As the Japanese government was encouraging people to eat *kokuminshoku*, it was important to show photographs of the POWs eating traditional Japanese food and working, encouraging others to do likewise. Food was now a form of national propaganda, not only as the "people's national food," but also because it showed the conquered how they should conduct their daily lives while under the administrative control of the Japanese. In fact, Japan could not afford to provide for the Allied POWs in the Western manner, and the government and military did not want that paraded in the open.

In May 1945, a British POW met with a Swiss foreign office representative to complain about conditions in his Yokohama POW camp, stressing the terrible food they were forced to eat.[43] What Allied POWs asked for – beds, milk, butter, bread – basic as such requests might seem to Westerners (and part of their own propaganda as seen in the US poster that exhorted citizens to eat well), seemed extravagant to the Japanese. These were items one might find in a foreign luxury hotel with all the Western amenities and a POW camp was not a hotel. This is not to deny the vicious cruelty foreign POWs met with in Japanese camps. But Western items were now luxuries, not necessities that established a nation's level of civilization. The Japanese officers in charge of Singapore when it fell were enraged when the surrendering British General Arthur Percival requested more bread and butter for his 80,000 men. "How dare he demand such items?" they apparently asked; "He is a damned POW! Especially at a time when we ourselves are making do with less. What arrogance."[44]

The social fabric broke down in wartime Japan within sectors dealing with foreign POWs as well as on the home front. Sometimes, though, it changed for the better in a sense but only at a local level. In the spring of 1944, the government had to produce school lunches as a necessity. The offering was small – just rice and miso soup – but it was something. Of course, Japan was not the only country to suffer food shortages. By 1945, forty percent of schoolchildren in England and Wales were also eating school lunches that provided close to one thousand calories a day to

---

[42] Nakao Tomoyo, "Sensō horyo mondai no hikaku bunkateki kōsatsu, (chū)," *Kikan sensō sekinin kenkyū*, dai 23gō, Spring issue 1999, p. 32.
[43] Ibid., p. 33.
[44] Ibid., p. 34.

hungry little mouths. War, since the turn of century, had been a catalyst for the introduction of such measures.[45]

Food and the Home Front

The military was not the only organization concerned about wartime cuisine. Women's magazines published hundreds of new recipes and devoted pages of recommendations to ways for wives and families to eke out a living and survive the war. A majority of these issues were only raised after the situation became dire in 1942 but prewar Japan had already witnessed a life-style gap between countryside and city. The city offered curry rice, croquettes, grilled beef and ginger pork, while rural areas could provide only brown rice, limp vegetables and lukewarm miso soup. Magazines created an "ideology of home cooking" and promoted the idea that taste "expressed a mother's love."[46] Along with an expanding range of meals to offer an increasingly poorly fed Japanese public, these women's journals provided recipes from the colonies where Japanese tastes mixed with local cuisine. The recipe names frequently evoked military victories and machismo, with dishes like "Iron Helmet Mashed Potatoes," and "Naval Destroyer Salad," similar to those early twentieth-century recipes that celebrated victory over Russia.[47] Readers were treated to a selection of Manchukuo Cuisine, as a way to prove the puppet country's existence and to rally in support. Recipes for dumplings and spring rolls (arguably Chinese staples) were now included and people on the home islands learned how to make them. These colonial dishes became part of Japanese cuisine through the Greater East Asia Co-prosperity sphere.[48] In 1940, as part of the national mobilization campaign, the government instructed everyone to consume twenty percent less rice. Another key feature of wartime menus were lists of substitutes for rice – mushrooms, chestnuts, etc. This was characteristic of British wartime cuisine as well, learning how to "stretch" a meal. With less rice as the main dish, bread and noodles were frequently suggested as meal alternatives. The June 1940 issue of "Women's Club" included an article about "Rising Asia Bread," the name a play on words that suggested Japan's efforts to raise Asia up from backwardness.

---

[45] John Burnett. "The rise and decline of school meals in Britain, 1860–1990," in John Burnett and Derek J. Oddy, eds., *The Origins and Development of Food Policies in Europe*, pp. 55–56.
[46] Saitō Minako, *Senka no reshipi taiheiyō sensōka no shoku o shiru*, pp. 31–32.
[47] Ibid., p. 41.
[48] Ibid., p. 45.

This bread recipe included wheat flour and people were encouraged to eat it once a week or month as a substitute for rice.[49]

By the end of the war the focus was just on survival food. In 1944, women's journals published detailed diagrams and instructions for cooking food in bomb shelters. Relentless US bombing campaigns all over the Japanese archipelago forced many urban populations to flee to the countryside or live their lives constantly running to air raid shelters or underground. Articles illustrated ways to cook without using a kitchen stove – making one in the field – as more people's houses and homes were destroyed.[50] In a complex move away from the urbanization that had continued since the 1870s, Japanese retreated from the cities near the end of the war and by 1944 urban landscapes (including bombed areas) began to turn into fields of produce, even in front of the imperial parliament. The authorities thought potatoes could be grown and used as fuel to extend the diminishing supplies of gas and oil. "Protect the nation potato" was one species attempted and there were many others.[51]

The war completely destroyed Japan's standard of living. Not until 1950 did the average caloric intake match what people had consumed before the war. For Japanese stomachs the war and its impact lasted a two full decades. Once people got their fill again, they gorged on rice; consumption reached a postwar peak in 1962 with 117 kilos per person per year. After that, rice consumption declined and remained in decline; by 1986, rice consumption had dwindled to 71 kilos per person annually.[52] People ate more bread and, of course, more noodle soup. Ramen was now just a heartbeat away from making its second national debut. The population had learned about the taste of delicious prewar only to have it removed from the table. Rice was slowly being replaced by other foodstuffs, including noodles and other wheat products. And the Japanese were experimenting with colonial cuisines more than ever before in the expansion of their empire.

Surrender and the Dissolution of Imperial Food

Japan's surrender on August 15, 1945, brushed away the idea of imperial food, changing Japanese cuisine forever. The postwar explosion of ramen shops in Japan was directly tied into wartime hunger; the search for an

---

[49] Ibid., pp. 56–57.
[50] Ibid., p. 153.
[51] Ibid., p. 137.
[52] Ishige Naomichi, et al., editors, *Shōwa no shoku*, p. 23.

alternative to starvation spurred the invention of instant ramen. War broke down any barriers to enjoying Chinese food, both through near-starvation and possibly also through Japan's long-term colonization and the impact of empire on concepts of suitable cuisine. For a time, Japan had conquered East Asia but the constituents of the empire and their cuisine inflicted consequences in return. Ramen was a result of this unlikely interaction. Ramen also made it possible for future Japanese people to dine alone. Judging from traditional constraints placed on those living in villages and less modernized hamlets, it is no surprise that small noodle soup restaurants would flourish. As cities later grew in the postwar period, ramen stores continued to prosper by offering single people living away from their families the opportunity to eat healthy meals.

Historian of Japanese cuisine, Katarzyna Cwiertka, says that although ideas about Japanese cuisine are "saturated with a sense of timeless continuity and authenticity," the reality is patently different.[53] What did the war create and destroy? It promoted an idea about the centrality of rice that drove up postwar rice consumption to unprecedented heights. The war also eradicated the notion that eating meat equaled civilization and revived the vegetarian origins and taste preferences of the Japanese diet. This idea offered Japan a healthier postwar life-style although it had delivered the opposite during the war. Finally, the war diet encouraged the idea that Japanese ate differently because they were different and that eating defined one culturally and ethnically. The argument was simple – Westerners eat bread and Japanese eat rice. This pushed all Westerners into the same category and gave the Japanese precedence in Asia in the rice-eating department. But there was a problem in the immediate postwar because a lack of rice, vegetables and such meant that the Japanese could eat little of what they were being told to, so they resorted to other non-rice-based meals, such as noodles. At last, ramen had a chance to reappear. Noodles were a culturally and socially acceptable alternative to rice, supported by decades of recipes in household magazines. Wives and mothers had been busy creating Chinese-style dishes while believing they were nationally Japanese. The colonial diet would now transform the postwar and modern Japanese diet into something entirely different from its traditional origins in Tokugawa and before. And yet it would still be known as Japanese cuisine. People were eating more bread and, of course, more ramen noodle soup. How they made that soup and why it became so suddenly popular is the topic of the next chapter.

---

[53] Katarzyna J. Cwiertka, *Modern Japanese Cuisine – Food, Power and National Identity*, p. 175.

CHAPTER NINE

HISTORY AT THE DINING TABLE: POSTWAR INSTANT RAMEN

On October 11, 1945, Japan's first postwar movie, "Gentle Breeze" (*Soyokaze*), starring popular actress Namiki Michiko, blazed across screens. The title song, "The Apple Song" (*Ringo no uta*), shot to number one almost immediately. Top-selling hits about food are unusual but indicative of something significant, symbolizing in Japan something more like feminine ripening and innocent yearning. The implication in the film of scenes in which a cute young woman sings about fruit was surely lost on no one. "The apple can't say anything but I understand how it feels," she sang. "Apples are cute! Apples are cute!" "That girl is a good girl, she's good-natured like the apple, she's a cute girl." Red apples embodied the sense of hope bursting forth after a long decade-and-a-half of war.

Politics in postwar Japan was intensely focused on food. It was slightly more complex than the "bread and circuses" of Roman times, but not by much. Any leadership that failed to provide the defeated nation with a robust food program would eventually face resistance.

In some ways it was ironic that consumers would spend their hard-earned cash being entertained by a song about fruit rather than actually eating it, but dreaming about food was probably almost as good as digesting it, especially when there was precious little of it around.

The early postwar era (1945–1955) introduced new thinking about national cuisine and new ideas about Japan's identity and place within the international hierarchy. Analyzing how changes in Japanese foodways regenerated ramen in the early postwar period illuminates three major points about modern Japanese food history: 1) Tasty and nutritious food psychologically equated with the concept of a new, strong nation, and generated pride that somewhat blunted the psychological and political trauma of military defeat; 2) Japan started to positively and proactively incorporate Chinese influence into Japanese cuisine, in contrast to the imperial era when the Japanese people and government made efforts to reduce or even denigrate such effects; and 3) Japan enlarged its concept of national identity through the incorporation and promotion of these new food products.

Figure 38. The postwar playbill for the song, "The Apple Song."

Initially, noodle foods, including ramen and other dishes, were sold at meager stands staffed by people impoverished by the war. No one could have predicted the long-term success and international influence of ramen on world cuisine. These new food products would become the international face of Japan as it rejoined the world market, making a trade footprint that continues to have an enduring impact today.

Early postwar life in Japan was arguably no better than wartime, the country having turned into what is termed *yakenohara*, or "burned out fields." Buildings were reduced to rubble and much of the urban population took refuge in the countryside, not returning *en masse* until the early 1950s. Tokyo's population dropped from seven to three million by the end of the war and that of Osaka plummeted from three million to one million. This massive decrease took a heavy toll on the nation's economic strength. *Katsugiya*, women who hauled produce around from market to market, took on the role of carts and mules to deliver goods since little other transportation was available.[1] It was difficult for Japanese postwar industry to muster a competent work force because workers took frequent "food holidays" to go to the countryside and scrounge. Absenteeism was rampant.[2]

Novelist Shiga Naoya depicted Japan's fall from imperial splendor in his short story *Ashen Moon*, penned in 1945, which described a defeated and demoralized people. At one point in Shiga's story a man stumbles around in the midst of a crowded train. On the train everyone tries to ignore him and no one offers any assistance – everyone assumes he is drunk. Only at the very end of the story are we are told that the man was not drunk but dying – from extreme malnutrition.[3] This was not mere fiction. In the first year after the war ended, people died at Tokyo and Ueno rail stations at an average of about twenty a day. In Osaka, about sixty people a month perished from starvation.[4] When Japan surrendered in August 1945, its food supply, perilously dependent on rice, reached only sixty percent of its prewar levels. Conditions continued to decline in 1946. The first issues of women's magazines after the war urged readers to develop new eating habits in articles with titles such as "How to Eat Acorns," and "Let's Catch Grasshoppers," though to be fair these had been eaten long before the war

---

[1] Gary Allinson, *Japan's Postwar History*, p. 49.
[2] Steven Joseph Fuchs, "Feeding the Japanese: MacArthur, Washington and the Rebuilding of Japan through Food Policy," PhD Dissertation at University of New York at Stony Brook, 2002, p. 79.
[3] Stephen W. Kohl, "Shiga Naoya and the Literature of Experience," *Monumenta Nipponica*, Vol. 32, No. 2., Summer, 1977, pp. 211–224.
[4] Harada Nobuo, *Washoku to Nihon bunka*, p. 201.

began.⁵ Rations were in such demand that the black market price was twenty-five times the official price. This disparity was one of the major reasons for people taking their belongings and going out to the countryside to trade their possessions for food.⁶

Japanese did not trade goods only with each other: a rich extracurricular exchange took place with the occupiers as well. According to Robert Whiting, a postwar American journalist, the US armed forces were guilty of soaring scales of graft and corruption. Within less than a year after the start of the occupation, "members of the armed forces had remitted back to America approximately $8 million a month, a sum exceeding the entire military payroll."⁷ Postwar Japanese movies frequently portray this sordid side of the occupation. The 1961 film, *Pigs and Battleships (Buta to gunkan)*, centers on the interaction between arrogant US service men, their voracious appetites (sexual and culinary) and the low-life Japanese scavengers who service them. The 1973 Japanese movie, *Battles Without Honor and Humanity (Jingi naki tatakai)*, opens with a scene where we witness the attempted rape of a Japanese woman that is thwarted only by the intervention of Japanese gangs who chase the American GIs away and keep order in the black market.

It was not just that Japan had depleted its own supply lines: it found itself on the fringes of even more difficult circumstances out of its control – in 1945 the depressed world food market threatened impending catastrophe far beyond East Asia.⁸ In 1948, over seventy percent of the British people believed they had a harder time making ends meet than during the previous year; prewar consumption patterns did not resume until the mid-1950s.⁹ Postwar British butchers frequently closed their shops five days a week because they had nothing to sell. Britain's Ministry of Food searched for alternatives to meat, experimenting with whale, snoek and even barracuda.¹⁰ By the fall of 1947, whale steaks were selling at the rate of six hundred a day at one London shop. As merchant shipping recovered, enthusiasm for such alternative protein sources abated and four thousand tons of blubbery whale carcasses lay rotting on the Tyne

---

⁵ John Dower, *Embracing Defeat*, p. 94.
⁶ Kano Masanao et al., eds., Iwanami kōza, *Nihon tsūshi*, Vol. 21, p. 240.
⁷ Robert Whiting, *Tokyo Underworld: The Fast Times and Hard Life of an American Gangster in Japan*, p. 15.
⁸ Christopher Driver, *The British at Table, 1940–1980*, p. 17.
⁹ Ina Zweiniger-Bargielowska, *Austerity in Britain, Rationing, Controls and Consumption, 1939–1955*, p. 85.
¹⁰ Christopher Driver, *The British at Table, 1940–1980*, pp. 38–40.

docks near the northeast city of Newcastle.¹¹ It was not all doom and gloom because the food situation did improve slightly in some areas. On December 31, 1946, the first shipment of bananas in six years arrived in Britain. But daily life was a nonstop grind of physical effort. A spring 1951 survey of the London suburbs calculated that most British housewives spent ten to eleven hours a day on household chores, with eight on Sunday. Cooking, cleaning and eating occupied the most time, consuming almost half a woman's waking hours per day.¹² This was similar to how wartime and early postwar Japanese housewives spent their days.¹³

THE SUDDEN POSTWAR

A half-century of Japanese imperial bravado evaporated in a few moments following surrender in August 1945. Perhaps without being aware of the source of their emotion, the Japanese people became suddenly less enthralled with their national cuisine. This was a turnaround from the wartime accolades and slogans lauding the superiority of Japanese over Western and Chinese diets. Compare the views of Kawashima Shirō, who championed the role of Japan's high-quality food in procuring medals at the 1936 Olympics, with those of Ozaki Yukio, postwar political statesman and writer who discussed the Japanese life-style in his writings on improving Japanese culture. Japanese culture, Ozaki implied, was outdated and could not respond adequately to the needs of the era. Kimono were nice but only in certain situations when one sat in the formal *seiza* position. Japanese clothing, he stated emphatically, was no good when you wanted to move around. Japanese food "is a feast for the eyes, but does not seem to take the mouth, namely taste, into consideration."¹⁴

In mid-December 1945, only a few months after surrender, Ishiguro Tadaatsu's testimony in the Upper House of the Diet captured Japan's anxious national mood at finding itself in an unimagined situation and

---

[11] Ibid., p. 44.
[12] Ina Zweiniger-Bargielowska, *Austerity in Britain, Rationing, Controls and Consumption, 1939–1955*, p. 108.
[13] David Earhart, *Certain Victory, Images of World War II in the Japanese Media*, p. 176, discovered the January 1945 work schedule from *Ladies' Companion* magazine. The timetable demonstrates that work was supposed to begin at 5 am and ended only at 9 pm. Housewives were responsible for all the cooking and cleaning but also worked in the factory or in agriculture.
[14] Kawashima Shirō, *Kessenka no Nihon shokuryō*, pp. 32–33. Ozaki Yukio, "Ishokujū no kaizen," *Ozaki gakudō zenshū*, Vol. 10, p. 223.

stripped of its empire. Ishiguro's pronouncements demonstrate that imperial thinking still lagged behind the new reality, i.e. that Japan was no longer able to rely on its colonies for sustenance: "Concerning using imports from abroad to augment this situation of insufficient food supply, I have heard that Korea has produced a rare abundant harvest. But our country is now placed in such a position that we are not free to bring such product here. These are the conditions in which we find ourselves," he announced to his equally worried colleagues.[15] The main postwar US investigator of wartime Japanese food management policies noted that Japanese were accustomed to pillaging their occupied territories. During the imperial era, the Japanese military had maintained a policy of living off the land: "[t]roops in Korea, Formosa and China secured all their rice locally."[16] It is obvious from Ishiguro's remarks that the Japanese faced something of a quandary in responding to their new situation, denuded of colonial supplies and no longer able to plunder. Ishiguro cogently described the fear that struck everyone as the ramifications of defeat sunk in – the nation was now forced to produce food on its own for the first time since 1895.[17] It was not only exhaustion but fear – fear of starvation, fear of dying hungry, fear of withering slowly away in the knowledge, perhaps, that Japan had brought defeat upon itself. Ishiguro skillfully avoided commenting on the taboo against discussing the reasons for Japan's defeat; his political comments made it seem as if the tragedy had occurred naturally. "Today," Ishiguro began, "because this fear threatens our nation's meals, our hearts are filled with a terrible darkness about tomorrow's fate.... [I]f we do not band together in a concerted effort and use all our means, we will be unable to keep the land from descending into chaos and disappearing altogether."[18]

Postwar Japan was hungry and the dire implications of this were not lost on the US military commanders charged with reforming East Asian security. US occupation officials understood clearly that newly defeated Japanese citizens suffering from an intense need to eat could be the fuse

---

[15] Ishiguro Tadaatsu, "Mushozoku kurabu," Upper House Diet Speech, December 14, 1945, ([001/058] 89 - 貴 - 本会議 - 11 号(回)). US authorities were also aware of how much wartime Japan had depended on food imports from its colonial holdings. See Ronald L. McGlothlen, *Controlling the Waves: Dean Acheson and U.S. Foreign Policy in Asia*, pp. 24–26.

[16] Bruce Johnston, *Japanese Food Management in World War II*, p. 153.

[17] In 1895 Japan acquired its first colony, Taiwan. Taiwan then became a net exporter of sugar, rice and varied fruits to Japan until the end of World War II.

[18] Ishiguro Tadaatsu, "Mushozoku kurabu," Upper House Diet Speech, December 14, 1945, ([001/058] 89 - 貴 - 本会議 - 11 号(回)).

for a political explosion. Bruce Johnston, the scholar of postwar Japanese economic analysis, noted in 1949:

> If Japan's new democratic government coincides for a prolonged period with economic instability and severe hardship, it will encounter great difficulty in winning a genuine acceptance in the minds of the Japanese people. The supply of food will be the most basic factor....[19]

Johnston pointed out that the only way Japan could procure enough food was to export something for foreign trade and import food based on the hard currency it received in exchange. This was easier said than done, because Japan's postwar financial and industrial structure had been cut off from the international network for over a decade. Although pre-surrender Japanese propaganda had incited social anxiety about rape and pillage by marauding bands of US soldiers, one historian of Japanese history noted that "fear of the Americans was replaced by anxiety about food."[20]

Regardless of the initial stern terms and conditions of the occupation, General Douglas MacArthur, leader of SCAP (Supreme Commander for the Allied Powers), which essentially managed the occupation of Japan, was adamant that the US should not financially aid Japan in its efforts to rebuild. In November 1945, he issued a directive that announced Japan was on its own: "You will not assume any responsibility for the strengthening of the economic rehabilitation of Japan or the strengthening of the Japanese economy," the directive read.[21] However, Japanese mismanagement, military hoarding and traditional ways of collecting and distributing rice and other foodstuffs, impeded the Japanese government's ability to adequately feed its people and forced a change in SCAP's plans. Although MacArthur had publicly announced that the US would not contribute money to support Japan's economic recovery, food was a different issue.

A Land without Food

At the end of the war, according to US government surveys, Japan was allocating rations to its military that exceeded what its budget could afford.

---

[19] Bruce Johnston, "Japan: The Race between Food and Population," *Journal of Farm Economics*, Vol. 31, no. 2, May 1949, p. 279.
[20] Simon Partner, *Toshie: A story of village life in Twentieth-Century Japan*, p. 105. Kimura Takuji, "Fukuin – gunjin no sengo shakai e no hōsetsu," in Yoshida Yutaka, ed. *Nihon no gendai rekishi, Vol. 26, sengo kaikaku to gyaku kōsu*, p. 92
[21] Bruce Johnston, "Japan: Problems of Deferred Peace," *Far Eastern Survey*, Vol. 18, No. 19, September 1949, pp. 221–225.

Consequently, prices for civilians, already skyrocketing, continued to escalate. From 1946 to 1947, the US occupation resorted to importing double the amount of foodstuffs it distributed to the defeated nation to maintain stability.[22] On March 15, 1946, General MacArthur ordered US occupation forces to hand over to the Japanese approximately seven million pounds of wheat flour declared "surplus" for US soldiers.[23] In a twist of fate, the flour was the same stock that had been delivered to the Philippines in anticipation of a pre-planned Allied invasion of Japan's home islands before the surrender. Japan benefited from US forward planning against an enemy the Americans were not even sure would surrender unconditionally.

The Japanese oscillated in their appreciation of assistance from the occupier. In August 1946, during the *Obon* festival (a Buddhist festival to honor one's deceased ancestors), crowds performed a "Thank you General MacArthur" dance for helping Japan out with the summer food crisis in Tokyo.[24] Just a few months prior, demonstrating how SCAP's rule depended on its ability to feed the population, on May 19, 1946, over two hundred thousand protesters staged a *Food Shortage May Day* in front of the imperial palace next door to the occupation general headquarters. May Day was not just a celebration of socialist ideals: for many Japanese, it was also about eating. The May Day demonstrators held up many signs with slogans such as, "Before The Constitution, First Food," a clear signal to US authorities not to focus on redrafting Japan's legal charter at the expense of its starving population. By the summer of 1947, the occupation authorities had taken the drastic step of recalibrating government bureaucrats' pay and setting new prices for goods. Unfortunately, inflation continued to soar and only SCAP's interference quelled strikes. American reports noted that, during the first three years of the occupation, urban residents were going hungry while farmers in the countryside were hoarding or selling rice on the black market for better prices.[25] By the fall of 1949, ex-secretary of the army Kenneth Royall was quoted in the American press, saying that he was worried about feeding the eighty million Japanese and warning

---

[22] T.A. Bisson, "Reparations and Reform in Japan," *Far Eastern Survey*, Vol. 16, No. 21, December 1947, pp. 241–247; R.P. Dore, *Land reform in Japan*.

[23] "Japan Gets Bread From Allied Flour," *New York Times*, March 15, 1946.

[24] Ōgushi Junji, "Sengo no taishū bunka," in Yoshida Yutaka, ed. *Nihon no gendai rekishi, Vol. 26, sengo kaikaku to gyaku kōsu*, p. 199.

[25] Jerome B. Cohen, "Japan's Economy on the Road Back," *Pacific Affairs*, Vol. 21, No. 3, September 1948, pp. 264–279.

that social problems could be exacerbated if the Japanese Communists won any more seats than they had in the January 1949 elections.[26]

Throughout the occupation, the US exported wheat to Japan, thus encouraging the consumption of different grains and less rice. The result had implications that went beyond economic ones. As the postwar Japanese were actually starving, it is difficult to criticize the SCAP measures, but a secondary impact (not lost on the nation's leaders) was a further massive shift in the Japanese diet.[27] Japan's Agriculture and Forestry Minister Akagi Munenori, speaking at a *Food for Peace* dinner in 1952, lamented that US aid would ultimately transform the way in which the Japanese ate: "At the same time that shiploads of American food were coming to our shores helping to stamp out revolution, a different kind of revolution is occurring in Japan. It is a revolution in eating habits. For centuries, our dietary habits were built around rice. Today we find people in the cities and even the farm communities eating bread...while rice consumption continues to decline."[28] There was a marked increase in bread consumption across Japan and school lunches included bread instead of rice until the early 1970s.

Along with Japan's post-1952 security arrangement with the US as part of the San Francisco Peace Treaty, food purchases were part of US-Japan postwar realignment. The 1951 Mutual Security Act allowed the US to maintain military bases in Japan and allowed Japan to manufacture weapons for the US, which assisted Japan's economic regeneration during the Korean War (1950–1953). This agreement provided Japan with sorely needed hard currency that it used to purchase US agricultural surplus. That surplus fed the growth of ramen consumption.

Repatriates and Food

In France *pied-noir* cookery reflects the experience of former colonials who lived in North Africa and returned to the south of France after the struggles of decolonization forced them to repatriate. Former British

---

[26] Bruce Johnston, "Japan: The Race between Food and Population," pp. 276–292. For the communist issue in early postwar Japan, see Robert Scalapino, *The Japanese communist movement, 1920–1966*.
[27] Harriet Friedmann, "The Political Economy of Food: The Rise and Fall of the Postwar International Food Order," *The American Journal of Sociology*, Vol. 88, Supplement: Marxist Inquiries: Studies of Class and States, 1982, p. 254.
[28] As quoted in Darrell Gene Moen, "The Postwar Japanese Agricultural Debacle," *Hitotsubashi Journal of Social Studies* 31, 1999, p. 36.

residents returning from India brought back their appetite for curry, which has uniquely altered the taste landscape of England. In the Netherlands, even the fairly stable Dutch diet changed somewhat in the 1960s with the loss of Indonesia; Chinese-Indonesian cooking is one of the few foreign cuisines to have gained a foothold.[29] Did Japanese repatriates, or *hikiagesha*, from Korea, Taiwan, China and elsewhere have an impact on taste patterns and the postwar Japanese diet? The city of Utsunomiya, in Tochigi Prefecture, is a good starting point for this analysis. Utsunomiya is home to more dumpling stores, *gyōza-ya*, than any other city. For a population of about 450,000 the city boasts approximately eighty-three dumpling stores.[30] It is not quite the ratio of ramen shops to people as in Kitakata but it makes Utsunomiya the first city that comes to mind when thinking about Japanese dumplings. The Japanese writer Kusano Shinpei believes that the Japanese word for dumplings was not a military invention but evolved out of conversations among expat Japanese housewives who had formerly lived in the three northeastern provinces of China.[31] Since the immediate postwar, *gyōza* had been eaten as a complement to ramen.

Historically, the most distinctive aspect of Utsunomiya was that people ate their dumplings as a meal and not as a side dish – arguably a traditional Chinese way of dining. Dumplings as *shushoku*, or a main dish, reflect a Japanese modern understanding of how food is eaten and arranged for a meal. In the current Japanese mindset, meals should center on a main starch, as in Tokugawa times; this could be rice or, if you were less well-off financially, millet or another grain. Around this central starch were small side dishes called *okazu*. This structure of a traditional Japanese meal may also explain why Japanese food tends toward salty/savory flavors, relying on soy sauce. The director of the Salt and Tobacco museum in Tokyo, Okawa Yoshihiko, informed me that salty foods were used as side dishes because of the large quantities of rice one had to ingest to gain sufficient vitamins to live a healthy life.[32] Adding a bit of salt to the meal, he explained, allowed people to cope with the monotony of digesting up to

---

[29] Catherine Salzman, "Continuity and Change in the Culinary History of the Netherlands, 1945–75," *Journal of Contemporary History*, Vol. 21, No. 4, October 1986, pp. 605–628.

[30] If we compare that figure with the east coast city of Shizuoka that has a larger population with 700,000, the numbers are striking. With almost forty percent more population Shizuoka enjoys only sixty-two *gyōza* stores.

[31] Kusano Shinpei, "Jingisu ryōri," in *Kusano Shinpei zenshū*, Vol. 10, 1982, p. 54.

[32] Interview at the Salt and Tobacco Museum in Shibuya, Tokyo, August 22, 2006.

one and a half pounds, if not more, of some kind of rice or cereal mixture throughout the day.

After Japanese military forces vanquished the Qing Empire in 1895 and the Russians a few years later in 1905, they stationed more battalions in central Japan, including Utsunomiya, as part of a general expansion of the military, in Utsunomiya's case reinvigorating what had been a slumbering backwater. In 1927, the Army's 14th Division stationed in Utsunomiya mobilized to China. In 1932, the troops were again sent to China, this time to Shanghai to quell the unrest that followed Japan's aggressive tactics on the mainland. (Many of these soldiers spent their formative years in China.) For the rest of the war, the division continued to deploy to China. One theory goes that, because the Army's 14th Division was based in China, soldiers brought back knowledge of, or at least the taste for, dumplings. However, this theory demonstrates a lack of understanding regarding the real extent of interaction between Japanese soldiers and Chinese civilians on the mainland. Most Japanese soldiers, beyond contact with coolies and military engagement, had little if any direct associations with the Chinese, let alone authentic Chinese cuisine. There was probably more sharing between Japanese expats and Chinese people on the civilian side, with exchanges of recipes for example, but there is no way to know how many such Japanese civilians in China repatriated to Utsunomiya.

Many repatriates met with derision when they came back to Japan after the war, since they were living symbols of Japan's failed imperializing project.[33] There are poignant stories about Japanese expatriate families having to set up food stalls on the street in liberated northern China at the end of the war. Hattori Sumiko, a Japanese mother trying to return from the city of Dalian in northeastern China, said in a letter to a repatriate association magazine that she owed her entire postwar survival and the lives of her three children to the selfless efforts of two Chinese entrepreneurs:

> And in the dire condition I found myself I thought, my young children are the future of Japan, the last treasures bestowed to me by my husband whom I do not even know is alive or dead. My greatest responsibility was somehow to manage to raise them and return safely to the motherland. However, I had no money whatsoever and I was at wit's end trying to figure out what to do… suddenly out of the blue two Chinese helped me out. They offered me money and food without looking for repayment. With their assistance my children and I opened a food stand on the west side of the central square. In the end,

---

[33] Lori Watt, *When Empire Comes Home: Repatriation and Reintegration in Postwar Japan*.

> we eked by a living and managed to repatriate. Of course, when we returned I had no opportunity to repay the Chinese kindness....

Obviously, moved by her plight and the fact she had no chance to repay the Chinese loans, the writer expressed her gratitude publicly:

> I want everyone to know how these two miraculous Chinese helped me and I write this letter praying every day that Sino-Japanese ties improve for the better.[34]

The imperial Japanese military's tactics in China and the resulting mass social upheaval influenced the mixing of Japanese and Chinese national appetites but postwar food policy was also key.[35] According to Kamiuma Shigekazu, a founding member of the local Utsunomiya dumpling association, wheat production was historically strong in Utsunomiya but after the war there was none, so it all had to be imported from America. The question on everyone's mind was: "Well, now what do we do with the wheat the Americans gave us?" The combination of surplus wheat, a certain flair for Chinese cooking and an expanded desire to experience international tastes (perhaps due to Japan's imperial expansion and the military and civilian experience in China) coincided with a new market – the hordes of repatriates returning from the Asian mainland after the war.[36] Repatriates from China did open several of the first *yatai*, or food stalls, and the increasing number of students and hard working laborers who fed postwar economic growth flocked to purchase cheap, oily, fattening and filling foods such as ramen and dumplings.

The Japanese now coveted rich flavors and convenience, two innovations that took postwar Japan by storm. By the mid-1950s, Japan's economic foundations were once again secure and the labor force was furiously rebuilding the national infrastructure. A 1953 article from a women's journal observed that most meals in villages offered little in the way of cooked dishes and tended to present foods in their natural state. Most of the time it was the mother who prepared the meal. At one mother's round-table meeting, children explained: "We do not want to be mothers. Mommy gets up early and cooks the rice and then she has to clean but

---

[34] *Dairen*, October 1, 1950, p. 13. See also "Hikiagesha seikatsu kondankai," in *Fujin no tomo*, dai 39kan, 12gō, reprinted in Maruoka Hideko and Yamaguchi Mieko, eds., *Nihon fujin mondai shiryō shūsei*, Vol. 7, seikatsu, 1980, pp. 595–599.

[35] Kamiuma Shigekazu, *Utsunomiya gyōza no yoakemae*, Kyōdō kumiai Utsunomiya gyōza, no date.

[36] Interview in Utsunomiya, Tochigi Prefecture with Gyōza Association members, August 11, 2006.

Dad just sits by the fireplace smoking."[37] Gender roles in the home were becoming more entrenched but eating out of the home was also becoming popular again, just as it had been before the war. In 1954, Hanamori Yasuji, the editor of *Kurashi no techō* (Notebook for Living) detailed this growing phenomenon in an article entitled, "Sapporo: the city of ramen" in the weekly *Asahi* magazine. The article detailed the proliferation of ramen shops around the city and that there were now more opportunities to dine outside. Ramen was not the only new item to attract consumers; the fatty part of tuna, known in Japanese as *toro*, was starting to be considered a delicacy whereas before it had just been thrown away. A six-day work week was in force and people worked long hours to save, rebuild their families and reform the country. New meals were needed to fuel such efforts.

The postwar era of instant food and convenience had not yet arrived but it seemed imminent. The women's magazine, *Housewife's Companion*, asked readers to take note of how they spent their day. The average reader replied that she allocated three hours and thirty minutes a day to preparing meals. Eating occupied less time, about two hours and ten minutes daily. A little less than seven hours was dedicated to sleeping. Clothing preparation, washing and mending also took two hours and a few minutes on average. The article noted that wheat and corn flour were now available and if made into bread as the "main dish" of a meal, could help housewives reduce the amount of time they devoted to housework. The article explained that stores would now accept flour or grains from customers and make bread or thick noodles, *udon*, on demand. In the conclusion, the article remarked that for Japan to advance in the world the country needed to improve its food technology, like the Americans, who could just add hot water to cornmeal and pop open a can of tomato juice for a satisfying and convenient meal.[38]

Housewives in postwar Japan played a significant role as a conduit for political change. The most influential of these groups, formed to remold the Japanese as consumers, was the Housewives' Federation, or *Shufuren* in Japanese. Consumers, mostly housewives, criticized the often arbitrary and poorly implemented postwar rationing and pricing system for sugar, potatoes, rice, kerosene and other daily staples. The group later grew into

---

[37] Kumagai Motoichi, *Mura no fujin seikatsu*, reprinted portions from the 1953 text reprinted in Maruoka Hideko and Yamaguchi Mieko, eds., *Nihon fujin mondai shiryō shūsei*, Vol. 7, p. 635.
[38] "Shufu wa 24jikan o dō kurashite iru ka," *Shufu no tomo*, dai 40kan, 10gō, reprinted in Maruoka Hideko and Yamaguchi Mieko, eds., *Nihon fujin mondai shiryō shūsei*, Vol. 7, seikatsu, pp. 599–608.

part of the "protect our life-style campaign;" its symbol was the rice paddle, *shamoji* or flat spoon used to scoop rice out of a kettle (consumerism in postwar Japan was also initially linked to rice).[39] Japan's concept of democracy and political enfranchisement for all in the postwar period came not through philosophical tracts and long-winded political speeches but through female control of the kitchen, the need to place food on the table and a reconceptualization of *Nihon ryōri*, or Japanese cuisine.

As part of the national "Improve Nutrition Campaign," founded on the prewar and wartime nutritional awareness movement, the government passed a law in 1952 under the sponsorship of the Health and Welfare Ministry to raise people's awareness of the importance of nutrition.[40] Liberal Democratic Party Member and Lower House Representative Yoshida Manji took the notion further in August 1954 by linking nutritious eating with political soundness. Yoshida stated in session:

> And secondly, to prevent illness and advance preventative health measures by improving nutrition, we need to increase knowledge about nutrition and implement ways to practice making meals, keeping one's hands clean, keeping cooking implements clean, learning how to chew, improving methods for making meals. And then we need to correct our unbalanced meals, improve the hygiene of the kitchen, *spread democratic ideals*, rationalize rural cuisine and lead social intercourse forward smoothly....[41]

In direct contrast to prewar notions of "national meals," *kokuminshoku*, and Kawashima Shirō's hollow rhetoric about Japanese cuisine, Yoshida Manji subtly connected political philosophy with national cuisine, including eating patterns, in the midst of his list of how to make good meals. His remarks are a fascinating example of the new political ideas about food and cuisine. Japan needed to alter its cuisine to rebuild the nation.

A Dream Come True – Instant Ramen

Although the roots of noodle soup, or ramen, run deep and wide in very early Chinese and Japanese history, *instant* ramen is inherently a postwar Japanese phenomenon. It belongs to a cuisine of the masses, a food that is part of the unstructured, egalitarian postwar Japanese society. Instant ramen is distinctly the result of several postwar phenomena – the

---

[39] Patricia Maclachlan, *Consumer Politics in Postwar Japan*, pp. 63–64.
[40] Harada Nobuo, *Washoku to Nihon bunka*, p. 204.
[41] Japanese Diet Debate, August 19, 1954 ([033/077] 19-参-文部委員会学校給食法案). (author's italics)

increased availability of wheat, changing food desires arising from civilian experiences in colonial China and elsewhere in the empire, and an expanding urban landscape where a larger number of hungry office and factory workers wanted filling meals that were not necessarily rice-based. People wanted new tastes in the afternoon, evening or very late night as the population's wealth grew and clubs, bars and other venues flourished as they had before the war. Customers wanted their meals quickly and no longer scorned Chinese cuisine. The meaty yet Japanese-style taste of wheat noodles floating in broth pleased crowds again, as it had started to do in prewar Japan. Ramen satisfied all these needs.

As Japan rebuilt and regained international stature, in 1958 a formerly bankrupt inventor near Osaka finally hit upon a formula to produce a remarkable new food product. It was an item long dreamed about but created in almost complete secrecy – instant ramen. When it first appeared on the market, eager customers purchased a thin cellophane-wrapped envelope, poured its dried contents into a bowl, added boiling water, covered the contents and then waited for three minutes. You could add tiny satchels of spices as well – and *voilà* – you had a full meal of a noodle soup. The packaging was clean, the contents quick and easy to use and the meal was tasty, nutritious and filling. The buzz about this new dish was palpable. More homes and offices and offices now had electricity, appliances made housework easier and women were returning to work (usually part-time). More and more people were pursuing employment, hobbies or other activities outside the home.[42] Nissin, the company incorporated in part to market this dramatic new product, promoted instant ramen as a fast and convenient meal that also, more importantly, offered filling calories. The Japanese advertisement read: "Just by adding water you can quickly enjoy 'instant ramen,' a nutritious and unparalleled delicious meal you can prepare without fuss."[43]

Famous chefs are not usually ex-convicts but the inventor of instant ramen, Andō Momofuku, had the dubious distinction of having been imprisoned twice. The Japanese military police incarcerated Andō in 1943 and the American military did so again during the occupation in 1948. After the second time Andō (whose first name means "tremendous

---

[42] Morieda Takashi, "Insutanto rāmen wa ikani shite kokusaiteki ni ukerareta ka," *Kokusai kōryū*, April 1998, p. 39.

[43] Nissin shokuhin kabushiki gaisha, *Shokusō isei: nisshin shokuhin sōritsu shijisshūnen kinenshi*, p. 27. Even the company name pays homage to Japan's relations to China because it is written with the characters (日清) for "Japan" and "China." The "shin" character refers to the Qing dynasty when China was at one point at its imperial apex in East Asia.

fortune") found himself penniless. Andō later reminisced in his memoirs about what kept him alive during those dark moments, when his lending company had foreclosed, and he was bankrupt: it was, he wrote, "thinking about food." he wrote. Food, during the later years of World War II in Japan was terrible and often inedible, especially in a Japanese prison. Meals were rotten and upon release some forty-five days after his wartime incarceration, Andō could barely walk. Severely malnourished, he was escorted by friends and family to a hospital for treatment. Five years later, while American military police controlled Japanese streets for six and a half years after the surrender, Andō again found himself in jail, this time for alleged tax evasion. To his great surprise, the meals were American, and tasty and nutritious. In Sugamo prison, a notorious facility that also held Japan's suspected and convicted war criminals, "everyone ate the same," he remembered, "even the guards." "It was like the difference between heaven and hell," Andō recorded in his autobiography, "The Magic of Ramen – A Story of Invention."[44]

Like many young Japanese of the early twentieth century, Andō grew up at the periphery of the Japanese empire, on the small island of Taiwan. His parents died when he was a child and his grandparents raised him in one of the southernmost idyllic settings, the quiet and backwater town of Tainan. In the early 1930s, he returned to Japan to seek his fortune and went into the textile and garment industry. In December 1941, he was back in Taiwan on business when he heard the announcement that Japan had attacked Pearl Harbor. The war years were not easy for Andō and by the early part of the American occupation he was penniless and unemployed. There was nothing left for him to do. He was hungry and the country and economy were in shambles. As a result, Andō went to work in the only remaining place he owned, the shed behind his house in Ikeda, a small hamlet just outside Osaka.

In 1958, when Andō first released his new creation, consumers clamored for more. Hungry crowds of businessmen and students marked their hearty approval not only by spending their hard-earned cash on the new product, but by writing letters and articles to newspapers and magazines and voicing their opinions on the street. So popular was instant ramen that many tried to cash in by copying or counterfeiting the product. On April 25, 1966, a company was caught trying to unload 350,000 fake packets

---

[44] Andō Momofuku, *Mahō no rāmen: hatsumei monogatari*, p. 51.

Figure 39. The package of the first type of instant ramen for sale, chicken flavored ramen. It was not yet referred to as "*insutanto*" in Japanese but used the more traditional word for instant, "*sokuseki.*"

of instant ramen by offering them at half price.[45] Andō's invention launched the contemporary ramen fever so dominant in Japanese popular culture today. However, instant ramen did not emerge from nothingness, like divine intervention. The history of instant ramen is intertwined with ramen and Japanese history in general. It is a history of the changes in tastes, traditions and attitudes over a century, and included two massive wars that reshaped Japanese society. Through this process of evolution, instant ramen became an immediate, popular meal or snack for students, office workers, housewives and children – eaten by everyone almost anywhere.

Why Invent Instant Ramen?

Andō created instant ramen as a solution to postwar Japanese hunger: as a product that could provide a quick and easy meal to urban residents struggling to wage a new kind of war against poverty, dislocation, fear and starvation. It took him ten years of trial and error but Andō achieved his dream. He had overcome all obstacles to create a noodle dish that tasted good, was relatively nutritious and could be quickly prepared by adding hot water.

Andō claims in his autobiography that Arimoto Kunitarō, Nutrition Bureau Chief for the Ministry of Health and Welfare, encouraged him to find some use for American surplus wheat flour. During the occupation, Andō consulted for the Ministry regarding the creation of new flour-based foods as part of a program to provide school lunches for children. According to Andō, he and Arimoto were fearful that, as Arimoto intimated: "Bread... will end up Westernizing our life-style." But then, apparently, Arimoto thought: "In Eastern culture there is a long tradition of noodles. Japanese like noodles, so why don't we encourage everyone to make noodles out of the wheat flour?"[46] With that encouragement and some financial backing, Andō rose to the challenge.

Allied commanders of the occupation had already tried to encourage the Japanese to use flour to bake bread, but such plans ended mostly in failure. Japanese kitchens rarely contain ovens, so there was really no way to bake bread at home, but few US officials were aware of this at first.

---

[45] *Asahi shimbun*, (Tokyo, evening edition), April 25, 1966.
[46] Andō Momofuku, *Mahō no rāmen: hatsumei monogatari*, pp. 16–17.

Figure 40. A cartoon from a 1950 American occupation report, "Survey of Bread and Flour Utilization by the Japanese People," shows how confused Japanese initially were about eating bread as a new part of their daily meal.[47]

Promoting bread as the new Japanese staple ran into problems early in the occupation. The Supreme Command for the Allied Powers grew worried enough about the initiative to investigate Japanese attitudes toward bread. The resultant report, created at the request of the Food Branch, Price and Distribution Division, Economic and Scientific Section, provided data for the American Wheat Utilization Mission that visited Japan from 1949 to 1950. The investigation underscored that: "The Japanese people are far from whole-hearted in their acceptance of bread and tend to regard it as a temporary expedient rather than as a permanently desirable part of their diet." One hundred Tokyo housewives were surveyed. The central problem, the mission ascertained, was that Japan was not food-sufficient so people had to look beyond rice for substitutes. Housewives' responses revealed that bread in the post-surrender period

---

[47] "Survey of Bread and Flour Utilization by the Japanese People," produced by the Public Opinion and Sociological Research Division, GHQ, SCAP, CIE Section, January 15, 1950, (On Microfiche – CIE(D) – 05320, Box 5872, National Diet Library, Tokyo.

was inferior and tasted coarse and sour. Forty percent of Tokyo housewives still made bread by steaming it in a pot (arguably a more Chinese style of bread – *mantou*); only two percent even possessed a Western-style oven. The occupation authorities' overall goal, after collating people's likes and dislikes in relation to bread, was to encourage housewives to use the rationed flour as efficiently as possible.

The bread survey results demonstrated that only a small portion of housewives, seven percent, wished to include more bread in their diet. Forty-two percent wanted less and thirty-three percent felt that the amount they currently consumed was sufficient. The report concluded: "If people were free to select foods, three out of every ten would use no bread at all and most of the others would use it only 'from time to time'." A very small minority, therefore, wanted to eat more bread. American authorities and businesses faced a steep challenge in shifting postwar Japanese eating patterns, despite believing it to be in Japan's own interest for economic and social stability. Housewives and their families clung to a strong belief in the superiority of rice as a source of nutrition, the report observed. One fifty-eight-year-old housewife remarked: "With bread alone, people like my husband, who does carpentry work, get tired. I think this is because bread is lacking in nutritious value. We are used to eating rice for a long time, so we cannot eat much bread. We get hungry from it."[48] Prewar and wartime convictions about national diet and "the people's national food" did not easily dissipate, even after unconditional surrender to America.

Between 1954 and 1964, Japan received from the US $445 million in "food aid." The shipments, mostly of wheat flour, were imported and then sold as part of the Ministry of Health and Welfare's wheat flour promotion program. This program provided milk and bread for Japanese school lunches and was an integral part of the Nutrition Improvement Campaign. Suzuki Takeo, a contemporary Japanese writer, believes this campaign was part of a conspiracy to force Japan into buying Western foods from the US, thus bringing the Japanese diet under US economic domination.[49] What better way, he argues, than shifting Japan's meals from rice to wheat? Suzuki paints an insidious picture of the relatively generous US plan to help Japan get back onto its own food-supply feet by pointing out that the US government gave money and food specifically for school lunches. Suzuki viewed this move as culinary imperialism, noting that children

---

[48] Ibid.
[49] Suzuki Takeo, *Amerika komugi senryaku to Nihonjin no shokuseikatsu*, p. 20.

who learn to eat certain foods will want to purchase those products for life. "It is said that you never forget the taste of what you ate as a child," he writes.⁵⁰ While Suzuki sees devious American culinary manipulation behind the changes in Japanese dining styles, an alternative view is offered by Ōno Kazuoki who provides a more balanced analysis. Ōno demonstrates that actual postwar changes in the Japanese food supply and dietary habits stem, in part, from the dismantling of Japanese agriculture that started after the war, despite shrill warnings that the agricultural sector was in jeopardy.⁵¹ Although the new US wheat imports had a significant impact on Japanese agriculture, America's plan to reshape Japanese cuisine in its own image for economic gain may be more a coincidental outcome than an actual goal, given the fact that, after all, what the USA sold to Japan was what it had as a surplus. One result of this proliferation of wheat was a growth in the sales of noodles and, of course, the rise in popularity of these noodles in a meaty soup – ramen.

The postwar issue of what to eat had cultural as well as economic implications that went to the heart of how postwar Japanese society perceived itself. A high-level official in the nutrition section of the Ministry of Health and Welfare, Ōiso Toshio, a prolific postwar author on nutrition and health, wrote that people who eat rice "exist and eat," while those who eat wheat "eat and therefore exist." In his analysis, rice-eaters are more passive, wheat-eaters more progressive. Despite a lack of scientific evidence to underpin this reasoning, Ōiso offered anxious postwar Japanese a convincing metaphysical argument that eating rice satiates one's inner drive, while wheat is unsatisfying. As a consequence, wheat-eaters are always looking for something tastier, which propels them to be more pro-active.⁵² Such a theory in some ways harks back to the late-nineteenth-century arguments between Fukuzawa Yukichi and Mori Ōgai about whether Japanese should eat rice or not. This postwar debate, picked up in the national media, similarly implies that it was what the Japanese ate that shaped their Japanese-ness.

In a real version of butter for guns the US pressured Japan to stop building up its own agricultural strength, to buy from the US and to use the

---

⁵⁰ Ibid., p. 25. NHK produced a documentary in 1978, *Shokutaku no kage no seijōki – beikoku to komugi no sengoshi*, which detailed the impact of the US and wheat on postwar Japanese eating habits and thus the postwar Japanese economy and identity.

⁵¹ Ōno Kazuoki, *Nō to shoku no seiji keizaigaku*, p. 27. For a description of this impact elsewhere see Jerome M. Stam, "The Effects of Public Law 480 on Canadian Wheat Exports," *Journal of Farm Economics*, Vol. 46, No. 4., November 1964, pp. 805–819.

⁵² Suzuki Takeo, *Amerika komugi senryaku to Nihonjin no shokuseikatsu*, p. 64.

surplus to spur domestic industry to rebuild Japan. A secondary goal was to allow Japan to slowly rearm and serve as a bulwark for the US against the spread of communism in East Asia. In spite of the negative reports on the consumption of bread, during the 1950s a nationwide campaign involving medical staff and nutritionists encouraged the Japanese to use flour for bread and wheat instead of rice. The US Wheat Association went so far as to deploy "kitchen buses" in 1955 to show Japanese housewives how to use imported white flour and teach them to make new food products with which many were unfamiliar.[53]

The re-emergence of ramen soup and instant ramen arrived on the market at precisely the time when wheat products were being touted as a substitute for rice. The actual process of making instant ramen is deceptively easy and requires only a handful of steps, even though the process took close to a decade to perfect. Andō used the wheat flour to make

Figure 41. A traveling "Kitchen Bus" parked at the side of the road where instructors would teach housewives new methods of cooking.[54]

---

[53] As quoted in Darrell Gene Moen, "The Postwar Japanese Agricultural Debacle," *Hitotsubashi Journal of Social Studies*, p. 35.

[54] *Asahi Shimbun*, (evening edition), July 28, 1952.

noodles by mixing in alkaline water to make them springy, like the Chinese noodles he must have encountered in the extended Japanese empire. When regular noodles are made from the dough, you can boil them, mix them in a bowl with a flavored soup and eat. That works if you eat the noodles fresh, but the problem was how to make them durable and long-lasting, and to distribute them all around the country? The last step is the most crucial and it is the one that took Andō the longest time to solve. How do you package the noodles in a way that preserves their freshness and maintains their shape?

After years of trial and error, Andō found the answer by looking at how tempura is made. The trick is to fry the noodles quickly enough and in hot enough oil that they fuse into a hard block. Because they are fried so quickly, adding hot water will "melt" them back to their original shape. Because the dough contains alkaline water, the noodles retain their springiness and do not fall apart or get soggy in water, like a piece of bread. Keeping the noodles springy and in one piece was the key to making successful instant ramen. During the initial years of marketing his product, Andō generally used the Japanese term for "instant," *sokuseki*. Later, marketing patterns shifted and items with Western-sounding names sold better. Perhaps in an effort to exploit Japan's new internationalism during the early 1960s as the economy boomed, Andō coined a new term for his noodles, *insutanto rāmen,* a corruption of the English word for instant and the Japanese term for the popular prewar noodle soup, *rāmen.* And with that invention, Andō forever changed the modern Japanese diet.

Japan and Instant Ramen

Instant ramen helped to spur Japan's third food revolution. The first revolution had been the beginning of the Tokugawa era with growing markets for white rice for the upper classes. The second came about during the time of the Meiji Restoration with new imperial banquet styles, and the third involved postwar transformations. Prewar education had been confined to select strata of society but with more avenues for advancement, training and night schools opened up. Postwar Japan saw more students studying longer to progress through high school and to university. These *jukensei,* or students about to take exams, had a voracious appetite for a quick and easy meal that could be devoured at their desks. Others, to promote their careers, extended their working hours in offices and factories and therefore also eagerly consumed mountains of instant ramen. As urban areas grew more densely populated and living expenses rose, companies sent their male employees around the country to take advantage of increasing economic opportunities. In a break with the past, these temporary bachelors started to live alone near their jobs during the week, often in some distant city, and commuting back to their families on the weekends. This phenomenon was encapsulated in the new Japanese term, *tanshin funin*, "single person deployment." Youths were also beginning to leave the hinterland to build careers in the new urban centers. The nuclear familiar might have grown more prevalent but throughout the 1960s and 1970s single people living by themselves gobbled up cartons of inexpensive instant ramen, coming home late and eating alone.[55]

The new cuisine and dishes were everywhere. Like the Taisho era, postwar Japan was a time of industrialization and rebirth, but society had become much more egalitarian, determined to reclaim what the war had extinguished. At the same time as Japanese began eating differently, they also began living differently, in smaller apartment blocks called *danchi*, which speeded the demise of the larger, multi-generational family homes that had been common in rural areas. Postwar city residents purchased homes rather than renting them, part of a new government push to expand the property-owning middle class.[56] These were the new, single-family and semi-cramped yet clean apartments that divided communal living into tiny spaces measured in square footage, complete with personal bathrooms, full plumbing, kitchens with running water and electricity. Postwar urban architecture and reduced family living space almost required that some meals be taken outside the home or at least prepared using processed food purchased in stores. Entire bedroom communities virtually sprang up overnight on the fringes of cities, extending the urban reach further and further into the countryside and lengthening commutes for many up to an average duration of close to an hour and a half.[57]

---

[55] Nihon shokuryō shimbunsha, *Shōwa to Nihonjin no ibukuro*, p. 421.

[56] Laura Neitzel, *Living modern: Danchi housing and postwar Japan*, PhD dissertation at Columbia University, 2003. Compare this with Jordan Sand's descriptions of late Meiji and early Taisho housing conditions and style in *House and home in modern Japan: architecture, domestic space and bourgeois culture, 1880–1930*, 2003.

[57] The influence that postwar urban planning had on food consumption and the increased emphasis on convenience is explored by Gavin Hamilton Whitelaw, "At your konbini in contemporary Japan: Modern service, local familiarity and the global transformation of the convenience store," PhD dissertation, Yale University, 2007.

The Ramen Boom

The public's enthusiasm for instant ramen was linked to the resumption of ramen-eating in an increasingly economically viable Japan. In 1954, the Rairai Ramen Shop, formerly in Asakusa and which had closed in 1943, reopened on a plot near the Tokyo station. It then remained in business until 1976. Its rebirth signaled the return of the noodle soup. At the same time, a "home" column started to appear in the main newspapers, commenting on menus, Western clothing and what was popular in fashion. It also included letters to the editor from women readers. By the mid-1950s the Japanese media began to shift from talking about food as a means to fill one's stomach to discussing meals that included Chinese recipes, the need to consume oily foods and to expand one's daily culinary choices in the house and outside. The Japanese were once again chatting about how to enjoy and appreciate food.[58] Just as wealthier Meiji Japanese became more choosy about which strain of rice they wished to eat, postwar Japanese, especially after 1956 when a government economic white paper proclaimed that "Japan is no longer in the postwar," championed new dishes that in both taste and content represented a break from wartime cooking. Ramen was perfect for these circumstances because a preference for it had clearly been established prewar and now at last the ingredients were readily available, as was the consumer base.

Rachel Laudan, renowned food historian and scientist, says that we should not always worry about changes in our diet, nor should we always recoil in horror at processed food. And certainly, the postwar Japanese did not. Laudan eschews the idea that authentic and traditional cuisine was fresh and natural. Fresh and natural, she writes, would have horrified our ancestors. As she explains, fresh often turned sour, putrid or inedible soon after storage and "natural was often indigestible." The belief of the day was that cooking foods "pre-digested them" and only the poor or stupid would prefer raw.[59] Laudan sums up why processed foods are not the bane of our existence but perhaps the root of our success. "Culinary Modernism has provided what was wanted: food that was processed, preservable, industrial, novel and fast, the food of the elite at a price everyone could afford. Where modern food became available, populations grew taller, stronger,

---

[58] Narukawa Hiroko, "Shimbun no kateiran kara mita sengo no katei seikatsu no henka," *Kanjōgakuin daigaku ronshū*, no. 8, 1968, pp. 27–33.
[59] Rachel Laudan, "A Plea for Culinary Modernism: Why We Should Love New, Fast, Processed Food," *Gastronomica* I, February 2001, p. 37.

had fewer diseases and lived longer. Men had choices other than hard agricultural labor, women other than kneeling...five hours a day."[60] We forget that the traditional foods so often cherished in cookbooks and in memoirs required hordes of servants and a life-style inaccessible to most and probably illegal in most countries today. The taste, speed, convenience and nutritional value of ramen, in both its regular and instant forms, satisfied Japanese social and political needs after the war in much the way Laudan describes.

Thus, ramen represented a certain sense of the new and processed but there were also demographic and structural issues that aided its rise. It was really after the 1960s that the Japanese diet saw its most dramatic changes. According to Japanese government statistics, in 1955 the average Japanese during the year ate 1.1 kilograms of beef a year, 0.8 kilograms of pork, 0.3 kilograms of chicken and 1.1 kilo of other meats. In addition, they consumed 3.4 eggs per capita and a staggering 110.7 kilograms of rice. By 1965, the amounts had risen slightly and the distribution was changing. Japanese ate about 1.5 kilograms of beef, 3.0 kilograms of pork, 1.9 kilograms of chicken, 11.6 eggs and 111.7 kilos of rice. Another ten years went by before the most drastic shift in 1978. Now Japanese were rich and fed on 8.7 kilograms of pork and 14.9 eggs per capita; there was a noticeable downward trend in rice consumption, which had decreased to 81 kilograms per capita.[61] Paralleling the trend to eat more meat and less rice, Japanese consumers used their increased national income, which had doubled under Prime Minister Ikeda Hayato's new economic growth plan, to invest in the "three sacred treasures." In the 1950s, these were a television, an electric washing machine and a fridge. By the 1960s, the three treasures had climbed up the capitalist scale to include a car, an air conditioner and a color television.[62]

Japan's postwar economic success also led to what I would label as the fourth major food revolution for Japan – an over-abundant, varied food supply and a corresponding weakening of traditional patterns of diet. Just twenty years after the war Japan was already becoming a nation of "solitary eaters," people who dined alone, exemplified best by the ramen consumers I described in the Introduction to this book.[63]

---

[60] Ibid., p. 40.
[61] Yuize Yasuhiko, Saitō Masaru, *Sekai no shokuryō mondai to Nihon nōgyō*, p. 161.
[62] Simon Partner, *Assembled in Japan – Electrical goods and the Making of the Japanese Consumer*, p. 233.
[63] Jon D. Holtzman, "Food and Memory," *Annual Revue of Anthropology*, no. 35, 2006, pp. 36–78.

Ramen and Food Tourism

To understand how ramen revived in postwar Japanese society, we need to briefly revisit Kitakata and its ramen boom of the late 1960s and early 1970s. Here we can see where history, tourism, transportation and local taste all merge in a culinary consensus supporting the re-emergence of ramen as a sign of Japan's postwar success. The city of Kitakata was not a prewar hub for ramen nor was it really a center for anything else. The growth of ramen shops in an unlikely town at the geographic core of Japan came about more through tourism and happenstance than through any innate Kitakata interest in the noodle soup. On both national and regional scales, the ramen story is a postwar phenomenon. Years after the war was over, a local photographer, Kawada Minoru, photographed majestic images of the large surviving *kura*, or storage houses, that dotted the town. His published collection helped the rest of Japan rediscover a heritage that had been ignored in the postwar and economic boom of the 1960s and 1970s. Kawada's pictures were broadcast in an NHK television program and suddenly Kitakata became a city of national interest. According to Onodera Mitsuo, a volunteer tour guide, until that moment Kitakata was just another small Japanese town. "There were about ten or so ramen shops but it wasn't a place known for its ramen," he told me one sleepy afternoon when I visited the town.[64] Mr. Onodera had a distinct country accent, with a slight slurring of the "s" sound and a tendency to say "e" instead of "ai." He certainly knew his local history so I asked him how the Chinese peddler's arrival made a difference in the 1920s.

Mr. Onodera paused, looked at me and explained: "Kitakata was the commercial center, the provision hub (*shōgyōchō*) for the castle town nearby. A large number of men (samurai and officials) were stationed near the center of the Aizu domain, which had enormous land holdings." The rise of ramen in Kitakata was due to a rare intersection of historical conditions, he explained. First, the general wealth of Tokugawa-era Kitakata residents and the region's prosperity during the Meiji and Taisho periods made the town an attractive location for a Taisho-era Chinese immigrant to risk a financial stake in opening a noodle stand near a rail station. The second factor was that prewar Kitakata was already producing miso, saké and rice and was accustomed to the commercialization of agricultural

---

[64] Interview on August 8, 2007.

products – there was already strong market demand for foodstuffs. But the real key was a postwar media campaign that put pressure on the Japanese to find the authentic, lost Japan that seemed to have perished postwar. Many Japanese and foreigners feel a regret that modern, postwar Japan has been superimposed over traditional, authentic Japan, which lurks somewhere in the hinterland regions, waiting to be re-discovered and re-studied. For the city of Kitakata, the real Japan could supposedly be found in the city's food and taste. For Japan's outlying regions, "authentic" Japan could be used as a vehicle to boost tourism and sell local food products, another postwar media-driven phenomenon.

As Onodera and fellow city historian Koyama Yoshiko explained, stimulated by the book of photographs and the TV show, tourists arrived *en masse* to view the stylish old storage houses (*kura*) that remained in use in Kitakata, although destroyed or left to rot in many other parts of Japan. Once the tourists completed the relatively short walk around the town they needed a place to eat. Day trippers usually came only for a couple of hours and those from Tokyo and other wealthy cities only wanted to stop, look and eat – the bullet train, or *shinkansen*, made such a quick journey possible. The real ramen boom was born because all of the necessary ingredients – fast trains, extra wealth, a desire to tour "authentic" Japan and the leisure time to do it – coalesced. Speed and expendable income only really existed after 1964, the bullet train's inaugural year. Kitakata was home to a few ramen shops but postwar entrepreneurs saw the opportunity ahead. As my two volunteer history guides explained, local government officials realized that tourists were coming to Kitakata for the sightseeing; as those numbers rose, so did the number of ramen shops to meet expanding demand.

Nowadays, travelers to Kitakata have somewhat reversed their preferences: they come to enjoy and peruse the large number of ramen shops as much as to view the *kura*. But the ramen still has to be tasty to draw fans and Mr. Onodera believed it was the water that made his city's ramen delicious. He claimed the town hall occasionally receives complaints from people who enjoyed tasty ramen in Kitakata and bought packages of local ingredients but were unable to recreate the taste at home.[65] The town is now in the process of bottling and selling its water; he showed me two sample bottles about to go on the market.

---

[65] Interview on August 8, 2007.

Figure 42. Banners hanging on the platforms in Kitakata rail station. The deep red curtains announce Kitakata as the "village of store houses" and on the right as the city of "Japan's number one ramen, rice, saké and water."

Branding the Local

Marketing local tastes to sell local identity as a tourist product is nothing new, but Utsunomiya, the dumpling capital, and Kitakata, the ramen capital, have taken the phenomenon to new heights. In postwar Japan, with its strong centralizing government in Tokyo and pork barrel politics that express the periphery's financial attachment to the center, many communities have lost what formerly made them unique. Alex Kerr laments this inexorable decline in his book *Dogs and Demons: Tales from the Dark Side of Japan*, an elegiac take on how a modernizing Japan has subsumed its traditional soul. Many critics note that Kerr pines fervently for a Japan that never existed in reality as much as it does in Kerr's dreams and was never as idyllic as he imagines. Nevertheless, his point is valid. Japanese who do not live in Kyoto, Osaka or Tokyo wonder the same thing. What shall we do, they pine? We cannot compete with the major cities for tourist attractions and we no longer have facilities or traditions that distinguish us from the mainstream. Wartime bombing campaigns had leveled much of what made many Japanese cities distinct and postwar city-planning policies further erased those distinctions. The need to carve out a unique identity in the homogeneous landscape of postwar Japan to encourage tourism can help to explain why disparate areas in Japan tout their own flavors and methods of producing ramen. Hinterland Japan has been emptying ever since the Japanese economic boom took off and millions flocked to the cities looking for excitement and jobs. Many local business associations and trade groups came together in the early 1980s to promote their vibrant local areas through specialty cuisine and national campaigns to promote local tastes. Occasional tourist campaigns market a "back to the heartland" idea that works for brief periods of time. Nowadays in Japan you can travel to virtually any point on the four major islands within half a day by the bullet train. Easy transportation has enabled Japanese from all over the islands to connect linguistically and culturally as they never could before, but it has also eroded local identity. Cuisine is one surviving resource that enables local regions to maintain a sphere of uniqueness; this too explains the continued popularity of ramen.

Ramen Finds Its Way Abroad – First to America

The first packets of instant ramen came in a sealed, thin plastic wrapping. That packaging still exists, but instant ramen today is more of a hybrid due to the demands of the international consumer. The evolution of *cup ramen*, the next stage in ramen evolution, where the envelope was discarded in favor of a styrofoam cup (and later a bowl) and a resealable lid, is a fantastic story of corollary invention and serendipity. Andō had traveled to the US in the late 1960s to promote instant ramen as a new foodstuff to Americans looking for an exotic "oriental" taste with the added convenience of quick preparation. What Andō came to realize was not only that the US diet was drastically different but that consumers ate with completely different utensils as well. In America, he saw people putting the noodles into styrofoam cups since most US homes at that point had shallow soup bowls but nothing like the Japanese *donburi*, a deep bowl for single servings of rice or noodles in broth. The American preference for styrofoam cups perplexed Andō. On his return flight home, through Hawaii as was customary in the early days of jet travel, he was sitting in the back of the plane eating macadamia nuts from a can with a plastic, resealable lid. Popping the lid on and off the container to pass time he suddenly realized that he had hit upon a solution. In one of his interviews Andō claims to have shouted out the Japanese equivalent of "Eureka!" at that moment. "The problem was that we had to invent the container" for noodles, he explained. Andō realized that he could not sell packets of instant ramen abroad in the way that he had done in Japan. Dining behavior and crockery were too different. The company needed to sell the product with its own delivery system, to offer it with its own container that one could eat out of.[66]

Cup Noodle as a concept seems fairly obvious but the construction of a container that can serve as both packing mechanism and heat retention unit is tricky. To keep the fragile noodles safe during transport but ready for boiling water once the container is opened led to a fateful discovery – you have to suspend the noodles in the middle of the cup. They cannot be allowed to settle on the bottom or float around the cup while being transported. Mid-cup suspension keeps the noodles from breaking while traveling. When the hot water is poured in, liquid pools at the bottom, cooking and steaming the noodles from below, back into edible form.[67] If the noodles were not kept in the center of the cup they would all mush up on the bottom when water was poured in, creating an unappetizing mess.

---

[66] Andō Momofuku, *Mahō no rāmen: hatsumei monogatari*, pp. 95–96.
[67] Ishige Naomichi, *Mendan tabemono no shi*, p. 111.

You Are *Not* What You Eat

The Japanese started to consume larger amounts of regular ramen in various forms and flavors around the country by the early 1960s and were exporting instant ramen abroad by the end of the decade. At the same time, Japan had already become a target for international fast food chains such as Dunkin' Donuts and McDonalds. These transformations illustrate an important, but often unacknowledged, change in the Japanese diet. Linda S. Wojtan, a Senior Advisor and Chair of the Advisory Board on the National Clearinghouse for US-Japan Studies, at one point wrote about the importance of, and supposedly obsessive Japanese affinity for, rice in the daily diet. "The language of a culture provides clues to important concepts and values," she writes. "This is true in the Japanese culture. The primacy of rice as a diet staple is echoed in the Japanese language. *Gohan* is both the word for *cooked rice* as well as *meal*." Wojtan asserts, "these multiple terms signal that it was almost impossible for most Japanese to think of a meal without rice."[68] Wojtan might have meant *imagine* rather than "think," since historically most Japanese could only dream of such a splendid meal with pure rice. But ramen has no rice in it, none whatsoever, and there are millions of Japanese who would consider a meal consisting of just ramen the epitome of being culturally Japanese.

Does the expansion of quasi-Chinese cooking within the accepted paradigm of Japanese cuisine change the discussion about what is culturally native or foreign? To be sure, rice is central to the idea (if not the practice) of Japanese food but we must remember that it is a recent phenomenon. There were many long periods when it just would not have been accurate to say that rice was central to Japanese cuisine. A less monolithic way of looking at modern Japanese food should ask when the internationalization of Japanese cuisine first began and whether this dominance of rice persists today. Considering the rise of Western fast food franchises in Japan and the popularity of convenience foods like ramen and instant ramen, the centrality of rice to Japanese identity may be more myth than actual tradition, at least in the postwar era.

This transformation of the Japanese diet had created a backlash of concerns about the risk to national health. Contemporary Japanese enjoy one of the longest life spans in the world and critics fear this is threatened by modern, processed foods like instant ramen. However, when I asked Takeo

---

[68] http://www.indiana.edu/~japan/digest6.html (accessed July 27, 2005).

Yutaka, director of the *Instant Ramen Memorial Hall* just outside of the city of Osaka, if instant ramen was bad for your health, he replied, "Andō Momofuku is over ninety-four years old [he was still alive then] and since 1958 he has eaten chicken flavored instant ramen every single day for lunch. It's all a matter of nutritional balance."[69] One should also add that the founder did not eat much else for lunch, aside from his instant noodles. Obviously, keeping calorie intake low is a factor as well. Andō died at the ripe old age of ninety-six, having lived a full life. Takeo's response reminded me of Robert Chesebrough, the inventor of Vaseline. He also lived well into his nineties and attributed his health to consuming a spoonful of Vaseline on a daily basis. I prefer to think that Andō Momofuku was a happier customer.

Sasahara Ken, director of the international division of Nissin Foods, told me in defense of instant ramen and to avert any criticism of its social benefits, that "instant ramen has provided people and perhaps most importantly housewives, with more leisure and free time."[70]

"Fighting for a Share of the Stomach"

Sasahara Ken provided interesting insights regarding instant ramen and food in general when asked about ramen in Japan. He said, "the focus on the noodles is misguided. Soup is the storage of culture." Sasahara's comments reminded me of what Kamada Shigeto, the Japanese owner of the Minca noodle shop in New York, told me about ramen. Kamada, a jazz musician cum restaurateur, revealed that "every owner puts his own personality into the soup and that allows him to make his mark on the dish. It's like a new sauce for spaghetti or something, if you want to think about it in terms of Western food."[71] Western fast food tends to emphasize uniformity in place of individuality. As products are standardized, consumers can relax in the knowledge that wherever they go – England, the United States, China, or Mexico – the eating experience will not change.

Sasahara admitted that, as Japan's population ages, the elderly are not eating as much instant ramen as younger generations have done, so Nissin foods will be focusing its future marketing and development on products that offer nutritional balance. From the end of the war and even up to the

---

[69] July 29, 2004, interview in Ikeda City, Japan.
[70] August 6, 2004, interview in Tokyo, Japan.
[71] Interview with Kamada in NYC, July 4, 2005.

1970s, after decades of military deprivation, the Japanese craved fattier foods, meals that put calories under their belt and warmth into their bodies. Modern Japanese consumers are growing larger and taller, to the point where even the average weight of sumo wrestlers is cause for concern in the popular media. Japan has not yet experienced anything like the calamitous rise in obesity that plagues the West, but there is certainly cause for concern. Based on data collected by the former physician to the Sumo Wrestling association, Hayashi Asaroku, one hundred years ago the average sumo wrestler stood five feet five inches tall and weighed around two-hundred-and-thirty pounds. Today, that same genre of wrestler stands approximately six feet tall and tips the scales at three-hundred-and-forty-two pounds.

Since the postwar rebirth of ramen noodle soup and the creation of its close cousin instant ramen in 1958, the boom continues. Ramen is now the preferred midday or midnight meal of millions of Japanese men and women. At the dawn of instant ramen production, factories produced thirteen million sachets. 2010 statistics show that the world currently buys over ninety-five billion packages of instant ramen a year and that Japan does not even top the list.[72] The selection is also immense. At first, there was only chicken flavor. Nowadays, in addition to all the flavors offered by small ramen shops across the Japanese archipelago, instant ramen can be found in hundreds of variations.

Is Ramen Part of Japanese Cuisine?

Postwar Japan is a hybrid conglomeration of tastes and cultural influences, just as it was during the early Meiji period, with Chinese compradors and Western businessmen. As the French bask in their gustatory glory and Americans ponder their national cuisine, not to mention the British, Japan's reactions to the international rise in stature of its national cuisine appear at best ambivalent. Ramen has taken the world by storm. But its popularity has also caused uneasiness. Do the Japanese feel threatened by the fact that their supposedly unique diet that has given them the longest lifespan in the world but is now under pressure? France has a long tradition of gastronomic delight yet its authorities do not appear to worry about how French food is prepared abroad. Anyone can make a *croque-monsieur* and call it what they want, while the Irish government does not

---

[72] http://instantnoodles.org/noodles/expanding-market.html.

seem overly alarmed at the proliferation of pubs that exploit its history. The French, however, are concerned with stemming international imitations of their regional cheeses and champagne which leads one to surmise that Japanese leaders seem genuinely worried about national image, not just about making money (as their French counterparts mostly appear to be). In recent years, Japanese politicians have suggested that Japanese cuisine is being adulterated abroad. I do not think that we have returned to the idea of *kokuminshoku*, the nationalistic meals of the 1940s, but some historical *frisson* may still be there.[73] Many Japanese believe that there is an inviolable Japanese cuisine that is not receiving its full dues abroad, especially if non-Japanese are crafting it.

According to the Japanese Ministry of Agriculture, Forestry and Fisheries, in 2005–7 the government was trying to coordinate a strategy to improve the quality of Japanese cuisine offered abroad during recent boom years.[74] The interesting aspect of these discussions about how to legally define Japanese cuisine is the traditional way in which it is still conceived. For example, the report said:

> Characteristics of our nation's food are that its main focus is rice, with side dishes and soup. There is a lot of vegetable matter and nutritional balance. Our nation's food reflects the fresh and rich variety of forestry, agricultural and water products and has advanced cooking traits from China, the West and our domestic practices. In addition, in adapting to our changing lifestyles the overall selection of what Japanese eat on a daily basis has grown.[75]

The report concludes with this fascinating observation: "In this way, our country's cuisine has transformed in synch with our history and culture so that currently there is no one definition for 'Japanese cuisine'."[76]

The Ministry was quite aware that, in contrast to the overabundant and unhealthy image of American and some European cuisines, internationally Japanese cuisine's reputation was all to do with being "healthy," "beautiful," "safe," and "of a high quality." This image was exceedingly important, the government argued, for the status of Japanese cuisine and the nation internationally.[77] Nevertheless, this success also caused anxiety, for what if

---

[73] "Kokuminshoku to wa," *Eiyō to ryōri*, Vol. 7, no. 4, 1941, p. 4.
[74] http://www.maff.go.jp/gaisyoku/kaigai/conference/01/index.html.
[75] http://www.maff.go.jp/gaisyoku/kaigai/conference/01/index.html.
[76] http://www.maff.go.jp/gaisyoku/kaigai/conference/01/index.html.
[77] The Japanese have a strong fear over becoming a food colony of China in the near future. Such anxiety gets full media play in the more strident conservative magazines like *SAPIO!*, which have followed the 2008 food scandals of imported tainted goods from China into the Japanese food market.

restaurants did not uphold this high standard and sold Japanese food that was below par? On November 2, 2006, the Japanese government announced its intention to consider a licensing system to standardize and authorize what Japanese politicians believed were "authentic and qualified" Japanese restaurants as opposed to those "wholly unconnected to Japan."[78] The ministry, in a somewhat stilted translation, established an advisory council to deal with this new situation. Its website explained:

> There are an increasing number of Japanese restaurants outside Japan providing Japanese cuisine that is removed from traditional Japanese cooking, i.e. do not use Japanese ingredients or cooking methods however continue to operate under the guise of a Japanese restaurant. For this reason, an advisory council... will be established to put into effect a certification system for Japanese restaurants outside of Japan for the purpose of increasing consumer confidence in Japanese restaurants and promoting the export of Japanese agricultural and marine products while also popularizing the food culture of Japan and further establishing the food industry of Japan in overseas destinations.[79]

Authorization could avert problems and promote good foreign sales of Japanese products. An interactive web link allowed patrons of any restaurant to report on the "Japanese" quality of their dining experience to help the department collect data.[80] What exactly denoted "Japanese" quality remained unclear and was never specified.

The government report correctly noted that Japan was not alone in its efforts to maintain standards, citing a recent Thai government policy to promote authentic Thai cuisine, the Italian restaurant association effort to award commendations for Italian cuisine and JETRO's seal of approval for Japanese cuisine in France. The Japanese cuisine seal of approval in France, the "Cuisine Japonaise Authentique 2007," was established by the Comité d'evaluation de la cuisine Japonaise. Some of the measures needed to gain authorization in France are quite revealing. Among other conditions that needed to be met: "at least one person in the restaurant should speak Japanese and the staff should be polite and respect Japanese alimentary customs," regulations that are so vague they are comical.[81] How does one exactly respect alimentary customs? Would ramen be served and would that be authentically considered Japanese? If so, on what basis?

---

[78] *Asahi shimbun*, (Tokyo edition) November 3, 2006.
[79] http://www.maff.go.jp/gaisyoku/kaigai/english.html.
[80] http://www.voice.maff.go.jp/maff-interactive/people/ShowWebFormAction.do?FORM_NO=59.
[81] See the website and guides for full explanation: http://www.cecj.fr/.

One last condition concerning ingredients, taste and aesthetics stipulated that, "the presentation should be well balanced and pleasing to the eye," which should normally be the aim of any reputable restaurant, not just an authorized official Japanese eatery. The counter-argument would be to investigate how many restaurants on the home islands of Japan could meet these criteria? Would all restaurants operated by Japanese nationals be exempt due to the racial makeup of the chefs? The policy petered out eventually, perhaps due to feasibility issues, but the initiative behind the policies underscores a larger social debate about food, ethnicity and postwar Japanese notions of national cuisine.

Ramen Is Japan

Now in the twenty-first century, Japanese no longer eat the cuisine that was standard during the early Meiji era or even the early postwar period, nor are appetites constrained by the wheat and rice debate that arose during the Meiji era. Chinese and other foreign influences are felt around the archipelago and a new surge in convenience store foods has further altered the national cuisine.[82] From postwar transformations and the rebirth of ramen, to the instant ramen that developed as an outgrowth, dietary changes have left an indelible mark on Japanese society and the world at large. In a 2000 questionnaire, adults twenty years or older in the Osaka region were asked: "Which made-in-Japan products have become popular all over the world? What aspects of Japanese culture are now universally practiced? What kinds of Japanese technology or industry should the nation be proud of?" Out of a great variety of responses including Pokémon, Sony walkmans and karaoke, the number one vote-getter by a clear margin was instant ramen.[83]

Ramen (regular and instant) permeates virtually all features of contemporary Japanese life. A life-style statistics investigation in 2004 showed that an overwhelming majority of Japanese prefer ramen to other noodle dishes. 48.5% of people prefer ramen to *soba*, *udon*, or pasta, a real change from the Tokugawa era when *soba* shops could be found everywhere, especially in Tokyo. Of the average man or woman questioned for the survey, about 50% admitted eating cup ramen about one-to-three times a month.

---

[82] Gavin Hamilton Whitelaw, "At your konbini in contemporary Japan: modern service, local familiarity and the global transformation of the convenience store," PhD dissertation, Yale University, 2007.

[83] *The Daily Yomiuri* (Tokyo edition) December 12, 2000.

Half of the respondents said when they ate instant ramen it was for lunch and 64.7% said they bought it for taste rather than the low cost. This is an interesting shift because instant ramen now seems to be competing with regular ramen on quality and not merely as a convenience food.[84]

Japanese "soft power," that elusive metric that tries to calculate the impact of a nation's popular culture internationally, contains many elements such as electronics, film, anime and manga. Equally important, if not more so, is Japanese cuisine and specifically ramen. Ramen in its various forms is one of the most consumed foodstuffs around the world; and its appeal does not appear to be diminishing. One reason for its continued popularity is that, unlike sushi, sukiyaki, yakitori and other Japanese dishes that have proven trendy abroad, ramen has embedded itself into postwar Japanese culture. We have traveled far from the roots of noodley delights in ancient Japan, through the Tokugawa *soba* boom to the hybrid Chinese-produced meaty soups with springy noodles that were popular during the Meiji and Taisho eras. These noodle soups all remained mere items on a menu. Today's ramen has evolved into something more – a symbol of Japan's food culture in general and Japanese foodways specifically. The ways in which this manifests itself today are explained in the next chapter on popular culture and in the conclusion.

---

[84] Seikatsu jōhō sentā henshū, *Shokuseikatsu dēta sōgō tōkei nenpō*, Bunkōsha, 2004.

CHAPTER TEN

RAMEN POPULAR CULTURE

My first encounter with ramen, as mentioned in the Introduction, was partly shaped by linguistic barriers. In my first year in Japan, I neither spoke nor read much Japanese. For weeks, each day after working as an assistant English teacher in a small fishing village in the northeastern prefecture of Iwate, I would walk through the tiny one-road town, exploring shops and sights, not really understanding any of the signs on the stores. To make things worse, the thick brogue of the local dialect rendered the relatively few words I called my "Japanese vocabulary" unintelligible to the town's residents. Among other obvious problems, I had a tough time finding places where I was sure I could eat. I explained my frustration to an English-speaking colleague who readily offered a solution: "Look for doors with *noren*, blue curtains, hanging over the entranceway. This curtain signifies that a restaurant is open for business."

Armed with that simple advice I began discovering restaurants where I previously thought none had existed. All went deliciously well until I discovered that not *all* blue *noren* meant "restaurant." One evening, as I was searching for an interesting-looking eatery, I noticed a blue *noren* hanging over the doorway of a traditional old house. I slid open the door, stepped in, took off my shoes in the sunken "genkan" entranceway and started down the hallway. I ignored the laundry hanging in the passage, a common sight in restaurants in small villages, which often dry towels, aprons and napkins wherever space permits. The tantalizing aromas led me down the hallway into a room where I stopped suddenly in my tracks. I had interrupted a family of five seated on the floor around a low table, happily eating their dinner. As this fact sank in, I backed up slowly, the family's faces undoubtedly as dumbfounded as mine. That evening's lesson was that, while I was beginning to appreciate Japanese food, finding a place to eat it was proving far more difficult than I imagined, even with my new understanding of the secret of the blue *noren*.

How to Eat Ramen – Slurp!

As every ramen expert will tell you, ramen must be eaten hot. Piping hot. As any good ramen shop-owner also knows, it requires perfect timing, setting the bowl down in front of the customer just after the noodles have boiled and the soup has been ladled out. Good ramen cannot under any circumstances be tepid and it must be served fresh. In short, good ramen is labor-intensive and time-consuming to make. Just how strenuous an activity it is can be seen from the grueling curriculum at the new center for studying how to make the freshest noodles and tastiest soup, located in the heartland island of Shikoku.

Fujii Kaoru's "institute for higher learning about ramen" college runs a week-long 8am to 6pm program, sometimes including night courses, to teach the uninitiated the basic techniques of making perfect ramen. The school reveals how to cook noodles and how to make the essential broth base, where to buy quality ingredients and – equally important – how to financially manage your capital and attract more investment. Fujii's goal in teaching the solid production values behind quality ramen and how to operate a good eatery is to raise the general level of noodle cuisine around Japan. He is relentless in this pursuit. He briefly explained his philosophy to me, early one morning before an onslaught of business meetings: "There are no limits to how tasty ramen can get and our duty is to pursue a better and tastier product. Ramen is slowly taking over the world and one can see that in our growing student body. We are taking in over 300 students a year from all over the world, including America, Thailand, Australia, Korea and other countries."[1]

But how do you eat ramen? Historically, diners sucked the noodles in as quickly as possible and then tipped up the bowl and drank the soup. Eating quickly in this fashion seems to have been a mainstay of Japanese culture even in early times. Sei Shōnagon, a female writer of the late-ninth and early-tenth centuries and author of the *Pillow Book*, a record of personal observations at court, described how the masses ate:

> The moment the food was brought out, they fell on the soup bowl and gulped down the contents. Then they pushed the bowl aside and polished off the vegetables. I was wondering whether they were going to leave their rice; a second later there wasn't a grain left in their bowls.[2]

While the "guzzling" approach is still in evidence in most ramen stores and fast-food eateries – both traditional and contemporary – the volume of slurping may have toned down a bit. Each group has an arsenal of tools at its disposal, including websites, books and a growing mountain of

---

[1] Interview July 27, 2009.
[2] Ivan Morris, *The World of the Shining Prince*, p. 86.

literature devoted to advice on how one should eat ramen. This wealth of information demonstrates that there really is no single method. There are many methods – and yet, perhaps the methods share a single concern. This concern is appropriate speed and pace for drinking the soup, slurping the noodles (sucking them up, but not too quickly) and appreciating the flavors. In today's Japan, ramen has developed into a gastronomic tradition with a certain etiquette that distinguishes the expert from amateur. The frenetic approach of some eaters endures, to be sure – but these are usually the amateur, late-night, drunken slurpers. Go to a quality ramen store and you will see experts eating their ramen with slowness and precision. These are the *tsū*, or connoisseurs. In truth, though, serious eaters of ramen are still divided over the correct manner of eating their noodles, like mutually disdainful music critics competing for the most correct interpretation. Many believe the meal should be eaten slowly and savored like a fine wine; other, more vocal critics, believe that ramen should be consumed rapidly to be properly appreciated. But all ramen-eaters, whether slow and contemplative, or fast and frenetic, still slurp.

Comedy and Ramen

Regardless of which dictates are followed, no ramen enthusiast can ignore the fact that ramen has firmly attached itself to all aspects of modern Japanese culture, perhaps one reason for its phenomenal postwar success. Popular entertainers have created their own personalized brands of ramen. Consultants publish reams of guidebooks and magazines to help orient the public amid an ever-growing industry of new ramen shops, some featuring complex instructions on how to eat ramen. The commentary of Hayashiya Kikuzō, a well-known Japanese *rakugo* performer, is a case in point. Nowadays, many *rakugo* performers show up on TV comedy programs and sell CDs/DVDs of their performances. Kikuzō, like many comedians, has also turned to product endorsement and publishing to further enhance his popularity and fame. There is no doubt that he loves ramen but selling and commenting on the dish ties his name to a successful product line. Some other traditional Japanese comedians also produce their own lines of ramen, based on the distinctive flavors of their hometown ramen soups. These are sold to fans and as local souvenirs, in complete noodle-and-soup kits. Kikuzō happens to consider himself a *bon vivant* and a true ramen connoisseur. He explains the correct form for eating ramen, perhaps a little melodramatically, for comic effect, in his book "Ahh...Ramen:"

> Pretend that the ramen bowl is like the stage of a Greek play; a holy spectacle awaits you. Sprinkle pepper on as an overture. Pull your chopsticks apart and imagine that the noodles are the hero and the soup is your heroine. Taste the soup. Next, gather up a portion of noodles on your chopsticks and with some soup left over in your mouth slurp them in. Then, without hesitation take a piece of naruto (fish paste) and bamboo shoot into your mouth. While chewing, bring a spoon of soup to your mouth and without missing a beat put a piece of pork slice in. Take a strand of noodles with your chopsticks and without leaving any behind eat them all up one by one. Last, drink the soup down until you can see the picture at the bottom of the bowl.[3]

To understand why traditional Japanese comedians are obsessed with ramen and base many routines around the act of eating it, I tracked down Hayashiya Kikuzō. On an extremely hot day in late August we met for coffee in a famous tea and dessert store near Ueno Park in northern Tokyo. The Wind-Moon Café has been around for almost one hundred years and its affluent clientele is so discreet that the sight of a short Japanese comedian enjoying iced coffee with a gangly American in shorts did not seem to draw much overt attention. Kikuzō is an immensely popular *rakugo* comedian in Japan. He has been performing for more than forty years, has a regular slot on the Sunday afternoon television *rakugo* show, *Shōten* ("Laughing Point"), and has published over fifty books on various topics. He now operates his own talent agency and markets a line of quality ramen, instant ramen products and gift cards. Such was his enthusiasm for bringing ramen to the rest of the world that he once tried, unsuccessfully, to open a chain of ramen shops in Europe.

I was particularly interested in why such a celebrity would bother to promote his own ramen – why ramen in general, not just in comparison with other possibly more lucrative dishes? Kikuzō explained that as a performer he traveled all around the country, eating out much of the time. He greatly enjoyed ramen and found it a convenient and tasty meal to eat while constantly on the go. In terms of his performances, Kikuzō explained that eating or mimicking the act of eating on stage is guaranteed to get laughs. Historically, Japan was poorly fed, he added, so "it's not hard to imagine people participating vicariously in the act of eating without really being able to always eat a delicious meal." Kikuzō explained that miming comedy on stage was also a good way to be understood.

---

[3] As quoted on the ramen website http://homepage1.nifty.com/momikucha/j/tabekata/tabekata-01.htm, but taken from Kikuzo's section on how to eat ramen in the out of print book, *Naruhodo za rāmen*, Saboten, 1981.

Historically, if you spoke the Edo dialect in the west of Japan you would not be fully understood and if you spoke the Osaka dialect as a comedian, you would surely be misunderstood. Including grand gestures of eating and such was a good way to make people laugh with visual gags.

Kikuzō does not believe in ramen connoisseurship and thus agrees with Ōsaki Hiroshi, the self-styled "ramen consultant." Both these men concur that the beauty of ramen is that it allows everyone to indulge their own personal taste preferences. Anthropologists of food culture would call ramen a "platform food," because it is a base on which other flavors can be placed and consumed, like the bagel or the sandwich. "It depends on where you were born and what you like," Kikuzō continued. He noted what many have said: "Western Japanese in Kyushu often prefer the pork-based soup, Tokyo-ites a light soy sauce taste, while a heavier miso-flavored ramen is popular in northern Hokkaido."[4]

Kikuzō is one of many ramen devotees who suggest that you drink a glass of cool water just before eating in order to refresh and "kickstart" the stomach to prepare for a ramen infusion. However, other camps are adamant that one should avoid drinking water, as it inhibits the taste buds

Figure 43. Author with *rakugo* star Hayashiya Kikuzō in Tokyo.

---

[4] Interview August 24, 2006.

and undermines the ramen-eating experience. Nonetheless, all ramen connoisseurs insist that when the ramen arrives at the table and as the chopsticks are taken up, one should first carefully observe the dish. Take note of the color and aroma of the soup. How are the eating utensils arranged? Be sure to take stock of the portions, shape and condition of the noodles in the *donburi*, or deep bowl. Remain still for about five seconds and look everything over. If the chopsticks are the disposable wooden ones that require the diner to split them apart, refrain from rubbing the split chopsticks together to make them smooth over the bowl. At a quality shop, fellow diners do not want to see people consume ramen with tiny slivers of wood in the soup. Next comes the real eating part. Generally speaking, one should first take a mouthful of soup and check the taste carefully with the tongue. Contrary to Kikuzō's exhortations, most ramen traditionalists do not sprinkle on the pepper right away. Spices and other condiments, such as garlic, onions and pickled ginger should be added only after the initial taste test.

From here the diner moves onto the noodles. It does not matter how many finely sliced scallions (green onions) garnish the soup, or how many pork slices the chef has stacked on top, as a newly-minted ramen aficionado one should concentrate on the noodles. Do not bite them in half as you slurp them in. Virtually all ramen eaters, both experts and amateurs, consider this a bad step that can ruin the pleasure of eating a sizeable mouthful of tasty ramen. History has come home. Instead, pull up a small portion of noodles with your chopsticks and make some noise – I mean *really* make noise – as you suck them in, ensuring that you also draw in lots of air. This is not a slurp for speed; this is a slurp for enjoyment, ensuring that some of the broth comes up with the noodles, accompanied by the cooling effect of air. Imbibing the noodles with such a sweeping whoosh in this way might mean droplets of soup splatter around your bowl or across the table. This is good form, although is not considered essential. After all, this is where the taste, texture, noodles and soup all blend together. It is the moment when a diner can reflect on the excellent taste of noodle soup and the relaxed atmosphere of dining in this manner. The ability to enjoy this complete experience reveals a true ramen master.

After eating the noodles, drink the soup. I personally find it difficult not to drink the soup between mouthfuls of noodles, but again, camps are divided on this practice. Whatever your preference, do not forget to pay attention to the soup. If the soup is not good, you can leave it; but if it is a broth that the chef has clearly put his heart and soul into, then drink it all down. Experts suggest leaving about 1–2 mm of soup at the bottom of the bowl, mainly to avoid the pork bone splinters or seafood shell fragments that often make up part of the broth base, as well as spice sediment. After finishing, take a breath and either call for the bill or, if you are in an establishment that requires upfront payment via a ticket machine, get up and leave. It is not considered good form to linger too long in a ramen shop. Ramen is a meal to be joyfully consumed but the shops themselves are rarely cozy or comfortable and they generally do not encourage drawn-out meals. In the eyes of a proprietor, if you have taken too long to finish, it means you did not eat the ramen while it was hot, which means that you do not know enough to enjoy the establishment's creations – or worse – that you do not think highly enough of the ramen to eat it in the correct manner. When you eat ramen, you enter into a relationship with the owner. In quality shops, the proprietors tend to be inordinately proud of their dishes. This may not sound important but, remember, even in Japan there are "ramen Nazis," similar to the "soup Nazi" made famous in the American television series *Seinfeld*. In that episode, a cook who ran a soup restaurant arbitrarily banished hungry customers from his store because he did not like their attitude. In Japan, some ramen stores enforce equally draconian measures. What is more, some ramen stores will only serve a strictly limited number of bowls of ramen a day, and if you do not behave correctly or demonstrate proper obeisance to the soup, you could be asked to leave and then barred from the premises. I personally have never seen this happen but popular anecdotes in the ramen world suggest that it does indeed occur.

Ramen Fanatics

Ramen has become so ubiquitous and loved in today's Japan that it now has what the Japanese call *otaku,* or "extreme fans." Over the last six decades, Japan has evolved from a country where malnutrition and famine were fairly common phenomena into a nation that thrives on watching, writing, talking about and glorifying food to mind-boggling levels. Postwar Japanese do not experience hunger but instead experience the *Iron Chef,* a television program where famous chefs pit their talents against one another in a quest to produce delectable dishes from a limited range of given ingredients. From the early history of gastronomy, when the Chinese were famous for discussing food, into the twenty-first century, the mantle of obsessive concern with cuisine has most decisively shifted to the Japanese. In a country now oriented toward producing the best and tastiest dishes, ramen has emerged as a top contender in the high-stakes game of competitive "mass" food production. Ramen fanatics reign supreme.

Ōsaki Hiroshi, the "ramen consultant," has what can only be described as an overwhelming dedication to ramen. He has virtually lived on the dish since 1976 and claims that, since 1995, he has eaten over 800 bowls of ramen per year. This means out of the 1,095 given meals in a year Ōsaki chooses ramen seventy-four percent of the time – virtually a bowl of ramen for breakfast, lunch and dinner every single day. (As Ōsaki explained to me, in his younger years he sometimes consumed as many as ten bowls of ramen in a single day.) As for the venues, Ōsaki claims that he has eaten at over 6,000 ramen shops throughout Japan. Indeed, the ramen industry is now massive enough to allow a "ramen consultant" like Ōsaki to dine at a different shop every day without having to revisit a store. Of course, he has his favorites but he also recounted to me the joy of continuing to discover and investigate new stores. Ōsaki is not a ramen snob, although after eating so many bowls of the noodle soup in so many locations, he easily could be. Rather, he is a pure and simple devotee, he says, noting that there is no such thing as the perfect bowl of ramen. Ōsaki explained to me that the truly great thing about ramen is that "there is a taste for everyone.... And that is what makes it such an interesting food. It's also fun to talk about and walk around looking for."[5]

Ōsaki is not alone. Sano Minoru, a ramen entrepreneur and self-proclaimed "ramenologist," sees it as his "duty" to raise the profile, quality and prestige of the ramen industry. Sano was at one point host of a reality show, *Competitive Ramen*, where "wannabe" ramen chefs competed against one another. First broadcast in 2001, the show achieved record-breaking ratings, watched by thirty percent of viewers nationwide. This success generated similar competitive ramen shows that pitted hopeful chefs against one another for the title of "best ramen." Sano is a frequent guest-host or commentator on such shows. He rarely smiles on camera, has perfectly coiffed and slicked-back hair and sports a crisp white uniform every day. Sano manages his own line of ramen shops and occasionally takes on protégés to whom he imparts his secrets of ramen making. In the TV shows, Sano is blunt and frequently berates competitors, mocking those who disagree – an abrasive approach that seems nevertheless to appeal to viewers. He wrote in his book, a manifesto on ramen, that when

---

[5] Interview, July 3, 2009.

making the stock, "...if you do not follow my instructions to the letter, you won't be able to make good soup."[6]

Sano Minoru lays out three steps for appreciating good ramen. "First," he says, "I smell the aroma. What ingredients are they using? If it smells good you'll want to eat it quickly. Next, I slurp the soup to the roof of my mouth. Here I can determine the technical ability of the cooks. Too much heat...too many spices...or mixed incorrectly...." "Last," Sano writes, "I taste the noodles. Do the noodles and the soup strike a distinct balance? Are the noodles domestic or foreign-made with imported wheat? What factory pressed them, or did the shop produce them?"[7] Sano claims to be able to deduce all these elements and says that when he encounters truly delicious ramen, he "feels moved." He is a harsh taskmaster and tough on his students but always with an eye to making a better-tasting ramen. This is one key reason that his stores remain popular with an equally knowledgeable population of ramen consumers.

Musée de Ramen

In Japan, there are ample opportunities to pay homage to ramen noodles. One of the top "temples" for ramen worship is the Yokohama Ramen Museum. A sprawling structure that celebrates all things ramen, its main attraction is a painstakingly detailed recreation of an urban Tokyo "eat street" of the late 1950s. The vibrant, bustling street transports visitors back to an era when vendors served hot bowls of savory noodles from open-fronted stalls, children ran along to the candy man and a veneer of grime covered a burgeoning society on the mend. In part, the museum's goal is to piggyback on the national obsession with ramen, while reminding the Japanese of the way life used to be in a simpler time with simpler food, before the high-rolling "bubble" era of the strong yen. The museum brochure announces that, "as you descend the stairs you encounter a street at dusk. You are suddenly standing on the street corner in 1958." At the Ramen Museum, the ground floor provides a simplified history of ramen, complete with the myth of Mito Kōmon (detailed in Chapter 4). The story is not true but the Ramen Museum is more concerned with creating a nostalgic picture of 1950s Japan than with researching how ramen really arrived in the country. Downstairs in the 1958 street scene,

---

[6] Sano Minoru, *Sano Minoru tamashī no rāmendō*, p. 27.
[7] Sano Minoru, *Sano Minoru tamashī no rāmendō*, p. 15.

numerous ramen shops compete for customers by offering a variety of tastes. Each specific flavor of ramen is associated with a different Japanese prefecture and the stalls change on a fairly regular basis.

When I visited, several stores were representing their prefectural food tastes: Wakayama on the east coast featured a pork and soy sauce soup. Sapporo, the main city of the northern island of Hokkaido, used a miso base with soy sauce and salt. Kuji, a city high in the northeastern prefecture of Iwate, represented the more rarified chicken-and-soy-sauce camp. The Tokyo stall offered traditional Tokyo ramen with a thinner, soy sauce-based soup, while Kumamoto, on the western island of Kyushu, boasted a thicker soup with a pork-flavored broth.

Some ramen museums and information centers also commemorate the modern off-shoot of ramen, instant ramen. The Instant Ramen Memorial Hall in Ikeda City celebrates Andō Momofuku's invention of instant ramen in 1958, when he irrevocably changed the gastronomic profile of East Asia. Instant ramen might be the most popular Asian food ever to have hit the market and its domination of the convenience-food market world-wide does not appear to be diminishing. But the Instant Ramen Memorial Hall does not just sell Andō's foodstuff – the hall markets his entire invention process, eagerly proclaiming in museum literature available on site: "Andō Momofuku completed his research for instant ramen in a small shed behind his house in the garden. All he had were regular kitchen appliances lying around but no great facilities were necessary. In order to do research and invent a new product, all he needed was the knowledge inside his head."

Andō captured a certain spirit of the time by linking instant ramen, his new invention, with the burgeoning idea of entrepreneurship in late 1950s Japan. As the Japanese government had declared in 1956 Japan no longer considered itself in the "postwar" era. The public wanted new ideas and a new life-style. They wanted to be forward-thinking. Japanese were busy rebuilding the nation and this new noodle meal, while not completely radical, was cheap and convenient, and definitely fit the bill.

Ramen Stadiums

Not to be outdone – not least because they are competing for tourists – other Japanese cities have followed suit and constructed ramen stadiums, generally large halls hosting numerous ramen shops. Osaka, historically a center for business where earlier generations used to greet one another with the phrase "Doing any good business today?," erected a Dōtonbori Ramen Eating Hall. It is similar to the more popular ramen stadium in Hakata in the north of Kyushu, but with eight shops offering different ramen tastes. The Dōtonbori Hall proudly proclaims that its shops are wider and more spaciously arranged so that visitors "can take their time to appreciate the moment and taste the ramen." The advertisement for the Hall even features a chart asking diners to quiz themselves and score their level of "ramen addiction." The questions include: "When you think of what you are going to eat this evening, do you think about what kind of ramen you will eat? Can you list more than three ramen places that you think are good? Do you quickly go out and buy new instant ramen products when they hit the market? When you eat ramen, do you become quiet and pay attention to consuming it before it gets cold?" The questions classify visitors on a scale ranging from those who "like" ramen, to those who "love" ramen and the ultimate ranking – "ramen fanatic." Many stores try to ascertain diners' needs and request visitors to complete questionnaires ranging from several check boxes to a series of pages asking everything from "How were the noodles?" and "Please describe a better soup stock that you would prefer" to "How was the service?" One store breaks down answers into five categories from "satisfied" to "unsatisfied," with three grades in between.

As of 2006, there were approximately twenty-four ramen "theme parks" in Japan, spread across more than sixteen of the forty-seven prefectures that make up Japan. They sport names such as the Ramen Atelier, Ramen Performance Hall, Noodle Café Eating Kingdom, Ramen Philosophers Hall and – my favorite, complete with an official seal – The Ramen Academy. Food theme parks in Japan are big business and the company behind the biggest names in the field is Namco. The company helped design Ice Cream City, Tokyo Cream Puff Field, the Yokohama Curry Museum, Relaxation Forest, Nagoya Dessert Forest, Kobe Sweet Harbor, Kyushu Ramen Stadium and the Gyōza Stadium in Osaka, to name but a few.

To understand the seemingly limitless Japanese love affair with food theme parks, I went to Namco's headquarters on the fringes of Tokyo to meet with two of the company's management executives, Ikezawa Mamoru and Takano Yuji. Both men explained to me that, like Las Vegas casinos and hotels, these food theme parks are designed to attract consumers who want to eat somewhere other than a normal restaurant. Their goal is to create a compact, self-contained entertainment complex similar to an outlet mall, a popular draw for consumers in Japan and Namco's original model. The Namco management team concluded that in Japan, many consumers historically shopped in department stores or large shopping malls and then dined in one of the basement or rooftop restaurants, or in a mall restaurant. It was a gap in the market that no business had focused on eating as its primary entertainment emphasis, with shopping as a secondary activity.

The Namco executives spoke about a new era of dining in Japan, in which people no longer merely wanted to eat to digest food but also wanted to be simultaneously entertained as if they were in Las Vegas or Disneyland. Gastronomic theme parks may be a peculiarly Japanese phenomenon. However, an interesting feature of their success is the way that communities on the periphery of mainstream tourist sites use local cuisine as a way to attract customers. *Shūkyaku sochi*, meaning "the technique to gather customers," was what the Namco executives called their strategy.

Namco does not build the theme parks: rather, it helps to design the themes around which the complexes are built. The business grew as an increasing number of smaller Japanese cities began requesting assistance on such projects as a way to attract tourists and build a consumer base, the two executives told me. Namco's company philosophy is encapsulated in the three-character slogan *anponraku*, which translates as "a good price,

Figure 44. Advertisement for a ramen competition hall, where six ramen shops compete for having the "strongest" or best ramen chef. Notice how the chefs are all standing in a somewhat macho pose with arms folded, in the same fashion as wrestlers in their posters announcing matches.

the chance to purchase quality food items in one place, and an entertaining atmosphere" – these are what will attract customers. "Basically, people spend about 1,000 yen (twelve dollars or eight British pounds) on lunch or 700 yen on a taxi ride. We want to create a world for them where for several hundred yen, they can select from several real food options," Ikezawa and Takano explained. Food, they said, has now become a "brand idea" in Japan, specifically linked in the minds of consumers to certain regional characteristics.

At the same time, a growing sense of nostalgia about Japan in simpler times has also served to popularize food theme parks. No one, certainly not the Japanese themselves, could have envisaged the economic bubble of the 1980s, or dreamed that one day Japan would seek to become a "normal" country with a permanent seat on the UN Security Council. For many contemporary Japanese, the 1950s remains a period when America and General Douglas MacArthur were *sugoi*, "cool," the Namco designers explained. Many theme parks attempt to exploit that myth, linking the dining experience with nostalgia. The men from Namco noted that the immediate postwar decade was, like the Edo and Meiji periods, the era of the *yatai*, or outdoor stall – since no one could afford high-class restaurants then. Instead of offering packaged and processed food like the gleaming convenience store on the corner near your tiny apartment, the food theme park of today tempts consumers with simple shacks and stalls. The Namco executives explained that the quaint names for these theme parks ("stadium," "museum" and "atelier," all written with *katakana*, Japan's syllabary alphabet for foreign words), were meant to evoke Japan's "emotional nostalgia for the 1950s."[8]

Manga and Ramen Music

On a bookshelf in my office is a full row of Japanese manga (comic books) devoted to ramen, a small part of the available popular literature concerning noodle soup. One series is dedicated to the culinary adventures of a noodle chef named Mantarō, a whimsical name that evokes the word for being fully satisfied after a meal, *manzoku*.

Readers eagerly devour each of Mantarō's adventures in these fat, relatively inexpensive volumes. In one volume, Mantarō is amazed at a rival ramen chef who demonstrates his prowess with a cooking knife by

---

[8] Interview, August 23, 2006.

Figure 45. The front cover of a popular manga about ramen with Mantarō enjoying a bowl of a form of noodle soup.[9]

shredding a large radish into a single long, translucent slice so that it "looks like a roll of tape." The graphics add to the tension of the moment with the swiftly drawn motion of a knife cutting through the air and thinly-sliced pieces of vegetable floating down into bowls carefully arranged on counters. Judging from these comic books, not only are there daring feats of culinary expertise but also a lot of hanky-panky in the fictitious ramen

---

[9] Biggu Jō, *Ippon hōchō Mantarō*. In this case the cover depicts a bowl of cold sōmen.

Figure 46. Mantarō falling, literally, in love with the naked female character of the story.[10]

world. At one point the female lead tells one of the rival chefs that "he is first rate at judging ramen but third rate at judging women," and asks if he wants to make her his own. She slides out of her kimono to reveal, in the next frame, that she is completely naked. At this point, the artist's talent shifts from drawing food to depicting a voluptuous young woman in all her naked glory. The next moment, the heroine jumps off a bridge, eventually ending up rescued in Mantarō's boat. She sighs, "Mantarō...please hold me and warm me up." Ramen, in some parts of the manga world, is not only good food, it is sexy as well.

Another series, entitled "Ramen Battles," features a ramen bully, a diner who is so confident about his understanding of gourmet ramen that he takes a baby lobster from a carefully prepared bowl of special, "deluxe" ramen and shoves it in the proprietor's face, angrily yelling, "I can't eat this crap!" to the amusement of other patrons in the store.

The longest running manga about ramen is entitled "Tales of a Ramen Genius" (*Rāmensai yūki*). One cold and blustery winter's day in Tokyo I went to interview Tanikawa Makoto, the editor of this manga series. Tanikawa explained that the series originally ran under a different title from 2000 to 2009 and then transformed into its existing form.[11]

---

[10] Biggu Jō, *Ippon hōchō Mantarō*, p. 199.
[11] The series used to be titled, *Ramen Discovery Stories* (Rāmen hakkenden).

The current version is also different in that the main character is now a young woman who drives the story forward. But, Tanikawa added, the series was not really only for ramen fans and like many manga it is not the ramen but the story and the characters that make the comic interesting; the stories just happen to take place where the noodle soup is present. That said, Tanikawa did admit when pressed that if the manga had been published during the 1980s, before the real manga and ramen boom, that it would have been tougher to gain a steady audience. Nonetheless, the real goal of any good manga, Tanikawa insisted, was the overall story and the tension it created. Most manga nowadays are produced by teams of people since their production (story-writing and drawing) involves a vast amount of effort, he explained. Many comic books also hired consultants for stories that required a particular expertise and their ramen series employed one as well. Each biweekly story is about twenty pages long and is published along with other short manga vignettes in a thick tome of a magazine called "Big Comics," which is published twice a month. These biweekly series of ramen stories are then later republished as longer comic books on their own.

An interesting point Tanikawa made was that during the 1980s there was a sameness about the ramen shops throughout Japan and there was nowhere near the variety and selection of different ramen that proliferate today. The explosion of tastes and varieties of ramen starting from the early 1990s also made writing manga on such a topic possible because the ideas continue to be fresh and interact with society in exciting ways. Tanikawa mentioned that the ramen boom was not limited to Japan and as testament to its growing appeal abroad the famed *Michelin* guide in Hong Kong had awarded one star to a ramen restaurant there. *The South China Morning Post* published an article about this store, noting: "Mist [the name of the store] is a rare outlet, with a Michelin star it earned in its first year in business in 2009. A franchise of the ramen specialist founded by Yasuji Morizumi in Japan, it focuses on pairing noodles of various thicknesses with different soups."[12] Given the international appeal and spread of ramen culture Tanikawa felt that in five years there would be no stopping ramen and that it would appear in Africa and "who knows elsewhere, maybe we will be writing stories along those lines," he said. "About

---

[12] (http://www.scmp.com/portal/site/SCMP/menuitem.2af62ecb329d3d7733492d9253 a0a0a0/?vgnextoid=bf4bd8a41165d210VgnVCM100000360a0a0aRCRD&ss=Food&s=Life) accessed on January 6, 2011.

four or five years ago," he told me, "there was even a real drama made about the ramen manga series, a two-hour special on TV."[13]

One sequence of the older ramen comic published before Tanikawa assumed position as editor is called "Ramen Flags." It recounts the story of colleagues forced to compete for prizes in a contest based on the flavor of ramen. Several bowls of ramen are placed in front of each contestant and competitors must deduce which region the ramen is from by sipping some of the soup and slurping a few noodles. After answering the questions, the contestants have to run through an obstacle course. A female contestant, a clear ramen expert, is about to win until she is attacked by a rival in the obstacle course who loosens her bikini top as she races for the finish line.

Figure 47. Contestants are asked to pick out the plate of noodles that are made in Tokyo, keeping in mind that the other three plates are noodles from outlying areas. This is the stereotype of a *tsū*, or connoisseur who is so adept he or she can taste regional differences.[14]

---

[13] Interview with Tanikawa Makoto, editor of *Rāmensai yūki* comic of Big Comics, which is published by Shogakukan, on January 7, 2011.
[14] Kube Rokurō et al., eds., *Rāmen hakkenden*, Vol. 9, p. 181.

Figure 48. The female contestant is about to win but a cheater loosens her top and so she fails at the last moment, even though she is more adept in ramen knowledge.[15]

Ramen may only be the background to this variety of comics but the literature continues to grow. On top of a vast selection of ramen-themed comic books are literally hundreds of guidebooks to help enthusiasts find the ultimate ramen restaurant. These describe national as well as local ramen "hotspots" and are published in book form on an annual basis and in special issue magazines virtually every month. Keeping up with the newest in *ramenology* could well be a full-time job.

---

[15] Ibid., p. 190.

Needless to say, the internet has added a new dimension to the appreciation of ramen, enabling fellow fanatics to contact one another, chat and even share their ramen-related artistic endeavors. Popular musicians have also left a deep impression on the field of ramen adoration. Yano Akiko's 1996 ballad, "I wanna eat ramen," contains repetitive yet catchy lyrics with some sexual overtones:

> I wanna eat ramen
> I wanna eat alone, I wanna eat it hot
> I wanna eat ramen
> I wanna eat delicious, I wanna eat it right now.
> I do not need the pork slice, do not need the fish slice
> I won't ask for anything fancy
> But...would ya, could ya, put in onions and some garlic and make it big!

The Komadori sisters, popular singers and film actresses in the early 1960s, sang a sweeter and more melancholic ode called "Ramen Tears," which went something like this:

> Warm ramen, unforgettable ramen,
> Even when you're poor you aren't broken, laugh away
> Ramen always soothes people
> Naruto, Chinese bamboo shoots, slice of pork
> Ahh, it fills one with an embracing taste
> The slippery saltiness cries out
> Is it my tears or maybe a dream.

Songs about ramen have even become theme songs for television shows, including this popular if tongue-in-cheek number entitled, "Chicken and Egg Ramen:"

> In the sky when the stars are asleep
> Somewhere a flute player in a rackety cart is calling
> The old man in the Chinese cap always laughs as he calls out:
> "Ramen! Ramen! Chicken and Egg Ramen."
> The old man would say,
> "There's an old saying in China,
> That everyone who eats ramen is good.
> That's why foreigners do not say ramen when they pray
> But...uh, amen."

Ramen songs are not just confined to the musical fringe in Japan. Mega-rock star Sharan Q blended sexual innuendo with noodles in the "Koike Loves Ramen Song," a track included on his 1996 "best of" album. Koike is a well-known character from a popular 1960s comic series, "The Ghost Q-tarō." The animators of the series were the same duo that developed the immensely popular cartoon "Doraemon," a twenty-second-century blue cat who has a gadget for every tough situation in which he and his fourth grade sidekick, Nobita, find themselves. In "The Ghost Q-tarō" series, Koike is a local elderly man who lives in the neighborhood and loves ramen. In virtually every scene, he can be seen with a bowl of ramen and chopsticks in his hands. The song recalls Koike's obsession, but with a different twist:

> Morning, noon and night, even in the evening too
> It's always nothing but you alone
> Your supple, sexy body is on my mind 24/7
> I take you wet and glistening, softly to my lips
> Yeah, Koike loves his ramen
> Koike, Koike, loves it, loves it.

In the cyber age, the fascination with ramen has spawned dozens of blogs devoted to charting, ranking, dissecting and reviewing ramen stores and new instant ramen products. Some blogs feature photographs of various ramen offerings with the authors' critiques. Other blogs contain personality quizzes to test how much a reader is obsessed with ramen, with a set of online questions ranging from question #11, "I keep a diary about ramen," to #19, "I have dreams about ramen," to #47, "I own the Sharan Q CD with the ramen song on it." Numerous blog authors specialize in posting images of the offerings in ramen shops, usually with cell phone cameras and post photos and reviews for all to read. One website predicts readers' fortunes depending on their choice of ramen broth and toppings. Noodle soup is now a topic to discuss, sing about, write about, blog about and make television shows and comic books about.[16]

For the Love of Sushi

If ramen culture is so highly appreciated in contemporary Japan, why has it failed to attract Western followers in the way, for example, that sushi has? To answer that question, I turned to Ted Bestor, an anthropologist at Harvard University, chronicler of the Tsukiji fish market (the world's largest) and author of a book on the culture and commerce of sushi.[17] Before writing that book, Bestor also penned an article detailing how sushi went global – and how, before the 1970s, it was considered "an exotic, almost

---

[16] www.misyuramen.com.
[17] Ted Bestor, *Tsukiji: the fish market at the center of the world*.

unpalatable ethnic specialty" in the West. I asked Bestor why sushi was more popular than ramen in the West – particularly since a hot and tasty noodle soup must be easier for Europeans and Americans to stomach than raw fish. "In part," he replied, "it may be the exoticism of the sushi that helps sell the product." Non-Japanese are already exposed to so many different noodle dishes – ranging from spaghetti to Chinese noodles – that ramen, although one of the most popular Japanese dishes, does not stand out in the foreign market as raw fish did in the early 1980s, when sushi began drawing acclaim outside of Japan. Bestor noted that the food industry and the profit motive could also be responsible for the popularity of sushi over ramen in the West. He said:

> To be crassly commercial, how much can you charge someone for a bowl of noodles? But with proper mystique, you can charge more for raw fish over rice. It's the marketing appeal of one versus the other and profitability is a key issue. If I were a Japanese sushi chef setting up in the US, to attract a crowd I could charge $30 per person... assuming I had the skills. On the other hand, noodles have the reputation of being inexpensive, which dampens the incentive to promote them as a restaurant food.[18]

In other words, its very affordability may explain why non-Japanese may prefer not to dine out on ramen. In the US, if people are going to go out for less expensive food, they will usually just grab a pizza or Chinese food (another formerly exotic food that is now common throughout many parts of the world but particularly in America).

At this point, it is probably worth reflecting on the insights that the sushi story provides us regarding the popularity of ramen in Japan. The fairly entrenched, yet traditional, image of sushi in Japan involves a sense of connoisseurship that, until recently, did not correspond to the ramen experience. There may be a formality to knowing which ramen is good and how to eat it, but ordering it is simple. In contrast, the nature of Japanese traditional dining etiquette is often daunting to younger generations not steeped in the codes of behavior that older generations took for granted. Because the rise of ramen was synonymous with the postwar, the dish is not associated with the same level of prescribed behavior. Groups may be arguing over how to eat it but fundamentally it does not require specialized knowledge to enjoy it. Ramen is the average dish for the average Japanese – and that is also part of its domestic appeal. On the other side of the spectrum, while sushi is far from exotic in Japanese eyes, it belongs

---

[18] Phone interview August 4, 2005.

more in the domain of the specialist. Sushi restaurant diners frequently employ a specialized vocabulary and terminology to ordering and the entire experience is much more formalized. To uncover how the average Japanese felt about sushi, I went southwest from Tokyo to the city of Shizuoka, about a two-hour train ride, partly on the high-speed bullet line. My destination was the Sushi Museum where I met with Aino Michiru, head of promotions for the museum.

Ms. Aino told me that during the Tokugawa era, Shizuoka had been one of the foremost fish-producing regions and Shimizu city, as it was known then, boasted the largest number of sushi restaurants in the country. By the 1990s, the region was in a downward economic spiral and most of the local shops had gone out of business. The local council's goal was to open a food theme park focused on sushi, exploiting the historic presence of sushi restaurants and relinking the region with its glory days. It was also a way, Aino said, for people who worried about the costs and the formality of proper sushi restaurants to comfortably sample offerings at the museum. "Look," she said, "here you can easily open the door and it won't be too expensive to sit down at the sushi counter and eat sushi. People come here to learn how to order correctly and make their 'counter debut' [kauntā debyu]", Aino said, meaning their first experience of ordering at the sushi restaurant counter. Sushi requires diners to know the name of the fish lying in the refrigerated window on top of the counter and often assumes knowledge about prices, styles and sushi terms. And usually, certainly at higher end places, there is no menu at all! If there happens to be a menu it can require customers to read a hand-written, Chinese-character-laden list – a feat that might daunt quite a few younger Japanese. At the sushi museum, on the other hand, Aino explained, "people can come in without fear and they do not have to be nervous."[19]

The Sushi Museum and my conversations with Aino-san revealed a significant factor behind the postwar development and success of ramen. The popular appeal of ramen over the last half century owes much to taste and the enjoyment of eating a savory noodle with a meat-based broth but it may also reflect the fact that ramen actually requires no special training or knowledge to enjoy. Unlike sushi and other traditional restaurants, where unique behavior and connoisseur knowledge are par for the course, ramen is a new food, available for any diner to enjoy. No "counter debut" is necessary for ramen – it truly is a meal for the masses. As Japan became

---

[19] Interview, August 16, 2006.

a less stratified and more equal society after World War II, ramen shops reflected these changes.

Ramen – With a New York State of Mind

Over the last twenty years Japanese food has extended its global reach. It is not uncommon today to find a Japanese restaurant in the smallest US town. Hungry foreign diners already gobble up sushi, miso soup and tempura, all Japanese dishes. Ramen, too, is steadily becoming better known abroad. A converse phenomenon may also be taking place – an American chef recently opened his own ramen shop in Tokyo. (More about "Ivan Ramen" follows in the Conclusion.) To see what inroads ramen was making in one of the biggest overseas markets for Japanese food, I went to New York City to meet Kamada Shigeto in his ramen shop on Manhattan's Lower East Side, and to uncover the story of one of the city's few individually owned and operated ramen restaurants.

The Minca Ramen Factory was opened in the summer of 2004. Kamada had originally been a jazz musician. He had come to America in 1981, worked in a variety of jobs, and then in 1997 began going back to Japan on performing tours, mainly during the summers. He had always loved ramen, he told me. "I was twenty when I came to Tokyo from Shimane Prefecture," he said, recalling the first time he ate in a small ramen shop in Shinjuku (west Tokyo). This first ramen experience in Tokyo was a shock to Kamada, who still remembers the thick tasty soup and *al dente* noodles. The store specialized in Kumamoto ramen stock, a creamy garlic-heavy broth with a pork base from the western island of Kyushu. The owner was so proud of his distinctive soup that he posted a sign boldly announcing it did not use any soy sauce in the recipe. Up till then, Kamada had only eaten his local ramen, which was served in a thinner, more watery soup broth with a chicken base. "To me," Kamada explained, "ramen was for *stamina*." "Stamina" is that almost immeasurable term the Japanese have appropriated to describe large meals full of vegetables and meat – food for energy, although not always the most savory. "Stamina" is also the word that Chen Pingjun, founder of the *champon* noodle empire in Nagasaki, first used to describe his noodle dishes. Kamada's first experience with ramen, like my own, was a shock to the system and provided an experience that literally forced him to change careers.

After Kamada moved to New York, he kept seeking the noodle soup he had so loved, or some form of good, casual Japanese food. But everywhere he ate he left unsatisfied. Once he started going back to Japan, "little by little," he said, "music tours began to evolve into ramen tours and I found myself searching for gigs in towns with well-known ramen shops that required a visit." It was a huge leap to change career paths from music to ramen. "At first I wrote to the Kumamoto store I was obsessed with and asked if I could open up a branch in the US. But they rejected that option," he recalled. He then asked if he could do an internship at the ramen shop, a request not completely uncommon in ramen circles, but the owner again refused. At the same time, the Kumamoto store patiently "let me pester and pepper them with relentless questions… I also read lots of the available literature on ramen." After a few false starts, he eventually saw an advertisement for a ramen chef and started making ramen from 12 am- 4 am in a restaurant in the St. Marks area of the East Village in New York City. For two weeks before he started serving ramen, he conducted tests – creating soup flavors and adding and subtracting ingredients until he produced the taste he had fantasized about.

Kamada eventually secured outside investors who believed in his project of a privately-owned and operated ramen store in the city. Although he changed careers to devote himself to ramen, in many ways he still sees himself as a musician: "Making ramen," he says, "is very much like creating a song. In jazz music everyone has their own style and this ramen," he said, pointing to his restaurant, "is my own particular style. It's tough though," he added, "because we have to sell several hundred bowls a day. But I think we can continue." At the end of our conversation Kamada passed me a bowl of the hearty soup that he hopes will draw fans in New York and beyond to Japan's most popular dish.[20]

The Global Impact of Japanese Food

Despite its rapid evolution, Japanese food was not particularly well known nor widely available outside Japan until the 1980s. That has changed in the last three decades along with the growth of Japan's economy and the spread of Japanese culture, including video games, anime, manga, horror movies and pop music. There is also a dark side to the explosion of Japanese popular culture abroad, namely the stagnation of the Japanese economy that set in after the bursting of Japan's so-called "bubble" economy in the early 1990s, which flattened skyrocketing salaries, land prices

---

[20] Interview, July 4, 2005.

and the Nikkei stock market. Paperbacks that prophesied the downfall of Western management techniques and the domination of Japanese business acumen were proven incorrect. In the later 1990s, Japanese banks began talking about underperforming loans and top-ranked companies did the unthinkable by laying off legions of salaried employees. The once-mighty Japanese economy began to take on characteristics of Third World uncertainty and economic doubt. In the midst of this downfall, middle-aged former desk-jockeys and managers found themselves with little outlet for their skills.

Japan's postwar economy had been a system in which workers entered a factory or business in their twenties and left when they retired. Companies went the extra mile for their employees, sheltering the less capable and the genius alike and refraining from laying off loyal employees who did not strike and worked long hours safe in the knowledge that their company would prioritize their welfare over short-term profits or stockholder interests. All that changed in the 1990s when economic downsizing began. This has been a major force behind the explosion of ramen businesses in twenty-first-century Japan. Thousands of unemployed white-collar workers began thinking that opening a simple noodle restaurant could give them a livelihood. The subsequent surge of ramen shops opening throughout the country helped further transform the business of ramen. In some ways, ramen noodles came to signify failure in other fields of business. In one stroke, customers were no longer sure if they were entering an actual shop that served good ramen, or one that a reluctant ex-businessman had opened as a bridge between careers. The proliferation of ramen shops in today's Japan reveals the soft underbelly of Japan's revolving economy and highlights the hard times that faced large numbers of salarymen.

The sharp increase in the number of ramen shops relates not only to economic restructuring but also to the Japanese fascination with speed, electronics and expanding wealth. As Japan rebuilt itself after World War II, the rapidly-evolving society that invented the world's fastest train, the *shinkansen* or bullet train, needed quick and hearty food. Ironically, even as Japan's economic base deteriorated, the influence of its cuisine on international gastronomy grew. Just as in the 1920s, when Japanese searched for a quick and tasty meal, today's faster paced society continues to require quick food that is tasty, nutritious and accessible to urban residents commuting by train to work and coming home late from the office. The economic transformation of Japan from agricultural to urban service influenced how Japanese ate and subsequently, how the rest of the world perceived Japan and its cuisine.

Ramen began as an innocuous Chinese noodle dish and advanced to become a staple of Japanese cuisine that has acquired strong international appeal. Technology and advanced electronics have allowed Nissin Foods and other Japanese food-processing giants to produce enormous quantities of ramen products and ship them all over the world. In the second half of the twentieth century, as the Japanese economy grew, Japanese food – not least, ramen – began to dominate new territories.

The Rise of Ramen and Japanese Popular Culture

Ramen is Japan! To many, it embodies the culmination of their country's postwar history. Ramen has left an indelible mark on Japanese society and fused itself so tightly to contemporary culture that a Japan without ramen is unthinkable. It is not just because the noodle soup is a tasty diversion and more because, as we have seen in comics, music and TV shows devoted to it, ramen itself has became a staple element of popular culture – and more importantly, one face Japan presents to the wider world. Like Sony, Toyota and Panasonic, the rise of ramen parallels Japan's rise from the ashes of World War II into an economic powerhouse. And it is not only Japanese who have made this connection between ramen and popular culture. A cursory look at how ramen is sold around the world, even in China and Korea, demonstrates that selling ramen as a *Japanese* product is good for sales. In Taiwan, a country with its own long noodle traditions, ramen is often expressly sold as "*rishi*" or in the "Japanese style," to set it apart from native competitors.

One can now find ramen shops in most of East Asia; they are also making inroads into Europe and America and future growth seems likely. But this is where ramen and the globalization of sushi are different. Ramen has spawned an entire subset of popular culture industries attached to it and yet it remains a food for the common person. Eating ramen requires no specialized knowledge and is, in fact, an activity that is hard to avoid given the sheer number of shops. While sushi may continue to gain popularity in the West, ramen will slowly and surely gain dominance. As the next generation sees it featured in their favorite programs, hears about it on the web or on CDs, the public's appetite will certainly be whetted enough to actually go out and try it. The stage is now set for the next wave of Japanese cuisine to sweep the world, led by a team of ramen chefs.

Figure 49. Typical Japanese-style ramen shop in downtown Seoul, Korea. The red sign on the right side of the entrance is in Japanese lettering while the signs above the outside facing counter are in English transliteration and Korean.

Competition for Original Ramen

As ramen has now become so popular in Japan, the stakes for claiming ownership of the supposed original recipes have grown. One shop in Tokyo has attempted to outstrip any rivals for this position by flying a massive red sign with bold white lettering on its storefront. The lengthy explanation on the sign extends virtually ten feet in height by six feet in width, and exhorts customers not to believe all they have heard elsewhere about the history and flavor of ramen. Real ramen, the banner claims, comes from the city of Kurume in Kyushu, and the true origins of ramen are derived from the pork-based broth, *tonkotsu* flavor, established by this shop in 1937. None of the other shops established before, therefore, were ever ramen shops in the true sense, and so to taste the best, and of course the most original ramen, the sign suggests, discerning slurpers should dine at their ramen restaurant. But there are even stranger fictions brought into play as well. Somehow the owners seem to have got it into their minds that until 1949 Japan's noodle soup dish was only called "*Shina soba*." The

People's Republic of China, they explain, requested the Japanese government to stop using this derogatory term, which led to the dish later being referred to as *Chūka soba*. Aside from making up history from a jumble of only loosely related elements, the store's managers facilely tap into a sensitive historical narrative and Japan's relationship with China to mold a story of ramen that conveniently underpins their marketing concept. Not only have the managers created a seemingly irrefutable place of origin for ramen, a feat undoubtedly appealing to many customers seeking authenticity; they also link their store to the changes in name applied to ramen throughout the twentieth century. If all this were true then this book would have been much shorter. However, as we have come to learn, we can be as discerning about the history of ramen as many marketers are liberal with the wording used in their sales tactics.

Figure 50. Image of the massive sign hanging outside the Fukuya Ramen Shop in Tokyo, not far from the Australian Embassy.

CONCLUSION

This history of ramen and East Asian cuisine and politics has given the lie to simplistic notions of national cuisine. How a nation conceives of itself through food is very often as much fiction as fact, and it is worth exploring the contours of both. Culinary beliefs and practices change over time, reflecting the interactions of certain groups with others, and politics and ideology. Food constantly reminds us about the history of the idea of the nation and plays a key role in supporting the ideology of the nation. Drawing on Benedict Anderson's discussions of imagined communities based on the notion of a common language and reinforced by the media, we might want to think about how equally imagined are our notions of national cuisine and shared dinner tables.[1]

Mogi Yūzaburō, former CEO of the soy sauce company Kikkoman and current head of the Strategy Council for the Commercial Promotion of East Asian Food Products, wrote an interesting if somewhat unusual argument that reveals how difficult it is to dispel deep-seated myths about Japanese cuisine. He wrote:

> Our country, from ancient times, is a country that has actively introduced the culture of world cuisine into our own specific national foodways. Our nation's people in addition to being extremely sensitive to delicious products, also pay keen attention to the shelf life of products, the safety of ingredients and taste and food security, and they have a tendency to demand high standards for packaging and appearance as well.[2]

There is a real belief in Japan that this has always been the case, an overarching idea that Japanese cuisine and tradition sets the Japanese apart and makes them Japanese. It is a sort of "I eat this therefore I think I am part of this nation" scenario. Ramenologists would strenuously disagree with such outdated notions of Japanese tradition, as would lovers of pork cutlet and tempura, because they know that historically the Japanese have eaten a much wider range of foods than is normally assumed.

---

[1] Anne Allison notes the same phenomenon in her article on boxed lunches, *bento*. "Japanese Mothers and Obentos: The Lunch-Box as Ideological State Apparatus," *Anthropological Quarterly*, Vol. 64, No. 4, Gender and the State, October 1991, p. 198.

[2] Mogi Yūzaburō, "Shokubunka no kokusai kōryū," *Myōnichi no shokuhin sangyō*, June 2007, p. 4.

Figure 51. It is not just ramen that inspires comic books but now also *soba*. This poster is for a newly launched series called "Soba-master," in which the protagonist undertakes "noodle adventures." The series is reminiscent of the Edo-era tour books about noodle shops that were written several hundred years earlier.

Food culture is similar to a perceived shared consciousness – people rally around culinary signifiers that make up a meal and then identify them as belonging to their group.[3] In the words of anthropologists, these linkages create an imagined authenticity. The idea of *washoku* as an overarching symbol of Japanese cuisine "implicitly alleges historical continuity and stability."[4] Even cutlery or its absence can be part of that. It may sound ridiculous but many professionals believe in such values, even in the absence of solid evidence. The South Korean scientist who gained short-lived fame from his apparent ability to manipulate genes, Hwang Woo Suk of Seoul National University, publicly claimed that the Korean custom of using thin, metal chopsticks while dining helped Korean scientists isolate DNA faster and more accurately than other nations, leading South Korea to become the first country to clone a dog.[5] The experiment was later proven fraudulent but Hwang did not retract his comment linking Korean food culture with scientific progress.

As a well-known folklorist notes, "people define events through food." I have argued in this book that cuisine defined Japan's modernity and relations with China.[6] And yet even with all the changes to Chinese and Japanese cuisine through the centuries, many of the interviews I conducted up and down the Japanese archipelago in my quest to understand how ramen fit into the history of food in East Asia were obfuscatory.

I encountered one strange example of this pattern when talking with junior research associate, Kawada Keisuke, at the Cattle Museum in Maesawa, Japan. Like many of the people I interviewed, Kawada interrupted himself at various points with the statement, "Well, you have to understand how the Japanese eat." This was said time and time again – regardless of the interview and location. The beef scientists, the soy sauce factory workers, the comedians all made statements and then backtracked, as if to demonstrate that – despite what they had just said, which made eminent sense – there was something essential and unchanging about Japanese cuisine. Sometimes I wondered if, unbeknownst to myself, each person knew about my next interview, had phoned ahead and said, "Hey, we are driving this point home, do not forget to tell him." So, even though we were sitting in the cattle museum and Kawada is a specialist on the science of raising cattle, he insisted on telling me that, historically, the

---

[3] Theodore Bestor, *Tsukiji: The Fish Market at the Center of the World*, p. 126.
[4] Ibid., p. 141.
[5] "The scientist behind stem cell success story," *San Francisco Chronicle*, May 29, 2005.
[6] Michael Owen Jones, "Food Choice, Symbolism and Identity: Bread-and-Butter Issues for Folkloristics and Nutrition Studies," *Journal of American Folklore* 120, 2007, p. 134.

Japanese did not really like meat. I found this immensely ironic. When I pointed out the inconsistency between where we were sitting (amidst large plastic models of cow parts) and the content of his statement, he stammered, "Well not exactly." He then remarked: "We Japanese do not like large pieces of meat, or cooked rare with so much blood. So, historically we liked *sukiyaki* because that's made from small pieces or *shabu shabu* where the meat is more marbled, thin and dipped in simmering water."[7] We had suddenly leaped from eating no meat at all to enjoying some meat dishes.

Another issue concerning the supposed timelessness of Japanese cuisine is the notion of food and hygiene. Patricia Maclachlan, a political scientist, asserts that in Japan a "cultural premium is placed on safety and cleanliness, particularly for food products."[8] Not many would disagree but we should add that this is mainly a postwar phenomenon, not unique to Japan. Decades of environmental spoilage led to the creation of so many of these consumer advocacy groups. Maclachlan herself notes that Japan's obsession with hygiene developed because, since 1945, Japanese food companies have been less than scrupulous in observing the health and safety guidelines so often praised by the media and government. From the late 1950s to the early 1960s, a flood of defective products soured the Japanese market. The 1955 arsenic poisoning of Morinaga's powdered milk affected more than 12,000 infants, while the 1968 Kanami cooking oil incident, involving PCB poisoning, caused 1,600 casualties. In 1970, an antidiarrhea medicine affected 11,000 users.[9] Japan has not always been a safe place for eating. In the well-known fake canned beef incident consumers complained and the authorities responded by inspecting the product. It turned out that the canned beef was actually whale meat.[10] The Japanese food industry also increased its use of risky synthetic additives in prepared foods between 1957 and 1969.[11]

The Dark Side of Food Greatness

The postwar, with its abundant food and expanding economy, has its dark side as well. At the end of the 1950s, Japan faced a poor food supply and shaky economic base but within a short while the problems had also

---

[7] Interview, August 9, 2006.
[8] Patricia Maclachlan, *Consumer Politics in Postwar Japan*, p. 15.
[9] Ibid., p. 87.
[10] Ibid., pp. 104–105.
[11] Ibid., p. 180.

become environmental. Cold War politics produced a level of environmental degradation in Tokyo not seen since the English novelist Charles Dickens described mid-nineteenth-century London. That same kind of damage is currently being replicated in many new areas of the Far East, with ironically some of the same technology and food trends. In China, this crisis is known as the *baise laji*, or "white trash problem." According to recent Chinese government statistics, railroads collect over two billion instant ramen styrofoam bowls yearly from customers. Previously, this trash was merely collected in the trains and then tossed out the window but the containers have harmful chemicals that do not degrade so companies are searching for different products that are more environmentally friendly.[12] Nissin and other food companies claim that they are working on less environmentally damaging products with biodegradable containers. However, the fact that international consumers buy large numbers of these convenient products to simplify life so that they can earn more money and buy more products appears somewhat self-defeating.

Not only are ramen and instant ramen reintroducing themselves to China but for the last several decades Japanese cuisine has been marketed in China as a symbol of civilization, in much the same way that Western food was in Japan one hundred and fifty years ago. There is an element of soft power behind this transformation; Japanese food is perceived as cool and healthy and many women believe it can help to maintain slenderness and beauty.[13]

The negative side of this mass exportation and promotion of modern Japanese cuisine is that it is causing severe environmental degradation both domestically and abroad. This problem, combined with China's immense pollution, could seriously damage world food supplies if the situation is left unmanaged. The continued expansion and popularity of Japanese and Chinese cuisines, often touted as healthy alternatives to the fatty Western cuisines, may not actually be to our benefit. Severe water shortages and poor agricultural practices are denuding the Chinese landscape, a worrisome scenario for a growing population that will need to eat more in the future.[14] Japanese dietary habits have inflicted a heavy

---

[12] *People's Daily*, March 11, 2005, (http://env.people.com.cn/GB/1073/3235463.html).
[13] The Japanese book came out following the success of its virtual twin that touted the French diet. Naomi Moriyama, *Japanese Women Do not Get Old or Fat: Secrets of My Mother's Tokyo Kitchen*; and Mireille Guiliano, *French Women Do not Get Fat*.
[14] Elizabeth Economy and Kenneth Lieberthal, "Scorched Earth: Will Environmental Risks in China Overwhelm Its Opportunities?" *Harvard Business Review*, June 2007, pp. 88–97.

environmental cost in Southeast Asia, as well, where countries have dedicated their fishing industries to feeding the insatiable Japanese appetite. In 1991, food imports to Japan amounted to approximately thirty-four billion US dollars, more than the nation spent on oil. Japan currently consumes one-third of the world's tuna and two-fifths of the world's shrimp harvest. Historian and political scientist Gavan McCormack paints a dismal picture of Japan's future, suggesting that the Japanese are "increasingly being fed on fantasy" and "similar images of success and the good life are being implanted among countless millions outside Japan."[15] Japan is draining or eating many of the resources in Asia, where half the factories are producing foodstuffs for Japan.[16] Until not long ago, the Japanese cherished rice. Laws concerning food freshness now force convenience stores and other businesses to discard perfectly edible products that have passed their sell-by dates. The average family is just as wasteful. According to official 1993 Japanese statistics, forty percent of household garbage is leftover food.[17]

The Future of Food in Japan

Japanese cuisine, generally speaking, is still relatively bland and uses fewer spices than most other national cuisines with the exception of Polish and Danish. Japanese cuisine is on par with England in using approximately four spices per dish. (Thailand and India use double that number.)[18] A lack of spice has not interfered with the proliferation of Japanese cuisine abroad, any more than spiciness has halted the explosion of Chinese restaurants in the West. Fred Balitzer, a professor of government, claims that the spread of Asian food to even small towns in America may prove that Americans are quite aware and receptive on many fronts to Asian values and culture.[19] While Japanese food purists lament the change and supposed decline of "Japanese cuisine," postwar Japanese live longer than any other national group on earth. Britain faces an entirely different set of issues – more people each year are eating alone, eating poorer fare and paying for it with declining health.[20] The Japanese diet has changed

---

[15] Gavan McCormack, *The Emptiness of Japanese Affluence*, p. 132.
[16] Ibid., p. 133.
[17] Nihon shōhisha renmei, edited, *Hōshoku Nihon to Ajia*, p. 17.
[18] Paul W. Sherman and Jennifer Billing, "Darwinian Gastronomy: Why We Use Spices," *BioScience*, Vol. 49, no. 6, June 1999, p. 454.
[19] Fred Balitzer, *Japan Times*, August 8, 1999.
[20] Joanna Blythman, *Bad Food Britain: How A Nation Ruined Its Appetite*.

immeasurably over the last century, as has the life-style, but the transformation has produced stronger citizens rather than weaker ones, with relatively less of the obesity epidemic experienced in the West.

Has this transformation of eating styles influenced Japan's postwar class structure? In France, cuisine means *haute cuisine* and that means striving for three Michelin stars. French wine, French food – the entire essence of high-class French dining – in many settings connotes snobbery. Until the late twentieth century, Japanese cuisine was not discussed or debated in glossy guidebooks that count stars and use impressive Latin phrases to label sauce reductions. Japanese food is debated in manga, on web blogs and in newspapers. Only recently has this changed, with famed French restaurant guide Michelin awarding stars to Japanese restaurants in a new series of guidebooks. Imagine the shift of Western attitudes toward Asian cuisine necessary for chief Michelin executive Michel Rollier to declare: "Japan is a country where fine dining is an integral part of the culture."[21] Such a statement would certainly never have been made prewar; that it is imaginable now is due in part to the spread of sushi. At the same time, ordinary Japanese food has crept into the lexicon of daily living throughout the world. This, of course, includes ramen.

Changes in the Contemporary Japanese Diet

Contrary to the international image of Japan as a healthy place to eat, modern Japan has its problems. The government has two major concerns: food safety and nutrition. Since 2005, increasing quantities of tainted food products have been imported from China. *SAPIO*, a right-leaning biweekly magazine, has published scores of articles decrying this issue. One particularly suggestive piece asked whether Japan risked becoming "a food colony of China" because it imported so many basic ingredients from the mainland.[22] Food security is an important issue for countries with low food self-sufficiency ratios. Japan currently produces about forty percent of its domestic calorie requirements – the lowest ratio among industrialized nations – and many people are concerned. Food security is one of the

---

[21] Associated Press, "Famed French restaurant guide extends reach to Japan," March 17, 2007.
[22] "Dokuiru gyōza jiken de wakatta [Nihon wa chūgoku no 'shokuryō shokuminchi' de aru]," *SAPIO*, February 27, 2008, p. 3.

basic roles that the government should manage.²³ In response to political and social anxiety concerning the source and safety of food, as well as fear over the effects from changes in diet, the national government passed The Basic Law on Shokuiku (Food Education) enacted in June 2005. *Shokuiku* is defined as "the acquisition of knowledge about food as well as the ability to make appropriate food choices." According to Japanese government surveys, approximately thirty percent of males and fifty percent of females in all age groups believe that they lack the necessary knowledge and skills to make good food choices and meals.²⁴

In 1993, Japan suffered its worst harvest in postwar history, prompting a major change in the food laws. In December 1994, the National Diet passed the New Food Supply Law, (*Shinshokuryōhō*), which superseded the older 1942 edict that kept the food markets heavily regulated. Food control in Japan concerns the belief that the state should plan and distribute staple foods; this system is essentially an outgrowth of the World War II rationing program. In 1942, the government made it illegal to sell rice and other grains outside the agency's framework. Wheat was released from the food control system in the 1950s but rice was and remains a special case. The 1960s were a turning point because the administration had to buy rice from farmers who at that time wanted to sell it at higher prices and encourage consumers to pay the elevated prices.²⁵

The Japanese government is anxious. The ministries that manage food and agriculture have made clear the official position on what constitutes Japanese food in a way perhaps only done in France and China. "Japanese food has come to be what it is today, blessed with an abundance of freshness and seasonality of the yearly climate, based on a Japanese sensibility of seasonal changes and feel for aesthetics and an adoption of foreign foods and culture," claims one ministerial report.²⁶ The goal is not only to raise Japan's international image through Japanese cuisine but also "to contribute to world richness in food life-style and food culture."²⁷

---

[23] *Some Key Issues for the East Asian Food Sector,* PACIFIC ECONOMIC PAPER, No. 305, JULY July 2000, The Australia—Japan Research Centre is part of the Asia Pacific School of Economics and Management, The Australian National University, Canberra, p. 1.10. This issue of food and security is being debated in numerous Japanese books as well. See Shibata Akio, *Shokuryō sōdatsu,* pp. 208–214.

[24] http://www.maff.go.jp/e/topics/pdf/shokuiku.pdf.

[25] Penelope Francks, "Agriculture and the state in Industrial East Asia: the rise and fall of the Food Control System in Japan," *Japan Forum,* Vol. 10, number 1, 1998, pp. 1–16.

[26] Japanese government website, 海外日本食レストラン推奨有識者会議, (http://www.maff.go.jp/j/shokusan/sanki/easia/e_sesaku/japanese_food/index.html).

[27] Ibid.

Figure 52. Abundant shelves of food products, including many noodle dishes, in the average corner convenience store in most Japanese urban areas.

Clearly, the authorities are now confident that Japanese cuisine is something to be admired on an international scale – it is no longer superceded by other national cuisines in diplomatic dinners. Because Japanese cuisine is increasingly popular in the world today, the international market is a potential "showroom" for Japanese culture and an opportunity to introduce Japanese products. Japanese bureaucrats have even developed a "Plan to Promote Japanese Restaurants Abroad." Japan has come far since debating whether to dismantle its own cuisine and mimic the West, over a century and a half earlier.

Did Japanese Food Create Japanese Identity?

For comparative purposes, let us ask the question: when did cuisine in France become French cuisine? One historian responds that, "In the last analysis French cuisine came from Paris, not because of products or dishes but because in the largest sense Paris supplied the template of French culinary civilization. Put another way, it brought every identifiable periphery in France into the center."[28] Japan's historical pattern was similar: we might remember the Edo preference for a heavier soy sauce dominating the market and pushing out the more refined and lighter, Kyoto version. And yet, at the same time, Japan's regional markets are trying to identify and market themselves as local brands in fierce competition for consumers numb to the sameness of urban offerings. Ironically, modern Japanese cuisine is marked by an intense capitalistic drive to separate the local from the mass, with the local considered superior by far. In France, cuisine offers "a model for national unity all the more powerful in that cuisine somehow exists beyond the political, beyond the material, in a realm of Frenchness all its own."[29] While there may be a Japanese-ness to Japanese cuisine, over time there has been little consensus beyond a general devotion to the supposed centrality of rice.

Even now ramen may be helping to buck a long-standing stereotypical idea that only Japanese people cook Japanese food as I learned from Ivan Orkin, one of the first non-Japanese to dare to open a successful ramen store in Tokyo. An intelligent and astute American businessman, Ivan realized that good food was so regardless of who made it; and that if he put his mind to it, he too could produce a great bowl of ramen noodle soup. It has not all been an easy road though he claims to be the "most recognized ramen shop owner in Japan" because he is Caucasian and thus does not fit the norm in Japan. "One customer took three sips of the soup and left," Ivan told me, "while another guy liked the meal so much, he licked the bowl." Orkin also feels that not only does his store stand out because he is a foreigner devoted to making great ramen every day, but also because he believes ramen so pervades Japanese society that "it is now mostly a corporate food." His "Ivan" brand, he asserts, is synonymous with quality and good service at a reasonable price.[30] I see Ivan and his ramen store as a symbol of the overall changes Japan is now experiencing. Noodle soup has almost come full circle from its days as a sort of Chinese hybrid creation in the late nineteenth century. Once again, non-Japanese are experimenting and forming new tastes and dishes in Japan, adding to the culinary landscape for the native population.

---

[28] Priscilla Parkhurst Ferguson, "Is Paris France?," *The French Review*, Vol. 73, No. 6., May 2000, p. 1059.

[29] Ibid., p. 1061.

[30] Interview October 13, 2009. See also his short book on the history of his store, Aiban Ōkin, *Aiban no rāmen*.

Figure 53. Ramen has become so popular in contemporary Japan that it headlines at mass exhibits of new tastes and stores, held in large convention centers. Above is just one example of a poster touting a 2009 show.

Food may not be discussed in the same sensual tones in Japan as it is in France but it does invoke memory. Mother's cooking, *ofukuro no aji*, is important. For Japan, cuisine is the locus of national identity and you can see this in the government's new plan to help people get healthier by eating better *Nihonshoku* – yet another term for Japanese cuisine. The government is pushing a concept of Japanese food that does not include too many sweets, is not fast food, is balanced and reduces over eating. This is an example of what the famous historian Eric Hobsbawm has labeled "the invention of tradition," a complex interplay of discourses that every nation indulges in, and that enable every nation to create a mythic or

Figure 54. Japanese readers can today select from dozens of weekly and monthly magazines reviewing restaurants, recipes, food travel tours and guidebooks.

non-existent past for itself, to justify elements that are in fact entirely modern. Cuisine set Japan historically apart from China and engaged it with the West. In the twenty-first century, Japanese eating patterns have come to symbolize a healthy life-style and the secret of a long life. A change in diet, as Japan is again experiencing, suggests that another major food revolution is in the works – an overabundant food supply and a corresponding weakening of traditional patterns of diet.[31]

Ramen and History

Japan has moved from a society that never had enough food to a society that ate well, to a contemporary society that wastes food. Historically, virtually everyone was malnourished. Only the wealthy few could afford a

---

[31] Jon D. Holtzman, "Food and Memory," *Annual Revue of Anthropology*, 35, 2006, pp. 361–378.

good nutritional balance. Looking at the long history of ramen, as the result of interaction between Japan and China and to a lesser extent Korea and the West, proves that Japanese cuisine is neither timeless nor unchanging. If one myth is clearly debunked, it is the idea that Japanese cuisine has unique traditions. What the Japanese eat has been immensely improved through interaction with its East Asian neighbors. The success of modern Japanese cuisine owes much to these linkages. Ramen was not born out of the blue but developed into a worldwide popular cultural phenomenon because of the Chinese influence and East Asian national debates about cuisine, health and hygiene. As many historians and food industry experts have also detailed, Japan's ability to further these inventions with its own additions and to transform these products into consumer delights – such as instant ramen and related foodstuffs – caught the fancy of those beyond its own borders and primed their further expansion and popularity. The fact that these dishes are now being re-exported back to the countries where many of their ingredients originated parallels the same exchanges that brought them to Japan centuries ago. National cuisines may be symbols of national pride and identity, but an intricate web of history belies the dishes that we see today. The very erudite French scholar Alain Corbin demonstrated that we have failed to grasp the growth of history from early modern societies because we no longer take smell historically into account.[32] I would say the same goes for taste, not only the aesthetic version but the physical taste of change. We need to move away from our narrow preoccupation with the high political, the decisions that affect the few and the mighty, and aim our sights a bit lower to what was happening at many levels of society at various times through some of its most basic functions to appreciate more fully the changes and undulations people experienced. I have hoped to provide such an angle through this research on ramen.

Now Go Eat History!

As I discovered on my trips around Japan, China, Taiwan, and Korea, national cuisine is not just the result of the intersection of history and economic need. It can be created as a tourist attraction to define the image of a local region in contrast to the often times oppressing uniformity of modern urban daily life. Change in diet came around due to a multitude of

---

[32] Alain Corbin, *The Foul and the Fragrant: Odor and the French Social Imagination.*

factors including migration, the search for delicious, the industrial landscape and labor, geographic forces, the quest for profit, shifting demography of the urban populations, war, and a host of other reasons. Ramen developed in response to these many factors; to understand its real provenance and continued vitality means analyzing the history of Japan in a wider context. In modern Japan, cuisine has become an integral part of the larger culture and is virtually inseparable from our modern concept of the nation. To many people, ramen plays a key historical role and its story illuminates Japanese history.

In the end, regardless of all the talk of international relations and Sino-Japanese culinary exchanges over the centuries, one thing should be clear – just by eating ramen you can digest history; the exercise can be nutritious and appetizing. So, go on, try it and see what you learn. Dip your chopsticks into that bowl of noodle soup and see what sort of history you can taste.

BIBLIOGRAPHY

ENGLISH LANGUAGE

Alcock, Rutherford. *The capital of the tycoon: a narrative of a three years' residence in Japan*, Vol. 1, London: Longman, Green, Longman, Roberts, & Green, 1863.

Allinson, Gary. *Japan's Postwar History*, 2nd edition, Ithaca: Cornell University Press, 2004.

Allison, Anne. "Japanese Mothers and Obentos: The Lunch-Box as Ideological State Apparatus," *Anthropological Quarterly*, Vol. 64, No. 4, Gender and the State, Oct. 1991, pp. 195–208.

Anderson, Benedict. *Imagined Communities: Reflections on the origin and spread of nationalism*, London: Verso, 1983.

Anderson, E.N. *The Food of China*, New Haven: Yale University Press, 1988.

Anderson, Warwick. "Excremental Colonialism: Public Health and the Poetics of Pollution," *Critical Inquiry*, Vol. 21, No. 3. Spring, 1995, pp. 640–669.

Aoyama, Tomoko. "Romancing Food: The Gastronomic Quest in Early Twentieth-Century Japanese Literature," *Japanese Studies*, December 2003, pp. 251–264.

—— *Reading Food in Modern Japanese Literature*, Honolulu: University of Hawaii Press, 2008.

Appadurai, Arjun. "How to Make a National Cuisine: Cookbooks in Contemporary India," *Comparative Studies in Society and History*, Vol. 30, No. 1, 1988, pp. 3–24.

Aston, W.G. (translation). *Nihongi: Chronicles of Japan from the Earliest Times to AD 697*, Vermont, Charles E. Tuttle and Company, 1972.

Baskett, Michael. *The Attractive Empire: Transnational Film Culture in Imperial Japan*, Honolulu: University of Hawaii Press, 2008.

Batten, Bruce. *Gateway to Japan: Hakata in War and Peace, 500–1300*, University of Hawaii Press, 2006.

Belasco, Warren and Philip Scranton, eds. *Food Nations: Selling Taste in Consumer Societies*, London: Routledge, 2002.

Bestor, Theodore. *Tsukiji: The Fish Market at the Center of the World*, Berkeley: University of California Press, 2004.

Bisson, T.A. "Reparations and Reform in Japan," *Far Eastern Survey*, Vol. 16, No. 21, December 1947, pp. 241–247.

Black, John. *Young Japan, Yokohama & Yedo*, Vol. I, 1858–1879, London: Oxford in Asia, reprinted 1968, (originally published in 1883).

Blythman, Johanna. *Bad Food Britain: How A Nation Ruined Its Appetite*, London: Fourth Estate, 2006.

Bodart-Bailey, Beatrice M, edited and translated. *Kaempfer's Japan: Tokugawa Culture Observed*, Honolulu: University of Hawaii Press, 1999.

—— *The dog shogun: the personality and policies of Tokugawa Tsunayoshi*, Honolulu: University of Hawaii Press, 2006.

Bodart-Bailey, Beatrice M. *The dog shogun: the personality and policies of Tokugawa Tsunayoshi*, Honolulu: University of Hawaii Press, 2006.

Bowring, Richard. *Mori Ogai and the modernization of Japanese culture*, Cambridge: University of Cambridge Press, 1979.

Braisted, William R. *Meiroku Zasshi: Journal of the Japanese Enlightenment*, Cambridge: Harvard University Press, 1976.

Breen, John and Mark Teeuwen. *Shinto in History: Ways of the Kami*, Honolulu, University of Hawaii Press, 2000.

Buell, Paul D. and Eugene N. Anderson. *A Soup for the Qan: Chinese Dietary Medicine of the Mongol Era as Seen in Hu Szu-Hui's Yin-Shan Cheng-Yao*, London: Kegan Paul International, 2000.
Burnett, John. "The rise and decline of school meals in Britain, 1860–1990," in *The Origins and Development of Food Policies in Europe*. London: Leicester University Press, 1994, pp. 55–69.
Burnett, John and Derek J. Oddy, eds. *The Origins and Development of Food Policies in Europe*. London: Leicester University Press, 1994.
Cadwallader, Gary Sōka and Joseph R. Justice. "'Stones for the Belly': *Kaiseki* Cuisine for Tea during the Early Edo Period," in Eric Rath and Stephanie Assmann, eds., *Past and Present in Japanese Foodways*, Chicago: University of Illinois Press, 2010, pp. 68–91.
Carpenter, Kenneth. *Beriberi, White Rice, and Vitamin B: A Disease, a Cause, and a Cure*, Berkeley: University of California Press, 2000.
Chang, K.C. *Food in Chinese Culture: Anthropological and Historical Perspectives*, New Haven: Yale University Press, 1977.
Chang, Richard T. "General Grant's 1879 Visit to Japan," *Monumenta Nipponica*, Vol. 24, No. 4, 1969, pp. 373–392.
Chehabi, H.E. "The Westernization of Iranian Culinary Culture," *Iranian Studies*, Vol. 36, no.1, March 2003, pp. 43–61.
Ching, Julia. "Chu Shun-Shui, 1600–82: A Chinese Confucian Scholar in Tokugawa Japan," *Monumenta Nipponica*, Vol. 30, No. 2, Summer, 1975, pp. 177–191.
Cohen, Jerome. "Japan's Economy on the Road Back," *Pacific Affairs*, Vol. 21, No. 3, September 1948, pp. 264–279.
Collingham, Lizzie. *Taste of War: World War Two and the Battle for Food*, London: Allen Lane, 2011.
Collins, Sandra. *The 1940 Tokyo Games: The Missing Olympics: Japan, the Asian Olympics and the Olympic Movement*, London: Routledge, 2008.
Corbin, Alain. *The Foul and the Fragrant: Odor and the French Social Imagination*. New York: Berg, 1986.
Cwiertka, Katarzyna J. *Modern Japanese Cuisine: Food, Power and National Identity*. London: Reaktion books, 2006.
—— "The Making of Modern Culinary Tradition in Japan," PhD Thesis at Leiden University, Holland, 1999.
Diamond, Jared. *Collapse: How Societies Choose to Fail or Succeed*, NY: Viking Press, 2005.
Dore, R.P. *Land reform in Japan*, London: Oxford University Press, 1959.
Dower, John. *Embracing Defeat: Japan in the Wake of World War II*, New York: W.W. Norton & Co., 2000.
Drea, Edward. *In the service of the Emperor: essays on the Imperial Japanese Army*, Lincoln: University of Nebraska Press, 1998.
Driver, Christopher. *The British at Table, 1940–1980*, London: Chatto and Windus, 1983.
Dung, Bùi Minh. "Japan's Role in the Vietnamese Starvation of 1944–45," *Modern Asian Studies*, Vol. 29, No. 3, July 1995, pp. 573–618.
Dunlop, Fuchsia. "Gastronomically Chinese: Culinary identities and Chinese modernity," MA Area Studies (China) of the University of London, September 1997.
—— *Revolutionary Chinese Cookbook: Recipes from Hunan Province*, London: Ebury Press, 2006.
Duus, Peter. *The Abacus and the Sword. The Japanese Penetration of Korea, 1895–1912*. Berkeley: University of California Press, 1995.
Earhart, David. *Certain Victory, Images of World War II in the Japanese Media*, NY: ME Sharpe, 2008.
Economy, Elizabeth and Kenneth Lieberthal. "Scorched Earth: Will Environmental Risks in China Overwhelm Its Opportunities?" *Harvard Business Review*, June 2007, pp. 88–97
Farquhar, Judith. *Appetites, food and sex in post-socialist China*, Durham: Duke University Press, 2002.

Farris, William Wayne, *Sacred Texts and Buried Treasures*, Honolulu: University of Hawaii Press, 1998.
—— *Japan's Medieval Population: Famine, Fertility, and Warfare in a Transformative Age*, Honolulu: University of Hawaii Press, 2006.
—— *Japan to 1600: A Social and Economic History*, Honolulu: University of Hawaii Press, 2009.
Ferguson, Priscilla Parkhurst. "Is Paris France?" *The French Review*, Vol. 73, No. 6, May 2000, pp. 1052–1064.
Fogel, Joshua A. "A Decisive Turning Point in Sino-Japanese Relations: The *Senzaimaru* Voyage to Shanghai of 1862," *Late Imperial China*, Volume 29, Number 1 Supplement, June 2008, pp. 104–124.
—— ed. *Late Qing China and Meiji Japan: political & cultural aspects*, Norwalk, CT: East Bridge, 2003.
—— Review of Lydia Liu, ed. *Tokens of Exchange: The Problem of Translation in Global Circulations*, Durham: Duke University Press, 1999, in "'Like Kissing through a Handkerchief:' *Traduttore Traditore*," *China Review International* 8.1, Spring 2001, pp. 1–15.
—— *The literature of travel in the Japanese rediscovery of China, 1862–1945*, Stanford, Calif: Stanford University Press, 1996.
—— Review of Stefan Tanaka, *Japan's Orient: Rendering Pasts into History*, *Monumenta Nipponica*, Vol. 49, No. 1, Spring, 1994, pp. 108–112.
—— *The cultural dimension of Sino-Japanese relations: essays on the nineteenth and twentieth centuries*, Oxfordshire, UK: Carfax Pub. Co., 1993.
Formanek, Susanne and Sepp Linhart, eds. *Written Texts – Visual Texts: Woodblock printed Media in Early Modern Japan*, Amsterdam: Hotei Publishers, 2005.
Forster, Robert and Orest Ranom, eds. *Food and Drink in History*, Selections from the Annales, Vol. 5, Baltimore: Johns Hopkins Press, 1979.
Francks, Penelope. *Japanese Consumer: An Alternative Economic History of Modern Japan*, Cambridge University Press, 2009.
—— "Agriculture and the state in Industrial East Asia: the rise and fall of the Food Control System in Japan," *Japan Forum*, Vol. 10, number 1, 1998, pp. 1–16.
Friedmann, Harriet. "The Political Economy of Food: The Rise and Fall of the Postwar International Food Order," *The American Journal of Sociology*, Vol. 88, Supplement: Marxist Inquiries: Studies of Class, and States, 1982, pp. 248–286.
Fritsch, Ingrid. "Chindonya Today - Japanese Street Performers in Commercial Advertising," *Asian Folklore Studies*, Vol. 60, No. 1, 2001, pp. 49–78.
Fruin, W. Mark, *Kikkoman: Company, Clan, and Community*, Cambridge: Harvard University Press, 1983.
Fuchs, Steven Joseph, "Feeding the Japanese: MacArthur, Washington and the Rebuilding of Japan through Food Policy," PhD Dissertation at University of New York at Stony Brook, 2002.
Fujitani, Takashi. *Splendid monarchy: power and pageantry in modern Japan*, Berkeley, California: University of California Press, 1996.
Fukutomi, Satomi. "Connoisseurship of B-grade culture: Consuming Japanese national food Ramen," PhD dissertation in the Department of Anthropology at the University of Hawai'i Manoa, 2010.
Garnsey, Peter. *Food and Society in Classical Antiquity*, Cambridge: Cambridge University Press, 1999.
Gatten, Aileen. "A Wisp of Smoke. Scent and Character in The Tale of Genji," *Monumenta Nipponica*, Vol. 32, No. 1, Spring 1977, pp. 153–185.
Gerth, Karl. *China Made: Consumer culture and the creation of the nation*, Cambridge: Harvard University Press, 2003.
—— *As China Goes, So Goes the World: How Chinese Consumers Are Transforming Everything*, NY: Farrar, Straus and Giroux, 2010.

Goody, Jack. *Cooking, Cuisine and Class: A Study in Comparative Sociology*, Cambridge: Cambridge University Press, 1992.
Gowen, Herbert H. "Living Conditions in Japan," *Annals of the American Academy of Political and Social Science*, Vol. 122, The Far East, November 1925, pp. 160–166.
Grappard, Allan. "The economics of ritual power," in *Shinto in History: Ways of the Kami*, edited by John Breen and Mark Teeuwen, Honolulu: University of Hawai'i Press, 2000, pp. 68–94.
Grew, Raymond, ed. *Food in Global History*, Boulder: Westview Press, 1999.
Guiliano, Mireille. *French Women Do not Get Fat*, New York: Vintage (Reprint edition), 2007.
Hall, Ivan. *Mori Arinori*, Cambridge: Harvard University Press, 1973.
Hall, John ed. *The Cambridge history of Japan*, volume 4, Early modern Japan, Cambridge: Cambridge University Press, 1991.
Hall, John. "Rule by Status in Tokugawa Japan," *Journal of Japanese Studies*, Vol. 1, No. 1, Autumn, 1974, pp. 39–49.
Hanley, Susan. *Everyday Things in Premodern Japan*, Berkeley: University of California, 1997.
Hardacre, Helen. "Creating State Shinto: The Great Promulgation Campaign and the New Religions," *Journal of Japanese Studies*, Winter 1986, pp. 29–64.
Harrel, Paula. *Sowing the seeds of change: Chinese students, Japanese teachers, 1895–1905*, Stanford: Stanford University Press, 1992.
Harrison, Henrietta. *The Man Awakened from Dreams*, Palo Alto: Stanford University Press, 2005.
Hayashi, Reiko. "Provisioning Edo in the Early Eighteenth Century," in James McClain et al., eds. *Edo and Paris: Urban Life and the State in the Early Modern Era*, Ithaca: Cornell University Press, 1994, pp. 211–233.
Hesselink, Reinier H. "A Dutch New Year at the Shirando Academy," *Monumenta Nipponica*, Vol. 50, No.2, Summer 1995, pp. 189–234.
Hoare, J.E. "The Chinese in the Japanese Treaty Ports, 1858–1899: The Unknown Majority," *Proceedings of the British Association for Japanese Studies*, Vol. 2, 1977, part 1, pp. 18–33.
Holmes, Colin and A.H. Ion. "Bushido and the Samurai: Images in British Public Opinion, 1894–1914," *Modern Asian Studies*, Vol. 14, No. 2, 1980, pp. 309–329.
Holtzman, Jon D. "Food and Memory," *Annual Revue of Anthropology*, 35, 2006, pp. 361–378.
Howell, David. *Geographies of Identity in Nineteenth Century Japan*, Berkeley: University of California Press, 2005.
—— "Fecal Matters: Prolegomenon to a History of Shit in Japan," in Ian J. Miller, Julia Adney Thomas, and Brett L. Walker, eds., *Japan at Nature's Edge: The Environment of a Global Power* (forthcoming from University of Hawaii Press.)
Huang, H.T. *Science and Civilisation in China Series*, Vol. 6, Biology and Biological Technology, part 5, Fermentations and Food Science, Cambridge: Cambridge University Press, 2000.
Igarashi, Yoshikuni. *Bodies of Memory: narratives of war in postwar Japanese culture, 1945–1970*, Princeton: Princeton University Press, 2000.
Iwaya, Saori. "Work and Life as a Coal Miner: the life history of a woman miner," in Wakita Haruko, Anne Bouchy and Ueno Chizuko, eds., *Gender and Japanese History*, Vol. 2: The Subject and Expression/Work and Life, Osaka: Osaka University press, 1999, pp. 413–448.
Jannetta, Ann Bowman. *Epidemics and Mortality in Early Modern Japan*, Princeton: Princeton University Press, 1987.
Jansen, Marius B. *The Cambridge History of Japan*, volume 5, The nineteenth century, Cambridge: University of Cambridge, 1989.
Johnston, Bruce. *Japanese Food Management in World War Two*, Palo Alto: Stanford University Press, 1953.
—— "Japan: Problems of Deferred Peace," *Far Eastern Survey*, Vol. 18, No. 19, September 1949, pp. 221–225.

—— "Japan: The Race between Food and Population," *Journal of Farm Economics*, Vol. 31, no. 2, May 1949, pp. 276–292.
Johnston, William. *The Modern Epidemic: A History of Tuberculosis in Japan*, Cambridge: Harvard University Press, 1996.
Jones, Michael Owen. "Food Choice, Symbolism, and Identity: Bread-and-Butter Issues for Folkloristics and Nutrition Studies," *Journal of American Folklore* 120, 2007, pp. 129–177.
Jung, Keun-Sik. "Colonial Modernity and the Social History of Chemical Seasoning in Korea," *Korean Journal*, Vol. 45, no. 2, Summer 2005, pp. 9–36.
Keene, Donald. *The Battles of Coxinga: Chikamatsu's Puppet Play, Its Background and Importance*, Cambridge: University of Cambridge Press, 1951.
—— *Modern Japanese Literature, an Anthology*, NY: Grove Press, 1956.
Kerr, Alex. *Lost Japan*, 2nd edition, NY: Lonely Planet, 2009.
—— *Dogs and Demons: Tales from the Dark Side of Japan*, London: Hill and Wang, 2002.
Kidder, J. Edward. *Himiko and Japan's Elusive Chiefdom of Yamatai: Archaeology, History, and Mythology*, Honolulu: University of Hawaii Press, 2007.
Kieschnick, John. *The Impact of Buddhism on Chinese Material Culture*. Princeton: Princeton University Press, 2003.
Kikunae Ikeda. "New Seasonings," (translated by Yoko Ogiwara and Yuzo Ninomiya) *Journal of the Chemical Society of Tokyo*, no. 30, pp. 820–836, 1909, in *Chemical Senses* 27, 2002, pp. 847–849.
Knechtges, David R. "Gradually Entering the Realm of Delight: Food and Drink in Early Medieval China," *Journal of the American Oriental Society*, Vol. 117, No. 2, April – June 1997, pp. 229–239.
Kohl, Stephen W. "Shiga Naoya and the Literature of Experience," *Monumenta Nipponica*, Vol. 32, No. 2, Summer 1977, pp. 211–224.
Kojiki, (translated and notes by Donald Philippi), Princeton: Princeton University Press, 1969.
Kunitake, Kume. *The Iwakura Embassy, 1871–1873: A True Account of the Ambassador Extraordinary and Plenipotentiary's Journey of Observation Through the United States of America and Europe*, (Graham Healey and Chushichi Tsuzuki, editors), several volumes, London: Routledge, 2002.
Kushner, Barak. "Sweetness and Empire: Sugar Consumption in Imperial Japan," in Janet Hunter and Penelope Francks, eds., *The Historical Consumer: Consumption and Everyday Life in Japan, 1850–2000*, London: Palgrave Macmillan, 2011, pp. 127–150.
—— "Imperial Cuisines in Taishō Foodways," in Eric Rath and Stephanie Assmann, eds., *Past and Present in Japanese Foodways*, Chicago: University of Illinois Press, 2010, pp. 145–165.
—— "Going for the Gold – Health and Sports in Japan's Quest for Modernity," in William Tsutsui and Michael Baskett, eds., *The East Asian Olympiads, 1934–2008: Building Bodies and Nations in Japan, Korea, and China*, Folkestone: Global Oriental, 2011, pp. 34–48.
Laudan, Rachel. "A Plea for Culinary Modernism: Why We Should Love New, Fast, Processed Food," *Gastronomica I*, February 2001, pp. 36–44.
Ledyard, Gari. "Galloping along with the Horseriders: Looking for the Founders of Japan," *Journal of Japanese Studies*, Vol. 1, No. 2, Spring 1975, pp. 217–254.
Levenstein, Harvey. *Revolution at the Table: The Transformation of the American Diet*, Berkeley: University of California Press, 2003.
—— *Paradox of Plenty: A Social History of Eating in Modern America* (revised edition), Berkeley: University of California Press, 2003.
Liu, Lydia. *Translingual Practice: Literature, National Culture, and Translated Modernity-China, 1900–1937*. Palo Alto: Stanford University Press, 1995.
—— Ed. *Tokens of Exchange: The Problem of Translation in Global Circulations*, Durham: Duke University Press, 1999.
Lu, David. *Japan: A documentary history*, New York: M.E. Sharpe, 1997.

Lu, Hanchao. *Beyond the Neon Lights: Everyday Shanghai in the Early Twentieth Century*, Berkeley: University of California Press, 1999.
Lynn, Richard John. "'This Culture of Ours' and Huang Zunxian's Literary Experiences in Japan (1877–82)," *Chinese Literature: Essays, Articles, Reviews*, Vol. 19, December 1997, pp. 113–138.
Maclachlan, Patricia. *Consumer Politics in Postwar Japan*, New York: Columbia University Press, 2002.
Masini, Frederico. *The Formation of Modern Chinese Lexicon and Its Evolution Toward a National Language: The Period from 1840 to 1898*, Special Issue of the Journal of Chinese Linguistics, Monograph Series Number 6, 1993.
McClain, James, et al., eds. *Edo and Paris: Urban Life and the State in the Early Modern Era*, Ithaca: Cornell University Press, 1994.
McCormack, Gavan. *The Emptiness of Japanese Affluence*, London: Allen & Unwin, 1996.
McGlothlen, Ronald L. *Controlling the Waves: Dean Acheson and U.S. Foreign Policy in Asia*, New York: Norton, 1993.
McOmie, William, ed. *Foreign Images and Experiences of Japan*, Vol. 1, First Century AD to 1841, Folkstone: Global Oriental, 2005.
Melnick, Daniel. "Monosodium Glutamate-Improver of Natural Food Flavors," *The Scientific Monthly*, Vol. 70, No. 3., March 1950, pp. 199–204.
Mennell, Stephen. *All Manners of Food: Eating and Taste in England and France from the Middle Ages to the Present*, Chicago: University of Illinois Press, 1996.
Mintz, Sidney W. *Tasting Food, Tasting Freedom: Excursions into Eating, Culture, and the Past*, Boston: Beacon Press, 1996.
Moen, Darrell Gene. "The Postwar Japanese Agricultural Debacle," *Hitotsubashi Journal of Social Studies* 31, 1999, pp. 29–52.
Montanari, Massimo. *Food is culture*, (translated by Aine O'Healy), NY: Columbia University Press, 2006.
Moriyama, Naomi. *Japanese Women Do not Get Old or Fat: Secrets of My Mother's Tokyo Kitchen*, New York: Delta, 2006.
Morris, Ivan. *The World of the Shining Prince*, New York: Alfred Knopf, 1964.
Morse, Edward. *Japan Day by Day*, Tokyo: Kobunsha, 1936.
Nakamura, Hirosi. "The Japanese Portolanos of Portuguese Origin of the XVIth and XVIIth Centuries," *Imago Mundi*, Vol. 18, 1964, pp. 24–44.
Narushima Ryūhoku. (translated by Matthew Fraleigh), *New Chronicles of Yanagibashi and Diary of a Journey to the West: Narushima Ryūhoku Reports from Home and Abroad*, Ithaca: Cornell University Press, 2010.
Neary, Ian. *Political Protest and Social Control in Prewar Japan: The Origins of Burakumin Liberation*, NJ: Atlantic Highland, 1989.
Neitzel, Laura. "Living modern: Danchi housing and postwar Japan," PhD dissertation at Columbia University, 2003.
Nestle, Marion. *Food Politics: How the Food Industry Influences Nutrition and Health* (revised and expanded edition), University of California Press, 2007.
Nishiyama Matsunosuke. *Edo Culture: daily life and diversions in urban Japan, 1600–1868* (translated by Gerald Groemer) University of Hawaii Press, 1997.
Nivison, David S. *The Life and Thought of Chang Hsueh-ch'eng (1738–1801)*, Palo Alto: Stanford University Press, 1966.
Notehelfer, Fred. "On Idealism and Realism in the Thought of Okakura Tenshin," *Journal of Japanese Studies*, Vol. 16, No. 2, Summer, 1990, pp. 309–355.
Offer, Avner. *The First World War: An Agrarian Interpretation*, Oxford: Clarendon, 1989.
Ooms, Herman. *Imperial Politics and Symbolics in Ancient Japan: The Tenmu Dynasty, 650–800*, Honolulu: University of Hawaii Press, 2009.
Partner, Simon. *Assembled in Japan – Electrical goods and the Making of the Japanese Consumer*, Berkeley: University of California Press, 1999.

—— *Toshie: A story of village life in Twentieth-Century Japan*, Berkeley, University of California Press, 2004.
Pastreich, Emanuel. "The Pleasure Quarters of Edo and Nanjing as Metaphor: The Records of Yu Huai and Narushima Ryuhoku," *Monumenta Nipponica*, Vol. 55, No. 2, Summer 2000, pp. 199–224.
Patrick, Hugh, ed. *Japanese Industrialization and its Social Consequences*. Berkeley: University of California Press, 1976.
Peters, Erica. "National Preferences and Colonial Cuisine: Seeking the Familiar in French Vietnam," *Proceedings of the Western Society for French History*, Vol. 27 1999, pp. 150–159.
Philippi, Donald (translated and with notes). *Kojiki*, University of Tokyo Press 1969.
Platt, Steve. *Provincial patriots: the Hunanese and modern China*, Cambridge, Mass: Harvard University Press, 2007.
Plutschow, Herbert. *A Reader in Edo Period Travel*, Folkstone: Global Oriental, 2006.
—— *Rediscovering Rikyu and the Beginning of the Japanese Tea Ceremony*, Folkstone: Global Oriental, 2003.
Pollack, David. *The Fracture of Meaning: Japan's Synthesis of China from the Eighth through the Eighteenth Centuries*, Princeton University Press, 1986.
Rath, Eric. "Banquets Against Boredom: Towards Understanding (Samurai) Cuisine in Early Modern Japan," *Early Modern Japan*, Vol. 16, 2008, pp. 43–55.
—— *Food and Fantasy in Early Modern Japanese Foodways*, Berkeley: the University of California Press, 2010.
Rath, Eric and Stephanie Assmann, eds. *Past and Present in Japanese Foodways*, Chicago: University of Illinois Press, 2010.
Reader, John. *The Untold History of the Potato*, London: Vintage, 2009.
Reardon-Anderson, James. "Chemical Industry in China, 1860–1949," *Osiris*, 2nd Series, Vol. 2, 1986, pp. 1–16.
Rimer, J. Thomas, ed. *Culture and Identity: Japanese Intellectuals during the Interwar Years*, Princeton: Princeton University Press, 1990.
Rogers, Ben. *Beef and Liberty: Roast Beef, John Bull and the English Nation*. London: Chatto and Windus, 2003.
Saaler, Sven, and J. Victor Koschmann, eds. *Pan-Asianism in modern Japanese history: colonialism, regionalism and borders*, London: Routledge, 2007.
Salzman, Catherine. "Continuity and Change in the Culinary History of the Netherlands, 1945–75," *Journal of Contemporary History*, Vol. 21, No. 4, October 1986, pp. 605–628.
Sand, Jordan. *House and home in modern Japan: architecture, domestic space and bourgeois culture, 1880–1930*, Cambridge, MA: Harvard University Press, 2003.
—— "A short history of MSG: Good science, bad science, and taste cultures,"*Gastronomica* 5, no. 4, 2005, pp. 38–49.
Sato, Barbara. *The New Japanese Woman*: Modernity, Media, and Women in Interwar Japan, Durham: Duke University Press, 2003.
Scalapino, Robert. *The Japanese communist movement, 1920–1966*, Berkeley: University of California Press, 1967.
Screech, Timon, annotated and introduced. *Japan Extolled and Decried: Carl Peter Thunburg and the Shogun's Realm, 1775–1796*, London: Routlege, 2005.
—— Annotated and introduced. *Secret Memoirs of the Shoguns: Isaac Titsingh and Japan, 1779–1822*, London: Routledge, 2006.
Serventi, Silvano and Francoise Sabban. *Pasta: The Story of a Universal Food*, New York: Columbia University Press, 2002 (translated by Anthony Shuugar).
Sheng, Annie. "Ramen Rage: Instant noodles in global capitalism and the production, reproduction and transformation of social meanings and taste," Undergraduate Thesis, International Studies Program, Spring 2006, Anthropology, University of Chicago.
Sherman, Paul W. and Jennifer Billing. "Darwinian Gastronomy: Why We Use Spices," *BioScience*, Vol. 49, no. 6, June 1999, pp. 453–463.

Silverberg, Miriam. *Erotic, Grotesque Nonsense – The Mass Culture of Japanese Modern Times*, Berkeley: University of California Press, 2006.
—— "The Café Waitress Serving Modern Japan," in Stephen Vlastos, ed. *Mirror of Modernity: Invented Traditions of Modern Japan*, Berkeley: University of California Press, 1998, pp. 208–225.
Smythe, Hugh and Yoshimasa Naitoh. "The Eta Caste in Japan," *Phylon*, Vol. 14, No. 1, 1953, pp. 19–27.
Solt, George. "Taking ramen seriously: food, labor, and everyday life in modern Japan," PhD dissertation in the History Department, University of California, San Diego, 2009.
Stam, Jerome M. "The Effects of Public Law 480 on Canadian Wheat Exports," *Journal of Farm Economics*, Vol. 46, No. 4, November 1964, pp. 805–819.
Steele, William. *Alternative Narratives in Modern Japanese History*, London: Routledge, Curzon, 2000.
Sterckx, Roel. *Food, Sacrifice, and Sagehood in Early China*. Cambridge: University of Cambridge Press, 2011.
Swislocki, Mark. *Culinary nostalgia: regional food culture and the urban experience in Shanghai*, Stanford, Calif: Stanford University Press, 2009.
Tannahill, Reay. *Food in History*, NY: Crown Publishers, 1988.
Tao, De-min. "Negotiating Language in the Opening of Japan: Luo Sen's Journal of Perry's 1854 Expedition," *Japan Review*, 2005, pp. 91–119.
Toby, Ronald. *State and Diplomacy in Early Modern Japan: Asia in the Development of the Tokugawa Bakufu*, Stanford, Calif: Stanford University Press, 1991.
Tomasik, Timothy J. "Certeau à la Carte: Translating Discursive Terroir in The Practice of Everyday Life: Living and Cooking," *The Atlantic Quarterly*, 100:2, Spring 2001, pp. 519–542.
Totman, Conrad. *Early Modern Japan*, Berkeley: University of California Press, 1995.
Tsurumi, Shunsuke. *A Cultural History of Postwar Japan*, NY: Columbia University Press. 1987.
—— *An intellectual history of wartime Japan, 1931–1945*, London: Paul Kegan International, 1986.
Tsutsui, William and Michael Baskett, eds. *The East Asian Olympiads, 1934–2008: Building Bodies and Nations in Japan, Korea, and China*, Folkstone: Global Oriental, 2011.
Vaporis, Constantine. *Tour of duty: samurai, military service in Edo, and the culture of early modern Japan*, Honolulu: University of Hawaii Press, 2008.
Vasishth, Andrea. "A model Minority – Chinese community in Japan," in Michael Weiner, ed. *Japan's Minorities – The illusion of homogeneity*, London: Routledge, 1997, pp. 108–139.
Vlastos, Stephen, ed. *Mirror of modernity: invented traditions of modern Japan*, Berkeley, University of California Press, 1998.
Walker, Brett. "Commercial Growth and Environmental Change in Early Modern Japan: Hachinohe's Wild Boar Famine of 1749," *Journal of Asian Studies*, Vol. 60, No. 2, May 2001, pp. 329–351.
Watt, Lori. *When Empire Comes Home: Repatriation and Reintegration in Postwar Japan*, Cambridge: Harvard University Press, 2009.
Weiner, Michael, ed. *Japan's Minorities: The Illusion of Homogeneity*. London: Routledge, 2009.
Wellington, A.R. *Hygiene and Public Health in Japan, Chosen and Manchuria*. Report on Conditions met during the tour of the League of Nations Interchange of Health Officers. Kuala Lumpur: Federated Malay States Government Printing Office, 1927.
Whitelaw, Gavin. "At your konbini in contemporary Japan: modern service, local familiarity, and the global transformation of the convenience store," PhD dissertation, Yale University, 2007.
Whiting, Robert. *Tokyo Underworld: The Fast Times and Hard Life of an American Gangster in Japan*, New York: Vintage, 2000.

Wilkinson, Endymion. *Chinese History: A Manual, Revised and Enlarged*, Cambridge: Harvard University Asia Center, 2000.
Wu, David Y.H. and Sidney C.H. Cheung, eds. *The Globalization of Chinese Food*. Honululu: University of Hawaii Press, 2002.
Xu, Guoqi. *Olympic Dreams: China and Sports, 1895–2008*, Cambridge: Harvard University Press, 2008.
Young, John Russell. *Around the world with General Grant: a narrative of the visit of General U.S. Grant, ex-President of the United States, to various countries in Europe, Asia, and Africa, in 1877, 1878, 1879; to which are added certain conversations with General Grant on questions connected with American politics and history*, New York: American News Co., Vol. 2, 1879.
Yue, Gang. *The Mouth That Begs*, Durham: Duke University Press, 1999.
Zweiniger-Bargielowska, Ina. *Austerity in Britain, Rationing, Controls and Consumption, 1939–1955*, Oxford: Oxford University Press, 2000.

Japanese Language

(Unless otherwise noted, all Japanese books are published in Tokyo)

Aiai Ryō, Shi Qian. *Kojiki shakai no seikatsu*, (originally published in 1925) Taipei, Taiwan: Taiwan minami shinpōsha, part of reprint of series, *Senzen senchūki Ajia kenkyū shiryō 2, shokuminchi shakai jigyō kankei shiryō – Taiwanhen*, Kindai shiryō kankōkai, 2001.
Amano Seisei. *Daidokoro kairyō*, Hakubunkan, 1907.
Andō Fujio. *Shina manyū jikki*, Hakubunkan, 1892.
Andō Momofuku. *Mahō no rāmen, hatsumei monogatari*, Nihon keizai shinbunsha, 2002.
Aoki Naomi. "Mito Kōmon no teuchi udon," *Rekishi kōkishin*, NHK publishers, June, 2007, pp. 48–62.
Aoki Setsuzō. *Harukanaru toki Taiwan: senjūmin shakai ni ikita aru Nihonjin keisatsukan no kiroku*, Osaka: Kansai tosho shuppan, 2002.
Aoki Toshisaburō. *Edo jidai no shokuryō mondai*, Keimeikai jimusho, 1942.
Arakawa Gorō. *Saikin Chosen jijō*, Yamagata: Shimizu shoten, 1906.
Biggu Jō. *Ippon hōchō Mantarō*, Shūeisha, 2004.
Bu Anryū, Yū Tatsuun, eds. *Chūgokujin no Nihon kenkyūshi*, Rokkōsha, 1989.
Catalogue House, eds. *Taishō jidai no mi no ue sōdan*, Chikuma shobō, 2002.
Chikamori Takaaki, "Roji ura no yashokushi," in Nishimura Hiroshi, ed. *Yashoku no bunkashi*, Seikyūsha, 2010, pp. 75–108.
Chinba Junji, ed. *Tanizaki Junichirō, Shanhai kōyūki*, Mimizu shobō, 2004.
Deguchi Kisō. *Zenkoku kōtō gakō hyōbanki*, Keibunkan, 1912.
Ego Michiko. *Nanban kara kita shokubunka*, Fukuoka: Genshobō, 2004.
Ema Tsutomu. *Tabemono no konjaku*, Tōkyō shobōsha, 1985.
Fujiwara Akira. *Uejinishita eireitachi*, Aoki shoten, 2001.
Fukuchi Genichirō. *Kaiō jidan*, reprinted in Bakumatsuhen, shinshiryō sōsho, Vol. 8, Jinbutsu ōraisha, 1968.
Fukuzawa Yukichi. "Nikushoku sezarubekarazu," in *Fukuzawa Yukichi zenshū*, Vol. 8, Iwanami shoten, 1970.
—— "Seiyō ishokujū," in *Fukuzawa zenshū*, Vol. 2, Jiji shinpōsha, 1898.
Harada Nobuo. *Washoku to Nihon bunka*, Shōgakukan, 2005.
Hayashi Reiko and Amamo Masatoshi. *Nihon no aji shōyu no reskihi*, Yoshikawa, 2005.
Higashikata Hakaru. *Hijōshokuryō no kenkyū*, Tōyōshokan, 1942.
Higuchi Kiyoyuki. *Taberu Nihonshi*, Asahi shinbunsha, 1996.
Hiraide Kōjirō. *Tōkyō fūzokushi*, reprinted in 1983, Nihon tosho sentā.
Hiraide Kōjirō. *Tōkyō fūzokushi*, Vol. 2, Fuzanbō, 1902.
Imai Saeko. "Mori Ōgai to Fukuzawa Yukichi no shokuseikatsuron," *Kyoto tandaigaku ronshū*, 30, 1, 2002, pp. 17–24.
Ishige Naomichi, et al., eds. *Bunka menruigaku koto hajime*, Fūdiamu komyunikēshon, 1991.

―― *Shōwa no shoku*, Domesu shuppan, 1989.
―― *Mendan tabemono no shi*, Bungei shunjū, 1989.
Itō Hiroshi. *Tsuru tsuru monogatari*, Tsukiji shokan, 1987.
Itō kinen zaidan ed. *Nihon shokuniku bunkashi*, Itō kinen zaidan sōritsu jūshūkinen publishers, 1991.
Itō Izumi. "Yokohama kakyō shakai no keisei," *Yokohama kaikō shiryōkan kiyō*, dai kyūgō, March 1991, pp. 1–28.
Iwanami kōza nō kyōgen. *Kyōgen no sekai*, Vol. 5, Iwanami shoten, 1987.
Kakinuki Ichiemon and Kojima Torajirō. *Shōkō Hakodate no sakigake: Hokkaidō hitori annai*, Osaka: Seikendō, 1885.
Kamiuma Shigekazu. *Utsunomiya gyōza no yoakemae*, Kyodo kumiai Utsunomiya gyōza, no date.
Kanagawa daigaku jinbun gakkai ed. *Chūgokujin Nihon ryūgakushi kenkyū no gendankai*, Ochanomizu shobō, 2002.
Kano Masanao. *Heishi de aru koto – dōin to jūgun seishinshi*, Asahi shimbunsha, 2005.
Kano Masanao et al., eds. Iwanami kōza, *Nihon tsūshi*, Vol. 21, Iwanami shoten, 1995.
Katō Eshō. *Nenbutsu daigo hyōzō*, Wakei shikai, 1885.
Kawakami Kōzō. *Nihon ryōri jibutsu kigen* (2 Vol. combined version) Iwanami, 2006.
Kawamoto Saburō. *Taishō genei,* Iwanami shoten, 2008.
Kawamura Yōjirō. *Umami mikaku to shoku kōdō*, Kyōritsu shuppansha, 1993.
Kawashima Shirō. *Kessenka no Nihon shokuryō*, Asahi shimbunsha, 1943.
Kikkoman edited series. *Food Culture*, Vol. 1, Watanabe Zenjirō, "Sekai o kakeru Nihongata shoku seikatsu no henbō," Kokusai shokubunka kenkyū liburarī, 2006.
Kikkoman shōyu kabushikigaisha ed. *Kikkoman shōyushi*, Kikkoman company, 1968.
Kimura Gorō. *Nihon no hoteru sangyōshi*, Kindai bungeisha, 1994.
Kimura Takuji. "Fukuin – gunjin no sengo shakai e no hōsetsu," in Yoshida Yutaka, ed. *Nihon no gendai rekishi, Vol. 26, sengo kaikaku to gyaku kōsu*, Yoshikawa kōbunkan, 2004 pp. 86–107.
Kobayashi Kazuo. *Kaikoroku*, Kyoto: Kawai bunkōdō, 1900.
Kodama Kagai. *Tōkyō inshōki*, Kanao bunendō, 1911.
Kodama Sadako. *Nihon no shokuji yōshiki: sono dentō o minaosu,* Chūōkōronsha, 1980.
Koishikawa Zenji, ed. *Kawaya to haisetu no minzokugaku*, Hihyōsha, 2003.
Kondō Yoshiki. *Gyūnyūkō tochikukō*, Nisshindō, 1872.
Kosuge Keiko. *Karē raisu no tanjō*, Kōdansha, 2002.
Koyama Hiroshi, et al., eds. Iwanami kōza Nō kyōgen, Vol. 7, *Kyōgen kanshō annai*, Iwanami Shoten, 1990.
Koyanagi Kiichi. *Nihonjin no shokuseikatsu: kiga to hōyō no hentenshi*, Shibata shoten, 1971.
Kube Rokurō et al., *Rāmen hakkenden*, Vol. 9, Shōgakukan, 2003.
Kumada Tadao. *Sessha wa kuen: samurai yōshoku kotohajime*, Shinchōsha, 2011.
Kumakura Isao, ed. Kōza shoku no bunka, Vol. 2, *Nihon no shokuji bunka*, Aji no moto no bunka sentā, 1999.
Kurano Kenji, Takeda Yūkichi. *Kojiki*, Nihon koten bungaku taikei, Vol. 1, Iwanami, 1971.
Kusano Shinpei. *Kusano Shinpei zenshū*, Vol. 10, 1982.
Lee Yeounsuk. *Kokugo to iu shisō*, Iwanami shoten, 1996.
Maruoka Hideko and Yamaguchi Mieko, eds. *Nihon fujin mondai shiryō shūsei*, Vol. 7, *seikatsu*, Domesu, 1980.
Masuda Yutaka. *Jūgun to senchū sengo*, Bungeisha, 2004.
Matsuda Makoto. *Takagi Kanehiroden*, Kōdansha, 1990.
Matsuhara Iwagorō. *Saiankoku no Tokyo*, Minyūsha, 1893.
Matsumoto Kendō, ed. *Nihon rekishi shaken mondai tōan*, Sekizenkan, 1892.
Meiji nyūsu jiten hensan iinkai, ed. *Meiji nyūsu jiten*, Vol. 8, Mainichi komyunikēshonzu, 1986.
Migita Hiroki, "Rāmenshi o yoru kara yomu – sakariba demae charume to senzen no Tōkyōjin," in Nishimura Hiroshi, ed., *Yashoku no bunkashi*, Seikyūsha, 2010, pp. 109–160.
Minami Hiroshi, ed. *Kindai shomin seikatsushi*, Vol. 6, Sanichi shobō, 1987.

Miyachi Masato et al., eds. *Bijuaru waido Meiji jidaikan*, Shōgakukan, 2005.
Miyagawa Masayasu. *Nihon zuihitsu zenshū*, Vol. 10, Kokumin tosho, 1927.
Miyoshi Yukio et al., eds. *Kōza Natsume Sōseki*, Vol. 1, Yūhikaku, 1981.
Mogi Yūzaburō. "Shokubunka no kokusai kōryū, *Myōnichi no shokuhin sangyō*, June 2007, pp. 3–12.
Mori Rintarō (Ōgai). "Nihon heishokuron taiyi," in *Mori Ōgai zenshū*, Vol. 28, Iwanami shoten, 1974.
—— Mori Rintarō (Ōgai). "Hi Nihon shokuron wa shō ni sono konkyo o ushiwan to su," originally published in 1888, in *Mori Ōgai zenshū*, Vol. 28.
—— "Zoku zoku hi Nihon shokuron shōshitsu sono konkyoron," originally published in 1889, in *Mori Ōgai zenshū*, Vol. 28.
Morisue Yoshiaki, ed. *Taikei Nihonshi sōsho*, Vol. 16, Seikatsushi II, Yamawaka shuppan, 1965.
Murai Gensai. *Kuidōraku*, Hōwasha, 1913.
Murakami Tadakichi. *Chōsenjin no ishokujū*, Seoul, Korea: Tosho shuppanbu, 1916.
Nagasaki kyōikuīnkai. *Chūgoku bunka to Nagasakiken*, Nagasaki: Nagasaki kyōikuīnkai, 1989.
Nagasaki meishō zue, Nagasaki: Nagasaki dankai, 1931.
Nakano Yoshiko and Ō Kōka. *Onaji kama no meshi: nashonaru suihanki wa jinkō roppyaku hachijūman no honkon de naze happyakumandai ureta ka*, Heibonsha, 2005.
Nakao Tomoyo. "Sensō horyo mondai no hikaku bunkateki kōsatsu, (ge)" *Kikan sensō sekinin kenkyū*, dai 23gō, Winter issue 1999, pp. 77–83. [There are three articles by Nakao on this topic.] See also Nakao Tomoyo. "Sensō horyo mondai no hikaku bunkateki kōsatsu, (chū)" *Kikan sensō sekinin kenkyū*, dai 23gō, Spring issue 1999, pp. 27–39.
Narukawa Hiroko. "Shimbun no kateiran kara mita sengo no katei seikatsu no henka," *Kanjōgakuin daigaku ronshū*, no. 8, 1968, pp. 27–33.
Nihon menruigyō dantai rengōkai. *Soba udon hyakumi hyakudai*, Shikita shoten, 1991.
Nihon shōhisha renmei, ed. *Hōshoku Nihon to Ajia*, Ie no hikari kyōkai, 1993.
Nihon shokuryō shinbunsha. *Shōwa to Nihonjin no ibukuro*, Nihon shokuryō shinbunsha, 1990.
Niijima Shigeru and Satsuma Uichi. *Soba no sekai*, Shibata shoten, 1985.
Nishikawa Takeomi and Itō Izumi. *Kaikoku Nihon to Yokohama chūkagai*, Taishūkan shoten, 2002.
Nishimura Hiroshi, ed. *Yashoku no bunkashi*, Seikyūsha, 2010.
Nishimura Kanebumi. *Kyōto ishiki kaii jōrei zukai*, no publisher given, 1876.
Nissin shokuhin kabushiki gaisha. *Shokusō isei: nisshin shokuhin sōritsu shijisshūnen kinenshi*, Osaka: Nissin shokuhin kabushiki gaisha, 1998.
Ōba Osamu. "Kinsei shinjidai no Nitchū bunka kōryū," in Ōba Osamu, Ō Gyōshū, eds., Nitchū bunka kōryūshi sōsho, Vol. 1, *Rekishi*, Taishūkan shoten, 1995, pp. 254–312.
Ōba Osamu et al., eds. *Nagasaki tōkanzu shūsei*, Suita: Kansai daigaku tōzai gakujutsu kenkyūjo, 2003.
Ōchō Enichi. *Nehankyō to jōdokyō: hotoke no ganriki to jobutsu no shin*, Heirakuji shoten, 1981.
Ōgushi Junji, "Sengo no taishū bunka," in Yoshida Yutaka. ed. *Nihon no gendai rekishi*, Vol. 26, sengo kaikaku to gyaku kōsu, Yoshikawa kōbunkan, 2004, pp. 185–226.
Okada Tetsu. *Rāmen no tanjō*, Chikuma shinsho, 2002.
Okamura Ayao. *Nihon menshoku bunka no sensanbyakunen*, Nōsangyo sonbunkakyōkai, 2009.
—— "Kodaishoku no fukugen," *Chōri kagaku*, Vol. 24, no. 1, 1991, pp. 67–70.
Ōkin, Aiban. *Aiban no rāmen*, Ritoru moa, 2008.
Okuyama Tadamasa. *Bunka menruigaku rāmenhen*, Akashi shoten, 2003.
—— *Rāmen no bunka keizaigaku*, Fuyōshobō shuppan, 2000.
Onishi Shirō, et al., eds. *Seikatsushi II*, Taikei Nihonshi sōsho 17, Yamakawa shuppansha, 1969.
Ōno Kazuoki. *Nō to shoku no seiji keizaigaku*, Ryokufū shuppan, 1994.

Orita Kinjō. *Rimen no kankoku*, Kōbunkan, 1905.
Ōtsuka Shigeru. "Ryōri no kaikoku," *Gengo*, Vol. 23, no. 1, 1994, pp. 72–89.
Ōtsuka Tsutomu, ed. *Shokuseikatsu kindaishi*, Yūzanka shuppan, 1969.
Ozaki Yukio. "Ishokujū no kaizen," *Ozaki gakudō zenshū*, Vol. 10, Kōronsha, 1955.
Saeki Tadasu. *Eiyō*, Eiyōsha, 1926.
Sai Ki ed. *Nihon ni okeru Chūgoku dentō bunka*, Bensei shuppan, 2002.
Saitō Minako. *Senka no reshipi Taiheiyō sensōka no shoku o shiru*, Iwanami Shoten, 2002.
Sakamoto Kazutoshi. *Dare mo shiranai Chūgoku rāmen no michi – Nihon rāmen no genryū o saguru*, Shōgakukan, 2008.
Sanetō Keishū. *Chūgokujin Nihon ryūgakushi*, Kuroshio shuppan, 1960.
Sano Minoru. *Sano Minoru tamashī no rāmendō*, Takeshobō, 2001.
Satō Torajirō. *Shina keihatsuron*, Yokohama: Yokohama shinpōsha, 1903.
Segawa Kiyoko. Nihon no shokubunka taikei, Vol. 1, *Shokuseikatsushi*, Tokyo shobō, 1983.
Seikatsu jōhō sentā henshū. *Shokuseikatsu dēta sōgō tōkei nenpō*, Bunkōsha, 2004.
Sekine Shinryū. *Narachō shokuseikatsu no kenkyū*, Yoshikawa kōbunkan, 1969.
Senryūdō Kobayashihen. *Kikyō gunjin shūshoku annai*. Senryūdō, 1906.
Shibata Akio. *Shokuryō sōdatsu*, Nihon keizai shinbun shuppansha, 2007.
Shimanuki Hyōdayū. *Shinkugakuhō*, Keiseisha, 1911.
Shinoda Osamu. "Shoku no fūzoku minzoku meicho shūsei," Vol. 2, *Kome to Nihonjin*, Tokyo shobō, 1985.
Shōwa joshi daigaku shokumotsu kenkyūshitsu, eds. *Kindai Nihon shokumotsushi*, Daibundō, 1971.
Son Ansoku. "Keihi wa yūgaku no haha de ari," in Kanagawa daigaku jinbun gakkai edited, *Chūgokujin Nihon ryūgakushi kenkyū no gendankai*, Ocha no mizu shobō, 2002, pp. 169–206.
Tabi no bunka kenkyūjo, ed. *Rakugo ni miru edo no shokubunka*, Kawade shobō, 2000.
Tamura Shinpachirō. "Sengo – heisei no shoku," *Gengo* (gekkan), Vol. 23, no. 1, 1994, pp. 80–85.
Taimon Sukurīchi, *Edo no ōbushin: Tokugawa toshi keikaku no shigaku*, Kōdansha, 2007.
Suzuki Takeo. *Amerika komugi senryaku to Nihonjin no shokuseikatsu*, Fujiwara shoten, 2003.
Takahashi Yoshio. "Nihonjinshu kairyōron," (originally published in 1884), republished in *Meiji bunka shiryō sōsho*, Vol. 6, Shakai mondaihen, Kazamashobō, 1961.
Tanaka Seiichi. *Ichii taisui – Chūgoku ryōri denraishi*, Shibata shoten, 1987.
Tanizaki Junichirō. *Tanizaki Junichirō zenshū*, Vol. 22, Chūō kōronsha, 1968.
Tatsuno shōyu kyōdō kumiai ed. *Tatsuno shōyu kyōdō kumiai yōran*, internally published, 2001.
Terada Yūkichi. "Shinkoku ryūgakusei mondai," *Chūō kōron*, January 1905, pp. 17–21.
Tō Ken. "Yūkō toshi Nagasaki e" *Nihon kenkyū*, 23, Kokusai Nihon bunka sentā kiyō, Kadokawa shoten, March 2001, pp. 77–102.
Tsurumi Yoshiyuki. *Banana to Nihonjin: Firipin nōen to shokutaku no aida*, Iwanami shoten, 1982.
Ujima Eishun. *Ame to ame uri no bunkashi*, Genshobō, 2009.
Yamagata Kōhō. *Ishokujū*, Jitsugyō no Nihon shamei, 1907.
Yamamoto Noritsuna. *Nagasaki Tōjin yashiki*, Kenkōsha, 1983.
Yamashita Tamiki. *Kawashima Shirō kyūjissai no kaiseinen*, Bunka shuppankyoku, 1983.
Yamawaki Izumi. *Izumiryū kyōgen daisei*, Vol. 4, Wanya ejima iheibei, 1919.
Yamazaki Kanei. *Chanchan kokkeigunka*, Nomura yōjirō, 1894.
Yanagita Kunio. *Meiji Taishōshi sesōshi*, Kodansha, 1976.
Yano Seiichi. *Rakugo nagaya no shiki no aji*, Bungei shunjū, 2002.
Yonezawa mengyō kumiai kyūjūnenshi kankō īnkai ed. *Yonezawa mengyōshi*, Yonezawa mengyō kumiai, 1989.
Yoshida Yutaka. *Nihon no guntai: heishitachi no kindaishi*, Iwanami shoten, 2002.
Yoshida Yutaka, ed. *Nihon no gendai rekishi*, Vol. 26, sengo kaikaku to gyaku kōsu, Yoshikawa kōbunkan, 2004.

Yuize Yasuhiko and Saitō Masaru. *Sekai no shokuryō mondai to Nihon nōgyō*. Yūkaisha, 1981.
Yunoki Manabu, eds. *Nihon suijō kōtsūshi ronshū*, Vol. 2, Bunken shuppan, 1987.
Wada Tsuneko. *Nagasaki ryōri*, Noa shobō, 1970.
Watanabe Minoru. *Nihon shokuseikatsushi*, Yoshikawa kōbunkan, 1964.
Watanabe Shōyō. *Meiryū hyakuwa*, Bunkindō, 1909.

Bibliography of Chinese Materials

Jia Huixuan. *Zhongri yinshi wenhua bijao yanjiu*, Beijing daxue chubanshe, 1999.
Li Shijing, ed. *Zhonghua shiyuan*, Vol. 6, Beijing: Zhongguo shehui kexue chubanshe, 1996.
Qiu Zhonglin (Chi-u Chung lin). "Huangdi de canzhuo: mingdai de guanshan zhidu ji qi xiangguan wenti," *Taida lishi xuebao*, di 34 qi, December 2004, pp. 1–42.
Zhong Shuhe, ed. *Zhou Zuoren wenleibian*, Vol. 7, Hunan: Hunan wenyi chubanshe, 1998.

Japanese Periodicals

Asahi Shimbun
Bungei shunjū
Chōri kagaku
Chūō kōron
Dairen
Eiyō to ryōri
Food Culture (*Kikkoman food series magazine*)
Gengo
Kanjōgakuin daigaku ronshū
Kikan sensō sekinin kenkyū
Kokusai kōryū
Kyoto tandaigaku ronshū
Myōnichi no shokuhin sangyō
Nihon kenkyū
Rekishi kōkishin
SAPIO
Shūkan tōyō keizai
SPA!
Yomiuri Shimbun

Other Periodicals

Annals of the American Academy of Political and Social Science
Annual Revue of Anthropology
Anthropological Quarterly
Asian Folklore Studies
BioScience
Chemical Senses
China Review International
Chinese Literature: Essays, Articles, Reviews
Comparative Studies in Society and History
Critical Inquiry
Early Modern Japan
Far Eastern Survey
Gastronomica

Harvard Business Review
Hitotsubashi Journal of Social Studies
Imago Mundi
Iranian Studies
Japan Forum
Japan Review
Japan Times
Japanese Studies
Journal of American Folklore
Journal of the American Oriental Society
Journal of Asian Studies
Journal of Contemporary History
Journal of Farm Economics
Journal of Japanese Studies
Korean Journal
Late Imperial China
Modern Asian Studies
Monumenta Nipponica
New York Times
Osiris
Pacific Affairs
PACIFIC ECONOMIC PAPER (Australia)
People's Daily (PRC newspaper)
Phylon
Proceedings of the British Association for Japanese Studies
Proceedings of the Western Society for French History
San Francisco Chronicle
South China Morning Post
Taida lishi xuebao (Taiwan)
The American Journal of Sociology
The Daily Yomiuri
The French Review
The Scientific Monthly
The South Atlantic Quarterly
The Trans-Pacific

Archives

Japanese Diet Proceedings
Ministry of Foreign Affairs Archives, Tokyo
National Archives, Tokyo
National Diet Library, Tokyo
Tōkyōto kobunshokan (Tokyo Metropolitan Archives)

Museums

Cattle Museum, Maesawa
Instant Ramen Memorial Hall, Ikeda City
Kimchi Museum, Seoul, Korea
Nagasaki Museum of History and Culture, Nagasaki
Ramen Museum, Shinyokohama
Salt and Tobacco Museum, Tokyo
Sushi Museum, Shizuoka City
Tatsuno Shōyu Museum, Tatsuno City

INDEX

Aguranabe 106
Ajinomoto 146–148
Akagi Munenori 199
Akiyama Tokuzō 166, 182
Alcock, Rutherford 91
alkaline 27, 31–32, 145, 156, 213
America 20, 89, 111, 171–172, 194, 202, 210, 220–221, 230, 241, 249, 251, 254, 262
American B-29 182
American Wheat Utilization Mission 209
Anderson, Benedict 257
Andō Momofuku 3, 205–206, 208, 212–213, 221, 223, 238
apple 191–192
Aoki Setsuzō 165
Aomori Prefecture 85
Arakawa Gorō 150
Asahi Newspaper (*Asahi shimbun*) 147, 162, 203
Asakusa 66, 157, 161, 163, 215

baise laji ("white trash problem") 261
bakufu 63, 72, 76, 94–95
banana 164, 195
Ban Kinsei 158
Batavia 48
Batten, Bruce 24
beef 22, 95, 99, 105–107, 148, 169, 187, 216, 259–260 (see also *Aguranabe*)
beefeaters 105
beriberi 80, 109, 111–113, 129
bing 17–20, 31, 35, 45
Bird, Isabella 128
Black, John 94
Bose, Rash Behari 143
botuo 27, 31
bread 10, 15, 18, 69, 109–111, 129, 152, 169, 176, 186–189, 191, 199, 203, 208–210, 212–213
Britain 9, 11, 104, 131–133, 143, 171, 175, 194–195, 262
bunmei kaika 96, 113
butter 29–30, 48, 62, 123, 129, 152, 186, 211

Calpis 154
caramel 154
castella 11, 51

Cattle Museum 259
Chamberlain, Basil Hall 128
champon 115–116, 133, 251
Chang'an 24, 30
charumela 166
Chen Pingjun 115, 251
Chiba Prefecture 3, 50
chindon 147
chocolate 18, 154
chopsticks 1–2, 15, 18, 56, 97, 114, 123, 232, 234, 248, 259, 270
Christian 25, 48, 52, 55, 86
Chūka soba 116, 256
Chūō kōron 138
coffee 98, 232
concubine 53
Confucianism 16, 77
courtesan 53, 60–61
Coxinga 76
cup ramen 227
curry rice 10–11, 144, 187
Cwiertka, Katarzyna 96, 103, 189

daikon 50
daimyo 48–49
Dalian 201
danchi 214
dashi 146–147
Deshima 52, 92
Diamond, Jared 13
Dōkōan 66
donburi 2, 7, 221, 234
Dunkin' Donuts 222
Dunlop, Fuchsia 11, 125
Dutch 48, 52, 54, 60, 62, 69, 76, 90, 92, 177–178, 200

Eichū 30
ekiben 126
Emperor Tenmu 23, 103
Engishiki 35–36
Enni 37–38
Ennin 31
Enryōkan 119, 122
erotic 160
"Essential Skills for the Common People" 17, 20, 27, 35 (see also *Qinmin Yaoshu*)

eta 80, 84
excrement 149, 151 (see also shit, *kuso*)

famine 13, 36, 51, 79, 235
fangbian mian 4 (see also instant noodles, pot noodles)
Farris, Wayne 36
food theme park 239, 241, 250
Formosa, 76, 196, (see also Taiwan)
French 6, 9, 81, 86, 120, 124, 151, 174, 177, 224–225, 263, 265, 269
Frois, Lois 48
fugu 99
Fujii Kaoru 230
Fujin no tomo 154
Fukuchi Genichirō 94–95
Fukui Prefecture 169
Fukuoka 3
Fukushima Prefecture 158, 183
Fukuzawa Yukichi 96–97, 99, 104, 106, 110, 119, 211

garlic 6, 162, 165–166, 234, 247, 251
Gen'e 37
General Tōgō Heihachirō 131
Genraiken 158
Gifu Prefecture 49
Grant, Ulysses 121–122
Great Kantō Earthquake 166–167
gyōza 31, 200, 239
gyūnabe 105 (see also *Aguranabe* or beef)

Hakata 1, 3, 24, 38, 52, 239
Hakodate 91, 116, 128
Hara Kei 177
Harada Nobuo 17, 108
Hayashiya Kikuzō, 231–234 (see also *rakugo*)
Heian 24, 33–34, 40, 52, 66
heroin 179
hikiagesha 200
Himiko 22
hishio 34
Hishiya Heishichi 54–55
Hokkaido 6, 40, 91, 116, 156–157, 233, 238
Hong Kong 90–91, 244
hōtō 27
Huang Zunxian 136
Hunan 11
huntunjiao 25
hygiene 99, 121, 126, 128, 132, 149, 151–152, 154, 159, 164, 204, 260, 269

ice cream 123, 239
ichizen meshiya 159

Ikeda Kikunae 146, 148
Imperial Army 109–111, 113, 144
Imperial Navy 109, 111
India 21, 124, 131, 177, 184, 200, 262
Indian 11, 29, 143
instant noodles 6, 223 (see also *sokuseki*)
instant ramen 3–4, 6–7, 160, 189, 191, 204–208, 212–215, 220–224, 227–228, 232, 238–239, 248, 261, 269
Instant Ramen Memorial Hall 223, 238
insutanto 207, 213
Iron Chef 8, 235
Ishiguro Tadaatsu 195–196
Ishiki kaii jōrei 101
Ishinpō 30
Itō Hirobumi 112
Iwate Prefecture 229, 238

jiang 35, 39
jochū 152 (see also maid)
Jōten Temple 37–38
jukensei 213

Kaempfer, Engelbert 69
kaiseki 43, 47
Kamakura 33, 36–37, 42, 47, 68
kamigata 42, 81–82
Kang Youwei 135
Kansai 22, 40, 50, 80–81, 147, 167, 179
Kantō 27, 50, 80–81, 91, 166–167, 179
Karafuto 130–131
katsugiya 193
katsuobushi 6, 145
Kawamoto Saburō 162
Kawashima Shirō 131, 178, 180–182, 195, 204
Kikkoman 42, 257
kirimen 45
Kitakata 3, 158, 200, 217–220
kitchen Bus 212
Kobe 91, 134, 239,
Kodama Kagai 155
Kōfuku Temple 54–55
Kojiki 25
kokugo 124
kokuminshoku 173–174, 186, 204, 225
Komadari sisters 247
konbu 6, 40–41, 145, 147
konnyaku 114
Kōrakuen 71, 73–74
Korea 3, 15, 24, 29, 36, 42, 44, 94, 109, 123, 127, 134, 144, 148, 150, 159, 164, 173, 178, 180–181, 196, 200, 230, 254–255, 259, 269

INDEX

kowaī 66
kudaranai 82, 156
Kuidōraku 129 (see also Murai Gensai)
kugaku 160
Kumamoto 39, 238, 251–252
kura 217–218
Kurume 3, 255
kuso 150 (see also shit, excrement)
kyōgen 40, 74, 145
Kyushu 1, 3, 6, 22, 24, 38, 47–48, 51, 53–54, 56, 59–60, 76, 91, 134, 233, 238–239, 251, 255

Laudan, Rachel 215–216
Liang Qichao 135
Luo Sen 90
Lu Xun 138

MacArthur, Douglas 197–198, 241
MAFF 12
maid 140, 152–153
makanai seibatsu ("blitzkrieg for more board") 114
Manchuria 73, 76, 130, 166, 168, 173, 178
manga 228, 241–245, 252, 263
Mazu (Maso) 55
Meiji Emperor 103, 112
Meiji Restoration 8, 13, 61, 89, 105, 114, 119, 154, 213
men (noodles) 20, 157
mian (noodles) 4, 13, 20, 157
Michelin Guide 244, 263
milk 29–30, 48, 99, 112, 154, 186, 210, 260
Ming 45, 52–53, 59, 72–73, 75–76,
miso 2, 6, 10, 35, 38–39, 45–46, 48, 51, 94–95, 108, 150, 152, 172–173, 178, 185–187, 217, 233, 238, 251
Mito Kōmon 72–75, 77, 79, 237
mochi 31, 159
Mongolia 15, 21, 184
Mori Ōgai 110–111, 113, 185, 211
Morse, Edward 128–129
MSG 146–148, 153, 167
Murai Gensai, 129–131, 143 (see also *Kuidōraku*)
Muromachi 44–45, 47, 80

Nagano Prefecture 66
Nagasaki 47–48, 51–62, 69, 72–73, 77, 89–92, 115–116, 134, 173, 251
Nanjing (or Nanking) 72, 76, 86, 116–117
Namiki Michiko 191

nanban ryōri ("southern barbarian cuisine") 54
Nanking soba 116–117
Narushima Ryūhoku 105
naruto 7, 232, 247
Natsume Sōseki 149
nattō 51
New York 13, 20, 223, 251–252
New York Times 143
niboshi 6
nighthawk 63 (see also *yotaka*)
Nihon ryōri 10–11, 125, 204
Nihon shoki 23, 25
Nihonshoku 125, 267
Niigata 91
Ningxia 27
Nirvana Sutra 29
Nissin 205, 223, 254, 261
nutrition 13, 17, 99, 126, 131, 134, 149, 154, 163, 174, 177–178, 181–182, 185, 204, 208, 210–211, 263

Oda Nobunaga 49
oden 160, 169
Okamura Ayao 30
Okita Kinjō 150
Ōkuma Shigenobu 113–114
Olympics 166, 169, 181, 185, 195
onigiri 169
Ōoka Shōhei 161
Ooms, Herman 24
Orkin, Ivan 251, 266
Osaka 3, 40, 50, 54, 63–64, 68, 72, 80–81, 91, 147, 167–168, 178, 193, 205–206, 220, 223, 227, 233, 238–239
Ōsaki Hiroshi 10–11, 233, 236
otaku 235
Ozaki Kanichi 158
Ozaki Yukio 195

pachinko 169
Perry, Matthew 89–90, 95
Pillow Book 230
pizza 11, 20, 249
Pokémon 227
pork 1, 6–7, 11, 54–56, 60–62, 85, 95, 155, 158, 169, 174, 187, 216, 220, 232–235, 238, 247, 251, 255, 257
Port Arthur 130–131
Portuguese 11, 47–48, 54, 166
potato 10, 12–13, 51, 171, 174, 176, 187–188, 203
pot noodles 4 (see also instant ramen)

POW (prisoners of war) 183–186
propaganda 175, 180, 186, 197

Qin Shihuang 15
Qing 34, 52–53, 59, 72–73, 76, 86, 91, 93, 123, 132–133, 135–136, 155, 166, 201
Qinmin Yaoshu 17 (see also "Essential Skills for the Common People")

Rairaiken 158, 161, 215
rakugo 82–83, 85–86, 105, 231–233 (see also Hayashiya Kikuzō)
Rāmensai yūki 243
Rath, Eric 16
Rogers, Ben 9
Rokumon 4
rōnin 79
Russia 21, 129, 130–132, 143, 154, 187
Russo-Japanese War 129, 131–132, 143
ryōsai kenbo 126
ryōtei 127

Saeki Tadasu 163
Saitō Gesshin 62
saké 4, 35, 43, 86, 217, 219
sakubei 31, 51
Salt and Tobacco Museum 200
samurai 33, 36–37, 40–41, 43–45, 59, 68–69, 74, 79–80, 83, 89, 92, 94, 106, 114, 145, 217
sankin kōtai 68
sanma 82–83
Sano Minoru 236–237
Sapporo 3, 6, 134, 156–158, 203, 238
Satsuma 53, 79, 95
SCAP 197, 199
Screech, Timon 71
scurvy 131
Sendai 3
seolleongtang 148
Seoul 109, 127, 148, 150, 255, 259
sesshō kindanrei 23
shamoji 170, 204
Shanghai 90–91, 148, 168, 201
Sharan Q 247–248
Shenyang 73, 162, 168
Shiga Naoya 193
Shiga Prefecture 30
Shimane Prefecture 251
Shina ryōri 57, 125, 155, 174
Shina soba 156–157, 161, 172, 255
shinkansen 218, 253
shogun 6, 48–53, 60, 62–63, 68–69, 71–72, 76–77, 81–82, 86, 94–95, 164

Shinto 17, 35–36, 106
shippoku 56–57
shit 112, 150 (see also kuso, excrement)
Shizuoka 250
shōjin ryōri 47
shokuiku 264
shōyu 6, 38 (see also soy sauce)
Shu Shunsui 73, 75–79
Shufu no tomo 152
shuho 172
shuiyin 20
Sino-Japanese War 93, 136
slurp 6, 18, 48, 97, 229, 231–232, 234, 237
soba 27, 31, 37–38, 42, 45, 51, 62–64, 66–68, 71, 75, 82, 104, 107, 116–117, 156–157, 159, 161, 172, 179, 227–228, 255–256, 258
Sōfuku Temple 54, 56
sokuseki 167, 207, 213
sōmen 41–42
Son Kitei 181
Song dynasty 20, 31, 37, 90
sonnō jōi 92
Sony 227, 254
soy bean 131
soy sauce 2–3, 6, 14, 34–35, 37–39, 42–43, 45–46, 50–51, 81–82, 94, 106, 113, 123, 140, 164, 178–179, 200, 233, 238, 251, 257, 259, 266 (see also *shōyu*)
Soyokaze 191
Spanish 11, 54
"stamina" 115, 133, 251
starvation 44, 180, 184–185, 189, 193, 196, 208
sugar 53, 164, 181, 203
sumo 3, 224
Sun Yat Sen 135, 143
sushi 45, 64, 66, 82, 84, 136, 228, 248–251, 254, 263
Sushi Museum 250
Suzuki Bunji 155
Suzuki Takeo 210

Taiping 86
Taiwan 3, 11, 76, 123, 127, 144, 148, 159, 162, 164–165, 173, 200, 206, 254, 269 (see also Formosa)
Takagi Kanehiro 111–113, 129
takuan 51, 127, 173
Talleyrand 95
Tampopo 7
tanshin funin 214
Tatsuno 42, 50, 81
tempura 11, 51, 64, 83, 213, 251, 257
terroir 124

INDEX

Tochigi Prefecture 200
Tōjin yashiki 52–53
Tōkaidō 68
tonkotsu 6, 255
Tottori Prefecture 113
Tōyama Mitsuru 143
Toyama Prefecture 38
tsū 81, 231, 245

udon 27, 31, 37–38, 42, 45, 51, 62, 68, 71, 156, 160, 172, 179, 203, 227
umai 145
umami 40, 45, 145–146
urine 150, 182
Utsunomiya 127, 200–202, 220

vaseline 223

walkman 227
Wang Wencai 156–157
washoku 10–11, 125, 259
weijing 148
wonton 45, 158
Wu Yunchu 148

Xian 30

Yamada machi 4
Yamagata Kōhō 133
Yamatai 22, 24
Yamato 22, 172
Yamazaki Eizan 68
Yanagita Kunio 107
Yano Akiko 247
yatai 202, 241
Yeoman Guard 105
Yokohama 3, 6, 33, 74, 91–94, 106, 108, 134, 156–158, 185–186, 237, 239
Yokohama Ramen Museum 237
Yokoyama Gennosuke 128
yotaka 63 (see also nighthawk)
Yōwaken 116–117

zanpanya 129, 159
Zen 30, 37–38, 41, 43–44, 47, 56, 169
Zhongcai 126
Zhongguocai 126
Zhou Zuoren 138

www.ingramcontent.com/pod-product-compliance
Lightning Source LLC
Chambersburg PA
CBHW070233230426
43664CB00014B/2294